Hearts and Minds in Guerrilla Warfare

Hearts and Minds
in Guerrilla Warfare

The Malayan Emergency 1948-1960

Richard Stubbs

SINGAPORE
OXFORD UNIVERSITY PRESS
OXFORD NEW YORK
1989

Oxford University Press

Oxford New York Toronto
Delhi Bombay Calcutta Madras Karachi
Petaling Jaya Singapore Hong Kong Tokyo
Nairobi Dar es Salaam Cape Town
Melbourne Auckland
and associated companies in
Berlin Ibadan

Oxford is a trade mark of Oxford University Press

ISBN 0 19 588942 8

Printed in Malaysia by Peter Chong Printers Sdn. Bhd.
Published by Oxford University Press Pte. Ltd.,
Unit 221, Ubi Avenue 4, Singapore 1440

To my parents, Joan and Graham Stubbs

Preface

WHILE working on various aspects of the Malayan Emergency during the 1970s, I became aware of the lack of any study which placed the 'shooting war' between the Malayan Government and the Malayan Communist Party (MCP) within the broader context of the social, political, and economic aspects of life in Malaya. In particular it seemed to me that there was a need for a review of the Emergency which detailed the full scope of the Government's 'hearts and minds' strategy and the impact of both government and MCP policies—including administrative, security, political, economic, and social policies—on what I considered to be the key factor in any guerrilla war, the sympathies, allegiances, and actions of the general population. Moreover, I was keen to use the Malayan experience to see if it was possible to compare the effectiveness of the hearts and minds approach with what I have termed in this study the 'coercion and enforcement' approach—an approach to counter-insurgency which continues to this day to be popular with nearly every government facing a guerrilla threat. I also felt that a broad-based analysis of the Emergency would contribute to a greater understanding of what I consider to be a critical period in the formulation of modern Malaysia.

It was not, however, until the late 1970s and into the 1980s when government files for the crucial period 1945-55 were opened that such a study became feasible. The files in the National Archives of Malaysia and especially in the Public Record Office in London, to which no previous analyst of the Emergency has had access, provide a wealth of data not only on government activities but also on the views and actions of the different communities in Malaya. Drawing on these and a variety of other sources I have been able to address the issues that originally prompted me to embark on this study.

In completing such a wide-ranging review of the events of the Emergency I have acquired a great many debts over the years. I would like to thank the staff of the following institutions for accommodating my many requests: Arkib Negara Malaysia (National Archives of Malaysia), Department of External Affairs Archives (Canada), Foreign and Commonwealth Office Library (Great Brit-

ain), Institute of Southeast Asian Studies Library (Singapore),
National Library of Singapore, Public Record Office (London),
Rhodes House Library (Oxford), Royal Commonwealth Society
Library (London), Royal Institute Of International Affairs Press
Clippings Library (London), Rubber Research Institute Library
(Kuala Lumpur), University of Malaya Library, and the University
of Singapore Library. Many people have provided information,
advice, and encouragement in various forms along the way. In
particular I would like to thank Geoffrey Edwards, David Glover,
the late David Gray, John W. Humphrey, the late Malcolm Mac-
Donald, Gordon Means, Ozay Mehmet, Stephen Milne, Peter
Nailor, Saleem Qureshi, Martin Rudner, Kernial Singh Sandhu,
Anthony Short, the late Michael Stenson, the late Sir Gerald
Templer, and C. C. Too.

I am indebted to the Social Science Research Council of Canada
for a Leave Fellowship in 1981-2 and for a Research Grant, covering 1981-3, which allowed me to undertake research in Malaysia
and Britain. It would have been impossible for me to have completed
my research in London without the help of friends and family. I
would like to thank Edward Milner, Simon Awde, and especially
Victoria and Geoffrey Edwards and my parents for all their help.
Finally, my greatest debt is to my wife, Grace Skogstad. She has
encouraged, advised, criticized, edited, and endured endless hours
of discussion on the Emergency and guerrilla warfare—often with
a high degree of tolerance.

The usual caveat concerning responsibility for the contents of
an analysis is of particular importance in this case. Many of the people
I have consulted have conflicting opinions about the Emergency
and certainly none would agree with everything I have written. It
must be emphasized, therefore, that I am solely responsible for any
errors of fact or judgement that may be found in the following pages.

Toronto   RICHARD STUBBS
October 1988

Contents

Map

Note

ALL dollar figures cited in this study are Malayan dollars unless otherwise stated. In order to avoid confusion I have employed the spelling of the names of people and places in general use at the time of the Emergency.

Abbreviations

ACAO	Assistant Chinese Affairs Officer
ADO	Assistant District Officer
ARO	Assistant Resettlement Officer
BDCC	British Defence Co-ordination Committee
BMA	British Military Administration
CAO	Chinese Affairs Officer
CPO	Chief Police Officer
DO	District Officer
IMP	Independence of Malaya Party
KVHG	Kinta Valley Home Guard
MAS	Malayan Administrative Service
MCA	Malayan Chinese Association
MCS	Malayan Civil Service
MCP	Malayan Communist Party
MIC	Malayan Indian Congress
MMEA	Malayan Mining Employers' Association
MNP	Malay Nationalist Party
MPAJA	Malayan People's Anti-Japanese Army
MPAJU	Malayan People's Anti-Japanese Union
MPIEA	Malayan Planting Industries Employers' Association
MRLA	Malayan Races Liberation Army
MSS	Malayan Security Services
PAP	People's Action Party
PMCJA	Pan-Malayan Council of Joint Action
PMFTU	Pan-Malayan Federation of Trade Unions
PMIP	Pan-Malayan Islamic Party
PUTERA	Pusat Tenaga Ra'ayat
PWD	Public Works Department
RIDA	Rural Industrial Development Authority
RO	Resettlement Officer
RS	Resettlement Supervisor
RSS No.1	Rubber Smoked Sheet No.1
SCA	Secretary for Chinese Affairs
SEP	Surrendered Enemy Personnel
SFTU	Singapore Federation of Trade Unions
UMNO	United Malays National Organization

The Federation of Malaya at the Time of the Emergency

Introduction

THE term 'the hearts and minds' first became associated with counter-guerrilla warfare during the 1948-60 guerrilla war in Malaya, commonly referred to as the 'Emergency'.[1] It was the British High Commissioner, General (later Field Marshal) Sir Gerald Templer who, shortly after his arrival in Malaya, in February 1952, coined the term–'that nauseating phrase I think I invented' as he was to refer to it some fifteen years after the event[2]–and made it popular. Indeed, within a few months the term had caught on to such an extent that it became the label by which everyone referred to the campaign plan that Templer adopted in the Malayan Government's battle with the Malayan Communist Party's (MCP) guerrillas. Although it took time for the details to emerge, the main themes of his strategy were apparent almost immediately. He called for a total effort on all fronts–political, economic, cultural, social, as well as military–and emphasized that there was no reason to distinguish between the peacetime activities of the Government and the Emergency activities. The Government's co-ordinated effort was to be concentrated on gaining the support of the people of Malaya by addressing their grievances and bringing them under the Government's administrative control. The aim was to isolate the guerrillas from their base of support and thus make them vulnerable to the security forces' operations.[3]

Although coined by Templer the term was clearly rooted in ideas that had been percolating for some time both internationally and within Malaya itself. At the international level such statements as the preamble to UNESCO's Constitution that, 'since war begins in the minds of men, it is in the minds of men that the defences of peace must be constructed', had contributed to the notion of the emerging cold war as 'a battle for men's minds'. For example, the American ambassador to China, J. Leighton Stuart, who, like other Western political leaders, was casting around for ways of countering the perceived threat of communist expansion, argued in early 1949 for a 'new approach' directed primarily at the 'mind and heart'.[4] In Malaya, both 'hearts' and 'minds' were being discussed with reference to the Emergency. Chinese community leaders talked not only of the old Chinese saying, 'Gain the people's heart', but also of the need to eradicate 'the fear of Government found in the people's minds and hearts'.[5] Sir Henry Gurney, the British High Commissioner in Malaya from 1948 to 1951, also spoke of the importance of the minds and hearts of Malayans in determining the outcome of the Emergency.[6] However, whatever its origins, there can be little doubt that it was the publicity that Templer gave the term, combined with the eventual success of the Malayan Government in defeating a full-fledged, and initially very effective, communist rural guerrilla army which has ensured that the idea of 'winning the hearts and minds' became well known as a strategy for countering rural guerrilla warfare.[7]

In focusing on cutting the link between the guerrillas and the population, the hearts and minds approach developed by the Malayan Government under Templer echoes what practitioners of guerrilla warfare have argued is the vital ingredient in any successful rural guerrilla campaign. T. E. Lawrence, using his experience in the Arab Revolt against the Turks between 1916 and 1918, has written that rebels 'must have a friendly population, not actively friendly, but sympathetic to the point of not betraying rebel movements to the enemy'.[8] Mao Tse Tung has stated that 'because guerrilla warfare basically derives from the masses and is supported by them, it can neither exist nor flourish if it separates itself from their sympathies and cooperation'. He urges guerrilla fighters not to neglect 'the question of the immediate interests, the well-being of the broad masses' and notes that revolutionary war 'can be waged only by mobilizing the masses and relying on them'.[9] In a similar vein, Luis Taruc, who led the Hukbalahap against the Government of the Philippines, said in 1948 that the Huk rebellion 'can only hold out as long as it is supported by the masses. No more, no less.'[10] Che Guevara has emphasized that 'The guerrilla fighter needs full help from the people of the area. This is an indispensable condition.'[11] And Hoang Quoc Viet, one of the senior North Vietnamese leaders, has said that 'in order to conduct a successful revolution you have got to involve the entire people. It is no use trying to run a revolution with the Communist Party alone.'[12]

To this list of practitioners may be added the host of scholars who have also dissected and theorized about revolutions. While there are a number of schools of thought as to why revolutions occur, as Skocpol points out, they all envisage the underlying revolutionary process in much the same way.[13] What is stressed is first, the social dislocation which gives rise to grievances, and second, the presence, or emergence, of an organizational framework which allows for the collective mobilization of those affected by the changes taking place in the social system. In other words, just as the originators of the hearts and minds approach and the practitioners of guerrilla warfare acknowledge that the link between the population and the guerrillas is critical for the pursuit of an effective guerrilla campaign, so theorists of revolution emphasize the juncture of similar factors in singling out the necessary conditions for open revolt.

Yet among those interested primarily in counter-guerrilla warfare, the hearts and minds approach has had a mixed reception. While some, especially British analysts who served in Malaya, have generally favoured this approach, others, particularly in the United States, have been more sceptical. In part this was because the approach became a casualty of the Vietnam War.[14] The label 'hearts and minds' was associated with a number of policies which were far removed from the original Malayan strategy. For some, winning the hearts and minds simply entailed a massive propaganda, or psychological warfare, assault on the general population. Faith in the approach was undermined when the policy proved ineffective. Even more damaging for the term's reputation was its association with the concept of 'pacification'. While they contained elements of the hearts and minds approach, the pacification programmes generally failed to include a satisfactory role for the armed forces, who appeared to be off fighting a separate war. And at times, as the term suggests, pacification seemed to be aimed more at addressing symptoms than causes. For example, pacification policies in Vietnam made little attempt to change the fundamental relationship between the people and the central government.[15]

However, this failure to appreciate fully the nature and significance of the hearts and minds approach used in Malaya is understandable. Sir Robert Thompson, who served in Malaya throughout the Emergency as an administrator, most notably as Deputy Secretary and then Secretary for Defence from 1957 to 1961, and who was later head of the British Advisory Mission to South Vietnam and an adviser to President Nixon, has pointed out that, while 'many Americans made studies of the British success during the Emergency in Malaya [they] were largely superficial and confined to particular aspects of the campaign. It was never comprehended as a whole.'[16] Indeed, analysts tended to use aspects of the Emergency campaign to buttress their own arguments without reference to the overall strategy of the Malayan Government.

Perhaps even more importantly, this general failure to understand the Emergency has been perpetuated by British analysts. While being quick to endorse the breadth of scope and fundamental tenets of the hearts and minds approach developed by the Malayan Government, they have tended to adopt a rather narrow focus when actually analysing the course of the guerrilla war itself. For example, Thompson, in his excellent theoretical study of counter-guerrilla warfare, argues that one of the five basic principles of counter-insurgency is that the 'government must give priority to defeating the political subversion, not the guerrillas'.[17] He also makes the point that a person 'can only be made to choose freely to support the government if the government can show him that what it has to offer is something better than the insurgents can offer him', and he stresses the 'importance of improving the standard of living of peasants socially, politically, economically and culturally as a war measure'.[18] Yet his analysis concentrates on the military and administrative aspects of the Emergency and pays little attention to economic, political, or social factors. Similarly, Richard Clutterbuck has stated that the resolution of the Emergency was concerned 'at least as much with social, political and economic factors as it was with military ones'; but although his two major studies of the Emergency touch briefly on some of the political, economic, and social factors, he too devotes his most detailed analysis to the way in which the Government's military and administrative techniques were developed.[19] Anthony Short's review of the Emergency is by far the most comprehensive to date and he takes pains to expand on what has become the traditional approach to analysing the Emergency. However, he too is more concerned, as he notes in the Preface to his book, 'with the framework of colonial decisions and activities' than with how these decisions and activities were received by the people of Malaya.[20] He also pays relatively little attention to the economic and political factors which influenced the course of the Emergency. Generally, other surveys of the Emergency have provided only minor variations on these same themes.[21] Somewhat surprisingly, then, in no account of the Emergency is the hearts and minds approach a central feature of the analysis.

This study undertakes to provide such an account. The traditional way of viewing the Emergency is broadened in two ways. First, the hearts and minds approach clearly suggests that the battleground of the Emergency was the general population. The focus of attention, therefore, will be not only the impact that the changing social, economic, and political environment had on the lives of the people of Malaya, but also the policies pursued by the Malayan Government and the MCP, the management and implementation of these policies, their consequences, and their effect on the relationship that each side in the conflict was able to establish with the different segments of Malayan society. Bearing in mind the importance that practitioners and theorists alike have attached to the link between the guerrilla organizations and the mass of the population, the question to be asked throughout the analysis will be: with whom, if anyone, did the sympathies of the various groups in Malaya lie? Secondly, taking as a cue one of Templer's first directives, that the Emergency element of the Government should not be kept in a watertight compartment separated from the normal practices of government,[22] the study examines the effect on the general population of social, economic, and political developments as well as military and administrative factors. This is not to say that the traditional view of the Emergency will be ignored completely. Indeed, the morale and cohesion of the Malayan Government, and the way in which it was able to operate, will receive a good deal of attention. Just as it has been argued that unattended grievances arising from social change and the presence of an organizational vehicle for channelling anti-government actions are both necessary for the emergence of a revolutionary movement, so it is argued that a further condition which has to be met in order for there to be a successful revolution—one to which the first two conditions may contribute but not always bring about—is the collapse of the existing regime.[23] This study, then, pursues the question of whether at any time the Malayan Government was likely to collapse under the weight of its own incompetence and self-doubt.

For the most part, the analysis proceeds chronologically. The period between the surrender of the Japanese in August 1945 and the declaration of the Emergency in June 1948 is reviewed in some detail because it was at this time that many of the attitudes which influenced the course of events during the early years of the Emergency were formed. Indeed, the initial success of the MCP guerrillas cannot be fully explained without an appreciation of the extent to which the post-War chaos and the Government's ineptitude shaped people's views of the British colonial administration. The striking feature of the first few years of the Emergency was the MCP's ability to gain the initiative despite the ill-co-ordinated launching of the guerrilla campaign. Placed on the defensive, the Government adopted what is labelled in this study as a 'coercion and enforcement' policy in which the military and the police were employed to search out the guerrillas and to try to intimidate the general population into abandoning their support of the MCP. The policy backfired. The mass of the rural population were caught in the middle between the increasing violence of the MCP, who were seeking a quick military victory, and the widely used intimidation tactics of the Government's security forces. For the rural Chinese, who had a long-standing distrust of the Government and who generally saw the MCP as a legitimate alternative to the Government, continued support for the guerrillas was viewed in many cases as the only reasonable course of action.

The change in the Government's policy from a coercion and enforcement approach to a hearts and minds approach was aided by three events. First, the onset of the Korean War generated a high demand for Malaya's two main commodities, natural rubber and tin. The resulting prosperity produced full employment and dramatically increased revenues from duties and taxes which the Government was able to use to full advantage. The economic boom, therefore, provided the Government with a reprieve as well as funding for key aspects of the hearts and minds policy. Secondly, the death of the High Commissioner, Sir Henry Gurney, in a guerrilla ambush gave the newly installed Conservative Government in Britain the opportunity to thoroughly review the Malayan Government's counter-guerrilla policy and to change senior personnel in the Malayan administration. The result was the appointment of General Templer as High Commissioner and the implementation of the hearts and minds approach. Thirdly, in late 1951, the MCP revised its policy of increasing military activity and put greater emphasis on political organizing. The resulting lull in attacks by the guerrillas allowed the Government time to start implementing their new approach and heightened the sense that the new High Commissioner was wresting the initiative away from the MCP. Despite these advantages, the main elements of the hearts and minds approach were only slowly put in place. In particular, the development of the New Villages, as the centres in which much of the rural Chinese population were resettled were called, was most uneven. As a consequence, and despite the widespread support for the Government and for the emerging political system which was created by the introduction of state and federal elections and the granting of independence in 1957, the MCP continued to receive support from pockets of discontented rural Chinese. However, by 1960 the concerted pressure of the Government forced the remnants of the guerrilla army to cross the border into southern Thailand and allowed the Prime Minister to declare an end to the Emergency.

Clearly, as in any other guerrilla war, the course of events in the Emergency was greatly influenced by factors unique to Malaya and to international events which occurred during the fifteen years after the end of the Second World War. Yet, just as each guerrilla war has its own specific characteristics, so too it has features that are common to all such wars. With this in mind, it is possible to compare the events in Malaya to the outcomes of other guerrilla wars–the Huk rebellion in the Philippines during the late 1940s and 1950s, and the wars in Vietnam, for example–and to derive some generalizations which will allow for a better understanding of current guerrilla wars in Central America, the Philippines, Sri Lanka, and Afghanistan. Certainly this analysis of the guerrilla war in Malaya gives a clear indication that while a coercion and enforcement policy may help a government to stay in power, it also ensures the continuation of a significant level of political violence. On the other hand, a hearts and minds approach adapted to local conditions, although often difficult to implement, stands a much better chance of eventually bringing about a relatively stable social, economic, and political environment.

1. The term 'Emergency' is derived from the Malayan Government's declaration in June 1948 of a State of Emergency. Two other 'emergencies' have overtaken Malaya/Malaysia since the Second World War: 'Confrontation' with Indonesia during the 1960s and the period directly after the 13 May 1969 racial riots. But the term is usually reserved for the guerrilla war of 1948-60.

2. *Straits Times*, 27 March 1968.

3. See Minutes of a speech to representatives of senior members of the Civil Service, 9 February 1952, P/PM1 Secretary to Government Y5, Arkib Negara Malaysia (National Archives of Malaysia, hereafter referred to as ANM), Kuala Lumpur, Malaysia. See also *Proceedings of the Federal Legislative Council*, 5th Session, p. 8, 19 March 1952, and John Cloake, *Templer Tiger of Malaya: The Life of Field Marshal Sir Gerald Templer* (London: Harrap, 1985), p. 477, fn. 1, Ch. 11.

4. See Ritchie Ovendale, 'Britain, the United States and the Cold War in South-east Asia', *International Affairs* 58 (Summer 1982), p. 449.

5. See, for example, 'Memorandum submitted to the Government of the Federation of Malaya by Yap Mau Tatt on behalf of the Chinese Community leaders in

Negri Sembilan', 21 December 1949, CO 537/6090, Public Record Office, London. All sources which include the prefix CO, FO, WO, or CAB to the file number are to be found in the Public Record Office, London.

6. Anthony Short, *The Communist Insurrection in Malaya 1948-1960* (London: Frederick Muller, 1975), p. 416.

7. Rural guerrilla warfare is here defined as a war which is carried on, by rural-based bands or groups, in an irregular manner with the objective of causing the fall of the government.

8. T. E. Lawrence, 'Guerrilla–Science of Guerrilla Warfare', in *Encyclopaedia Britannica*, 14th edn., Vol. 10.

9. Samuel B. Griffith, ed., trans., *Mao Tse-tung on Guerrilla Warfare* (New York: Praeger, 1961), p. 44, cited in Eqbal Ahmed, 'Revolutionary War and Counter-Insurgency', *Journal of International Affairs* 25 (No. 1, 1971), p. 2, and Mao Tse Tung, *Selected Military Writings*, 2 vols. (Peking: Foreign Language Press, 1966), Vol. 1, p. 147.

10. Benedict J. Kerkvliet, *The Huk Rebellion: A Study of Peasant Revolt in the Philippines* (Berkeley: University of California Press, 1977), p. 247.

11. Che Guevara, *Guerrilla Warfare* (New York: Vintage Books, 1961), p. 4.

12. Quoted by P. J. Honey in Royal United Services Institution, *Lessons from the Vietnam War: Report of a Seminar held at the Royal United Services Institution on Wednesday, 12 February 1969* (London: RUSI, 1969), p. 11.

13. Theda Skocpol, *States and Social Revolutions: A Comparative Analysis of France, Russia, and China* (Cambridge: Cambridge University Press, 1979), pp. 14-15. In making this point, Skocpol identifies four major families of social scientific theories of revolution: Marxist theories, represented by the works of Karl Marx; aggregate-psychological theories, represented by Ted Gurr's *Why Men Rebel* (Princeton, NJ: Princeton University Press, 1970), systems/value consensus theories, represented by Chalmers Johnson's *Revolutionary Change* (Boston: Little Brown and Co., 1969), and political-conflict theories represented by Charles Tilly's *From Mobilization to Revolution* (Reading, Mass: Addison Wesley, 1978). See Skocpol, *States and Revolution*, pp. 6-14. In discussing these approaches, Skocpol does not clearly distinguish between the necessary conditions for the rise of revolutionary movements and the necessary conditions for a successful revolution (see pp. 16-17). To Skocpol's list of approaches to the study of revolution which see the revolutionary process in the same way, add John L. S. Girling, *America and the Third World: Revolution and Intervention* (London: Routledge and Kegan Paul, 1980), pp. 89-100, and Samuel Huntington's institutional approach as set out in his *Political Order and Changing Societies* (New Haven: Yale University Press, 1968). One might also argue that, despite their disagreement, both James C. Scott, *The Moral Economy of the Peasant: Rebellion and Subsistence in Southeast Asia* (New Haven: Yale University Press, 1976), and Samuel P. Popkin, *The Rational Peasant: The Political Economy of Rural Society in Vietnam* (Berkeley: University of California Press, 1979) subscribe to the prevailing view of the underlying revolutionary process.

14. There is an interesting division between those US counter-guerrilla warfare analysts writing before the Americans got deeply embroiled in the Vietnam War and those writing in the mid- to late 1960s. Those writing before the mid-1960s generally favoured the hearts and minds approach. See, for example, Peter Paret and John W. Shy, *Guerrillas in the 1960s* (New York: Praeger, 1962), and David Galula, *Counterinsurgency Warfare: Theory and Practice* (New York: Praeger, 1964). See Nathan Leites and Charles Wolf, Jr., *Rebellion and Authority: An Analytic Essay on*

Insurgency Conflicts (Chicago: Markham, 1970) for a typical post mid-1960s American analysis.

15. See Robert Thompson, *No Exit From Vietnam* (London: Chatto and Windus, 1969), p. 153. It is interesting to note that Leites and Wolf in *Rebellion and Authority* cite the Malayan experience as refuting the hearts and minds approach—or at least their version of it—and confirming an approach which proved to be little more than a rationale for the continued use of the US Army's disastrous 'search and destroy' tactics.

16. Thompson, *No Exit From Vietnam*, p. 131.

17. Robert Thompson, *Defeating Communist Insurgency: Experiences from Malaya and Vietnam* (London: Chatto and Windus, 1966), p. 55.

18. Ibid., p. 143.

19. See 'Reviews: Insurrection in Malaya', *Modern Asian Studies* 11 (1977), p. 150; *The Long, Long War: Counterinsurgency in Malaya and Vietnam* (New York: Praeger, 1966), and *Riot and Revolution in Singapore and Malaya 1945-1963* (London: Faber and Faber, 1973).

20. Short, *The Communist Insurrection*, p. 1.

21. See, for example, Harry Miller's two books, *Menace in Malaya* (London: Harrap, 1954) and *Jungle War in Malaya: The Campaign against Communism, 1948-60* (London: Arthur Barker, 1972); also Edgar O'Ballance, *Malaya: Communist Insurgent War 1948-1960* (London: Faber and Faber, 1966). Two books which touch on a few of the social and economic issues are Victor Purcell, *Malaya: Communist or Free?* (London: Gollancz, 1954) and J. B. Perry Robinson, *Transformation in Malaya* (London: Secker and Warburg, 1956).

22. See his discussion of this point in his speech to Division One officers, 9 February 1952, in P/PM1, Secretary to Government Y5 (ANM).

23. See the discussion in Girling, *America and the Third World*, pp. 50-1. Girling (p. 232, fn. 17) quotes Acheson's report on the communist victory in China: 'The Nationalist armies did not have to be defeated; they disintegrated. History has proven again and again that a regime without faith in itself and an army without morale cannot survive the test of battle.' Secretary of State Dean Acheson's forward to *United States Relations with China, 1944-49*, August 1949, (no author given). See also Skocpol, *State and Social Revolutions*, p. 17.

I
The Return of the British

WHEN the British returned to the Malay Peninsula at the close of the Second World War they were given a warm reception. After landing forces at Penang, the main liberation convoy reached Singapore on 5 September 1945. The troops and officials who went ashore that evening were applauded wherever they went. One 'old Malaya hand' who made his way to the pre-War Chinese Secretariat found a crowd of several thousand blocking the streets and cheering 'themselves hoarse'.[1] On the Peninsula, the British forces were accorded similarly emotional receptions. F. Spencer Chapman, who had lived with local guerrilla bands during the Japanese Occupation, has recorded that when he arrived in Kuala Lipis, the capital of Pahang, 'The people especially the Chinese, literally wept with joy to see Englishmen again and we had an unforgettable welcome.'[2] But perhaps the predominant feeling was one of relief. The hardships and deprivations of the three and a half years of the Japanese Occupation had been considerable. The economy had deteriorated rapidly, food shortages and malnutrition were widespread, and harsh laws had been brutally implemented. The general expectation was that the relative order and prosperity which had characterized British colonial rule and which had been shattered by the Japanese invasion would be restored. The miseries of the Occupation would end.

Inevitably, such expectations could not be met, and the impossibility of restoring the old order soon became apparent. After the humiliating retreat from the Peninsula and the surrender of Singapore, the British could no longer claim to be the protectors of Malaya. Indeed, the Malays referred to this period as 'the time the white man ran'.[3] Equally, while they were clearly defeated by the Japanese in 1942, the British were not so clearly the victors in 1945. They did not retake the region in battle; indeed, it was nearly four weeks after the Japanese surrendered before British forces reached Kuala Lumpur, and well over six weeks before they reached some of the more remote areas of the East Coast. As well as undermining the prestige of the British, the success of the Japanese had acted as a catalyst to Asian nationalism and the political consciousness of the people of South-East Asia. Obviously the old order could not be reinstated; a new relationship had to be worked out between the returning colonial power and the local population. Some tensions between the rulers and the ruled were therefore only to be expected.

Yet few would have predicted the widespread antipathy towards, and even contempt for, the colonial regime which emerged in the months and years following the return of the British. It was quite evident that the Government faced a difficult task. The Japanese Occupation had cultivated dissension among the various racial communities in Malaya and left a legacy of physical destruction which severely dislocated the normal process of governing. Moreover, His Majesty's Government (HMG) was in no position to deal with these problems. The British economy was so devastated by the Second World War that only very limited funding could be spared for reviving the colonies. Nor was the necessary manpower with a knowledge of Malaya and the languages of its people available to administer the country. By themselves these limitations should not have caused the Malayan population to become so disaffected. However, in combination with inept and poorly implemented policies, they led to the alienation of significant portions of nearly every section of Malayan society.

These attitudes towards the Malayan Government and the relations which the Government developed with the people of Malaya are crucial to understanding the course of events during the early years of the Emergency. They acquired a momentum which carried them past the declaration of the Emergency and made them a key ingredient of the context within which the Government's counter-guerrilla policy took shape and was implemented. These attitudes also help to explain the lack of success that the Government encountered in its initial attempts to deal with the threat posed by the MCP-led guerrillas.

The British Military Administration

The British got off to a bad start. Their plans for governing the area had been based on the assumption that Malaya would be reclaimed in a piecemeal fashion after an invasion and an extended battle against the Japanese. Hence, the sudden end to the War brought about by the dropping of the atomic bombs on Japan left British forces ill-prepared for their task of immediately restoring British authority to the whole region. The initial form of government which ruled the Malay Peninsula and Singapore from September

1945 to April 1946 was known as the British Military Administration (BMA). As its name implies the BMA was primarily a military organization and, although there were civilian advisers and many of the military officials were civilians in uniform, it too often appeared indifferent to popular concerns. A complicating factor was that the BMA had few seasoned professional administrators on whom to call. Nearly three-quarters of the senior staff had no previous experience in government and only a quarter of the Civilian Affairs senior staff had any knowledge of Malaya.[4] The BMA was not particularly well prepared for the enormous task it faced.

Superficially, Malaya was the same country that the British had so hastily left in 1942. The population had increased only marginally to just under five million people of whom 44 per cent were Malay, 38.5 per cent Chinese, 10.5 per cent Indian, 5.5 per cent aborigines, and 1.5 per cent 'other' (including the returning Europeans).[5] Apart from those who lived in the few towns on the East Coast, most Malays continued to live primarily as subsistence padi farmers, with their religion and their kampong (village) as the focus of their daily lives. Despite the dislocation caused by the Japanese, the Chinese population, which was made up of five linguistic groups–Hokkien, Cantonese, Hakka, Tiechu, and Hainanese–originating in four of China's south-eastern provinces–Kwangtung, Fukien, Kwangsi, and Hainan–was still concentrated mainly in the Straits Settlements of Malacca and Penang and throughout the West Coast of the Peninsula. The Indians–who included a large number of Tamils from South India, a sizeable Sikh community, a number of Indian Muslims, and a distinct Ceylonese community–populated the European-owned rubber estates, with a small group of the more educated working in commerce, the professions, and for the Government. The relative social, linguistic, and religious isolation of the major communities was still accentuated by the physical environment.

The Malay Peninsula itself is about the size of England or New York state. A range of mountains runs down its spine and these, combined with a dense tropical forest, which in the immediate post-War period covered two-thirds of the land, served to make travel from the East Coast to the West Coast extremely difficult. Along the broad western coastal plain, the endless miles of rubber plantations that had replaced the jungle were interrupted only by the scars from the many tin mines that chewed up the landscape. It all looked the same. But beneath the surface, the regular rhythm of life that had characterized pre-War Malaya had been changed drastically by the Occupation. The British, however, seemed unable and at times unwilling to appreciate the nature of these changes.

The problems began not long after the BMA was installed. First, the armed forces were the source of innumerable complaints. As one disgusted British observer noted, 'In general the Army behaved, and this goes for the officers also, as if they were in conquered enemy territory.'[6] The best buildings were requisitioned, sometimes without the proper authority, and the troops were billeted in private residences–much to the inconvenience of the original occupants. Theft was widespread. A number of BMA officers went around during the first few days collecting radios, furniture, refrigerators, valuable carpets, and other movable objects.[7] Despite protest meetings, it took a long time to curb the worst excesses and little was done to bring the officers responsible to justice. Troops engaged in gun-play against unarmed civilians and sold their arms to local gangsters, and there were many reported instances of rape.[8] Nevertheless, as in the case of the officers, senior BMA officials seemed reluctant to act against the culprits. While only a small minority of soldiers were responsible for these activities, too many Malayans and Singaporeans were mistreated or harmed for there to be any restoration of the pre-War respect for British authority.

Secondly, a few days after the British arrived in Malaya, it was announced that the Japanese currency, or 'banana money' as it was called, was 'worth no more than the paper on which it is printed'.[9] As a result, nobody had any money with which to buy necessities such as food and fuel. Individuals' savings which had been carefully and often painfully husbanded during the Japanese Occupation were completely wiped out. Stall-holders had to give away food in order for people to eat. In sum, the events which occurred within the first few weeks of the BMA's establishment created a great deal of bitterness among the general population.

As the BMA slipped into a routine it became clear that corruption was widespread. Because of the inculcation of a strong sense of loyalty and the adherence to a strict code of behaviour, corruption had been virtually absent in pre-War administrations. Under the Japanese, however, bribery, smuggling, extortion, black market dealings, and other unsavoury habits had become a way of life and were much too ingrained to be changed without a strenuous effort once the British returned. But there was no concerted attempt to deal with these problems. While officials who had been in the administration before the War were generally honest in their dealings with the public, many of the new recruits fell in with prevailing practices.[10] And with so much of Malayan life regulated by the

BMA, there were plenty of opportunities (for example, the issuing of licences and exit permits, the imposition of food and price restrictions as well as export and import controls) for officials to extract bribes in return for their services. Especially damaging for the reputation of the BMA was the extent to which some of the European government officials not only condoned but openly participated in these practices. The high level of integrity which had characterized pre-War British rule was gone.

This general problem of corruption was compounded by the BMA policy of circumventing the shortage of trained government officers by assigning the import and distribution of key relief and industrial supplies to virtually autonomous agencies made up of private British traders and plantation and tin mine owners and managers. With the acute shortages of all goods and the consequent need for rationing and strict allocation of imported supplies, local entrepreneurs—mainly Malayan Chinese—complained that European interests received the lion's share of these goods. For instance, in the rubber industry, it was the Malayan Rubber Estate Owners Company which was given the task of ensuring that supplies from overseas were properly distributed at a fair price. However, after the demonetization of the Japanese currencies, few local owners had the money to subscribe to the Company and it became dominated by the British. Most local owners were, therefore, forced 'to acquire their materials at higher, and sometimes exorbitant, prices on the "free market"'.[11] Furthermore, the Rubber Buying Unit, which was the official organization for channelling supplies to small-holdings, was so inefficient and corrupt that materials were left undistributed in warehouses, put into the hands of the Malayan Estate Owners Company, or placed on the black market. Indeed, the whole system seemed to encourage a massive black market, and it was perhaps not surprising that disgruntled Malayans referred to the BMA as the 'Black Market Administration'.

The BMA also had to deal with the contentious issues associated with the treatment of those who had collaborated with the Japanese as well as those who had helped Allied personnel during the Occupation. Initially, Malays were distrustful of the BMA, fearing that they were to be hounded because they had been forced to collaborate. The Chinese, on the other hand, pressed for quick and decisive action against suspects. In general, the BMA found that, faced with the mammoth task of reviving Malaya's fortunes, many collaborators were far too useful to be tried and sent to prison. Indeed, some of the most notorious collaborators were given conspicuously favourable treatment. This inevitably led to rumours that almost any-one could get what they wanted if they had the money to pay for it. By contrast, those who had helped Allied fugitives and internees during the Occupation–often at great personal risk–were given short shrift by officials.

Even in the one area where the military government might have been expected to be most successful–that of ensuring personal security–they were found wanting. First, the BMA were incapable of curbing what was widely referred to as 'gangsterism'. Over 600 murders were reported during the BMA period, and it was generally acknowledged that the actual number was much higher.[12] Kidnapping and extortion were common throughout the Peninsula, as was piracy along the West Coast. The victims were Malayans, mostly Chinese, and there was a good deal of resentment that so little was done to restore law and order. Secondly, the Administration was unable to contain the racial clashes that broke out throughout the Peninsula. During the interregnum between the surrender of the Japanese and the arrival in force of the British, a good many old scores were settled between Malays and Chinese. Much of the racial violence that ensued was rooted in the Japanese policy of incorporating Malays into an administration which was very harsh in its treatment of the Chinese community. Later, the tensions produced by the experiences of the Occupation were exacerbated by the terrible economic conditions. The violence was sparked by Chinese guerrillas, mostly from the MCP-sponsored Malayan People's Anti-Japanese Army (MPAJA), who emerged from the jungle, took control of certain areas, and in a few cases instigated aggressive and sometimes bloody searches for collaborators, a number of whom were Malays. Malay communities retaliated. There were numerous victims: the BMA estimated that in two early incidents alone, at Muar and Batu Pahat, about 400 people were killed and thousands were made homeless.[13] Racial clashes continued to flare up throughout the period of the BMA, and both Chinese and Malay communities were upset that, despite considerable efforts, the authorities were unable to protect innocent people.

Similarly, the BMA's handling of the growth of left-wing activities was widely criticized. The Administration appeared uncertain as to how to deal with the emerging confrontation with the MCP and its actions were generally considered inappropriate or inept. Many Europeans and some Malayans were surprised that the MCP was not declared illegal and that left-wing anti-British activity was tolerated by the authorities. This group expressed a good deal of relief when, in response to the general strike of 15 February 1946, the BMA began to clamp down on such activity in a systematic fashion. On the other hand, on the occasions when the BMA did try to put the MCP on the defensive by closing newspapers or arresting key officials, the result was the arousal of considerable sympathy among the Chinese community for the heroes of the Occupation. The most prominent case was that of Soong Kwong, the General Secretary of the MCP's MPAJA in Selangor, who was arrested in October for an incident that took place in Malaya in September 1945, before British authority had been re-established. He was acquitted twice by local assessors before being convicted by an all-British panel. The Soong Kwong case became a rallying point for the MCP cause and, when added to the deteriorating economic conditions, allowed the communists to mount a number of demonstrations throughout the Peninsula as well as a major strike on 29 January 1946 in which 150,000 took part in Singapore alone.[14]

Hence, by April 1946 when the BMA handed over the reins of power to civilian governments in Kuala Lumpur and Singapore, many sectors of Malayan society had become disenchanted with the returning colonial power. Their hopes of restoring a sense of normality had been dashed. As one commentary on this period notes, 'Those who understood the roots of British prestige in Malaya appreciated that it was 1945 at least as much as 1942 that undermined the confidence of the public.'[15] There might have been some hope of improvement with the advent of the new civilian government. However, two areas continued to be the cause of friction between the British administration and the general population: the economy and the political restructuring of the Peninsula.

Reviving the Economy

The Japanese Occupation left the Malayan economy in disarray. The fighting during the invasion of late 1941 and early 1942, and especially the British use of a 'scorched earth' policy as they retreated down the Peninsula, combined with the Japanese regime's neglect, had ruined much of the country's economic infrastructure. The important tin and rubber industries had also suffered. Of course, Malaya was fortunate to have been saved from further destruction by the sudden surrender of the Japanese, but the damage already done was considerable. It was estimated, for example, that $105 million would be needed to restore the railway system to its pre-War condition.[16] Ports were very run down; key bridges had been destroyed, and many of those that had survived were unsafe; and town roads and water and sewage systems were in a dilapidated state. Some tin mines required a good deal of work in order to get them back into operation, and a number of rubber estates had no housing for their labourers. To revive the Malayan economy, an injection of investment capital, both public and private, was clearly needed.

But public and private investment was extremely scarce. The primary reason for this was to be found in the policies pursued by HMG. London's post-War policies severely restricted the funds that were available to the Malayan Administration and limited the ability of Malayan industry to import vital machinery.

First, the British Government had no funds to spare for refurbishing the economies of the colonies and made it quite plain to the Malayan Administration that Malaya was to finance her own rehabilitation. With revenue only just covering very modest recurrent expenditures, extraordinary non-recurrent expenditure to revive the Malayan economy had to come out of the reserves that had been built up over the years. As a result, the reserves rapidly diminished from $210 million on 1 April 1946 to under $43 million by 1 January 1948.[17] The rapid dwindling of its resources acted as a brake on the Malayan Government's spending and consequently its ability to rejuvenate the economy. Some thought bankruptcy a possibility. Further compounding this shortage of funds was a Bank of England policy which, until 1948, discouraged colonial governments from floating loans on the London market.[18]

Secondly, Malayans were forced to help the British Government to ride out the successive crises which beset the sterling area. At the heart of the problem was that the sterling area countries, most notably Great Britain, did not have enough United States (US) dollars with which to pay for imports from non-sterling areas, such as Canada and the US. As a result, the Secretary of State for the Colonies imposed what he called 'a regime of war time austerity as regards imports'.[19] Only those goods considered absolutely essential–and this term was given a very narrow definition–could be imported from outside the sterling area. In 1947, colonial governments were told to restrict imports from the United Kingdom (UK) as well as from foreign countries. The resulting acute shortages of important supplies and machinery hampered Malaya's economic growth and created friction between Malaya's businessmen, who wanted the restrictions lifted, and the Administration, which had to defend Whitehall's policies.

Perhaps the most frustrating aspect of the whole affair for Malayans was that Malaya was the 'dollar arsenal' for Britain and the Empire. The dollar earnings from Malaya's export of rubber and tin to the US were piled up in London for the use of all sterling area countries but primarily Great Britain. In 1946, for example, Malaya's net contribution to the gold/dollar pool was US$118 million, while the net contribution of all the other colonies combined was only US$37 million.[20] So important was Malaya's contribution that one authoritative source has noted that 'without Malaya the sterling currency system as we know it would not exist'.[21] It was no wonder, then, that Malayans fretted over British policies, believing they should be exempt from the restrictions and able to import goods from wherever they wished.

Thirdly, the sale price set by the British Government for Malaya's key commodities, rubber and tin, were considered by most producers to be artificially and unrealistically low. There was a suspicion that the low prices were maintained to ensure that Britain did not have to compete in a free market with US companies who were prepared to pay higher prices. The free market was restored for rubber in 1946, but the Ministry of Supply continued to be the sole buyer of tin for a further year. Certainly this policy proved to be generally irksome and elicited many complaints from all quarters.[22]

Fourthly, the British Government put great pressure on the Malayan economy by re-establishing the rate of exchange at the pre-War level of M$1 to 2s. 4p. The Malayan dollar, however, rapidly depreciated in value in the post-War period, and the newly re-imposed exchange rate served to deflate Malaya's income from the export of its commodities. This led, for example, to a situation in which in 1947 a pound of rubber bought less than a fifth of the rice, a quarter of the flour, half of the milk, a fifth of the sugar, or a sixth of the textiles, it had bought before the War.[23] In reviewing the consequences of this policy, the economic historian Martin Rudner has argued that 'By forcing Malaya's post-War money-cost structure to adjust to the pre-War sterling exchange rate, rather than the reverse, Malayan planners doubtlessly contributed to the political unrest culminating in the Emergency.'[24]

Finally, in order to increase their revenue from domestic sources the British Government instructed the Malayan and Singaporean Administrations to introduce an income tax. This policy encountered fierce resistance from Malaya's business communities, especially from their representatives on the Malayan Union's Advisory

Council and Singapore's Legislative Council. It was argued that before imposing an income tax, more economies in administration should be undertaken. The Finance Review Committee of the Advisory Council indicated where cuts in expenditure could be made in the Malayan Union's budget. In their report, the Unofficials on the Committee (members of the general public who were appointed to the Council by the Governor) singled out what they considered to be the high cost to the Government of the Governor-General's office, the region's broadcasting service, and the Malayan Security Service. The majority of the members of the Committee also argued that an income tax would take 'the country's wealth away from it and [put] it into the dead hand of government'.[25] The Income Tax Bill was defeated in the Malayan Union's Advisory Council and suffered the same fate in Singapore. But the Colonial Office, with the support of labour leaders and left-wing politicians, insisted that an income tax be introduced. Eventually, in December 1947, the Governors of the Malayan Union and Singapore were forced to take the unusual step of overriding their respective Councils and enacted the Income Tax legislation by order.

Hence, in the first few years after the return of the British, the economic strategy of the British and Malayan Governments exasperated the country's business leaders. They were greatly dissatisfied with some key policies. In particular, Malayan businessmen, who were mostly Malayan Chinese, were critical of the way in which Britain's interests were placed above the interests of Malaya. There was also some concern expressed that the return of British rule was used primarily to pave the way for the return to dominance of British commercial interests.

The general mass of the population faced rather different problems. For most of the people the major preoccupations were the low wages and the high cost of living. These conditions squeezed unfortunate wage-earners and created considerable hardship throughout Malaya. Even for those not directly tied to the relatively low wage levels, the high cost of living was a major burden. In the months immediately after the return of the British, the BMA, in an attempt to restore the economy to the 'normality' of the pre-War days, pegged wages at just over pre-War levels. This was done despite the spiralling cost of living which was prompted first by the demonetization of the Japanese currency, and then by the recognition of the widespread shortages of almost every item of everyday life—from food and clothing to medical supplies and building materials.

The high cost of living, shortage of labour, and rising commodity prices produced a sustained pressure on employers to raise wages. However, led by the Government, most major employers, especially the large European-owned estates, were intent on resisting this pressure. Wage levels did rise gradually but they did not nearly compensate for the high cost of living. It was widely believed that the Government and the major European employers were conspiring to keep down wages. As a union representative in the Government-appointed Legislative Council noted in early 1948, 'There is a feeling in the working class that there is a kind of unholy alliance between Government and employers.' He went on to point out that 'The working class feel that they are always consistently and continually at the wrong end of the stick.'[26]

However, of all the economic hardships which beset Malayans during the post-War period, none was more aggravating and none caused more consistent criticism of the Malayan Government than the shortage of rice and the consequent high prices. The British Government encountered many difficulties in its quest to provide Malaya with rice. The primary problem was that the traditional rice-growing areas of South-East Asia had been devastated by the Second World War and, as a consequence, the production and distribution systems were unable to respond to the tremendous demands placed on them in the post-War period. The main sources of rice for Britain's Asian dependencies were Thailand and Burma.[27] Thailand proved to be most unreliable reneging on its shipping commitments on a number of occasions. Burma was inside the sterling area and, therefore, its rice could be bought without digging into the dwindling US dollar pool. But Burma had been especially hard hit by the fighting and was plagued by political problems after the War. It was in no position to fill all the region's needs. Moreover, in order to increase its revenue, the Burmese Government levied a substantial export tax, a move which angered British officials but one about which they dared not complain in case the Burmese decided to sell their rice for US dollars on the world market. The British also had to decide how to distribute the scarce shipments of rice among the British dependencies. On more than one occasion, shipments originally destined for Malaya were diverted elsewhere by Whitehall. To make matters even worse, Malaya's own limited rice production was slow to revive.[28] The overall result was a crippling shortage of Malaya's most important staple.

Despite rationing, the Malayan Administration was unable to ensure that each person received a reasonable minimum daily amount of rice. Before the Japanese Occupation the average consumption of rice was 15 oz per person per day. Plans drawn up in London for post-War Malaya estimated that the 'minimum tolerable per diem rice ration was 12 ounces per capita' and that anything lower would cause 'disease and unrest'.[29] However, the British could only provide 4.6 oz per day in the months after their return, and by late 1946 this amount had fallen to a derisory 2.5 oz. Rations were increased to 5.6 oz per person per day in early 1947, only to be reduced back to 4.6 oz later in the year when a complete breakdown in rationing threatened. Even by mid-1948, the per capita daily ration of rice was a mere 7.6 oz.[30] Moreover, increases in ration levels invariably came with an unwelcome increase in price. While the price of officially rationed rice fluctuated from week to week and from region to region, it was generally five times the pre-War level. Black market rice was available, but only in relatively limited quantities, and at exorbitant prices which were sometimes as much as five or six times the official price of rationed rice.[31] Indeed, the cost of buying food was so high that one official report estimated that it consumed up to 70 per cent of the budget of many families.[32] As the British wartime planners had predicted, the results of these shortages and high prices were a continuation of the malnutrition which had occurred during the Occupation, as well as widespread unrest.[33] There were numerous demonstrations throughout the Peninsula and many of the strikes which broke out during the months after the return of the British were initially prompted by the rice shortages. It was widely acknowledged that these shortages were responsible for much of the strong undercurrent of anti-Government feeling which was to be found in many parts of the country.[34]

By 1948, despite the frustrations that were encountered, Malaya's two main industries, rubber and tin, were on their way to recovery. Indeed, the production in the rubber industry in 1948 exceeded pre-War levels, and the price–though not particularly good–had stabilized at just over $0.40 per pound. The tin industry revived at a rather slower pace because of the problems of obtaining both the needed capital and machinery. Nevertheless, here too progress was being made. Generally, however, the recovery of these two industries ameliorated only some of the economic problems faced by Malayans and did not restore the living standards to pre-War levels. For example, in 1948, rice still cost over five times as much as it had in 1941, while the standard wage rate in the rubber industry, Malaya's largest employer, was only $1.30 a day compared with $0.55 a day before the War.[35] Hence, although the economic position improved in the years following the return of the British, the economic situation in 1948 still left many Malayans disillusioned with the British colonial administration. The Malayan Government, however, had more to worry about than the country's economic predicaments, bad though they were.

Constitutional Crises

In the years following the re-establishment of British rule, the Malayan Government blundered its way through a series of constitutional and political crises. In the process, it managed to alienate not only most of the country's political élite but also many of the growing numbers in all of Malaya's racial communities who were becoming politically aware.

The Second World War provided the British with an opportunity to review their position in the region. Prior to the Japanese invasion, the British had developed a rather odd patchwork of political authority. The three Straits Settlements (Singapore, Malacca, and Penang) were crown colonies run from Singapore. The Federated Malay States (Selangor, Perak, Pahang, and Negri Sembilan) were each officially ruled by a legally sovereign sultan; however, they were effectively ruled by British administrators who acted on the basis of guidelines laid down in Kuala Lumpur. Finally, the Unfederated Malay States (Johore, Perlis, Kedah, Kelantan, and Trengganu) were less overtly under British control; administrators were accepted as part of the governments of each state, but their roles were not always clearly defined and their effectiveness tended to depend on the personalities involved. A special committee which was set up in London during the War decided that there was a need to rationalize this disparate collection of states and colonies, and put in its place a secular modern Malayan state. The committee, known as the Malayan Planning Unit, drew up a plan under which one centrally governed political unit covering Peninsular Malaya was to be created, while Singapore would be retained as a Crown Colony under separate administration. This amalgamation of Malacca and Penang with the various Malay states was to be named the Malayan Union. The Malayan Planning Unit also recommended conferring equal political rights on Malays and non-Malays by introducing a broadly applicable common citizenship.[36]

In order to implement the new plan, it was necessary to persuade the sultans to surrender their sovereignty. Accordingly, just a few weeks after the BMA was installed, Sir Harold MacMichael was sent out to Malaya and, accompanied by Brigadier A. T. Newboult,

Deputy Chief Civil Affairs Officer, Malaya, he did the rounds of the state capitals. While a number of sultans had qualms about relinquishing their sovereignty, MacMichael was able to secure their agreement to the terms of the Malayan Union with remarkably little fuss.

There were some hints of a growing opposition to the Malayan Union but on the whole it was not unreasonable for the British Government to expect to inaugurate the Malayan Union without creating too many ripples. Although the Second World War had acted as a catalyst on the political life of the country and in the first few weeks after the surrender of the Japanese political activity in the Peninsula had blossomed, much of its focus was on events that were taking place outside Malaya. The Chinese and Indian communities appeared preoccupied with events that were unfolding in their respective mother countries. Similarly, those Malays who were politically active seemed to be more interested in Sukarno's August 1945 declaration of independence for the revolutionary Republic of Indonesia than in issues that were intrinsically Malayan. And so, when in late January 1946 the British Government published its White Paper on the Malayan Union in which it set out publicly for the first time the details of the new constitutional arrangements, it was quite unprepared for the flood of criticism from both Malays and former Malayan civil servants that swept over Kuala Lumpur and London.

Malay opposition to the British proposals coalesced around three particular concerns. First, Malays were very uneasy about the extent to which the sultans were to be stripped of their sovereignty. The sultans were a crucial element in the cohesion of Malay communities. Each sultan held not only temporal authority, standing as he did at the head of the social and political hierarchies, but also spiritual authority arising from Malay religious traditions. The advent of British colonial rule in the nineteenth century had changed the structure of Malayan society surprisingly little, and British administrators had been very careful not to undermine the position of the sultans. Indeed, traditionally, the British had formally respected a sultan's sovereignty even if they felt that for most purposes it was irrelevant. Viewed from War-time London, it seemed reasonable to end this somewhat anomalous relationship. A centralized government would allow for more efficiency and even for the flowering of the democratic process. But by relieving the sultans of their sovereignty, the Malayan Union struck at the heart of the Malay identity. It appeared to the Malays to open up Malay society

to the vagaries of the economic and social changes that had threatened the Malay way of life for some time but from which the sultans,
with a little help from the British, had been able to shield them.

Tied in closely with this question of the loss of the sultans' sovereignty was the role that the states were to play under the Malayan
Union. If the sultans forfeited their sovereignty and Malaya was
administered centrally from Kuala Lumpur, then the states would
lose their relative autonomy as well as some of their highly valued
and distinctive characteristics. For the Unfederated Malay States,
most notably Kedah and Johore, which had always fought strongly
against any form of administrative centralization, this was a particularly galling turn of events. Moreover, members of the Malay
élite in each state were fearful that they would lose their positions
as members of the state governments and state councils and thus,
most importantly from their point of view, lose much of their political power and social standing. Once the Malayan Union was prom-
ulgated and in operation for a short time, the worst fears of the Malay
élite were confirmed: the states had only a very limited role to play
in the new scheme of things. All of this was made even more un-
palatable by the memories of the extensive political power which
some members of the Malay élite had wielded during the Japanese
Occupation, and by the events unfolding in the newly proclaimed
Republic of Indonesia where the local population was asserting
its independence from the old colonial regime rather than allowing
it to gain an even firmer grip on the levers of government.

Secondly, Malays feared the extension of political rights to non-
Malays as set out in the British Government's White Paper. The
provision that caused the most unease was the proposal to grant
citizenship automatically to non-Malays who could claim to belong
to the country through birth or residence for ten of the previous
fifteen years, and to grant citizenship by naturalization to those
who had resided in Malaya for five of the preceding eight years and
who had a knowledge of Malay or English.[37] Malays viewed this as
a betrayal of past British commitments. Over the years, the Malay
leaders and the British administrators had shared the common belief that the political development of the Peninsula would be based
on the pre-eminence of the Malays and the conservation of Malay
values. To allow Malays to maintain their predominant position,
Malays were accorded special educational opportunities and were
brought into the administrative structure of the Peninsula through
the Malayan Administrative Service. A few Malays had even been
allowed into the predominantly British Malayan Civil Service. But

clearly the new citizenship proposals signalled a major change in policy. Non-Malays were to be treated in the same way as Malays. This made Malays very nervous about the erosion of their special position and the possibilities that the constitutional changes would undermine Malay customs and values.

In particular, Chinese incursions into Malay society had long been a source of irritation. For example, the Depression of the 1930s had caused a great deal of indebtedness, especially among those who relied on small rubber holdings for their livelihood. A large portion of these people were Malays while the vast majority of the creditors were Chinese. Registered and unregistered indebtedness in the Federated Malay States on reservation lands (lands allocated to Malays) alone was officially said to total $5 million.[38] This acquisition and control of land by the Chinese caused much anxiety for, of course, land was at the core of Malay subsistence existence. Moreover, the racial clashes that had flared up throughout the Peninsula exacerbated Malay fears of what would happen when they had to share Malaya with the Chinese. Rather than accept the British Government's view that everyone could benefit from the new constitutional arrangements, Malays tended to hold the belief that benefits accruing to an individual from society were fixed and constant and that any gain to a person or a group could only come at the expense of another person or group. This 'constant pie' view of society obviously made the Malays very suspicious of any redistribution of power that might work to the advantage of other groups.[39]

Finally, Malays were angered by the method by which the British Government had gained the agreement of the sultans to the new constitutional arrangements. MacMichael was accused of having used intimidation on his tour of the state capitals. There was some truth to this charge. MacMichael and Newboult had exerted, albeit in the most gentlemanly fashion possible, a great deal of pressure on the rulers, some of whom had signed only because they saw no other option open to them. The Sultan of Kedah was even driven to remark that 'although the manner was much more polite, the technique adopted by His Majesty's Government appeared to be not unlike the familiar Japanese technique of bullying'.[40] It was also thought that the somewhat cavalier attitude of the British Government towards the sultans was symptomatic of a change in the way British administrators in Malaya treated Malays in general. Gone were the old established relationships and the traditional ways of conducting affairs between HMG and the rulers. All this added to the frustrations already generated by the inability of the BMA

and the Malayan Union Government to provide such basic requirements as food and security.

The opposition to the Malayan Union was organized around,
first, the Pan-Malayan Malay Congress and then the United Malays
National Organization (UMNO), and was spearheaded by Dato
Onn bin Jaafar, the Mentri Besar (Chief Minister) of Johore. At its
initial meeting in early March 1946, the Congress passed a series of
resolutions condemning British policy. These were telegraphed to
the Prime Minister and others in Britain who had an interest in
Malaya and were thought to be influential. The Congress also
pressed for a total boycott of the Malayan Union by Malays. Dato
Onn persuaded the sultans not to attend the ceremonies inaugu-
rating the Malayan Union but rather to acknowledge the cheers of
the large crowd–many of whom were dressed in traditional mourn-
ing clothes–which had gathered outside their hotel.[41] The UMNO,
which formally came into existence at the May 1946 meeting of the
Pan-Malayan Malay Congress, took the lead in organizing massive
demonstrations of Malays throughout the Peninsula. What was
most impressive was that the UMNO was able to mobilize not only
men but also women–an almost unheard of occurrence–from nearly every kampong. The mass of the Malay population had become
politically conscious in a matter of months and it was no longer possible for the British Government or the Malayan Government to
assume the automatic acquiescence of Malays to whatever policies
these governments saw fit to introduce. The overwhelming expression of Malay antagonism towards the Malayan Union, in combination with the pressures exerted by former members of the
Malayan Civil Service as well as other Malayophiles living in
Britain, forced the British Government to reconsider its policy.

In July 1946, the Colonial Office reversed its previous stand and
the British Government authorized the negotiation of a successor
to the Malayan Union. Accordingly, representatives of the Malayan
Government, the rulers, and the UMNO formed the Constitutional
Working Committee, and by December 1946 they had drafted a
new set of constitutional proposals. The Working Committee of
pro-Malay British officers and moderate-conservative Malays not
unnaturally produced proposals which married the British Government's wish for a more centralized administration than had
existed before the War to Malay demands for a recognition of the
sovereignty of the sultans and for the imposition of strict limitations
on the granting of citizenship to non-Malays. Recognizing that the
non-Malay communities had not received much of a hearing on

these important issues, the British set up in 1947 a Consultative Committee through which a wider spectrum of views could be solicited. In the end, however, the views of the Consultative Committee were ignored. The new Federation Agreement was based almost entirely on the proposals originally put forward by the Constitutional Working Committee. On 1 February 1948, the Federation of Malaya was proclaimed, and with its introduction the British hoped that they had put the battle with the Malays firmly behind them.

But the Malays found it impossible to restore their trust in the British and Malayan Governments. The fact that the Malayan Union had been implemented without consultation, the initial inflexibility of the British Government when confronted with Malay opposition to their proposals, and the long delay—from July 1946 to February 1948—in promulgating a successor to the Malayan Union, all raised doubts in the minds of Malays about the extent to which the British could be trusted in the future. In addition, the two most senior members of the new Federation of Malaya Government, Sir Edward Gent, the High Commissioner, and Sir Alexander Newboult, the Chief Secretary, had been closely associated with the implementation of the Malayan Union. As head of the Eastern Department of the Colonial Office during the War, Gent was one of the key architects of the Malayan Union and was sent out in 1946 to be the first Governor. Although he changed his mind about the appropriateness of the Malayan Union once he arrived in Malaya, Malays had good reason to look on him with a great deal of suspicion. Newboult had also been involved in the Colonial Office's planning for the Malayan Union and had subsequently used his prestige within the Malay community and his personal friendship with the rulers to help MacMichael obtain their signatures. As Raja Tun Uda of Selangor is reported to have noted later, they had trusted Newboult to their cost.[42] It was not surprising, then, that the Malays had major reservations about placing their confidence in the new Government.

The scepticism with which Malays viewed the Malayan Administration was reflected in the attitudes of Dato Onn, the President of the UMNO. During the negotiations leading to the Federation Agreement, Onn constantly reminded Gent of the Malay frustrations and the Government's need to demonstrate its good faith in order to regain Malay support.[43] Even after the Malayan Union was abandoned in favour of the Federation of Malaya Onn still distrusted the Government. Onn was at his most acerbic in letting Colonial

Office officials know of Malay dissatisfaction when he visited London in late 1948. He chastised the Colonial Office for the loss of the states' reserve balances, and declared that the British Government had virtually 'stolen' the funds when they handed them over to the Malayan Union and allowed them to be squandered away. Onn demanded restitution. In a similar vein, he reminded the Colonial Office officials of the need to respect the newly won authority of the states. Onn's querulousness clearly surprised the Colonial Office. Shortly after Onn's departure, J. J. Paskin, a senior official, wrote that they were not 'prepared either for the degree of bitterness, under which he still labours, at what was done in 1945/6 or for (and especially this) the strength of his assertion (constantly repeated—or suggested in a wide variety of connections) that HMG has not yet regained the confidence of the Malays'.[44]

The Malays were not the only ones to react adversely to British attempts to change the constitutional arrangements. However, for the non-Malays—that is the Malayan Chinese and the Malayan Indians—it was the introduction of the Federation of Malaya in February 1948, rather than the Malayan Union, which aroused their anger.

Despite the benefits it conferred on them, the non-Malay communities were generally indifferent to the Malayan Union. A few people criticized the separation of Singapore from Malaya while leaders of left-wing groups felt that it did not go far enough in assuring Malaya of an independent, democratic future. But on the whole, the non-Malays did not anticipate that the Malayan Union would have much impact on their lives. Of course, in the past, the Malayan Government had not usually sought support for their policies from the Chinese and Indian communities and these communities were not in the habit of expressing a coherent opinion on major political issues. Thus their relative silence was not perhaps surprising. Most people in Malaya were simply trying to survive the economic hardships or busy making money through the black market. And even if they had wanted to give vocal support to the Malayan Union, the Chinese community in 1946 had no channels for doing so. Politically as a group, the Chinese were, as Sun Yat Sen was often quoted as saying, 'like a plate of loose sand', and apart from the Malayan Communist Party, there was no obvious means of pulling Chinese opinion together in a concerted fashion. Few Chinese had good contacts with the Government. Many of the Chinese community's former leaders had either fled the country or moved away during the Japanese Occupation and were slow to return to their old haunts after the Japanese surrendered. Indeed, many Chinese were loath to assume a leadership position because, given the prevailing state of lawlessness, to do so was to invite kidnapping and demands for money. Within the Indian community, people were slow to advance any public expression of opinion because they were either caught up in the momentous events that were taking place in their motherland or wary of being accused of stirring up further racial tensions.[45]

In late 1946, the non-Malay communities began to mobilize support for the Malayan Union and to argue strongly against a British reversal of policy. The first expressions of opposition to the abolition of the new constitutional arrangements came from left-wing groups which banded together to form the Pan-Malayan Council of Joint Action (PMCJA).[46] The PMCJA is thought to have been initiated by the MCP but it was able to broaden its base of support when a noted Malaccan businessman and widely respected leader of the Chinese community, Tan Cheng Lock, was persuaded to join the coalition. Tan Cheng Lock's intervention stemmed from his long-standing commitment to an independent Malaya in which members of all races would be treated fairly. Also joining this group was the Malay Nationalist Party (MNP) which was headed by left-wing Malays. The MNP had been excluded by Dato Onn from the UMNO-led Malay nationalist movement; they were critical of the Anglo-Malayan Constitutional Working Committee for its willingness to uphold Malay feudalism and for undermining prospects for democracy and independence. The MNP were first part of the PMCJA and then partners with the PMCJA after they had decided to set up their own umbrella organization for left-wing Malay groups, the Pusat Tenaga Ra'ayat (PUTERA). It was this partnership which led the fight against the Working Committee's proposals.

During 1947, opposition to the idea of replacing the Malayan Union with a new constitution mounted within the non-Malay communities. Chinese newspapers discussed the issue at some length and did not hide their fear of a Malaya dominated by the Malays. The Consultative Committee which was established by the Government to mollify non-Malay opposition and to solicit non-Malay opinion was considered unrepresentative (one contemporary European observer who was sympathetic to the non-Malay cause has called the European members of the Committee 'rabidly pro-Malay')[47] and was boycotted by the PMCJA. Moreover, the recommendations of the Consultative Committee, when they appeared in early 1947, ignored many of the submissions it had received, and were considered more of an anodyne than a constructive critique of the Working Committee's proposals. Even the conservative Associated Chinese Chambers of Commerce which had originally endorsed the establishment of the Consultative Committee became embittered by the process. When the draft Federation Agreement was published in May 1947, they reluctantly decided, despite major misgivings, to join with the left-wing PMCJA-PUTERA in order to battle the Government.

A number of points angered the members of the Associated Chinese Chambers of Commerce. First, it appeared that Singapore and Malaya would continue to be separate entities and that a merger could only be achieved if the sultans and the UMNO agreed. Secondly, the citizenship provisions were to be severely restricted, leaving many Malayan Chinese–for example those who were born in Malaya but who spoke only Chinese–ineligible for citizenship.[48] The Straits Settlement Chinese, or 'King's Chinese' as they called themselves, were especially distressed that their status would be changed so that they now became subjects of the sultans. Thirdly, arrangements for introducing self-government and elections were to be postponed and in the meantime the new Federal Council would have a built-in Malay majority. But perhaps what proved to be the unkindest cut of all was that, despite the way in which the Chinese community had aided the British in fighting the Japanese, and despite the vital role the Chinese played in developing the US dollar-producing Malayan economy, when the British had to make the hard choice between a pro-Malay position and a pro-Malayan position–that is, one which guaranteed equal treatment for all Malayans–they chose to support the Malays. From the Chinese point of view it appeared as if the British were not willing to arbitrate fairly among Malaya's communities and were not interested in the well-being of the Chinese.

The campaign against the introduction of the Federation of Malaya culminated in October 1947 with a hartal. Up to this point, anti-Federation activists had mounted rallies, sent letters and petitions to the Government, and used the Chinese and the Indian press to express their frustrations. However, it was all rather ill-organized and by no means matched the concerted efforts of the Malays. The hartal was looked upon as an answer to the Malay boycott of the Malayan Union. The idea of a one-day hartal was put forward by Tan Cheng Lock, who had come across this method of protest while living in India during the War. It entailed bringing the economy to a halt by closing shops and other commercial establishments. The first hartal staged in Malacca, Tan Cheng Lock's home base, in September 1947, proved successful, as did one later that month in Ipoh, Perak. Buoyed by these examples, the Associated Chinese Chambers of Commerce, together with the All-Malaya Council of Joint Action (the new name for the PMCJA) and PUTERA, decided on a country-wide protest which would include Singapore, to take place on 20 October, the day on which it was thought that the Federation Agreement would be debated in the British Parliament. Although the English-language press and Government leaders played down the success of the hartal, the Secretary for Chinese Affairs reported that it 'was effectively carried out with markets, shops, amusement parks, cinemas, factories and street stalls going out of business for the day'.[49] Victor Purcell, who had been Principal Advisor on Chinese Affairs with the BMA, has written that 'virtually all business and transport were at a standstill and Singapore was without buses, trams or taxis and no employees of the Harbour Board were at work', and that 'at the request of the organisers, the Chinese community of Singapore as a whole stayed at home'.[50]

But in the face of British determination to put the new constitution into effect, this dramatic show of unity could not be sustained. The action was continued in Singapore where elections were boycotted; however, in the Peninsula, the strange set of political bedfellows who opposed the Federation Agreement disagreed over what course of action to take. Despite talks of boycotting the Federation Agreement when it came into being on 1 February 1948, conservative Chinese organizations decided to accept appointments to state, settlement, and federal councils, and some Indian trade unionists followed suit.

Yet the hartal had left its mark on the non-Malay communities. It had certainly proved to be a 'unique method of political education'.[51] People throughout Malaya and Singapore were made aware of what the British and Malayan Governments were doing and, even if not all Chinese and Indians were sure of the complete details of the substantive points at issue, they and their leaders were henceforth alerted that they should be highly suspicious of the actions and motives of the new Federation of Malaya Government.

MacMichael's mission to Malaya opened up a Pandora's box. Acting with little appreciation of the rising tide of political consciousness that had been released by the Japanese Occupation the British managed, in quick succession, to alienate first the Malays and then the non-Malays. In the end, it was perhaps not surprising that faced on the one hand by a united Malay community led by the Malay élite, and on the other by a more fragmented, primarily Chinese grouping, seemingly manipulated by left-wing extremists, the British chose to side with the interests of the Malays. But this decision had long-term consequences as the bitterness generated by the constitutional battles lingered on well after the inauguration of the Federation of Malaya.

Government Morale

Following the re-establishment of British authority in Malaya in 1945, the Government was plagued by low morale. In the pre-War years the British had built up a fairly efficient and smooth-running administrative machinery manned by a relatively homogeneous group of British officers, a small number of Malay officers drawn from the Malay élite, and a locally recruited support staff. During the Japanese Occupation, this machinery was severely dislocated. When the civil Government took over from the BMA in April 1946, they were confronted with the enormous task of reconstructing in a few months what had taken years to develop. To make matters worse, there was a crippling shortage of funds, equipment, and manpower as well as some divisive issues remaining from the Japanese Occupation.

In stark contrast to the pre-War years, those attempting to reconstruct the administration in post-War Malaya found both their living and working conditions to be atrocious. As has already been mentioned, the price of all food—especially rice—was very high, and it was often difficult—even for Europeans—to get the quantities they required. There was also the general feeling that salaries for European officers were totally inadequate given the very high cost of living. Housing was so scarce that officers, many of whom brought with them their wives and children, had either to live in cramped hotel rooms or to share houses with at least one other family—sometimes two. A lack of doctors and nurses put health care facilities under considerable pressure. These problems were most acute in Kuala Lumpur where, compared to the pre-War years, the centralization of government under the Malayan Union had markedly increased the number of British personnel in the capital. Those posted in the states had their own peculiar frustrations as they 'were not paid their salaries for months', faced a 'lack of support and funds from the centre', and believed their views were being ignored in the capital.[52] In conjunction with such irritants, the loss of records, lack of transportation, dilapidated telephone and telegraph systems, and a generally increased volume of routine work created enormous strains on both personal and working relationships.

Underlying this malaise was the general problem of post-War exhaustion. This issue came to the fore when Field Marshal Montgomery, on a stopover in Singapore, was told by senior military officers that the civilian bureaucracy was inefficient and ineffective because of the number of ex-internees in its middle ranks. Montgomery passed the information on to the Prime Minister and the Colonial Office was invited to investigate the matter. Reporting to the Colonial Office, R. B. MacGregor, Director of Medical Services, Malayan Union, compared the pre-War and post-War bureaucracies and stated, 'The most striking feature is, I think, the deterioration in the quality of work and in the length of time which it takes for the work to be done.' However, he felt that the conditions were so different to those prevailing in the pre-War years that this was not surprising. He noted that there was a sense of exhaustion in other places, including England, and that this was not something confined to Malaya.[53] Gent wrote to the Colonial Office in a similar vein, but added that while a few were obviously not wholly physically or mentally fit, the rest worked harder than before in very adverse conditions.[54] On the whole, although an abnormally high suicide rate among ex-internees was alluded to, this group was not singled out in these reports as being a particular drag on the efficiency of the administration; it was recognized that post-War exhaustion had taken its toll on nearly everyone.

Yet the concerns of the senior military officers were not completely without foundation: a few of the ex-internees were a source of considerable discord. Because of the shortage of people with experience of Malaya, the Prisoners of War (POWs) who had returned to Britain directly upon release from Changi Gaol and who were judged physically fit were, after only a short period of recuperation, shipped back to Malaya. The long leave which they needed after the hardships of imprisonment had to be delayed for a year to eighteen months. Many, not surprisingly, had some initial difficulty adjusting to the new conditions and new attitudes; some harboured gnawing grievances which tended to undermine their morale. There was resentment that those who had escaped capture by the Japanese–a few ex-POWs referred to them as 'runaways' or 'deserters'–were promoted after their return to Malaya; some ex-internees refused to stay in the same room as 'runaways', let alone talk to them. The resulting tensions made life difficult for everyone. Other grievances felt by POWs have been listed by W. F. N. Churchill, who was adviser to the Sultan of Kelantan after the War, in a memorandum dramatically entitled 'Why be loyal?' He was especially incensed that government officers who had been ordered in 1941 to stay put in the face of the Japanese invasion or forfeit all rights to pay and pension and who had been promised full pay for the period during which they were interned had had '10% filched for "income tax"' in 1946, despite there being no income tax in Malaya. Churchill was also upset at the Government's repudiation of the financial guarantees given to those who had volunteered their services. Churchill's conclusions that members of the Malayan Civil Service had little confidence in their senior officers may have been somewhat extreme but was not without foundation.[55]

The ill will produced by the introduction of the Malayan Union and the switch to the Federation of Malaya opened up another contentious division within the European community. Each member of the Malayan Civil Service was required to learn one of the three main languages of Malaya: Malay, Chinese, or Tamil. This tended to balkanize the Service, and individual officers were prone to look at problems through the eyes of those whose language they spoke. Most of the officers learned Malay and many of this group were 'shocked and disgusted by the Malayan Union proposals which we considered to be a betrayal of our old Malay friends'.[56] Those who spoke Chinese found themselves clearly in the minority on the Malayan Union issue and could only fight a rather weak, rearguard action. The Chinese-speaking officers had been particularly hard hit by the Japanese invasion and the Occupation, and were spread very thinly across the country. Few were posted in Kuala Lumpur, and there was a feeling among them that, as a group, their views were not taken seriously in policy-making circles. This sense of frustration was underlined by the exclusion from the Executive Council of the Secretary for Chinese Affairs, the most senior official dealing with the Chinese community.

The mixture of 'old Malaya hands' and officers new to the country created further tensions. Only just over half the senior officers of the Malayan Civil Service (MCS) had served in Malaya before the War. This number was further decreased by late 1947 when those who had returned to Malaya directly after the War for an emergency eighteen-month tour departed to take their long leave or to retire. The 'old Malaya hands' fretted that the traditions of the MCS were being eroded and that their views were not being given the weight they deserved. The butt of many of their criticisms was Sir Edward

Gent, Governor of the Malayan Union and later High Commissioner of the Federation of Malaya. Considered responsible for the policies so disdained by the old guard and because of his background in Whitehall, Gent 'symbolised for them the triumph of the Colonial Office over the man on the spot'.[57] One other important official who was treated with suspicion, especially by the old guard, was Malcolm MacDonald. In 1946 he became Governor-General of Malaya, Singapore, and British Borneo, and then in May 1948 he was elevated to the position of Commissioner-General in South-East Asia with the personal rank of Ambassador. MacDonald had no experience of Malaya; he rarely wore a coat and tie; he tended to fraternize with members of the local population; and he was an ex-politician rather than a civil servant. It was no wonder that the generally conservative MCS officers were wary of him.

Gent also came under attack from the wider European community in Malaya. The planters, the miners, and the traders were highly critical of the Government's inability to stem the rising tide of lawlessness. The raids on villages, the highway robberies, the kidnappings, the extortion and murders, all served to envelop Malaya in an atmosphere of fear and tension. The planters and miners considered the use of intimidation to be at the heart of the wave of labour unrest and demanded firmer action. They advised Gent to restore banishment as a punishment and to come down hard on the law-breakers. This perception that the Government could not maintain law and order was particularly damaging to its reputation; from the very beginning, acceptance of the British presence and authority in the region had been predicated on its ability to establish peace and order. Unable to perform this function the Government could not command the respect of either the Europeans or large sections of Malaya's other communities. An editorial in the *Straits Times* put it bluntly: 'The Governor of the Malayan Union can have no conception of the cynical bitterness with which his administration is regarded as a result of the failure to suppress criminal elements.'[58]

A key reason for the Government's lack of success in combating lawlessness was the disastrous impact of the Japanese Occupation on the police force. Upon returning to their former posts after the War, British police officers found 'the dregs of a police force, badly equipped, shabbily dressed with no morale and carrying its share of the hatred and contempt which the Japanese system of secret police, working through spies and informants, had called down upon the force'.[59] The Japanese use of the Malays on the force to harry the Chinese community had increased racial tensions and meant that there was little respect among Chinese for the police. Moreover, the low pay and the habits acquired during the Occupation made corruption widespread. Indeed, the problem was so bad that a special section of the Criminal Investigation Department was set up just to look into it. Lack of public confidence in the force meant that the victims of extortion and theft were unwilling to give the police information for fear that the perpetrators would not be caught and that the victims themselves would instead be vulnerable to reprisals. The difficulties of rebuilding the police force were compounded by an acute shortage of suitably qualified police officers, especially those with a knowledge of Malay, let alone Chinese. Overall, the police force in the years following the surrender of the Japanese was patently incapable of maintaining order throughout the Peninsula.

Morale was low not only among locally recruited members of the police force but also among locally recruited members of the administration. Officers of the Malayan Administrative Service were demoralized, first, by the fact that the responsibilities they had been given by the Japanese were downgraded when the British returned; secondly, by the threat which seemed to hang over their heads that they were liable to be investigated as collaborators; and thirdly, by having to work under a regime, the Malayan Union, to which they and their fellow Malays were bitterly opposed. The Asian staff demanded back pay for the time of the Japanese Occupation, but the Government refused their request and paid out money on a very limited scale only to members of the volunteer forces. As a result, in order to augment the very low levels of pay in the post-War period, the support staff—many of whom were caught in a web of indebtedness—resorted to accepting 'tea money' or 'coffee money,' a practice that had developed under the Japanese.[60] The *Straits Times* in an editorial underscored the consequences of this situation by saying: 'High-level policy has been singularly lacking in imagination and a true appreciation of the significance of such bribery and corruption as we have in Malaya. No Government can afford the ridicule, contempt and slander that is the order of the day in this country.'[61]

Summary

By mid-1948, Malaya had been ruled by the returning British for nearly three years. It had not been a very pleasant experience for anyone. The British could no longer automatically command the respect of the people of Malaya. Tan Cheng Lock, the Malayan Chinese leader, put the British presence in Malaya in context in 1948 when he wrote: 'One of the greatest events in human history, which is taking place at the moment, is the revolt of Asia, where the prestige of the white man *per se* has gone.'[62] Nor were the British able to win the support and confidence of Malayans through their policies. Partly because of the crises which beset the sterling area, notably Britain, and partly because of poorly planned and executed policies, the economy of Malaya limped along. The cost of living caused special problems for everyone. As the *Financial Times* of London said in June 1948, 'To some extent it has been a miracle that Malaya with all her economic troubles has been so quiet for so long.'[63] The vacillation over Malaya's constitutional arrangements soured the Malayan Government's relations with both the country's leaders and the large numbers of people mobilized to oppose the Government's policies. The succession of new political arrangements also took its toll on the already shaky administration. One contemporary commentary on the Malayan Union and the Federation of Malaya noted that: 'The first was workable but not very popular, the second was not very popular and so far appears to be not very workable.'[64] The Government itself was riven with divisions. Everyone from Gent at the top to the local support staff at the lowest levels seemed to be involved in one controversy or another. The people of Malaya had little confidence in the Government and the Government had little confidence in itself.

In a scant three years, the Government had succeeded in alienating practically every section of Malayan society. The whole population was directly and disastrously affected by the shortages and high prices of rice, and by the generally high cost of living. Labourers were especially angered because they felt squeezed by unrealistically low wage levels imposed by employers with the connivance of the Government. Chinese and Indian as well as some European commercial leaders were unhappy with the incompetent way in which the economy was run and with London's seemingly excessive interference. Malays were outraged by the imposition of the Malayan Union, and the Chinese and the Indian communities felt abandoned after the switch to the Federation Agreement. Even the Straits Settlement Chinese, Britain's most loyal supporters, became disaffected after they realized that their traditional relationship with Britain would be severed by the new citizenship laws. Finally, the Chinese, who bore the brunt of the wave of violence that hit the

Peninsula in the post-War period, and the Europeans, who were personally confronted with the threat of violence on a large scale for the first time since their arrival in the region, were highly critical of the Government's failure to bring the situation under control.

Except for the first few days after they returned to Malaya, the British never really regained the confidence of the general public. Certainly the hearts and minds of Malayans were not with the Government. To what extent, then, were they with the Malayan Communist Party, the Government's opponents in the Emergency?

1. Hugh T. Pagden, 'Unrest in Malaya', para. 72, CO 537/3757.

2. F. Spencer Chapman, The Jungle Is Neutral (London: Chatto and Windus, 1949), p. 419.

3. Charles Allen, ed., Tales from the South China Seas: Images of the British in South-East Asia in the Twentieth Century (London: Futura, 1983), p. 254.

4. Martin Rudner, 'The Organisation of the British Military Administration in Malaya', Journal of Southeast Asian History 9 (March 1968), p. 103.

5. M. V. del Tufo, Malaya: A Report on the 1947 Census of Population (London: HMSO, 1949), p. 40. The terms Malaya, Malayan, and Malay should not be confused. Malaya refers to the geographical entity, Malayan refers to a person of any racial origin who is a permanent resident of Malaya, and a Malay is a person of the Malay race who speaks the Malay language.

6. Pagden, 'Unrest', para. 81, CO 537/3757. This section owes much to Pagden's account. See also the observations of other disgusted British officers who observed the behaviour of their peers, in Malayan Union Secretariat Files 356/46 and 364/46, quoted in Khong Kim Hoong, Merdeka! British Rule and the Struggle for Independence in Malaya, 1945-1957 (Petaling Jaya, Malaysia: Institute for Social Analysis, 1984), pp. 42-3.

7. See Pagden, 'Unrest', para. 73, CO 537/3757, who also suggests that the BMA Mess in Singapore was rumoured to be full of loot.

8. T. H. Silcock and Ungku Abdul Aziz, 'Nationalism in Malaya', in William L. Holland, ed., Asian Nationalism and the West (New York: MacMillan, 1953), p. 299, and Pagden, 'Unrest', para. 80, CO 537/3757.

9. Straits Times, 8 September 1945. See also the discussion of this action in F. S. V. Donnison, British Military Administration in the Far East (London: HMSO, 1956), pp. 222-3. The term 'banana money' was used because of the banana trees printed on the notes.

10. Pagden, 'Unrest', paras. 87-90, CO 537/3757.

11. Colin Barlow, The Natural Rubber Industry: Its Development, Technology and Economy in Malaysia (Kuala Lumpur: Oxford University Press, 1978), p. 77.

12. Donnison, British Military Administration, p. 158.

13. Cheah Boon Kheng, The Masked Comrades: A Study of the Communist United Front in Malaya, 1945-1948 (Singapore: Times Books International, 1979), pp. 17-19.

14. Cheah Boon Kheng, Red Star Over Malaya: Resistance and Social Conflict During and After the Japanese Occupation of Malaya, 1941-1946 (Singapore: Singa-

pore University Press, 1983), pp. 252-65; Pagden, 'Unrest', para. 25, CO 537/3757, and Khong, *Merdeka!*, pp. 54-8.

15. Silcock and Aziz, 'Nationalism', p. 300.

16. 'Statement', 1948, Item 100, CO 717/153. All currency references in this book are to Malayan dollars unless otherwise stated.

17. 'Federation of Malaya–Financial Position', 1948, CO 717/153.

18. Martin Rudner, 'Financial Policies in Post-War Malaya: The Fiscal and Monetary Measures of Liberation and Reconstruction', *Journal of Imperial and Commonwealth History* 3 (May 1975), p. 326. War Damage compensation insurance was never paid out even though Malayans had been charged for this statutory insurance right up to the fall of Singapore and the Japanese victory. Moreover, the Colonial Welfare and Development Act excluded support for the reconstruction of war-damaged colonial territories. See ibid., *passim*.

19. Telegram to all Colonies, etc. from the Secretary of State, Colonies, 5 September 1947, CO 537/2974.

20. Memorandum from C. F. Cobbold to Sir Wilfred Eadey, 11 November 1947, CO 537/2974.

21. 'War in Malaya', *British Survey* (Main Series No. 39, June 1952), p. 17.

22. See the discussion of this issue in J. B. Perry Robinson, *Transformation in Malaya* (London: Secker and Warburg, 1956), p. 35.

23. Malayan Union, *Interim Report on Wages by the Joint Wages Commission* (Kuala Lumpur: Government Printer, 29 July 1947), p. 6.

24. Rudner, 'Financial Policies', p. 326.

25. Malayan Union, *Report of the Financial Review Committee* (Kuala Lumpur: Government Printer, 1947), pp. 11-12 and 38.

26. R. Ramani, Federation of Malaya, *Proceedings of the Federal Legislative Council*, 1st Session, p. B251.

27. The information in this paragraph relies heavily on CO 537/3004 and CO 537/2996.

28. Martin Rudner, 'The Malayan Post-War Rice Crisis: An Episode in Colonial Agricultural Policy', *Kajian Ekonomi Malaysia* 12 (June 1975), pp. 1-13.

29. Francis Kok-Wah Loh, 'Beyond the Tin Mines: The Political Economy of Chinese Squatter Farmers in the Kinta New Villages, Malaysia' (Ph.D. dissertation, Cornell University, 1980), p. 71.

30. See CO 537/3004 and P/PM1, Chief Secretary 530/48 (ANM).

31. Barlow, *The Natural Rubber Industry*, p. 438 and Special Annex Tables, Table 1.1.; Loh, 'Beyond the Tin Mines', p. 74, and Pagden, 'Unrest', para. 113, CO 537/3757.

32. 'Economic Position of the Federation of Malaya', p. 5, P/PM1, Chief Secretary 530/48 (ANM).

33. A survey in the Malacca area in 1947 showed that a minimum-level diet cost an adult $15.00 per month but in poorest households only $7.00-$8.00 per month per adult was spent and their diet was seriously deficient in protein and calories. P/PM1, Chief Secretary 530/48 (ANM).

34. See, for example, Richard O. Winstedt, 'What's Wrong in Malaya', *The Spectator*, 16 July 1948; Loh, 'Beyond the Tin Mines', pp. 71-9, and Martin Rudner, 'The Political Structure of the Malayan Union', *Journal of the Malaysian Branch, Royal Asiatic Society* 53 (Part 1, 1970), p. 12.

35. *Federation of Malaya Annual Report*, 1948, p. 46.

36. This section owes much to A. J. Stockwell's study, *British Policy and Malay*

Politics During the Malayan Union Experiment, 1942-1948 (Kuala Lumpur: Malayan Branch of the Royal Asiatic Society, Monograph No. 8, 1979).

37. Due to the War, calculations were to be made as of February 1942. See the discussion of this issue in Victor Purcell, *The Chinese in Southeast Asia*, 2nd edn. (Kuala Lumpur: Oxford University Press, 1965), pp. 317-20.

38. W. R. Roff, *The Origins of Malay Nationalism* (New Haven: Yale University Press, 1967), p. 205.

39. See G. M. Foster, 'Peasant Society and the Image of the Limited Good', *American Anthropologist* 62 (April 1965), and J. C. Scott, *Political Ideology in Malaysia: Reality and the Beliefs of an Elite* (New Haven: Yale University Press, 1968), pp. 105-7 and 249-52.

40. Stockwell, *British Policy*, p. 57.

41. William Shaw, *Tun Razak: His Life and Times* (Kuala Lumpur: Longman, 1976), p. 63.

42. Stockwell, *British Policy*, p. 50.

43. Ibid., pp. 95-6.

44. Paskin to Gurney, 22 December 1948, CO 537/3746.

45. See M. R. Stenson, *Class, Race and Colonialism in West Malaysia: The Indian Case* (Vancouver: University of British Columbia Press, 1980), pp. 152-3.

46. See Yeo Kim Wah, 'The Anti-Federation Movement in Malaya, 1946-48', *Journal of Southeast Asian Studies* 4 (March 1973) pp. 31-51. This section owes much to this study.

47. Pagden, 'Unrest', para. 98, CO 537/3757.

48. According to the criteria set out for citizenship under the Federation Agreement, 3.1 million people qualified automatically; of these 78 per cent were Malay, 12 per cent Chinese, and 7 per cent Indian. Federation of Malaysia, *Federation of Malaysia Annual Report* (London: HMSO, 1963).

49. Secretary for Chinese Affairs, *Annual Report*, 1947, Chief Secretary 376/A/48 (ANM).

50. Purcell, *The Chinese in Southeast Asia*, p. 327.

51. Yeo Kim Wah, 'The Anti-Federation Agreement', p. 45, citing the Minutes of the Third Delegates' Conference of PMCJA-PUTERA in Kuala Lumpur on 3 November 1947 (Tan Cheng Lock Papers) (no document number cited).

52. Noel Ross to High Commissioner, Sir Gerald Templer, 21 August 1952, P/PM1, Chief Secretary 23/1 (ANM).

53. 'Efficiency of ex-internee officers', CO 537/2179.

54. Gent to Lloyd, 11 September 1947, CO 537/2179.

55. British Association of Malaya, file IV/33 (Royal Commonwealth Society Library).

56. Stockwell, *British Policy*, p. 78.

57. Ibid., p. 79; see also a speech by E. D. Shearn, President of the Malayan Association, in which he called for Malaya to be run by men on the spot and not by directives from Whitehall, *Straits Times*, 1 October 1947.

58. *Straits Times*, 15 September 1947.

59. S. W. Jones, *Public Administration in Malaya* (London: Oxford University Press, 1953), p. 169.

60. *Straits Times*, 9 December 1947, and Department of Labour, *Monthly Report*, March 1948, p. 4.

61. *Straits Times*, 6 October 1947.

62. Tan Cheng Lock, 'A Chinese View of Malaya' in David R. Rees-Williams,

Tan Cheng Lock, S. S. Awberry, and F. W. Dalley, *Three Reports on the Malayan Problem* (New York: International Secretariat, Institute of Pacific Relations, 1949), p. 21.

63. *Financial Times*, 11 June 1948.

64. E. D. Shearn quoted in the *Straits Times*, 9 June 1948.

2
The Path to Revolution

The Impact of the Japanese Occupation

WHEN the Japanese surrendered in August 1945, the communist guerrillas emerged from the jungle as victors. The MPAJA, the guerrilla arm of the MCP, had provided the only resistance to the Japanese Occupation forces and gained great kudos in the process. The mass of the people in Malaya had little appreciation of what was taking place outside their immediate area, and no knowledge of the momentous events that were unfolding in the international arena. During the Japanese Occupation, the only information people received had been disseminated by the Japanese and the communists; thus they were quite prepared to accept that the MPAJA was responsible for the defeat of the Japanese. Further support for the communists' claims came in the euphoria of the post-surrender days when the major Chinese newspapers extolled the virtues of the guerrilla army and even the *Straits Times* reported that the exploits of the Resistance Army had demoralized the Japanese forces and had 'become almost legendary during the past three and a half years'.[1]

This popularity was quite a change from the pre-War years when the MCP had struggled to get itself established. Communism was introduced into the Peninsula by Chinese immigrants who were members of a left-wing faction of the Kuomintang. Mirroring the mainland purge the communists were expelled from the Kuomintang in 1927. In 1928, under the tutelage of the Comintern's Far Eastern Bureau in Shanghai, the Nanyang (South Seas) Communist Party was put in place only to wither and be superseded, in April 1930, by the MCP. A year later, the organization suffered a major reversal when a French communist, sent by the Comintern to aid the MCP, was arrested by the Singapore police and promptly provided them with the names of Party members. In March 1934, a constitution for the MCP was drawn up, and following a reorganization, the Party came back to life, establishing branches in the Malay Peninsula and building ties with labour. The MCP's activities were given impetus, first, by the outbreak of war between Japan and China in July 1937, which stirred Chinese nationalist feelings and brought in new recruits and, secondly, by a growing sense of frustration among Malaya's labour force–a factor which was exploited in order to increase anti-British sentiment.[2] Yet the MCP remained relatively ineffective: skirmishes with the Kuomintang, organizing anti-Japanese activities, and mobilizing discontent against the British spread its resources very thinly. The British administration found the MCP to be little more than an increasingly persistent nuisance.

All this was changed when the Japanese invaded Malaya on 8 December 1941. Offers of co-operation from the MCP, which had been prompted by the German invasion of the Soviet Union in June 1941 as well as by fears of Japanese intentions, and which had originally been turned down by senior British officials, were now quickly accepted. Arrangements were made for the MCP to provide young Chinese volunteers who could be trained in guerrilla warfare. Leading communists who were in gaol were released by the Government in order to organize resistance to the advancing Japanese among the Chinese community. The MCP and the Kuomintang put aside their differences and joined in a common war effort under the leadership of the Overseas Chinese Resist-the-Enemy Mobilization Committee. Using their considerable organizational skills and the network that they had built up throughout the Peninsula, the communists were able to give valuable support to British plans for 'stay behind' parties and the formation of guerrilla groups based on local volunteers. Communists also played a major part in Dalforce, a Chinese volunteer organization which, although poorly armed and trained, put up a strong resistance to the Japanese and fought on until the formal surrender of Singapore. Once the Japanese took over, members of the MCP tried to find their way into the jungle to continue the fight. Hence, because of their intense hatred of the Japanese, Malaya's communists became an integral part of the Allied cause in South-East Asia.

After an uncertain beginning, the MCP established a guerrilla organization which grew in strength during the Japanese Occupation. In the initial stages, quite a few guerrilla groups were formed, but not all lasted. Lack of experience and discipline, poor leadership, and the presence of high quality front-line Japanese infantry units eliminated some units and forced the rest on to the defensive. At the core of most of the guerrilla groups that survived were the trainees who had gone through No. 101 Special

Training School immediately before the surrender of Singapore. They became the guerrilla leaders. Within a few months five main guerrilla groups were in operation in North Selangor, the Negri Sembilan-Malacca border, North Johore, South Johore, and Perak. Later three more groups were set up in West Pahang, East Pahang, and Kedah. Originally named the Anti-Japanese force, the guerrillas then became known as the Anti-Japanese Army, and thereafter as the Malayan People's Anti-Japanese Army or MPAJA. This last appellation was purely for political effect, to give the impression that the guerrillas represented all of Malaya's races. In a similar vein, the three stars worn on the caps of the communist guerrillas were said to represent the three races of Malaya: Malay, Chinese, and Indian. The MPAJA, however, was about 90 per cent Chinese, with Mandarin the 'official' language. A parallel political organization, known as the Anti-Japanese Union and later as the Malayan People's Anti-Japanese Union (MPAJU), provided the MPAJA with links to, and support from, the local community–primarily the Chinese. Both the political and guerrilla organizations were tightly controlled by the MCP. Nothing was done without the permission of general headquarters, and communist propaganda was pervasive.[3]

The MCP was able to gain considerable prestige from its leadership of the resistance movement and its numbers grew accordingly. The Sino-Japanese War had, of course, set the stage for the Japanese Occupation of the Peninsula. The Japanese distrusted and in many cases hated the Chinese, a sentiment which was reciprocated by the Malayan Chinese. As the Japanese swept down through Malaya, all racial communities suffered; however, it was the Chinese community who bore the brunt of the brutality inflicted on civilians. Cases of rape, torture, and summary executions were common. Once Singapore fell, most of the male Chinese residents were marshalled into identification parades where hooded informers picked out anti-Japanese activists. Communists were especially sought out. Estimates of the numbers killed in the Singapore massacres vary from the official figure of 5,000 to one unofficial Japanese estimate of 25,000 and Chinese estimates of 30,000–40,000.[4] Whatever the number, the impression left behind seemed to reinforce the antipathy felt by Malayan Chinese for their erstwhile liberators. As a consequence, respect for the one group which appeared to stand up against Japanese repression grew steadily. While the anti-Japanese activities of the guerrillas were not spectacular, they did prove to be enough of a thorn in the side of the Japanese to keep them jittery and guessing. Raids were made on isolated posts and a few patrols were ambushed. There were also reports of daring releases of prisoners held by the Japanese authorities. Traitors and collaborators of all races were hunted down by units of the MPAJA and among the general Chinese population the guerrillas gained widespread popular support. By 1945, there were 7,000-8,000 members of the MPAJA and thousands of people in the cells of the supporting MPAJU.[5]

Like everyone else, the MCP leadership was caught by surprise by the abrupt ending to the War. The lack of any plans to cover such a turn of events had long-term consequences for the communists. In the weeks immediately after the surrender of the Japanese and before the British could deploy their military forces and get their administration functioning, the Japanese were expected to maintain order in the main urban centres, while the MPAJA, the only other organized force, was given responsibility for the small towns and the rural areas. The tensions which had built up during the Occupation when the predominantly Malay police force was used to suppress the predominantly Chinese guerrillas, led to a number of racial clashes. The MPAJA took full advantage of their new-found power to set up road blocks, stop trains and buses, and enter Chinese villages and Malay kampongs in order to seek out policemen, detectives, informers, and other collaborators. Impromptu 'people's trials' were carried out in many small villages. Invariably, the verdict was 'guilty' and the punishment a slow and hideous death. Perhaps the most common characteristic of the retribution that was meted out during this interregnum was its barbarity. Malays described it as the 'reign of terror', and those who found themselves to be the primary targets banded together for defence and, in some notable cases, mounted counter-attacks against Chinese villages.[6] Most clashes were minor, but major incidents occurred in Johore and Negri Sembilan in August and November 1945, and in Perak and Pahang in the early months of 1946. In these cases alone, well over 600 people were killed.[7]

For the MCP, these clashes proved to be a disaster, dashing any hope they may have had of gaining support among all of Malaya's racial groups. Many Malays and Indians who had been recruited into the MPAJA quickly left the organization as news of the racial fighting became widely known. Antagonism was further exacerbated by the MPAJA's announcements that the Chinese were going to rule Malaya, and by the general displays of Chinese chauvinism exhibited across the Peninsula. It was during this period that the MCP became known among Malays as the 'Chinese Party'.[8]

United Front Strategy

The sudden surrender of the Japanese could have provided the MCP with an excellent chance to launch a full-scale revolution. Organizationally, however, the MCP was in no position to undertake such a course of action. First, the original plan had been to combine with Allied troops in an attack on the Japanese and to aid the British authorities as the Peninsula was reoccupied. However, as the rather chaotic events of late August and early September 1945 attest, it would have been exceedingly difficult to communicate any change in strategy to all the MPAJA units, and almost impossible to co-ordinate a concerted take-over of the country. Secondly, the MCP faced the prospect of opposing a relatively formidable British force, known to be prepared for a full-scale invasion. Moreover, the British could have called on the Japanese forces in Malaya for assistance against the MCP and, as the racial clashes demonstrated, they would have had the support of the vast majority of the Malay population. Finally, the policy of adopting an 'open and legal' struggle through 'peaceful agitation' was one endorsed by the Comintern and, for reasons which will become clear shortly, was strongly advocated by the MCP leader, Lai Tek. The MCP, therefore, embarked on a strategy of building up its organizational base; working for social, economic, and political change, and attacking the legitimacy of the British colonial presence.

Initially, the relationship between the communists, particularly the MPAJA, and the British was occasionally strained but not totally antagonistic. On 13 September 1945, a contingent from the MPAJA participated in a ceremonial parade in Kuala Lumpur to mark the signing of surrender terms. On 6 January 1946, Lord Mountbatten presented campaign ribbons to some of the communist guerrilla leaders in a ceremony which took place on the steps of the Secretariat in Singapore. Later, in the spring of 1946, a group of MPAJA leaders was sent to London to take part in the Easter victory parade. Furthermore, the BMA, as part of its initial liberal policy of allowing freedom of speech and of association, invited members of the MCP and their satellite organizations as well as those from the Kuomintang, the Malay Nationalist Party, and many business and professional groups, to serve on advisory councils that were set up in Singapore and throughout the Peninsula. At the same time, some Chinese-speaking British administrators developed good contacts with a few communist leaders.[9]

But the relationship quickly soured. The more radical elements of the MCP were soon using their rapidly expanding organizational base, especially among the urban labourers, to stir up anti-British sentiment. The chaotic living conditions and the initially inept attempts by British authorities to exercise control, especially the fiasco of the arrest and trial of Soong Kwong, proved to be major irritants and significantly aided the relatively small group of dedicated and determined militant activists.[10] The number of strikes and work stoppages increased, culminating in a twenty-four-hour general strike at the end of January 1946, and a second general strike set for 15 February 1946, the anniversary of the fall of Singapore to the Japanese. Spurred by the clear intention of the MCP to humiliate them, the BMA acted in an uncharacteristically decisive manner. A series of arrests were made prior to the 15 February deadline, and military and armed police units were used to confront those who chose to follow the call to strike. The arrests and show of force—a number of people were killed both on the Peninsula and in Singapore—had a salutory effect on the MCP. While undoubtedly they benefited from what many considered to be the unnecessary violence used by the authorities, the communist leaders were also criticized for their role in the course of events. Even more importantly, however, the MCP realized that it had become too exposed and vulnerable. For the next two years the Party stayed well in the background, concentrating on building its base of support by means of a united front strategy.[11]

The organizational structures that the MCP set up in order to implement its united front policy may be thought of as a set of concentric circles. At the centre was the MCP. In the next circle were the satellite organizations. These included: the New Democratic Youth League, which appears to have been formed when the MPAJU surfaced and was reorganized at the end of the Occupation; the Ex-Servicemen's Association, to which ex-MPAJA members were expected to belong; and the Chinese Women's Association, in which some able and energetic women, notably Lee Kiu, were employed in the work of the Party. In the outer circle were the front organizations which were controlled or influenced by the Party to varying degrees. The large number of front organizations and their great variety was a deliberate Party policy which was rooted in the assumption that the more organizations there were, the more recruits would be attracted to the cause.

It was through the front organizations that the MCP gained control over much of the region's labour force. Where possible, old, well-established unions were infiltrated and taken over. More often, however, new structures were set up. At the village or local level, workers' organizations were formed which grouped together such people as coffee-shop workers, or barbers, or rickshaw pullers. These organizations were federated at the local level and tied to state federations. The state federations were in turn tied first to the General Labour Union and later, when Government pressure forced a division, to the Pan-Malayan Federation of Trade Unions (PMFTU) and the Singapore Federation of Trade Unions (SFTU). There were also state-wide organizations made up of similar local workers' groups such as the coffee-shop workers which were in turn represented in the PMFTU and SFTU. By placing people in official leadership positions and as informal opinion makers within these overlapping pyramids, the Party was able to steer the policies and actions of the various unions in the desired direction.[12]

Outside the trade union organizations, the MCP attempted to exert its influence through social welfare groups and, when possible, political parties. An interesting example of the social welfare groups was the Ex-Political Prisoners Old Comrades Union through which the Party helped to rehabilitate many of those who had been held in Japanese prisons. This organization eventually proved to be an excellent source of recruits for the communists.[13] Most of the political parties were to be found on the periphery of the concentric circles. The Malayan Democratic Union, a non-communal English-speaking left-wing group, was a good example of an organization which the Party infiltrated and influenced and which generally followed the communist line. Among Malay groups, the Angkatan Pemuda Insaf, a radical youth organization, and the Angkatan Wanita Sedara, a radical women's organization, were both controlled by the MCP. The Malay Nationalist Party was, at times, greatly influenced by the MCP. And, of course, through its front organizations, the MCP was able to manipulate the policies of such organizations as the AMCJA-PUTERA coalition.

Recruiting

As Lee Ting Hui has argued in his study of the MCP, 'manpower was crucial to the movement'.[14] People were slowly drawn into the Party's organizational structure. Recruits of good character and with some organizational or vocational skills were gradually given more responsibility, moved to satellite organizations, made probationary members of the Party and, finally, became full members. Of course, few reached the centre of power; there were only about 3,000 members of the Party in the years immediately following the Occupation.[15] However, the overall strategy of pulling as many people as possible into the Party's network of front and satellite organizations was fairly successful.

The key to the recruiting process was personal contact. Recruits became associated with front organizations either through 'existing friendships', such as family ties or friendships made at work or at school, or through 'created friendships', such as those resulting from one neighbour, worker, or student helping another. As one informant told Lucian Pye: 'It didn't matter what I was doing, there always seemed to be a Communist hanging around trying to become my friend.'[16] In the schools, it was not just students who recruited for the communists, but many teachers—especially the younger ones—used their influence to encourage an interest in communism. And once having been persuaded to attend a meeting of a satellite or front organization many found themselves swept along by the communist rhetoric. The MCP's propaganda machine was perhaps the most effective part of their organization, and their speakers were invariably dramatic and persuasive. One communist who was recruited at this time likened the experience to taking a drug: 'After you have had their fierce propaganda you can't do without it. It gives you so much strength that you feel weak when you don't have it.' Another talked of being 'dragged into the communist whirlpool'.[17]

The communists had some significant advantages in their recruiting drive. First, Chinese society has traditionally been honeycombed with groups, associations, and societies. For many Chinese, membership in such organizations is an essential part of their lives. Indeed, the Chinese community in Malaya was especially susceptible to what may be called the 'secret society complex'. The MCP and its satellite organizations had many of the characteristics of a powerful secret society—'underground pressure, intimidation, the impalpable influence which no one dares to defy'[18]–which served to attract recruits. To be associated with the members of such a group, particularly the group which was considered to be the most powerful, was to acquire prestige and status.

Secondly, the MCP was able to tap the nationalistic, xenophobic, and revolutionary sentiments which had become an integral part of the Malayan Chinese education curriculum. From the early 1920s onwards, the teachers and text books used in Chinese-language schools of Malaya were suffused with the revolutionary ideas of Dr Sun Yat Sen and the nationalistic sentiments which had been fostered by the Kuomintang. Text books were generally based on Sun Yat Sen's book, *Three People's Principles* and preached the superiority of the Chinese race and a hatred of the foreign powers.[19] British treatment of China during the nineteenth century, particularly in the 'Opium War', was described in a way which inevitably invoked hatred of the British authorities. As Victor Purcell has observed, even relatively contemporary events were quickly incorporated into text books: 'For example, a drawing in a text book intended for children of about twelve years of age showed the "May 30th Incident" at Shanghai in 1925 with British and Sikh policemen in uniform shooting down an unarmed crowd.'[20] At the same time, literature in a colloquial style was being produced and was very popular. Most notable was the 'Proletarian Literature Movement', whose books had themes such as the oppression of the masses and the need for courage in the face of poverty and adversity, and which overall 'had a widespread influence on the rising generation of students and teachers'.[21]

Thirdly, an added bonus for the MCP was the fact that the chaos induced by the Japanese Occupation put a great deal of pressure on the limited school system in the immediate post-War years. The dramatic increase in the numbers of school-age children, most of whom had not been able to attend school during the Japanese Occupation, meant that a large number of students were in their late teens and early twenties.[22] These circumstance made infiltration of the schools by Party supporters and workers much easier. For the older students, communism, coming as it did after the experiences of the Occupation and reinforced by the indoctrination they received in the schools, must have had considerable appeal. And, of course, because of the shortages of both teachers and suitable buildings in the post-War period, there were many who were unable to attend school.

The MCP was quick to capitalize on this by promising free schooling for potential recruits. Boys and girls between fourteen and sixteen, who had difficulty getting jobs and who could not attend school, were very willing to take advantage of any opportunity the Party may have been able to offer to advance their education.

Fourthly, in gaining the support of the workers for their trade union front organizations, the MCP was able to exploit the many real grievances which were widely felt by estate and mine workers throughout the Peninsula. Not all of these grievances were the product of the Occupation. Many had their origins in the years immediately before the Japanese invasion. Low wages at times when the cost of living as well as profits were high, 'brutal' actions by estate staff, inadequate medical facilities, and denials of the right to form associations to represent workers' interests were all ingredients in the pre-War labour troubles, notably on estates.[23] In the post-War years, the high cost of living was fully exploited by the Party. The initial problem of finding employment seemed to be solved by becoming a member of a union.[24] Later, as the problem became one of trying to extract fair wages and decent living conditions from employers, the Party encouraged workers to let the unions lead them in the battle.

These grievances were compounded by the post-Occupation turmoil. European estates and tin mines had great difficulty recruiting European managers and relied heavily on Asian staff. Workers claimed that these 'Black Europeans'—as they were called—'had betrayed and exploited them during the Occupation'.[25] Even the Europeans who were recruited often had little knowledge of the languages and customs of their workers and found it difficult to deal with the problems that materialized. Problems also arose because of the shortage of labour.[26] The Malayan Planting Industries Employers' Association (MPIEA) and the Malayan Mining Employers' Association (MMEA) tried to prevent the competition for labour from driving up wages. They insisted on the settlement of the terms and conditions of employment on a national basis and tried to keep fairly tight control over their members so as to maintain uniformity.[27] Workers, recognizing that wages were higher on some small Asian-owned estates and tin mines as well as in factories, pressed for higher rates. In particular the Chinese, who had 'a better appreciation of their value as workers to an individual employer',[28] and many of whom had the option of making good money working their private gardens,

were more willing than other workers to strike for better conditions. To counter any possible increase in the bargaining position of workers because of this shortage of labour, managers
looked to the Malay community for supplementary labour and
to provide a less volatile work-force. There was also a general feeling among workers that European managers used intimidation,
such as calling in the police or dismissing whole work-forces
at a day's notice, to keep employees in line and so minimize any
increased bargaining power they might have gained from the
prevailing limited supply of labour.[29]

Grievances also arose out of the way in which wages in the
plantation and mining industries were tied to the fluctuating international market prices of rubber and tin. For example, during
the middle of 1947, low rubber prices resulted in a general reduction of 20 per cent in contract tapping rates and a substantial reduction in wage rates and earnings. This caused a sharp increase
in the number of strikes and disputes; a one-day strike called to
protest against the reduction 'had the effect of closing down about
seventy percent of rubber estates in the country'.[30] All this was
grist for the MCP propaganda mill. As the Government and the
MPIEA and the MMEA believed, communist agitators were indeed at work among the labour force; but most workers wished
only for a quiet life, and the success of the MCP in organizing the
unions and turning people against the Government and employers
must be attributed in good part to a desire to alleviate the many
very real hardships that were inflicted on the labour force during
this period. While the labour unrest may have been used by the
communists, it was not always their creation; often they were
simply conduits for the expression of widespread frustration.

Finally, the MCP's ability to expand its base of support was
made much easier by the relative lack of competition the Party
faced in recruiting Malayan Chinese. Most importantly, the Malayan Chinese community had no real alternative organization
other than the MCP to which to look for leadership. The primary
reason for this was that the Japanese Occupation had so severely
dislocated Malayan society, especially the Chinese community,
that much of the old social fabric was irreparably torn. The old
Chinese *towkays* (leading businessmen) had lost their positions of
leadership within their communities. Some had fled the country
and were slow to return, others had moved to remote areas to
avoid the attention of the Japanese authorities, and a few had become collaborators. The old patron–client relationships, which

provided a network linking ordinary Chinese families to the Chinese business élite through reciprocal actions of support, and which had been an integral part of pre-War Chinese society, were, therefore, left in tatters. Similarly, the many associations and societies which had developed in pre-War Malaya had been the target of Japanese repression. Even the secret societies had been broken by the Japanese and were slow to re-establish their presence in the post-War years. The Kuomintang and its youth wing, the San Min Chu Yi Youth Corps, were sporadically active but were largely preoccupied with events in China and displayed little interest in immediate local issues. Chinese consuls tried to play an active role in Malayan Chinese society but were generally rebuffed by the Chinese, and their actions were carefully circumscribed by the Malayan Government. For example, reports circulating in mid-1947 that there would be elections among the Chinese in Malaya of representatives to the National Assembly of China were quickly laid to rest.[31]

But, from the perspective of later events, the most notable absentee in the competition for the support of the Chinese community was the Malayan Government itself. The value of maintaining good links with the Chinese community had been recognized fairly soon after the British established their authority in the region. Such relations had been developed in the pre-War years through the Chinese Protectorate. The Secretary for Chinese Affairs had his headquarters in Singapore and each state and Straits Settlement had a Protector of Chinese Affairs. The Protectorate dealt with all aspects of the life of the Chinese community, including labour and family matters, and the registration of societies. The Protectors of Chinese Affairs tendered advice to the British Residents or Advisers. The general information that was collected by the Protectors was passed up the chain, sifted and collated, and presented to the Government by the Secretary for Chinese Affairs. The Protectorate was well known to all Chinese and 'respected and appreciated by law-abiding Chinese and feared by wrong doers'.[32] However, during the War, it came under the scrutiny of the Malayan Planning Unit and became a casualty of the Malayan Union scheme. The move to a common Malayan citizenship, it was argued, would be inconsistent with one part of the Government dealing exclusively with one section of the population.

Unfortunately for the Government, the post-War administrative structure failed to compensate for the elimination of the Protectorate. The District Officers and Assistant District Officers

who had the closest contact with the general population were usually
Malay speakers. Almost none spoke Chinese. Former officials in
the Protectorate were dispersed around the rest of the Administration; most went to the Labour Department where their understanding of the Chinese language and customs was not always fully
employed. Nor were they always in a position to pass on any information they might receive to those who might make the best use of
it. The position of Secretary for Chinese Affairs (SCA) was kept,
but as the Chinese put it, he was a 'head without a tail', having no
field officers and hence limited information and no line duties. His
office was also very short-staffed; at one point in 1947 one officer
was trying to cover three duty posts. As a consequence, the SCA
had 'no face with the Chinese' and the field was left open for the
MCP.[33]

With all these advantages it is not surprising that the MCP
acquired considerable support throughout the Peninsula and became a dominant force in post-War Malayan society. Why, then,
did the Party abandon the policy of peaceful agitation and embark
on a policy of armed struggle?

The Call to Arms

The initial MCP policy outlined in its August 1945 statement was
most reasonable and moderate; indeed, many British officials noted
how close it was to their own Government's policy for the region.[34]
But in the months after the British returned, the militants within
the MCP gathered strength and began to effect some changes in
the Party's policies. The most notable early change came about
after the Government's decision to arrest labour leaders and use
the police and the army to counter the general strike of 15 February
1946. Cheah Boon Kheng has argued that as part of the recon-
sideration of its strategy the MCP decided 'to prepare for the
eventuality of armed struggle, the timing of which was to be determined by the extent of the Government's further repressive
measures'.[35] Although this was a clear demonstration that the
militants were gaining ground in their continuing debate with
the moderates, no revolutionary programme was prepared at this
time.

One of the keys to this debate was the role of the Secretary-
General and leader of the MCP, Lai Tek—or Mr Wright as he was
sometimes known. Leadership, of course, is crucial for any organization, but particularly so when the organization has to deal with

crises induced by external threats. Under such circumstances, the members of an organization look for strong leadership and will happily give a successful leader all the power he requires.[36] This was certainly true of the MCP. Decision-making was highly centralized, and members were enjoined to be loyal to the Party and to obey the leader without question. All those who knew of the MCP were in awe of the power of 'Central', the personification of which was Lai Tek. One Party document described him 'as a mysterious "hero" and a man of superhuman ability and all Party members worshipped him as an idol and obeyed and followed him blindly'.[37] Similarly, F. Spencer Chapman, who lived with the MPAJA guerrillas for much of the Japanese Occupation, has recorded that all the guerrillas 'knew the name of the Secretary-General, who was credited with innumerable attributes, being able to pilot an aeroplane, drive a tank, speak many languages and hoodwink the Japanese in any way he desired'.[38] It was not surprising, then, that Lai Tek held unchallengeable power within the Party at the time of the Japanese surrender.

The other reason for Lai Tek's pre-eminent position, and no doubt a factor in persuading him to encourage the pursuit of a cautious policy, was that he was a triple agent. A communist, he worked for both the British and the Japanese. Lai Tek was Vietnamese— some say half-Vietnamese and half-Chinese, others that he was half-Vietanmese and half-French—and had learnt his trade as a secret agent working for the French in Indo-China. When his position was compromised he moved on to Hong Kong and, then, under the sponsorship of the Special Branch in Singapore, he joined the MCP some time around 1934. Lai Tek's own version of how he had arrived in Singapore was rather different. He claimed to have been a founder of the Indo-China Communist Party, a representative of the Communist International, and to have visited Moscow. He also claimed that his activities in Indo-China would have led to his execution had he not managed to escape to Siam and, eventually, Malaya. Lai Tek was able to work his way up the Party hierarchy until in 1939 he became Secretary-General of the MCP Central Committee. He achieved this partly through his own initiative—he was said to have a strong personality, a keen brain, and good administrative skills[39]—and partly through the efforts of the Special Branch who, working with the information supplied by Lai Tek, were able to remove anyone who barred his path to the top or seemed likely to expose his double identity.

During the Japanese Occupation, Lai Tek simply exchanged

one set of masters for another. Once the Japanese took over Singapore, he quickly came to the attention of Major Sartoru Onishi, second-in-command of the Kempeitai, the Japanese equivalent of the Special Branch.[40] In exchange for the information he provided he was given freedom of movement–he was often to be seen riding around Singapore on his red bicycle–and a large sum of money with which he set up a café on Orchard Road and a restaurant near by.

The most important consequence of Lai Tek's co-operation with the Japanese authorities was that during the Occupation over sixty senior Party members and hundreds of others from the lower ranks died at the hands of the Kempeitai or the Japanese Army. The most spectacular Japanese success came on the night of 31 August-1 September 1942 when senior Party members and guerrilla leaders converged on a small village near Batu Caves, a limestone outcrop a few miles outside Kuala Lumpur. At dawn the Japanese launched a well co-ordinated and devastating attack: at least eighteen MCP and MPAJA members were killed, more than eight of whom were senior leaders, and up to twenty more captured.[41] Later, at least ten were beheaded and their heads displayed in public. Some reports suggest that Lai Tek was in the area and was stopped by a Japanese patrol but released on the production of a pass, while others say he was safely at home in Singapore.[42] Other successes followed for the Japanese and, by April 1943, as Cheah notes, 'there was neither a proper central committee nor politburo'.[43] Lai Tek was in sole command.

Lai Tek was clearly the architect of the post-War policy of peaceful agitation. Indeed, one British intelligence report stated in 1948 that 'but for him an attempt would have been made in 1945 or 1946 to organize a more militant campaign by the Communists in Malaya'.[44] His influence was a major barrier to any changes in policy proposed by the more militant factions within the Party. It is in this light that the unmasking of Lai Tek as a traitor must be viewed.

Towards the end of 1945, a letter appeared in the Chinese-language newspaper *Modern Daily News* accusing an unnamed person, a high official of the MCP, of deliberately betraying his comrades to the Japanese. It transpired that the author of the letter was a senior Party member, Ng Yeh Loh, also known as 'Yellow Wong'. But Ng's own credibility was widely questioned as many believed he himself was a traitor. Ng's defence was that he had been trapped into witnessing the arrest of one person in such a way as to appear that he had betrayed the man. Ng suggested that he and another senior MCP official, Ah Ning, were manoeuvred into being scapegoats so that Lai Tek could explain away the complete collapse of the Singapore Town Committee. Ng requested that 'all AJA Comrades recollect how many times their H.Q. and transport centres got into trouble after Lai Tek's inspection'.[45] Ng's letter and his persistence in trying to get to the bottom of the affair began to pay off. Others started to take up the matter and gradually more and more people questioned Lai Tek's loyalty. In early 1947, his past activities and policies began to be scrutinized in some detail by the Party's leadership. Eventually his position became so untenable that he missed a crucial Central Executive Committee meeting held on the evening of 5 March 1947, and went into hiding in Singapore. He left the country some months later.

Breaking the news of Lai Tek's treachery to the Party obviously posed problems. His prodigious reputation within the Party following the surrender of the Japanese was enhanced even further when, in late 1945, in order to counter the rumours of his treachery, an extensive public campaign of adulation was mounted. The Chinese-language press was full of letters and telegrams of praise and 'he was hailed as saviour and preserver of the MCP'.[46] Faced with the task of telling the Party and the general public that the Secretary-General and their 'saviour' had been a Japanese agent, the new leaders moved cautiously. An account by the MCP of what they called 'The Mr. Wright's Affair' indicates that after Lai Tek failed to appear at the 5 March 1947 meeting, a formal enquiry was instigated. In May, the Central Executive Committee met, set up an Enquiry Commission, and convened a Plenary Session of the Central Committee at which the former Secretary-General was dismissed from the Party. State and working committees were told of the turn of events in July 1947, but the ordinary Party members were not informed until February 1948, and a public report of the whole incident was not released by the MCP until 28 May 1948.[47]

The news of Lai Tek's treachery increased pressure on the Party's leadership to adopt a policy of armed struggle. First, Lai Tek's departure produced a reaction to the policies with which he had been associated and tipped the scales in favour of the militants within the Party's leadership. By mid-1947, the question became not one of 'if' but 'when' and 'how', to implement a strategy of armed struggle. Anthony Short has argued that there 'is some evidence to suggest that the majority of "Central" were in favour of an immediate resort to arms'.[48] It seems, however, that after much deliberation Central decided that a new line could not be adopted until they had survived any repercussions resulting from the spread of the news of Lai Tek's expulsion from the Party.[49]

Secondly, the inexperienced leadership which Lai Tek left behind enabled the more radical members of the rank and file to exert greater influence. In alliance with first the British and then the Japanese, Lai Tek made sure that by mid-1946 none of the old guard of the top leadership and very few of the middle level officers were left. For example, there was a complete turnover of the Central Committee on at least two occasions between 1935 and 1945: one just prior to Lai Tek's accession to the position of Secretary-General in the late 1930s, and another in the first fifteen months of the Japanese Occupation. In Singapore, the primary centre of communist activity in the region, so many of the Town Committee's original and replacement members were eliminated by the British and the Japanese that by 1944 it had completely collapsed. In the years immediately after the return of the British, a significant number of Party members were arrested and deported or imprisoned. This meant that when the MCP and Lai Tek parted company in 1947, the Party's organization fell into the hands of a young and relatively untested leadership. For example, Chin Peng, who replaced Lai Tek as Secretary-General, although generally recognized as highly competent, was only twenty-six and had been a member of the Party for less than eight years. Many of the others who moved into leadership positions in the middle and upper levels of the Party during the post-War period were not nearly so able. Chapman, who had first-hand experience of the MCP and MPAJA organizations during the Occupation, said of the guerrillas in particular that 'There were never enough natural leaders to go around and no attempt was made to encourage or train this quality.'[50] Chin Kee Onn, author of *Malaya Upside Down*, has commented that the communists did not 'have the brains'; he felt they were 'amateur revolutionists'.[51] Clearly, the lack of good quality leaders in the senior and middle level ranks of the Party led to much of the uncertainty which dogged the Party after Lai Tek's defection.

Thirdly, when Lai Tek decamped, he took with him a substantial portion of the Party's funds. The Party had been chronically short of funds since the end of the Occupation when the British demonetized the Japanese currency. Some money was acquired when the MPAJA was demobilized in December 1945. Upon handing over their arms, each member of the MPAJA received $350 from the Government, a sum which one contemporary account says was fixed by the MPAJA leadership and which was not thought to be unreasonable given that they considered themselves volunteers fighting for an ideal.[52] Out of this $350, the MCP collected $100 or more for joining the MPAJA Ex-Service Comrades' Association. The main source of funds, however, was the communist-led union movement which was able to bring in money from subscriptions. But once Lai Tek had departed with $130,000 and a lot of valuables, and the Malayan Government had started, in late 1947, to clamp down on the MCP's front organizations such as the unions, the Party suffered from an acute shortage of funds. Lack of money severely undermined the MCP's practice of maintaining discipline in part by paying members and making them dependent on the Party for their income.[53]

Finally, the unmasking of Lai Tek clearly led to a weakening of Central's authority. How could the leadership have let this happen? Was Central to be trusted in the future? Perhaps a more decentralized Party would be a stronger one? Hence, from early 1948 onwards, the rank and file of the Party felt less constrained to conform to the policy laid down by the MCP leadership than they had in the past. At the March 1948 Central Executive meeting, one of the three resolutions passed stressed the need to restore party discipline.

From early 1948 onwards, then, the pressures to adopt a strategy of overt armed struggle increased rapidly. Much of the Party leadership was leaning in this direction; indeed, many of the new group of leaders had been trained in the jungle during the Occupation and had risen within the Party because of the reputations they had gained in the resistance movement. Relatively few were well versed in the peaceful agitation techniques adopted in the post-War period; it was not, therefore, surprising that most were more than willing to return to the old haunts and their old ways. The more militant members of the rank and file were stepping up their activities. Undoubtedly, news of the successes of the Chinese Communist Party in their guerrilla campaign provided an important example for all Party members and especially for the militants, who still avidly followed events in China. Moreover, the Party was finding it more and more difficult to maintain the impetus of the peaceful agitation policy. The anti-Federation movement spearheaded by the AMCJA-PUTERA coalition had been ignored by the Government, there was clearly to be no progress in terms of the political development of Malaya, and the activities of the united front union organizations were increasingly restricted by Government actions.[54]

It was against this background that Chin Peng called a meeting of the Central Executive Committee for 17–21 March 1948. At this meeting a decision was taken to move to a policy of armed struggle, and the final barriers to the adoption of a policy of armed struggle were removed. News of a major reorientation in Soviet and Cominform policy was delivered to the MCP by a voluble Australian communist named Lawrence Sharkey. Sharkey, whose criticism of the weak-kneed policies of the British Communist Party had been made known to the MCP leadership on his way to the Southeast Asia Youth Conference held in Calcutta in February 1948, visited Singapore again on his way back to Australia. Fortified by the detailed discussions at the Calcutta Conference of the new 'two camp' policy and the need actively to resist imperialism, Sharkey had extensive talks with members of the Central Executive and addressed the Fourth Plenary Session of the Central Executive Committee. The traditional, official British view is that during these discussions, the MCP was ordered into the jungle as part of a revolutionary strategy for Asia which was developed in Moscow and set in motion at the Calcutta Conference.[55] But this view appears to have exaggerated Sharkey's role. By informing the MCP's Fourth Plenary Session of the Cominform's policy, Sharkey left the Central Committee free to follow their own predelictions without having to worry about flouting general Cominform policy. In other words, he spurred the MCP leadership on to follow a course of action they were already inclined to take.[56] Out of the March meeting came two key resolutions: one stated that the struggle for independence must ultimately take the form of a 'people's revolutionary war', and the other that the masses must be prepared for 'an uncompromising struggle for independence without regard to considerations of legality'.[57]

The next few months saw a spiralling of the reciprocal pressure tactics used by both the colonial authorities and the MCP. The number of MCP-inspired strikes increased dramatically; at the same time, the Singapore Government increased the number of police raids and made widespread arrests. Recognizing that the Malayan and Singaporean Governments were gearing up for a full-scale assault, not just on the front and satellite organizations but also on the MCP itself, the Central Committee at a hurriedly called meeting on 10 May 1948 in Singapore, confirmed 'that without resolute action, concerted struggle and the use of violence when necessary' they could not 'repel the enemy and achieve victory'.[58] This proved to be the last meeting of the Central Committee before the Party took to the jungle, and as Short has noted it produced 'an unmistakable call to clear the decks for action'.[59]

Nevertheless, there was no clear-cut call to take up arms, move into the jungle, and initiate the armed struggle immediately.[60] The intent of the decisions taken at the Fourth Plenary Session seems to have been to increase the type of pressure already being exerted on the Government. However, the message was obviously open to interpretation, and the resulting confusion says much about the inexperience and lack of leadership at the top and the impetuosity and lack of discipline in the lower ranks of the Party. The leadership found it impossible to co-ordinate their campaign and control the actions of the rank and file. A number of lower level cadres appear to have taken matters into their own hands. At least two MPAJA units had maintained a state of semi-mobilization and it was these groups which in May and June began to resort to murder and other acts of violence. Certainly, violent acts increased markedly. There is also evidence that the shortage of funds led groups to use extortion and robbery–the traditional means of collecting money–in order to sustain their political activities.[61]

Whatever the reason, the increasing use of violence by a number of communist guerrilla groups resulted in mounting pressure on the Malayan Government to take decisive, retaliatory action. On 16 June 1948, three British planters in the Sungei Siput area of Perak were killed in two apparently separate attacks by different guerrilla units. The Government declared a State of Emergency in parts of Perak and Johore, and extended the State of Emergency to the whole of these two states the next day. On 18 June 1948, a State of Emergency was proclaimed for the whole of Malaya. The MCP was caught by surprise. Although some of its membership had gone underground in May and early June, many others were left to fend for themselves and to escape the attention of the police as best they could. Some cells were not called into action until well after the declaration of the Emergency and the police were able to make a number of significant arrests. There can be no doubt that from the MCP's point of view, their guerrilla campaign went off at half cock.

The confusion which surrounded the move into the jungle and

the actual initiation of the armed struggle strategy did not auger well for the MCP. In addition, they had been unable to 'mobilize the masses' as they had hoped. Indeed, their support generally had been weakened by the increased use of violence and by the way in which members of the Party had on occasion manipulated the union movement. Yet it would be misleading to underestimate the sympathy for the MCP among the Chinese community. Intriguingly, despite the treachery of its leader and all the problems this created, the Party remained strong. Pye's assessment that the MCP 'emerged from the War as probably the best organized and most experienced party in Southeast Asia'[62] is undoubtedly an exaggeration given the extent to which Lai Tek, the British, and the Japanese had severely depleted the ranks of the MCP leadership. But it is true that at the level of the rank and file the MCP had few problems attracting recruits. Certainly, the MCP's general popularity among the Chinese community gave it a significant base from which to mount its guerrilla campaign.

1. *Straits Times*, 11 September 1945 and 13 September 1945.

2. A good discussion of the early years of the MCP is to be found in J. H. Brimmell, *Communism in South East Asia: A Political Analysis* (London: Oxford University Press, 1959), pp. 88-96 and 146-50. See also Gene Z. Hanrahan, *The Communist Struggle in Malaya* (Kuala Lumpur: University of Malaya Press, 1971), pp. 19-60.

3. See the account of life with the guerrillas behind the Japanese lines in F. Spencer Chapman, *The Jungle is Neutral* (London: Chatto and Windus, 1949).

4. See Victor Purcell, *The Chinese in Southeast Asia*, 2nd edn. (Kuala Lumpur: Oxford University Press, 1965), p. 306, and Cheah Boon Kheng, *Red Star Over Malaya: Resistance and Social Conflict During and After the Japanese Occupation 1941-1946* (Singapore: Singapore University Press), pp. 20-4.

5. Purcell, *The Chinese in Southeast Asia*, p. 310; and Zakaria Haji Ahmad and Kernial Singh Sandhu, 'The Malayan Emergency: Event Writ Large', in Kernial Singh Sandhu and Paul Wheatley, eds., *Melaka: The Transformation of a Malayan Capital c.1400-1980*, 2 vols. (Kuala Lumpur: Oxford University Press, 1983), Vol. 1, p. 417. For an account of the MPAJA, see Hugh T. Pagden, 'Unrest in Malaya', para. 19, CO 537/3757.

6. See the discussion in Cheah, *Red Star Over Malaya*, pp. 133-5 and 177-84, and Chin Kee Onn, *Malaya Upside Down* (Singapore: Jitts, 1946), pp. 203-4.

7. Cheah, *Red Star Over Malaya*, pp. 195-240; William Shaw, *Tun Razak: His Life and Times* (Kuala Lumpur: Longman, 1976), pp. 56-60, and A. J. Stockwell, *British Policy And Malay Politics During The Malayan Union Experiment, 1942-1948* (Kuala Lumpur: Malayan Branch of the Royal Asiatic Society, Monograph No. 8), p. 148.

8. Cheah, *Red Star Over Malaya*, pp. 127-9; M. R. Stenson, *Class, Race and Colonialism in West Malaysia: The Indian Case* (Vancouver: University of British

Columbia Press, 1980), pp. 107-8, and M. R. Stenson, 'The Ethnic and Urban Bases of Communist Revolt in Malaya', in John Wilson Lewis, ed., *Peasant Rebellion and Communist Revolution in Asia* (Stanford, California: Stanford University Press, 1974), pp. 131-3.

9. Cheah, *Red Star Over Malaya*, p. 257; Cheah Boon Kheng, *The Masked Comrades: A Study of the Communist United Front in Malaya, 1945-1948* (Singapore: Times Books International, 1979), pp. 49-50, and Pagden, 'Unrest', paras. 11-13, CO 537/3757.

10. On the arrest of Soong Kwong, see F. S. V. Donnison, *British Military Administration in the Far East* (London: HMSO, 1956), pp. 389-90, and Cheah, *Red Star Over Malaya*, pp. 261-2.

11. See Secretary for Chinese Affairs, *Annual Report*, 1947, P/PM1, Chief Secretary 376/A/48 (ANM), and Cheah, *Masked Comrades*, Ch. 4.

12. See Lucian Pye, *Guerrilla Communism in Malaya: Its Social and Political Meaning* (Princeton, NJ: Princeton University Press, 1956), pp. 75-9, and interview with C. C. Too, June 1979.

13. Pagden, 'Unrest', para. 70, CO 537/3757.

14. Lee Ting Hui, *The Communist Organisation in Singapore: Its Techniques of Manpower Mobilizition and Management, 1948-1960*, Field Report Series No. 12 (Singapore: Institute of Southeast Asian Studies, August 1976), p. 6.

15. Pye, *Guerrilla Communism*, p. 80.

16. Ibid., p. 199.

17. Ibid., p. 187, and Lee, *The Communist Organisation*, p. 15.

18. Memorandum by T. P. F. McNeil (Secretary for Social Welfare), G. C. S. Adkins (Secretary for Chinese Affairs), and G. W. Webb (Secretary for Internal Affairs), Singapore, 24 November 1948, CO 537/3758.

19. See the general discussion in the W. L. Blythe Papers, mss. Ind Ocn S 116 (Rhodes House Library), and A. S. Haynes, British Association of Malaya, History Division IV/34 (Royal Commonwealth Society Library).

20. Purcell, *The Chinese in Southeast Asia*, p. 280.

21. See 'The Chinese in Malaya: Cultural Background', prepared for the Carr-Saunders Commission on University Education in Malaya in April 1947, in Blythe Papers, mss. Ind Ocn S 116 (Rhodes House Library).

22. M. V. del Tufo, *Malaya: A Report on the 1947 Census of Population* (London: HMSO, 1949), pp. 174-5. There were well over 1.3 million children between five and fifteen years of age compared to 1 million pre-War. See also Purcell, *The Chinese in Southeast Asia*, p. 281, and Pye, *Guerrilla Communism*, p. 175.

23. H. E. Wilson, *The Klang Strikes of 1941: Labour and Capital in Colonial Malaya*, Research Notes and Discussion Paper No. 25 (Singapore: Institute of Southeast Asian Studies, 1981), pp. 12-13, and M. R. Stenson, *Industrial Conflict in Malaya: Prelude to the Communist Revolt of 1948* (London: Oxford University Press, 1970), Ch. 2.

24. Lucian Pye, *Lessons from the Malayan Struggle Against Communism* (Cambridge, Mass: Center for International Studies, Massachusetts Institute of Technology, 17 February 1957), p. 9.

25. Stenson, *Class, Race and Colonialism*, p. 135.

26. It was officially estimated that in 1948 there was a shortage of some 25,000 workers. See *Proceedings of the Federal Legislative Council*, 1st Session, p. B534.

27. Department of Labour, *Monthly Report*, April 1948, pp. 2 and 4.

28. *Federation of Malaya Annual Report*, 1948, p. 8.

29. The Department of Labour seemed very pleased when a temporary surplus of labour in one area produced an 'improved discipline among estate workers'. Department of Labour, *Monthly Report*, March 1948, p. 3.

30. *Malayan Union Annual Report* (Kuala Lumpur: Government Printer, 1947), p. 4.

31. See Secretary for Chinese Affairs, *Annual Report*, 1947, pp. 5-9, P/PM1, Chief Secretary 376/A/48 (ANM), and 'A Note' by Mr H. J. Banard, mss. Ind Ocn S 26 (Rhodes House Library).

32. Memorandum by McNeil, Adkins, and Webb, CO 537/3758. See also Lennox A. Mills, *Malaya: A Political and Economic Appraisal* (Minneapolis: University of Minnesota Press, 1958), p. 30.

33. Memorandum by McNeil, Adkins, and Webb, p. 5, CO 537/3758; Minute by Gent, 26 May 1947, Chinese Affairs (MU) 1600/159 (ANM), and 'The Chinese Protectorate and the Chinese Affairs', Chinese Affairs (FM) 1626C (ANM).

34. Cheah, *Red Star Over Malaya*, pp. 192-3, and Pagden, 'Unrest', para. 10, CO 537/3757.

35. Cheah, *Masked Comrades*, p. 43.

36. See, for example, Ralph M. Stogdill, *Handbook of Leadership* (New York: The Free Press, 1974), pp. 402 and 419-20.

37. Document issued by the Central Executive Committee of the MCP on 28 May 1948, translated by the MSS HQ Singapore, 30 June 1948, Political Intelligence Journal, 30 June 1948, Serial No. 12/1948, Appendix 'B', CO 537/3752.

38. Chapman, *The Jungle is Neutral*, p. 158.

39. Harry Miller, *Jungle War in Malaya: The Campaign against Communism, 1948-60* (London: Arthur Barker, 1972), p. 35.

40. See the accounts of Lai Tek's activities during the Occupation in Cheah, *Red Star Over Malaya*, pp. 82-100, and Ng Yeh Loh to H. T. Pagden, October 1945, Hugh T. Pagden Papers SP7/3 (ANM).

41. Anthony Short, *The Communist Insurrection in Malaya 1948-1960* (London: Frederick Muller, 1975), p. 22, puts the number attacked at 'forty-odd'. Gene Z. Hanrahan, *The Communist Struggle in Malaya*, p. 74, states that 'the MPAJA reportedly lost over a hundred men, including at least half its political commissars'.

42. Pagden, 'Unrest', Appendix 1, CO 537/3757, and Cheah, *Red Star Over Malaya*, p. 88, who cites Major R. J. Isaacs: 'Wright helps Japs to trap Reds at Batu Caves', in *Malay Mail*, 31 August 1953.

43. Cheah, *Red Star Over Malaya*, p. 90.

44. Political Intelligence Journal, 30 June 1948, Serial No. 12/1948, p. 443, CO 537/3752.

45. See Pagden, 'Unrest', Appendix 1, CO 537/3757. Pagden's comments on Ng's letter in the newspaper and the letter he received from Ng are as follows: 'It may well be argued that, having been betrayed by Lai Tek, or having a grudge against him, and having been expelled from the MCP as a traitor–he probably did talk under torture–Ng Yeh Loh was trying to get his revenge. This document, however, had the ring of sincerity and I could never accept the belief that Ng was just out for revenge and nothing more.' Pagden was an entomologist who had worked for the Department of Agriculture since the 1920s and who had established excellent contacts within the Chinese community. During 1945-6 he was seconded to the BMA in Singapore as Adviser on Chinese Affairs becoming Acting Secretary for Chinese Affairs on 1 April 1946 with the resumption of civil government. At the end of April

1946 he resumed his scientific work travelling throughout the Peninsula. This gave him an excellent opportunity to continue to maintain his contacts within the Chinese community.

46. Cheah, *Red Star Over Malaya*, p. 244.

47. Document issued by the MCP, 28 May 1948, CO 537/3752.

48. Short, *The Communist Insurrection*, p. 41, fn. 8. See also the discussion in M. R. Stenson, *Industrial Conflict in Malaya: Prelude to the Communist Revolt of 1948* (London: Oxford University Press, 1970), p. 216.

49. 'A Review of Malayan Communist Party Policy', Political Intelligence Journal, 31 July 1948, Serial No. 14/1948, Supplement No. 9, CO 537/3753.

50. Chapman, *The Jungle is Neutral*, p. 161.

51. Chin Kee Onn to H. T. Pagden, 9 August 1948, CO 537/3757.

52. Pagden, 'Unrest', paras. 27-8, CO 537/3757.

53. The MCP claimed that as well as the post-War embezzlement during the Occupation Lai Tek 'misappropriated from the Party organizations in Perak and Selangor $290,000 (Japanese currency), 170 gold pounds and 23 tahils of gold'. Document issued by the MCP on May 28, 1948, CO 537/3752. The practice of paying party members is noted in Lucian W. Pye, *Lessons from the Malayan Struggle Against Communism*, p. 8. The MCP's shortage of funds is noted, for example, in Political Intelligence Journal, 30 June 1948, Serial No. 12/1948, p. 442, CO 537/ 3752, and in 'Malaya–Political Intelligence Summary for May 1948', notes by D. J. Kirkness, Colonial Office Eastern Department, CO 537/3755.

54. On the impact of Government restrictions, see Stenson, *Industrial Conflict in Malaya*, pp. 214-35.

55. See Pye, *Guerrilla Communism*, pp. 83-4; Brimmell, *Communism in South East Asia*, p. 210; Robert Thompson, *Revolutionary Warfare in World Strategy, 1945-1969* (London: Secker and Warburg, 1970), pp. 62-3, and the discussion in Short, *The Communist Insurrection*, pp. 43-9 and 52-3.

56. See the argument in R. T. McVey, *The Calcutta Conference and the Southeast Asian Uprisings*, Interim Report Series, Modern Indonesia Project (Ithaca: Cornell University, 1958). Interestingly, Charles B. McLane, *Soviet Strategies in Southeast Asia: An Exploration of Eastern Policy under Lenin and Stalin* (Princeton, N.J: Princeton University Press, 1966), pp. 390 and 399, has suggested that a greater external influence may have been exercised by the Chinese Communist Party.

57. See McLane, *Soviet Strategies*, p. 386, and Short, *The Communist Insurrection*, pp. 50-1.

58. Short, *The Communist Insurrection*, p. 56.

59. Ibid., pp. 56-7.

60. C. C. Too argues that the revolt was to begin in earnest some time in August or September (interview, January 1973), while Purcell says that the 'declaration of a Communist Republic of Malaya was timed for 3 August 1948': *The Chinese in Southeast Asia*, p. 330.

61. See Brimmell, *Communism in South East Asia*, p. 211. Cheah, *Red Star Over Malaya*, p. 259, notes that units were active in Johore and Perak as early as 1946. The lack of co-ordination is noted by Anthony Short, 'Communism and the Emergency', in Wang Gungwu, ed., *Malaysia: A Survey* (New York: Praeger, 1964), p. 153; Stenson, *Industrial Conflict in Malaya*, p. 230, and John Weldon Humphrey, 'Population Resettlement in Malaya' (Ph.D. dissertation, Northwestern University, 1971), p. 62.

62. Pye, *Guerrilla Communism*, p. 11.

3
Between Two Millstones

WITH the declaration of the Emergency on 18 June 1948, each side began to formulate its strategy and to mobilize in earnest. The Government adopted a policy which can best be termed as one of 'coercion and enforcement'. It sought to stop or discourage Malayans from joining or aiding the communist guerrillas by searching out and punishing those who did. While the Government was able to continue governing, this ill-conceived and poorly implemented policy resulted in many people, particularly among the Chinese community, being driven—both metaphorically and literally—into the guerrillas' camp. At the same time, the communist organizations were not averse to using violence to eliminate their Kuomintang opponents, to disrupt the economic life of the country, to dissuade people from aiding the Government, and to persuade Malayans to provide the guerrillas with money, food, and supplies. Caught in the middle, 'between two millstones' as Tan Cheng Lock put it, were the people of Malaya.[1]

Law and Order

The immediate response of the Malayan Government to the communist guerrilla threat was to view it as a question of restoring law and order. This assessment was rooted in the traditional role that British authority had played in the Peninsula. The British had originally extended their influence throughout the area by being able to maintain order and stability in the face of conflicting Malay and Chinese interests. The narrow legalistic definition of the situation which confronted the Government in June 1948 was, therefore, consistent with the historic functions performed by the colonial administration.[2] Moreover, this perception of the task at hand was reinforced by two other factors.

First, as the number of violent incidents increased during the early months of 1948, various vocal and influential individuals and groups became more and more insistent that the 'criminal elements' be suppressed and that the Government act to stem the rising tide of lawlessness. By the end of May this criticism had reached a cres-

cendo. In a debate in the Legislative Council which took place on
31 May, the Government was roundly attacked. Dato Onn, to much
applause, chastised the Government, saying that the Malay states
in agreeing to the Federation had permitted the Federal Government to have the fullest powers so as to maintain peace and order,
and he demanded that they live up to their side of the bargain.[3] On
4 June one of the leading English-language newspapers, the *Straits
Times*, printed a list of thirty-three 'terrorist incidents' which had
taken place since 1 May. A few days later, armed with demands
from several state planters' organizations for immediate and decisive
action, representatives of commerce and industry–mostly European–
discussed the question of 'lawlessness' with the High Commissioner, Sir Edward Gent, and his senior advisers. At the same time,
another English-language paper, the *Malay Mail*, kept up a barrage
of criticism over what it considered to be the weakness of the Government's actions. Moreover, pressure was being put on London
to have Gent recalled.

Given this sustained attack, especially by the European community, on the Government's handling of the mounting threat to
law and order, an official reaction to the events of 16 June was virtually mandatory. The early morning murder of three British
planters in the Sungei Siput area of Perak was answered later
that day by a declaration of a State of Emergency in parts of Perak
and Johore. The next day, no doubt urged on by the *Straits
Times*' stinging front page editorial entitled 'Govern or get out',
the State of Emergency was extended to the whole of Perak and
Johore, and on the following day to all of Malaya. The context for
the declaration of 'the Emergency', as it became known, clearly
indicated that the Government considered its task to be the capture and punishment of those responsible for the spate of criminal activities, and the restoration of law and order.

Secondly, the law and order approach both informed and was
reinforced by the operations of the Malayan Security Service
(MSS), the intelligence arm of the Government. The traditions
of intelligence-gathering in Malaya, the shortages of agents
and staff, and the predelictions of its head, Lieutenant-Colonel
John Dalley, combined to give the MSS a rather narrow definition
of its intelligence-gathering role. It concerned itself essentially
with the potential for criminal activities of the major figures in
the various groups under its surveillance. Little was done to assess
the political, social, and economic conditions upon which these
groups fed. As a consequence, the information passed on to the

Government concerning the two main groups that preoccupied the MSS–the radical Malay nationalists and the communists–was too often ambiguous or misleading.[4] Dalley was particularly concerned about the strong influence that events in Indonesia were having on radical Malays. Their threat was overestimated. While undoubtedly there were individuals and factions within the Malay Nationalist Party and other radical Malay groups who were actively promoting Pan Malayanism or communism, or some combination of the two, and thus needed to be watched, they lacked a wide base of support within the Malay population. On the other hand, the threat posed by the MCP was underestimated. There were a number of possible reasons for this: the departure of Lai Tek left the MSS without a good source of information on communist activity; a lack of manpower made it impossible for the MSS to monitor the more decentralized activities of the Party; and the MCP itself was ambiguous and confused as to the timing of its initiation of all-out revolutionary action. 'Operating at the fringes of the subversive movement',[5] the MSS's assessments failed to appreciate the strong roots that the MCP had put down within the Chinese community.

Information received by the Colonial Office in London was indicative of the Malayan Government's inability to anticipate either the outbreak of the Emergency or the strength of support for the MCP and, hence, to warn the Colonial Office of what was in store. For example, on 28 May 1948, a senior official minuted: 'I do not think that any information which has reached Eastern Department during the last month would lead us to suppose that any serious trouble is brewing in Malaya.'[6] The failure of the MSS reports to place the mass of details they contained in a wider context frustrated the Colonial Office before the declaration of the Emergency, and clearly exasperated them as they began to get an inkling of the magnitude of the threat posed by the guerrillas. As one letter to the Commissioner-General for South-East Asia noted: 'We study the Malayan Security Service's reports with care but we find them lacking in [an] essential appreciation, on a wider scale, of the future developments which would be useful to us here.'[7] It became clear to the Colonial Office that the Malayan Government had little idea of 'what the ordinary law-abiding person in the different communities [was] thinking and feeling'.[8]

The impression that the Government was not fully aware of the true nature of the events which were taking place was accentuated by the use of the term 'bandits' to refer to all 'criminals' or 'bad hats'.

While this practice was fully in accord with the traditions of the law and order approach, it failed to make any distinction between the activities of non-political groups, such as secret societies and independent criminal gangs (which were taking advantage of the prevailing confusion), and the activities of the political organizations, such as the Kuomintang, with its base in Northern Perak, and the MCP. The term 'bandit' was essentially an appellation which covered all sorts of evil deeds and its continual use by the Government only served to confuse and mislead people. It appeared not only to deny that the communists could be politically motivated but also to ignore the fact that the MCP had widespread support within certain sections of the population.[9]

The law and order approach, then, was consistent with colonial traditions but failed to take into account the changed times. The generally accepted assessment of the situation within the Malayan Government and the European community in Malaya was that the strikes, the widespread violence, and the spread of anti-government sentiment were the work of a few agitators and extremists, probably directed from outside the country. Although there were undoubtedly people within the Government who appreciated the true nature of the threat, the prevailing view did not acknowledge that the communists were proving to be so persistent a problem because they were able to tie their assault on the Government to the many real grievances harboured by Malayans. As J. B. Perry Robinson has written: 'There was a pronounced tendency among Government officials to assume that the bandits were supported by a limited and ascertainable number of misguided sympathisers who could be cajoled or threatened into giving up their support.'[10] It was within this context that the Government developed its coercion and enforcement policy.

Coercion and Enforcement

The basis of the Government's use of coercion and enforcement to restore law and order was the Emergency Regulations under which the State of Emergency was maintained.[11] The powers thus acquired by the Government included the right to raise a force of special constables, the right to control movement on the roads, increased rights with regard to search and arrest without a warrant, the right to order detention, the right to register the entire population, and the right to try all but capital offences *in camera*. Those societies thought to be in support of subversive activities were proscribed. And people who aided or were suspected of aiding guerrillas were just as liable to arrest by the security forces as those who actually became guerrillas. From time to time, as circumstances warranted, other powers were added to the Government's arsenal. In themselves these powers were mostly not unreasonable given the situation. Problems arose, however, because of the manner in which they were implemented. The powers of Government were exercised more against the general population than for its benefit.

Confusion arose almost immediately. Just over a week after the declaration of the Emergency the High Commissioner, Sir Edward Gent, was recalled by the Colonial Office for 'consultations'; in effect he was to be relieved of his post. As the aircraft in which he was travelling was about to land in London it crashed and Gent was killed. It was not until 6 October, three months later, that the new High Commissioner, Sir Henry Gurney, was sworn in. During this interregnum, the lack of any overall direction to the Government's counter-guerrilla policies became apparent. Malcolm MacDonald, as Commissioner-General for South-East Asia, carried much of the burden of trying to get the Malayan Government's campaign under way; however, he had no executive authority within the Federation and could only advise and try to prod officials into action.[12] Within Malaya the newly arrived General Officer Commanding (GOC) Malaya, Major-General C. H. Boucher, tried to co-ordinate the 'anti-bandit' campaign. He seems to have assumed this role largely by default. The Commissioner of Police, H. B. Langworthy, was incapacitated by ill-health and on the verge of resigning, and the Administration was in the hands of 'acting' officials, with the Chief Secretary, Sir Alexander T. Newboult, as interim Head of Government. Boucher, portraying himself as the expert on guerrilla warfare since he had fought the Greek guerrillas, reassured everyone that the army would have no difficulty dealing with the situation: 'I can tell you this is by far the easiest problem I have ever tackled. In spite of the appalling country and ease with which he can hide, the enemy is far weaker in technique and courage than either the Greek or Indian Reds.'[13]

But Boucher and his fellow officers soon showed that they had little idea of how to fight a successful counter-guerrilla campaign. Having just won a major conventional war, it was their experiences in the battles in Europe and North Africa which appeared to be the basis for their tactical operations against the guerrillas. Large-scale 'sweeps', designed to locate and trap the guerrillas and carried out by men trained on the wide-open flats of England's Salisbury Plain, were vigorously employed. The major effect of these mass movements of troops was to telegraph their advance so that the guerrillas were alerted well before the troops arrived. The guerrillas melted into the jungle or the troops were caught in an ambush. The success rate of these operations was very low.

Immediately after his investiture as High Commissioner in early October 1948, Sir Henry Gurney tried to rein in the military. In line with the notion that the Government was engaged in a campaign to restore law and order, he gave overall authority for the conduct of the Emergency operations to the new Commissioner of Police, Colonel W. N. Gray, and directed that the military should act in support of the civilian power. Although the Colonial Secretary agreed with this ranking of responsibilities,[14] General Boucher did not. He felt it was completely unacceptable for a general to accept orders from a policeman, and he was supported in this view by a new Commander-in-Chief of Far East Land Forces, General Sir John Harding.[15] Moreover, the lines of authority encouraged Boucher's obstinacy. On the one hand, the Police Commissioner derived his authority from the High Commissioner, who in turn was responsible to the Colonial Secretary; on the other hand, the GOC Malaya was responsible through the various levels of the army command to the War Office. The civilian authority had no clear-cut right to give orders to the military.

The question of the respective roles of the police and the army was further complicated by the obvious weaknesses of the police force. Indeed, it seemed to be somewhat fanciful to expect that a force which had been singularly unsuccessful in maintaining law and order in the preceding three years could immediately cope with the intensified assault of the MCP. These weaknesses were exacerbated by the need to expand the size of the police force as rapidly as possible. From a total strength of just under 11,000 in 1947, the force tripled in size over the next two to three years. By far the largest percentage of recruits among the rank and file were Malays. Too often, new recruits—particularly the special constables—received virtually no training. This shortcoming, in conjunction with their newly acquired power, led to some unpleasant incidents which accentuated the friction between the Malays and the Chinese. As a community, the Chinese were very reluctant to join the police force.[16] While a few Chinese were recruited as officers or detectives in the first months of the Emergency, it was not until December 1950 that Chinese started to join the rank and file. And when they did so it was only because their pay was supplemented by Chinese organizations. With so few ordinary policemen being able to speak Chinese, the police force in general had great difficulty maintaining good contacts with Chinese communities. All these liabilities undermined the capacity of the force to play its allotted role.

Further problems were also caused by the influx of European policemen. Nearly 400 ex-Palestine recruits arrived towards the end of 1948. They were supplemented by European officers and sergeants from India and Hong Kong. The new arrivals were immediately put into service with only a minimum of training in professional police work, no knowledge of the Malay, Chinese, or Tamil languages or the customs of the country, and little appreciation of the standard of work and conduct expected of them. This lack of instruction in the local culture led to at least one case of a Malay who was being verbally abused 'stepping out of the ranks and hitting his senior officer, knocking him down'.[17] Nevertheless, while the new recruits created many problems, the Government's general attitude was that they were better than nothing. Indeed, Gurney was constantly badgering London to find and send out more sergeants and officers for without them, he argued, the rapidly expanding force could not be supervised and its effectiveness would be minimized.[18] Moreover, the heavy load placed on those already in Malaya meant that good men were taxed to the limit.

Newly recruited officers and sergeants without proper training and a rapidly expanding and poorly supervised rank and file provided fertile ground for corruption. The Emergency made extortion and bribery much easier for those who wished to line their own pockets. If bribes were received there were no arrests, but an uncooperative 'donor' could always be shot as a communist sympathizer.[19] Some Chinese detectives became particularly adept at employing such forms of persuasion. Secret societies were very good patrons of the detectives in the major towns, and gained some insurance against too much police attention in this way. But corruption was not confined to detectives; it pervaded every aspect of police work and included such diverse activities as petty theft, personal revenge, and the control of gambling and prostitution. Most officers, however, regarded it as a 'minor and ineradicable failing' and did little to control it.[20]

The police also gained a well-deserved reputation for brutality. One group of Chinese reported that detainees were hit with rifle butts and kicked as they got off buses at police stations; people held for screening were given a 'hammering' in full view of others in the villages; and suspects held in jail were tossed in the air, allowed to fall on the floor, and were then stepped on.[21] These were not isolated incidents. Much of this behaviour was fostered by the new recruits, especially those who had formerly served in Palestine. Harry Miller, a reporter for the *Straits Times*, recalls that there were 'some rough types and adventurers who arrived in the country with fixed ideas of how to treat the natives, notions fostered in Palestine where a heavy hand had been used on Jew and Arab without discrimination and the butt-end of a rifle had more effect than an appeasing tongue'. These attitudes, when transferred to Malaya meant that 'every Chinese was a bandit or a potential bandit and there was only one treatment for them, they were to be "bashed around". If they would not take a sock in the jaw, a kick in the gut might have the desired result.'[22]

Similar attitudes prevailed in police and military operations in areas in which communists were known to operate. Faced with a scared, sullen population and with no understanding of Chinese ways, and consequently with no hard evidence on which to act, the security forces tended to suspect everyone. Too often, after minimal success in tracking down a guerrilla group, the security forces would assume local complicity and vent their frustrations on those nearest at hand. A favourite tactic on these occasions was to burn the huts of suspects or even indiscriminately burn whole villages. In August 1948, the entire village of Pulai in Kelantan was burnt to the ground after it had been briefly occupied by guerrillas. Perhaps the most infamous example of this policy, however, was the burning of Kachau village in Selangor. On 2 November 1948, with a warning of only an hour or so, the whole village, together with valuables that had been removed from the houses but which caught fire in the general conflagration, was reduced to ashes. Sixty-one houses were destroyed and about 400 people were left homeless. Although Pulai and Kachau were the worst incidents, they were by no means the only examples of such tactics. Large numbers of houses were burnt in Jalong, Lintang, Tronoh, and in the Cameron Highlands, and in October 1948 the security forces expelled nearly 5,000 people from the Batu Arang area of Selangor after the town had been attacked by guerrillas.[23]

The army—and to a lesser extent the police force—were also prone to shoot people who appeared to be acting suspiciously. Given the army's training and tactics, the prevailing attitude that the army was fighting a war, and General Boucher's view that soldiers should fire to kill, it was not surprising that many Chinese who were merely suspects were shot and killed. One such incident gained special notoriety. In December 1948 at Batang Kali in Selangor, jittery British soldiers shot to death twenty-four Chinese villagers being held on suspicion of aiding the guerrillas. Interestingly, this incident, which was initially advertised as the shooting of twenty-four communist guerrillas, was hushed up by the Government. Gurney denied any knowledge of the incident to the Colonial Office, who were being pressed by questions in the House of Commons and enquiries from a *Daily Worker* reporter. It was assumed that the questioners must be referring to the Kachau case.[24] And, like Kachau and Pulai, Batang Kali was merely one of the starkest examples of how the leadership of the security forces prosecuted the Government's campaign through the use of its superior firepower. Despite court rulings that flight from security forces by uneducated people was far from proof of guilt and that anyone who was not armed was entitled to the full shelter of the law in the matter of arrest and custody, many frightened people were shot while running away from patrols. The Chief Police Officer of Johore was particularly concerned that there were many cases in which rounds of ammunition were placed on bodies in order to justify such shootings.[25]

Initially, a key adjunct to the actions of the security forces was the use of detention and banishment. This relatively 'ruthless operation', as Gurney described it, involved 'the wholesale arrest and detention and possible repatriation of all persons found residing within certain areas in which the bandits are and have been living among and on the population'.[26] After just over a year of the Emergency, the Government had rounded up more than 15,000 people, nearly 10,000 of whom had been sent to China. The High Commissioner had aimed at banishing and repatriating 2,000 people per month but, towards the end of 1949, as the new communist government in China restricted deportation, the Malayan Government found it very difficult to round up and house in detention camps all those who were in areas where they might be susceptible to guerrilla demands for aid.[27] This policy caught large numbers of innocent people in the detention net. Moreover, the committees of review were required to accept the advice of the police in doubtful cases, although it was recognized that police information was often based on flimsy evidence and that some members of the police force were not above reporting people as suspects for personal reasons. As a result, many of those who proved to be guiltless suffered considerable hardships because there were major bottlenecks in the review of individual cases, and it often took a long time for innocent people to be released.[28] The detention policy, therefore, had major flaws.

The Government clearly recognized that it was embarked on a campaign of coercion and enforcement which included a good measure of what Thomas Perry Thornton has termed 'enforcement terror'.[29] In a telegram to the Secretary of State for the Colonies, Gurney stated that the Chinese 'are as you know notoriously inclined to lean towards whichever side frightens them more and at the moment this seems to be the Government'.[30] This point was reiterated at a meeting of the British Defence Co-ordinating Committee (Far East) in Singapore in January 1949. Gurney stated that an alternative object of affiliation needed to be introduced which the Chinese would recognize as 'stronger than the bandits and at the same time inspiring greater fear'.[31] The High Commissioner also appeared unperturbed by the fact that at 'the present time the police and army are breaking the law every day', for he felt that it was 'most important that police and soldiers, who are not saints, should not get the impression that every small mistake is going to be the subject of a public enquiry or that it is better to do nothing at all than to do the wrong thing quickly'.[32]

Stories of the brutality of the army and the police, and of what one European official with good contacts to the Chinese community labelled their 'sadistic' activities,[33] spread quickly through family and friendship networks and via the lorry drivers and others who travelled the Peninsula. It was not unheard of for the Chinese, who lived along the jungle fringes and who had suffered greatly during the Occupation, to say that the British were more brutal than the Japanese. The Japanese, they said, had never burnt whole villages, arrested women and children, and destroyed their livelihood. Rumours were quick to circulate and were widely discussed within the Chinese community. For example, it was said that the security forces had burnt down a hut over the head of a woman who was in labour, forcing her to run out to safety; that villagers were left to fend for themselves after their villages had been destroyed; that innocent men were hanged after they had been forced at the point of a guerrilla gun to carry arms; and that women were raped by European soldiers and members of the Flying Squad. Some referred to this period as the 'Feast of the Passover', and the expression was 'used with real bitterness'.[34]

The Chinese community resented the predicament in which the Government had placed them. The security forces were clearly unable to protect the bulk of the population, especially those in the more remote rural areas, from guerrilla pressure, but at the same time they expected full co-operation from these people in rooting out the communists. The unreasonableness of the Government's demands for support, the distrust of the Government which had become ingrained during the post-Occupation period, and a sense of the need to help out those who had suffered at the hands of the security forces, all combined to unite the Chinese community in defence of those whom they considered more worthy of sympathy than of the full weight of the law. Indeed, the Government's law and order approach and its attendant assumption that everyone must take sides in the conflict were totally alien to the Chinese. They were particularly perplexed and angry that the Government could not appreciate that many Chinese were neither guilty nor innocent but associated with the communists because of the patriotic common front during the Japanese Occupation or because they were geographically exposed to guerrilla pressure.[35]

One issue which symbolized the difference in outlook between the Chinese community and the Government was the paying of protection money. The payment of protection money was not something which had started with the Emergency. It had a long if somewhat dishonourable history within Chinese society. In Malaya it had come to be regarded as an almost inevitable part of business life. The practice was said to be almost universal even down to the smallest farmer. The Chinese businessmen, commonly referred to as *towkays*, usually paid on the basis of an assessment made by the local communist 'subscription' collector. Failure to pay not only put their mines, plantations, or crops at risk but also the safety of their families. The Emergency simply made extortion that much easier, and the need to comply more necessary. The Government felt the Chinese were 'paying the bandits hundreds of thousands of dollars a month. With this money the bandits buy their food at good prices and employ new recruits. Without it, they could do neither.'[36] To put a stop to this practice, the Government made it known that where evidence was obtained of the payment of protection money, the offender would be 'dealt with with the utmost rigour of the law'.[37] A number of people were arrested and some fairly well-known Chinese leaders were questioned. It certainly frightened the *towkays* but it did not necessarily stop the threats and the use of extortion by the communists and others.

The Chinese felt trapped by the Government's policy. The Government could not ensure the protection of property, nor would it allow unauthorized individuals to carry arms for their own protection. By contrast, European estates were given protection by police officers and special constables, and most Europeans were authorized to carry arms. As one *towkay* said later: 'I too could have been a hero with such protection.'[38] Morale among Chinese and Indian estate managers was generally extremely low. Few dared to venture outside the safety of the nearest large town, and most left the labour on their estates largely unsupervised, allowing the communists a free rein. Given the atmosphere of lawlessness, the Government's exhortations to stand up and denounce the payment of protection money seemed inappropriate at best. In default of proper protection, payment was the only course open to anyone who wished to protect his livelihood and ensure the safety of himself and his family.

It would be a mistake either to imply that no government official appreciated the predicament in which the Chinese found themselves, or to suggest that all the actions of the Government's security forces entailed the use of force against the general population. There were certainly people within the Government who tried to alleviate the problems faced by the Chinese. And in many cases, members of the police and the army acted with considerable restraint. Nonetheless, it must be emphasized that the Government's initial strategy was clearly to reimpose law and order through the use of coercion and enforcement.

Administrative Failings

For large sections of the Malayan Chinese community, their growing sense of isolation and their resentment at the injustices inflicted upon them by the security forces were reinforced by their limited knowledge of the role of the Government, their lack of personal contact with Government representatives, and their traditional uneasiness in any dealings with authority. Most rural Chinese, for example, had only a vague notion of what the Government was or did. During the first few years of the Emergency, Labour Department officials who toured rural areas found Asian estates previously unknown to the Government as well as Chinese who had not seen a Government official for two or three years.[39] Lucian Pye reports that of the surrendered communists he interviewed, over 70 per cent 'indicated that they perceived the colonial administration as existing completely apart from the Chinese community in Malaya'.[40] There were some rural Chinese who thought that the Japanese currency still had value and others who believed that the communists had been ceded control of the non-urban areas by the Government after the defeat of the Japanese.[41] It gradually became clear, then, that the Government had been unable to administratively reoccupy key areas of rural Malaya. In particular, there were large numbers of rural Chinese who received no administrative benefits which might offset the harm caused by the security forces.

Although this gap in the Government's administrative structure was not altogether new, its dimensions and importance became starkly apparent as the communist guerrillas took up residence along the jungle fringes. Before the War, most of the work of the Chinese Protectorate–that part of the Government which had supervised the activities of the Chinese community–was concerned with the urban Chinese. In the rural areas the Chinese communities were supervised, usually in an indirect fashion through the good offices of the local *towkays*, by the District Officers (DO). However, after the British returned, the new set of DOs who were sent into the field were generally much less experienced, were not nearly so well-trained, and could not call on a long-standing personal relationship with local Chinese leaders. Indeed, the DOs had to re-establish their authority after the traumatic events of the Occupation–which had forced many Chinese to flee from the main centres into the jungle fringes–and amidst the chaos and hardships that characterized the post-War period. Perhaps the most serious deficiency was the scarcity of Chinese-speakers among the DOs. Almost none of them spoke Chinese, a fact which was particularly noticeable in predominantly Chinese areas such as Perak's Kinta Valley.

However, it was not just the DOs who could not speak Chinese. By the end of 1949, out of a total of 256 MCS officers, only 23 had passed the Chinese language exam and only 16 were learning Chinese, the language of over 38 per cent of the population.[42] Besides the district offices, the Labour Department, the Social Welfare Department, the police, and the Education Department also suffered from a shortage of Chinese-speaking officers. The Education Department was unable to supervise properly the Chinese schools, which were known to be forcing grounds for communist recruits and from which both teachers and students organized local support groups for the guerrillas. Indeed, there was only one Chinese-speaking European officer in the Education Department and there were over 1,300 Chinese schools.[43]

An additional obstacle to the Malayan Government's re-establishing its control over the rural Chinese population was created by the attitudes of the sultans (Rulers) and the Malay élite, especially those in the state governments. After the bitterness and frustrations that had arisen over the Malayan Union, the state governments were very much on their guard. An important irritant was the procedure for replacing Sir Edward Gent. Much to their annoyance, the Rulers and their advisers were told that they had no right to be consulted over the appointment of a new High Commissioner, only a right to be informed. The Rulers were apprehensive about Gurney's appointment because they feared his experience in Palestine might lead him to think that Malays and Chinese should be treated like Arabs and Jews. They were also concerned that so few of the top people under Gurney had experience of Malaya.[44] The concern that the Rulers and their Mentris Besar (Chief Ministers) felt over the newly evolving federal-state relations was reflected in the strenuous complaints they made about the protocol for Gurney's installation as High Commissioner. The original plans had to be revised to allow the representatives of the Malay Rulers to arrive just before Gurney and to be seated on each side of the High Commissioner, 'denoting as it should be, a partnership', as one Mentri Besar put it. Altogether it was not a propitious beginning for the new High Commissioner.

Even after their success at having the plans for the installation ceremonies changed, the state governments continued to be suspicious of what they viewed as British attempts to re-establish, by way of the Federal Government, their position as 'Tuans' or the masters of the Malays. Any perceived intrusion into what was considered to be state jurisdiction was hotly contested as a matter of principle. The state governments put as much pressure on the Federal Government as they could in order to maintain what they felt to be their legitimate sphere of authority. For example, Dato Onn, the Mentri Besar for Johore, gave notice in the Federal Legislative Council of a strongly worded resolution that charged the Federal Government with endeavouring to force upon State and Settlement Governments directives of policy on matters affecting and within the jurisdiction of the State and Settlement Governments. He asked the Council to deplore the manner in which the Government of the Federation was implementing the spirit and intention of the Federation Agreement.[45] The *Straits Times* supported Onn, noting that 'Directives have been received in Johore Bahru from Kuala Lumpur which read more like orders from a pre-war British Resident to his District Officers than communications to a Government, which is still very much a Government whatever powers it may have voluntarily sacrificed to the Federal Government for the sake of Malayan unity.'[46]

These procedural tensions led to battles over the substance of policy. For example, state governments were very slow to agree to do anything which might involve allocating land to the Chinese. They also felt strongly about the lack of money being spent on Malay education. Most upsetting for them was that a high proportion of the 50 per cent of school-age children who could not attend school—over 500,000 of these were of primary school age—a high proportion were Malays. They threatened that no more money would be spent on non-Malays until expenditure on the education of Malays had been increased by 50 per cent.[47] Other issues which occupied the Malay élite were the need to recruit more Malays to the MCS to promote the Malays who were already there, to appoint a Malay to head a Federal Department, to promote Malays to senior posts in the Malayan Police Service, to provide more scholarships for Malays, to increase the number of Malay battalions, and to help Malay kampongs economically. At the same time, the state governments were not very keen to see Chinese or Indians brought into the administrative services as they felt this could undermine Malay political power.[48] But perhaps most importantly, the Malay élite did not accept that the state governments had a crucial role to play in the fight against communism. They considered this to be the task of the Federal Government.

Gurney became very frustrated by the lack of co-operation from the state governments. He felt that the Federation Constitution had been brought in with the assurance that the principle of strong central administration would be retained. What he now saw, however, was that much of the administration of policy was in the hands of state governments which, he felt, took a parochial view of important issues and did not have the interests of the Chinese at heart.[49] He pointed out that, for example, although it dealt with little else but Chinese affairs, the Perak State Security Committee had no Chinese member, and the Malay DOs were generally too frightened to interfere with Chinese squatters, and received no support from their state government by way of needed measures such as new roads and police posts.[50] Interestingly, he blamed not only Malays within the state governments but also Malay-speaking senior MCS officers. In this assessment he was supported by David R. Rees-Williams, Parliamentary Under-Secretary of State, Colonial Office, whose tour of Malaya convinced him that the High Commissioner was supported by some very inferior senior officers, a number of whom were disloyal to the Government.[51]

At the same time, the queries and confusion which resulted from the new federal structure created a great deal of extra work for the Federal Administration, especially the Chief Secretary. This added burden, plus the problems associated with acclimatizing a new High Commissioner, dealing with the Rulers' Conferences (which were designed to be a forum for consultation between Rulers—the sultans and their advisers—and the High Commissioner), and accommodating the increasing demands of the Emergency, all produced an administrative bottleneck which did much to undermine the efficiency of the Federal Government. It was not surprising, therefore, that the Government found almost impossible the task of administratively reclaiming the Chinese-inhabited rural areas.

Underlying these problems and handcuffing the Government's attempts to expand its administrative authority was the critical financial position in which the Government found itself. This had caused considerable concern even before the declaration of the Emergency; after June 1948 it deteriorated rapidly. As Sir Henry Gurney noted in the Legislative Council: 'Terrorism is the most expensive form of illness from which any community can suffer and becomes more so the longer it is permitted to drag on.'[52] The rapid expansion of the police force and those parts of the Administration considered to be directly involved in the 'anti-bandit' campaign drained the Government's coffers. 'Personal Emoluments', for example, increased from $60 million in 1947 to $140 million in 1948 and to $166 million in 1949. And with over $50 million spent on 'Public Order, Defence and the Emergency' in 1948 and $109 million in 1949, the guerrilla war was costing the Malayan Government over $250,000 per day.[53] This had to be set against revenues which, despite the introduction of income tax, were not nearly enough to cover the increasing costs. The resulting deficits amounted to over $55 million in 1948 and over $52 million in 1949, with the Government's estimated Surplus Balance reduced to dangerously low levels. And, moreover, during the post-War period the Government had spent $112 million in loan funds—$61 million from the 1946 Malayan Union Loans and $51 million from the 1949 Federation of Malaya Loan—and could not expect to raise any more loans to ease the financial position.

Under these circumstances, the pressure on His Majesty's Government to help alleviate the Malayan Government's predicament steadily grew. However, the Colonial Office, the Malayan Government's spokesman in Whitehall, found the Treasury very unresponsive. In an unusual display of testiness, H. T. Bourdillon of the Colonial Office characterized the Treasury's inactivity as 'nothing short of criminal'.[54] The Treasury, of course, was beleaguered by Britain's own financial problems and did not wish to move until it absolutely had to. There was also some concern within the British Government that the British taxpayer was being called on for a contribution without the Federation doing all it could to raise revenue.[55] Finally, however, the Treasury made provision in 1949 for the Malayan Government to float a loan in London and agreed to contribute £5 million (nearly $42 million) of the £7.5 million asked for for 1949 and later agreed to make available £3 million of the £5 million asked for for 1950.[56]

The financial stringencies and the debate over who should make up the shortfall in revenues caused a good deal of friction within Malaya. During a debate on this issue in the Federal Legislative Council in September 1948, Dato Onn, in a very sarcastic speech, termed the British Government's announced contribution to the 1949 budget of £5 million as 'lousy'. There were a good many people less outspoken than Dato Onn who felt that all expenditure directly due to the Emergency should be met by the British Government.[57] The introduction of income tax had generated a fear on the part of the business community that the Government would dip deeper and deeper into their pockets in order to finance the Emergency. Moreover, Malaya's businessmen still chaffed at the continued restrictions on their ability to buy goods from outside the sterling area. Despite the low sterling prices received for Malaya's rubber and tin, and the major contribution Malaya made to the sterling area's US dollar earnings, both the Malayan and Singapore Governments, along with other colonial governments, were asked in 1949 'to suspend the issue of licences for imports from the dollar area except in exceptional cases where such suspension would have grave effects'.[58] For the critics of the British Labour Government, it all seemed to underscore the failure of London to appreciate the gravity of Malaya's position and to confirm for them that there was too much interference by HMG and too little leeway given to the 'man on the spot'.

The man on the spot while sympathizing with the problems faced by Malaya's rubber and tin producers, did not necessarily disagree that more revenue could be extracted from the Malayan economy. Gradually the Malayan Government started to explore ways of revising the tax structure. The major obstacle was the need to co-ordinate any tax changes with the Singapore Government so that they would be introduced simultaneously in both jurisdictions. There were, of course, rumblings of opposition to such moves, but the actions of the European planters and miners in particular seemed to belie their protestations. The planting industry, for example, was quick to lower wage rates when rubber prices went down but slow to raise them when prices rose. Even the Labour Department, which invariably took the side of the employers, was provoked, in early 1950, to rebuke the Malayan Planting Industries Employers' Association, saying that they 'were ill-advised to take advantage of their strong position and to force the workers to accept a new agreement only from April 1950' when rubber had been selling at a high price (over $0.50 per pound) since the beginning of the year.[59]

But what caused most consternation in Government circles were what the *Daily Herald* called the 'phenomenal' dividends of the tin producing companies.[60] In December 1949, Malayan Tin Dredging, South Malayan Tin Dredging, Ayer Hitam, and Sungei Besi announced dividends of 50 per cent, 60 per cent, 65 per cent, and 60 per cent respectively. A little later, Petaling Tin declared a dividend of 100 per cent. At the same time the chairman of one company complained that the labour employed on his mines appeared to have an insufficient sense of 'social duty'. This prompted a Colonial Office official to note that the dividends were 'quite unjustified when the Federal Government cannot balance its budget and HMG is having to make large contributions in aid of the territory's expenditure'. The Governor of Singapore pointed out that, '[I]t must be obvious that success against Communism in Malaya and the continuance of such exploitation on behalf of the United Kingdom interests are mutually exclusive.'[61] Corporate tax rates in both Singapore and Malaya were quickly increased.

Faced with the mounting cost of the Emergency the 'gloomy financial position' of 1949 had, by early 1950, turned into 'a very serious financial crisis'.[62] Throughout the first two years of the Emergency, calls for economy became a familiar refrain, and departments not directly concerned with restoring law and order were cut back, often severely. Draft estimates of expenditures were carefully reviewed and pruned; the resulting atmosphere of uncertainty made planning difficult and often caused bitterness and resentment. The Federal Government reduced its already very limited budget for social services by as much as 25 per cent, and although the state governments took up some of the slack, this aspect of the administration was given short shrift.[63] Curiously, a number of reports noted that this diversion of funds perpetuated 'conditions favourable to the growth of communism', but the caveat was always entered that nothing could be done to change the situation until the budget could be balanced.[64] Indeed, so scarce were the Malayan Government's resources that cutbacks were ordered in such crucial areas as Public Works, Drainage and Irrigation, Telecommunications, Railways, and Electricity.[65] Limitations were even placed on the recruiting of police officers in that only single officers could be sent out to Malaya because there was no housing for families.

With financial considerations so pressing in the first two years of the Emergency, there was only one major attempt to extend control over the general population other than by means of the police and the army. In early 1948, the Controller of Immigration prepared a scheme in which a 'filter area' would be created along the Thai border in order to prevent the infiltration of guerrillas. All Chinese in the filter area were to be registered. In July 1948, the Federal Executive Council decided to extend the scheme to the whole of the Federation. This was done by March 1949.[66] Registration proved useful to the police in their screening operations, to the Immigration Department in controlling illegal immigration, and to the large European estates for establishing who exactly were residents on their property. But the registration system was, as the Chief Registration Officer himself reported, 'far from perfect'.[67] In particular, the system of reporting lost identity cards and acquiring new ones was cumbersome and expensive and virtually invited corruption. It certainly aroused a great deal of antagonism among the general population.[68] Moreover, the fear of going through the registration process and being arrested because of past association with communist organizations induced many, who otherwise felt little antipathy towards the Government, to join the MCP.

The failure of the Government to re-establish its administrative presence in the predominantly Chinese area of the jungle fringes had a number of important consequences. First, because of the lack of direct contact with the Chinese population, the Government was cut off from the information and intelligence which only good personal relations can elicit and which was essential for successful police and army operations. Secondly, the Government found it had little influence over a population that derived its information in large part by word of mouth. Rumours abounded. For example, the fact that the British were arming large numbers of Malays–primarily as special constables–was widely interpreted among the rural Chinese population as evidence that the British would soon be leaving and handing over the country to the Malays. Thirdly, the Government's propaganda effort proved to be particularly ineffective. The Public Relations Department did little more than drop leaflets along the jungle fringes—many of which lodged in the tree canopy or quickly rotted once they reached the ground—and send out loud-speaker vans which were described by the Chinese as 'loud but empty voices'.[69]

This inability to reach the mass of the Chinese public proved to be particularly costly as news of the victory of China's Communist Party began to circulate in late 1949. Broadcasts from Peking urging support for the 'Liberation Armies' in their struggle to drive out the British Imperialists fuelled speculation that the Red Army would send troops to aid the MCP guerrillas. In these circumstances, and remembering the 'justice' which had been wrought by the communists when they took over the countryside after the Japanese surrender, who could afford to openly work against the MCP? And on top of all this came the British Government's decision, announced on 6 January 1950, to recognize formally the Chinese People's Government. Informed Chinese opinion felt that the British had suddenly weakened their position in Malaya for the sake of Hong Kong. The move certainly raised questions in their minds about Britain's commitments to Malaya. More generally, Britain's recognition of the new Chinese Government raised fears among many Chinese in Malaya that communist consuls would replace the nationalist ones, and that pressure would be exerted on members of their families remaining in China if they did not co-operate with the MCP.[70] Certainly HMG's decision did nothing to gain Chinese help in returning the country to law and order.

The one form of administration which was maintained in the rural areas was that provided by the European planters, and to a lesser extent, the miners. In many areas their supervision of their employees was the only means by which large sections of the population knew that a British presence still existed in Malaya. About 1,500 members of the European planting community were spread very thinly across the Peninsula. The casualty rate among this group was very high despite their having the protection of special constables and, in some cases, even ex-Palestine, European sergeants. Perhaps naturally these tense conditions encouraged some planters and assistants—or 'creepers' as they were called—to leave Malaya so as to find more peaceful environs in which to work. Nonetheless, enough stayed on to provide an important network of authority throughout the plantation areas. The courage of these men and their wives and families was a great boon to the Malayan Government.

However, because they, like the Chinese community, felt themselves to be on the front line of the battle, the planters became increasingly upset with the Government as the threat from the guerrillas mounted. They became convinced that the Government did not appreciate the gravity of the situation. Some ill-considered pronouncements by Sir Henry Gurney fuelled this perception. In one speech to the Legislative Council, he declared he was 'convinced that given certain conditions which we are doing our best and hope shortly to achieve', peace and order could be effectively restored in a comparatively short time. He also stated that 'in any case we cannot contemplate the present state of affairs dragging on for two years or any similar period. Were it to be allowed to, it would get worse'.[71] It did drag on, and it did get worse. Confidence in the Government was in short supply.

Nor was it restored as the government had hoped, by the 'Anti-Bandit Month'. This was an effort, which was mounted in early 1950, to mobilize on a voluntary basis and over a period of about a month all the civilian resources that could be made available to assist the security forces in an intensified combined operation.[72] Nearly a quarter of a million people put their names forward as volunteers for the occasion. But it proved to be 'a prize fiasco'.[73] The Government was not administratively prepared to cope with the influx of people, few constructive operations had been devised, and little of a permanent nature was achieved. Not long after the Anti-Bandit Month, dissatisfaction with the Government's ability to subdue the MCP guerrillas gave rise to a Legislative Council resolution which stated: 'This Council...views with grave concern the slow rate of progress being made so far to end the terrorist menace in this country.'[74] This virtually amounted to a motion of no confidence and although it was not carried, it had support among all racial communities, especially among Europeans, and reflected the widespread disenchantment with the conduct of the counter-guerrilla campaign.

The Communist Campaign

When the Emergency was declared, the Malayan Communist Party was only partially mobilized. Although by mid-June many members had already gone underground, there were a significant number

who were caught in the open. A few key leaders of front organizations were arrested by the Government while others found temporary hiding places before making contact with those already in
the jungle. The first few weeks and months of the Emergency, then,
were occupied with trying to get organized. Generally, confusion
was the order of the day. The experience of the nucleus of ex-MPAJA
guerrillas proved to be valuable, but even they found it difficult to
overcome the fact that too few of those new to the jungle knew how
to use their weapons, how to conduct guerrilla warfare, or even
how to dress for the occasion—many went 'inside' wearing clogs
rather than boots. Everyone faced the problems of getting used to
a communal, disciplined existence as well as organizing themselves
to acquire food and other supplies. To complicate matters further,
good leaders and administrators were scarce and poor communications were a critical obstacle to any major co-ordinated campaign.

This is not to say that the guerrillas were incapable of decisive
action. Where the leaders were competent and energetic, and where
a large group of ex-MPAJA guerrillas could be mustered, the guerrillas were able to launch some major attacks. Relatively large-scale
operations included attacks on the coal mine and town of Batu
Arang in Selangor and the 'capture' of the town of Gua Musang
on the border of Pahang and Kelantan in July 1948. Considering
that the initial guerrilla strength was generally estimated to be
over 4,000, it was perhaps remarkable that there were not more
major incidents.

Gradually, the guerrillas appreciated the need to become properly organized and trained. In early 1949, the main fighting force,
initially called the Malayan People's Anti-British Army, later named
the Malayan Races Liberation Army (MRLA), retreated deeper
into the jungle. There they went through a more intensive period
of political and military training. At the same time, the MCP started
to build up the Min Yuen or 'Masses' Organization'. Although there
were variations in the way in which the Min Yuen were organized
in the different states, their functions were usually the same. They
were to provide the MRLA units in the field with food, funds, information, and recruits. More generally they were responsible for
communications throughout the Peninsula as well as for propaganda. The purpose of their work among the rural population,
primarily the Chinese 'squatters', was to organize opposition to
the Government in the form of Self-Preservation Corps, Cultivation Corps, or some other similar groups. The Min Yuen were
often issued with arms if they wished, and could direct the special

units formed to eliminate traitors or even establish their own units for this purpose.[75] In many ways, it was the Min Yuen which became the key to the MCP's campaign against the Government.

Organizationally, the Party, the MRLA, and the Min Yuen were separate entities, with each having a hierarchical organization.[76] The Party filled the important positions in the other two organizations and in this way maintained their control over the overall conduct of the campaign. The MRLA units were based in jungle camps while the Min Yuen occupied the jungle fringes, moving among the people in order to undertake their work. By mid-1949 this new structure started to pay dividends, and the campaign against the Government was intensified.

At the heart of this successful reorganization was the MCP's ability to attract and absorb recruits, and generally to gain the support of a significant portion of the population. People joined the MCP campaign against the Government for many reasons. There were clearly some who genuinely believed that communism could release the mass of the population from oppression and the many economic, social, and political ills which beset Malayan society. For a few, no doubt, their positive view of communism was reinforced by news from relatives in China where the communists were painted in a very favourable light, especially in contrast to the Kuomintang Government. Some joined the MCP cause for the excitement and adventure or to escape personal difficulties—in other words, for the same reasons that young people join any army. Others saw the MCP as an organization through which their frustrated ambitions for power or for a better life could be realized. And still others joined out of a sense of loyalty to the MPAJA leaders they had known during the Occupation.[77]

Perhaps the most important reason why many joined the ranks of the MCP was because they saw themselves as 'refugees' from the Government. The Malayan Government's policy of arresting everyone suspected of being a member of a communist front organization forced a large number of people, who were only marginally associated with the MCP, to choose between arrest, with the distinct possibility of deportation, and going 'inside' with the guerrillas. In these circumstances, it was not surprising that many people, who would rather have stayed out of the fray altogether, joined the MCP.[78] Once part of the guerrilla organization, of course, they not only came under strict discipline but were faced with the brutality of the security forces and with the harshness of the Emergency Regulations. They were inclined to believe their leaders when they were told that they would meet certain death at the hands of the security forces or the police if they were to desert.

Moreover, the communists were able to garner support among the rural Chinese population, and in some isolated cases among Malays and Indians, not just because of the heavy-handed policy of the Government. There was a large measure of goodwill towards the MCP because of its role in the Japanese Occupation and because of its propaganda efforts in the post-War period. Indeed, many of the economic grievances which had turned Malayans against the Government lingered on. For instance, although the cost of living had declined, the price of food remained relatively high and continued to make living conditions difficult. The fluctuating and generally low prices for rubber and tin, to which the wages of plantation workers and tin miners were tied, and on which the whole economy depended, continued to create uncertainties and to cause frustrations. The MCP propaganda teams were skilful in highlighting these and other issues, such as corruption, land tenure, and high rents. Furthermore, there was a long and honourable tradition in Chinese culture of groups going into the countryside to fight injustice and corruption. Hence, for example, Chinese in Malaya whose families originated from Kwangtung province, which had a history of dissident groups battling a discredited authority, found the actions of the MCP understandable and not particularly extraordinary or wrong.[79]

The MCP was also able to benefit from the social structures and values which pervaded Chinese society. For example, for the Chinese who had relatives or friends who had 'gone inside', there was no question where their allegiance lay. Because the family occupies such a central place in Chinese life, a son, daughter, brother, or nephew who joined the guerrillas would invariably be supported. And for the vast majority of Malayan Chinese who had left most of their families behind when they emigrated to Malaya, friendship networks were as important as kinship relations. In a world which was seen as essentially hostile, the personal friendships with which an individual surrounded himself acted as a bulwark against the threats to his safety and well-being.[80] The breaking of a friendship relationship was, therefore, seen as a 'serious fault' and there was a great deal of social pressure to support a friend no matter what the circumstances. Consequently, Chinese would come to the aid of someone, even though he was a guerrilla or communist sympathizer and labelled a 'criminal' by the Government, simply because he was a friend.[81] It was because of the strength of these friendship ties that the many associations and societies that the MCP had assiduously formed during the post-War period began to pay off for them in the initial stages of the Emergency. As well as kinship and friendship ties, loyalties associated with districts, provinces, and common family name could also be called upon. As Duncanson has noted, at least in the early years of the Emergency, the MCP had little difficulty in 'seizing upon the natural organization of village society and exploiting it for its own end'.[82]

As the Emergency progressed, the MCP had few problems finding recruits to man the rapidly expanding Min Yuen, as well as maintaining and even expanding the number of MRLA units.[83] Full advantage was taken of the propaganda value of the Government's coercion and enforcement policy. News of such incidents as the burning of Kachau were made the subject of special circulars and word of mouth propaganda campaigns. In many rural areas, MCP propaganda was generally believed, and what limited Government propaganda reached inhabitants was often considered only a rumour and discounted. The Min Yuen became particularly adept at recruiting young people whose families had been affected by the security forces' habit of clearing 'squatter' areas, detaining and deporting large numbers of villagers, and burning huts. The one major difficulty that inhibited more recruits from being absorbed into the various Party organizations was a severe lack of good leaders.[84] The relatively few competent people that were available were hard-pressed, occupying three or four leadership positions at one time. The MCP did institute a training programme for political and administrative cadre but it did not necessarily produce people with leadership qualities. Indeed, this weakness, caused by a combination of Lai Tek's treachery, the colonial administration's deportation policy, and Japanese thoroughness in pruning the MCP leadership during the Occupation, was to haunt the MCP throughout the Emergency.

Perhaps because of the inexperience of the MCP leadership, the Party's strategy was slow to emerge. After the flurry of activity in the first weeks of the Emergency, during which the guerrillas were able to mount a few large-scale operations, the overall plan of operations for the next year seems to have been to build up support in particular rural areas and to try to disrupt the economy of the country. Although there were a number of violent attacks by guerrillas, there is some evidence, as one Government analysis put it, that 'the MCP prefers to woo rather than to murder'.[85] The Min Yuen, for instance, concentrated on trying to persuade labour to move away from European-owned estates and into rural areas where there was a strong MRLA presence. Such areas where the Government's presence was transitory and weak at best, and often non-existent, could then be considered akin to 'liberated zones'. Additionally, attacks that were made on European estates in order to encourage such an exodus also served to disrupt the economy. There were also attacks on Kuomintang members and others who were considered to have sided with the Government, but generally the pressure exerted on the population was inconsistent.

In June 1949, however, the Central Committee decided to step up its military actions. Whether this was because they felt that they had brought their support among the rural population up to a satisfactory level, because they were influenced by events in China, or because they wanted more tangible evidence of progress towards the elimination of the Government is not clear. The consequences of the decision were, however, a militarization of the Min Yuen and a more aggressive role for the MRLA. During the first half of 1949, the number of security forces and civilians killed by the guerrillas dropped markedly. However, during the last half of 1949, the numbers rose again, and in the first six months of 1950 more deaths were produced by guerrilla action than in the initial hectic months of the Emergency.[86] The resulting pressure on the general population did nothing to ease their anxieties about their increasingly precarious predicament.

Summary

Almost as a reflex action to what was seen as the work of a few agitators, the Government sought to restore law and order by adopting a policy of coercion and enforcement. But the Government clearly underestimated the extent of the threat they faced. Malcolm MacDonald's hope 'that the worst of the Emergency may be definitely behind us by the end of September',[87] was indicative of the extent to which senior officials were operating in the dark. This was largely because of the Government's total lack of contact with, and therefore information about, the rural Chinese population on whom the MCP depended for their support. The Government's use of force in these circumstances proved to be at best inappropriate and at worst self-defeating.

As far as the Chinese community was concerned, the coercion and enforcement policy adopted by the Malayan Government was disastrous. They felt harried on all sides. The natural tendency was to adopt the traditional Chinese notion of 'law-abidingness'– namely to keep out of trouble and not interfere in matters which were not their immediate concern. However, as a Department of Chinese Affairs report noted, this attitude brought the Chinese community into direct conflict with the Emergency Regulations which insisted that those who withheld information from the police were themselves infringing upon the law.[88] Yet without a guarantee that they would be protected by the security forces, the risks of openly siding with an unpopular government were all too apparent to most of the rural Chinese population. In a world in which the security of his family was constantly threatened, both by the guer- rillas and by the security forces, and his livelihood–often marginal at best–subject to the machinations of economic and social forces beyond his control, all the average Chinese 'squatter' wanted to do was to minimize his losses. Taking unnecessary risks, such as de- nouncing the communists as the Government wanted him to do, was for him a completely irrational act. There was also a very good chance that, if pressed, his sympathy was probably with the MCP.

The guerrillas did not overrun the country; the Government was maintained. Although the confusion within the ranks of the MCP and the inexperience of its leadership clearly had something to do with this, from the Government's point of view the credit had to be given to the army and the police, as well as to those planters and miners who continued to supervise their employees.

Yet in keeping the guerrillas off balance by their sweeps, their large-scale operations, and their sometimes brutal treatment of the population, the army and the police were alienating more and more of the Chinese population and creating stronger and stronger bonds between the communist guerrillas and their supporters. Moreover, there was no compensating administrative structure which could mitigate the damage done by the security forces, deliver the much- needed social services, or establish some measure of supervision of the general population. Indeed, there were very few Government officials who could speak Chinese and to whom the Chinese could go in order for their grievances to be heard. The result was that the MCP's base of support grew and, after the reorganization of early 1949, the Party was able to intensify its guerrilla campaign. What confidence the Malayan Chinese population had in the Malayan Government was rapidly diminishing.

But it was not just the Chinese community who were losing con- fidence in the Government. Malay leaders felt that the problems of their community were being ignored while the Government concentrated its efforts on dealing with the Chinese. Moreover, the predominantly Malay state governments were still suspicious of the Federal Administration and were often critical of its actions. And as the guerrilla threat waxed and waned the pronouncements of the senior officials of the Federal Government seemed ill-considered and their policy ineffectual. This also seemed to be the view of the European population, although opinion was divided as to why. Most seemed to think that the Government's policy was not being pursued with enough vigour. Others, for example one MCS officer in the field, felt that 'The Government is being pressed into strong repressive measures which will do little but manure the ground for the next phase of the communist attack.'[89] There was, however, a general concensus that the Government was not doing very well. Many agreed with a writer in the *Straits Echo* who argued that 'The handling of the Emergency since its declaration [has not] shown efficiency or vision. It requires a very generous assessment to make the campaign against banditry appear as even a qualified success.'[90] Indeed, all reports showed that for the Government the situation was steadily deteriorating.[91]

1. Tan Cheng Lock to Rt. Hon. Lord Listowel, Minister of State for Colonial Affairs, 24 July 1948, Tan Cheng Lock Papers, Item 133 (ANM).

2. See the discussion of this legalistic approach in Lucian Pye, *Lessons from the Malayan Struggle Against Communism* (Cambridge, Mass: Centre for International Studies, Massachusetts Institute of Technology, 17 February 1957), pp. 11-16.

3. *Proceedings of the Federal Legislative Council*, 1st Session, pp. B246-7.

4. See the discussion in Anthony Short, *The Communist Insurrection in Malaya 1948-1960* (London: Frederick Muller, 1975), pp. 77-90; the MSS's Political Intelligence Journal for the immediate pre-Emergency period may be found in CO 537/3752.

5. This is how one Colonial Office official saw the activities of the MSS after receiving the Political Intelligence Journal for mid-July 1948. See O. H. Morris, CO 537/3752.

6. J. B. Williams, CO 537/3755.

7. G. F. Seel to Malcolm MacDonald, 23 June 1948, CO 537/3752.

8. T. I. K. Lloyd to Sir Franklin Gimson and Sir Alec Newboult, 23 August 1948, CO 537/3758.

9. Lucian Pye, *Guerrilla Communism in Malaya: Its Social and Political Meaning* (Princeton, NJ: Princeton University Press, 1956), p. 88, fn. 5, notes that the Chinese community was sceptical about the use of the term 'bandit' because it was associated in their minds with the unsuccessful attempts by the Japanese and the Kuomintang to defeat Chinese communism.

10. J. B. Perry Robinson, *Transformation in Malaya* (London: Secker and Warburg, 1956), p. 78.

11. The Emergency was originally declared under the BMA (Essential Regulation)

Proclamation. This was replaced by legislation which passed through all stages in the Legislative Council on 5 July 1948. *Federation of Malaya Annual Report*, 1948.

12. See CO 537/6083 for a discussion of MacDonald's duties.

13. Harry Miller, *Menace in Malaya* (London: Harrap, 1954), p. 92.

14. See Griffiths in reply to a written question in the House of Commons. Great Britain, Parliament, *Parliamentary Debates* (Commons), 5th Series, 472 (1950), c. 116.

15. See Harry Miller, *Jungle War in Malaya: The Campaign against Communism, 1948-60* (London: Arthur Barker, 1972), p. 40, and Noel Barber, *The War of the Running Dogs: The Malayan Emergency, 1948-1960* (London: Fontana, 1972), pp. 57-8.

16. See Zakaria Haji Ahmad, 'Police Forces and Their Political Roles in Southeast Asia: A Preliminary Assessment and Overview', MIT/National University of Malaysia, mimeograph, n.d., p. 18.

17. See Sir Kerr Bovell papers, mss. Brit Emp S 397 (Rhodes House Library).

18. See, for example, Despatch No. 4 Gurney to Creech Jones, 11 April 1949, CO 537/4751, and Gurney to Creech Jones, 28 February 1949, CO 537/4750.

19. See anonymous MCP subscription collector to Tan Cheng Lock in Dato Sir Cheng Lock Tan, 'A Collection of Correspondence' (University of Malaya Library), and Tan Cheng Siong to Tan Cheng Lock, 18 May 1950, CO 537/6090.

20. Federation of Malaya, *Report of the Police Mission to Malaya*, 1950, p. 22.

21. 'Meeting of 10 ex-MPAJA communists with Hugh T. Pagden to discuss propaganda', 1 March 1949, Hugh T. Pagden Papers SP 7/9 (ANM).

22. Miller, *Menace in Malaya*, p. 89.

23. Short, *The Communist Insurrection*, pp. 162-6; James D. Clarkson, *The Cultural Ecology of a Chinese Village: Cameron Highlands, Malaysia* (Chicago: Department of Geography, University of Chicago, 1968), pp. 107-8, and John Weldon Humphrey, 'Population Resettlement in Malaya' (Ph.D. dissertation, Northwestern University, 1971), pp. 67-8. The Malayan Government's justification for the Kachau action is given in Savingram 11, CO 537/4750.

24. See CO 537/4750. For reviews of the incident, see Short, *The Communist Insurrection*, pp. 167-9; *The People*, 1 February 1970; *Straits Times*, 3 February 1970, and *Morning Star*, 3 February 1970.

25. Short, *The Communist Insurrection*, p. 161.

26. 'Law and order in the Federation', Annexure 'A' to Minute of BDCC(FE), 16th Mtg., 28 January 1949, CO 537/4773.

27. See Federation of Malaya, 'Speech to the Legislative Council, 29 September 1949', in *Communist Banditry in Malaya: Extracts from the Speeches of Sir Henry Gurney, October 1948 to December 1949* (Kuala Lumpur: Government Press, n.d.), and Gurney to Lloyd, 8 October 1948, CO 537/3758.

28. See Minutes of the Malaya Committee Meeting held at the House of Commons, 19 June 1950 (MAL.C.[50] 6th Meeting), CO 717/199. This file contains much discussion of the issues associated with detention.

29. Thomas Perry Thornton, 'Terror as a Weapon of Political Agitation', in H. Eckstein, ed., *Internal War: Problems and Approaches* (New York: The Free Press, 1964).

30. 19 December 1948, CO 537/3758.

31. Annexure 'A' to Minute of BDCC (FE), 16th Mtg., 28 January 1949, CO 537/4773.

32. Ibid.

33. Pagden to Morris, 27 October 1948, CO 537/3757.

34. Ibid., and 'Notes of a meeting', Hugh T. Pagden Papers SP 7/9 (ANM). One person made the point that 'Government is this sort of people and this sort of people are Government.' See anonymous MCP subscription collector to Tan Cheng Lock in Dato Sir Cheng Lock Tan, 'A Collection of Correspondence' (University of Malaya Library).

35. T. P. F. McNeil, G. C. S. Adkins, and W. G. Webb, 'Memorandum', 24 November 1948, CO 537/3578.

36. Gurney to J. J. Paskin, 10 December 1948, CO 537/3758.

37. 'Note of a meeting between representatives of the Perak Chinese Miners Association and the British Adviser, Perak, in the Office of the British Adviser on 6 December', 1948, CO 537/3758.

38. Interview with the author, May 1973. There were also rumours among the Chinese that Europeans were paying protection money.

39. See Department of Labour, *Monthly Report*, 1946–7.

40. Pye, *Guerilla Communism*, p. 201.

41. Department of Chinese Affairs, *Annual Report*, 1948, CO 717/157.

42. See 'Memorandum' by the Chief Secretary, 28 October 1949, P/PM1 Federal Secretariat 425/49 (ANM). By comparison, in 1939, out of 220 MCS officers thirty-four had passed the Chinese language exam and seven were learning Chinese.

43. Gurney to Creech, despatch No. 3, 12 January 1950, CO 537/5974, and 'Memorandum referring to communism in Chinese Schools, Brief for the visit to the UK of the Director of Operations and the Secretary for Defence', CO 537/6013.

44. Papers on Sir Henry Gurney's appointment may be found in CO 537/3687.

45. *Straits Times*, 27 October 1948. This issue contains a report of Onn's resolution which he withdrew after receiving assurances that the High Commissioner was cognizant of the problems.

46. Ibid.

47. Minutes of the Advisory Committee on Education in the Colonies. Abstract of a Statement by R. Holgate, Director of Education, Federation of Malaya, on 'Education in Malaya', 16 June 1951, CO 717/190.

48. See Minutes of the 7th Meeting of the Conference of Rulers, 1 September 1949, CO 537/4792.

49. See 'Notes in a Meeting with Mr Rees-Williams', 7 December 1949, CO 537/4870.

50. Gurney to Lloyd, 8 October 1948, and Gurney to Paskin, 10 December 1948, CO 537/3758.

51. 'Notes of a conversation with Mr Rees-Williams on the 18th November and subsequent days', 21 November 1949, CO 537/4870.

52. *Proceedings of the Federal Legislative Council*, 1st Session, p. B528.

53. 'Statement of the Financial Position of the Federation of Malaya since April 1, 1946,' P/PM1, Chief Secretary 530/48 (ANM).

54. H. T. Bourdillon to Gorell Barnes, 18 August 1948, CO 717/153.

55. A. H. Poynton to Gurney, 22 February 1950, CO 717/203. It was also pointed out that the extra cost of UK forces in Malaya for which London had assumed responsibility was in excess of £3 million (over $25 million).

56. 'Notes of a Meeting at King's House, Kuala Lumpur, at 9.00 on June 3, 1950', CO 717/155. Without the loan and the contribution from London, Malaya's Surplus Balance would have fallen to around $25 million or well under one-tenth of annual revenue.

57. See Onn's speech, *Proceedings of the Federal Legislative Council*, 2nd Session, p. 28, and *Times of Malaya*, 3 September 1948.

58. See Circular No 53, Secretary of State to all Colonies, 4 July 1949. The frustrations of the local businessmen are cogently argued in Telegrams 565 and 566, Sir F. Gimson to Secretary of State for the Colonies, July 1949. These restrictions continued on into 1950. See CO 537/4485. Malaya's balance of payments with the rest of the world is detailed in CO 537/4479.

59. Department of Labour, *Monthly Report*, March 1950.

60. *Daily Herald*, 22 March 1950.

61. See A. H. Poynton to Gurney, 22 February 1950, and Despatch No. 3, Gimson to the Secretary of State for the Colonies, 12 January 1950, CO 717/201.

62. *Draft Development Plan of the Federation of Malaya* (Kuala Lumpur: Government Printer, 1950), p. 3, and 'Notes of a Meeting at King's House, Kuala Lumpur, at 9.00 on June 3, 1950', 717/155.

63. 'Financial position of the Federation of Malaya since 1 April 1946', P/PM1, Chief Secretary 530/48 (ANM); Gurney noted in the Legislature that the medical facilities in 1948, even in the towns, were below the standards of 1938. See *Proceedings of the Federal Legislative Council*, 1st Session, p. B535.

64. 'Memorandum by the Colonial Office on the Security Situation in the Federation of Malaya', April 1949, CO 537/4751, and 'The Economy in the Federation of Malaya', 11 April 1949, P/PM1, Chief Secretary 530/48 (ANM).

65. Department of Public Works, *Annual Report*, 1948, pp. 3 and 7, and O.A.G. to the Secretary of State for the Colonies, 22 August 1948, CO 717/153.

66. E. C. G. Barrett, *Report of the Registration of Residents for the year 1949* (Kuala Lumpur: Government Printer, 1949).

67. Ibid.

68. Speech by F. G. H. Parry, *Proceedings of the Perak Council of State*, 1 August 1950, Leong Yew Koh Papers SP 3/3/5 (ANM).

69. Meeting on 1 March 1949, Hugh T. Pagden Papers SP 7/1 (ANM).

70. See the Commissioner-General's Office, 'Political Summary for January and May 1950', CO 537/6087. For Gurney's repeated expressions of concern and the replies of the Foreign Office, see CO 537/6021.

71. *Proceedings of the Federal Legislative Council*, 1st Session, p. B771. This speech was widely reprinted in the English-language press. See, for example, the *Sunday Gazette*, 13 February 1949.

72. *Straits Times*, 15 April 1952.

73. Ibid. See Short, *The Communist Insurrection*, pp. 216-18, for a more generous viewpoint.

74. *Proceedings of the Federal Legislative Council*, 3rd Session, p. 133.

75. See the comments of W. N. Gray, 16 February 1950, CO 537/5974; 'MCP Administrative Areas of Selangor', 26 May 1949, and 'What Are We Fighting?', 19 February 1950; Hugh T. Pagden Papers SP 7/6 (ANM), and 'Abstract of Intelligence', 1-15 July 1951, CO 537/7300.

76. Pye, *Guerrilla Communism*, p. 92.

77. See 'Surrendered Enemy Personnel', memorandum to OC CID Selangor, 18 December 1949, Hugh T. Pagden Papers SP 7/2 (ANM), and W. D. Horne, 'The Bandit Movement: The Outlook and Ability of Personnel', mss. Ind Ocn S 128 (Rhodes House Library).

78. See Judith Strauch, *Chinese Village Politics in the Malaysian State* (Cambridge, Mass: Harvard University Press, 1981), p. 66; Tan Cheng Siang to Tan

Cheng Lock, 18 May 1950, CO 537/6090; anonymous letter to Tan Cheng Lock, translated 23 May 1950, in Dato Sir Cheng Lock Tan, 'A Collection of Correspondence', n.d. (University of Malaya Library), and 'Surrendered Enemy Personnel', Hugh T. Pagden Papers SP 7/2 (ANM).

79. Dennis J. Duncanson, 'Impressions of Life in Malaya Today', *Journal of the Royal Central Asian Society* 38 (1951), p. 68.

80. James C. Scott, *Political Ideology in Malaysia, Reality and the Beliefs of an Elite* (New Haven: Yale University Press, 1968), pp. 100-1, and Pye, *Guerrilla Communism*, pp. 168 and 198.

81. William H. Newell, *Treacherous River: A Study of Rural Chinese in North Malaya* (Kuala Lumpur: University of Malaya Press, 1962), p. 171. One is reminded of E. M. Forster's assertion in *Two Cheers for Democracy* (1951): 'If I had to choose between betraying my country and betraying my friend, I hope I would have the guts to betray my country.' For the Malayan Chinese, the choice was somewhat easier because they had a very limited notion of Malaya as a country.

82. Duncanson, 'Impressions', p. 68.

83. Recruits first joined the Min Yuen as unarmed assistants, then, if they proved satisfactory they would be considered for transfer to an MRLA unit. See 'Malayan Intelligence Summary', CO 537/7291.

84. Among the many who mention the problem of leadership, see W. D. Horne, 'The Bandit Movement', December 1949, mss. Ind Ocn S 128 (Rhodes House Library).

85. See 'Present Attitude of the Chinese Population', Appendix to 'Memorandum by the Colonial Office on the Security Situation in the Federation of Malaya', April 1949, CO 537/4751, and 'Meeting on March 1, 1949', Hugh T. Pagden Papers SP 7/9 (ANM).

86. Police Force, *Annual Report*, 1955, p. 4 (ANM).

87. MacDonald to Secretary of State, 1 September 1948, CO 537/3687.

88. Department of Chinese Affairs, *Annual Report*, 1948, CO 717/157.

89. G. C. Dodewell, 'Diary as Malayan Civil Service Officer, 1948-52', mss. Ind Ocn S 224 (Rhodes House Library).

90. C. W. H., Taiping, 'Dare We Take Stock', *Straits Echo*, 10 November 1949.

91. See, for example, the Department of Labour, *Monthly Report*, March 1950.

4
Resettlement, Fear, and Prosperity

BY early 1950, it was becoming evident that the Government was losing ground to the MCP. As one official analysis put it, communism was 'getting a more and more serious hold' and incidents were increasing to dangerous proportions, 'affecting the morale of the country and threatening its economy'.[1] In February 1950, after reviewing their weakening position, the High Commissioner and senior members of the military in Malaya made a series of recommendations of which the most important was that a Director of Operations should be appointed to co-ordinate the activities of the police and the military. This recommendation was supported by the Chiefs of Staff and by the Colonial Office, and it was agreed that the new position should be held by an army officer who reported to the High Commissioner.[2] As the Secretary of State for the Colonies noted in a letter to the Prime Minister, this put the Director of Operations in a very delicate position and it was important that they selected someone with the right personality.[3]

The man chosen for the job was Lieutenant-General Sir Harold Briggs. He had served as a divisional commander in the 14th Army and as GOC Burma after the Japanese surrender, and he was generally considered 'a man of immense charm, the best kind of soldier and gentleman'.[4] Once Briggs was persuaded to take on the post, he was whisked off to London for discussions and then flown out to Singapore, arriving towards the end of March. Again he was thoroughly briefed before travelling up to Kuala Lumpur in the first week of April. During the next month, Briggs toured Malaya, soliciting advice from the different communities, business groups, and government departments, as well as from senior members of the armed forces and the police. Towards the end of May, Briggs set out his recommendations for action in a report to the British Defence Co-ordination Committee (BDCC). The value of the report lay in its distillation into a coherent and comprehensive plan of a number of proposed strategies, parts of which had been tried out at the local level.[5]

The Briggs Plan, as it was popularly known, was initially a rather general document. The overall strategy was to clear the country from south to north by 'dominating' and building up a feeling of complete security in the populated areas, breaking up the Min Yuen within the populated areas so as to isolate the bandits from their sources of food and information, and, finally, destroying the bandits by forcing them to attack the army and the police on the security forces' own ground. The police, army, and civil administration were each assigned their own general roles in the strategy. Most attention was given to the need to expand the civil administration in order to secure administratively those areas that had been cleared of guerrillas by the army and police. An ambitious timetable was posited in which troops, police, and the civil administration would begin operations on 1 June with the hope that Johore, the southern-most state, would be cleared of guerrillas by 1 November 1950. South Pahang and Selangor were scheduled to be cleared by 1 April 1951. No forecast was made for the remaining states. The whole operation was to be financed by state governments curtailing normal expenditure and passing on savings for use in operations directly related to the overall plan. In addition, a lump sum was to be allocated by the Federal Government to those states most directly affected.

It was not until the strategy began to be implemented and the flesh was put on the strategic bones that the key aspects of the Briggs Plan became apparent. First, Briggs consolidated a coordinating structure which gave the civil administration, the police, and the army the chance to meet regularly and to cooperate. This structure had the additional benefit of bypassing the often unresponsive state administrations and gave the Federal Government more flexibility in putting its policies into effect.[6] Briggs proposed to run the Government's campaign through a chain of committees. At the top was the Federal War Council which was composed of the Director of Operations, the General Officer Commanding, the Air Officer Commanding, the Commissioner of Police, the Chief Secretary, and the Secretary for Defence. At the next level, each state and Straits Settlement–Penang and Malacca–had a War Executive Committee on which sat the Mentri Besar, the British Adviser, the Senior Army Commander, the Chief Police Officer, and usually a full-time secretary. District War Executive Committees were made up of the District Officer and senior police and army representatives. This structure allowed general policy made at the highest level to be handed down through the War Executive Committee chain and adapted to local circumstances, and also for day-to-day operations to be co-ordinated in the field. Moreover, if disputes arose at the district level, they could be sent up the chain for consideration and a binding decision.

The second key aspect of the Briggs Plan emerged as the means by which the civil administration could reassert its authority were explored. It became apparent that this could only be done if a concentrated effort was made to move the entire rural Chinese population into fortified and defended compounds. This entailed a massive resettlement programme. But such a programme was a dangerous undertaking and by no means guaranteed success. It could just as easily increase support for the communist guerrillas as aid the Government's cause.

Resettlement

The primary target of the resettlement programme was the rural Chinese population. This group was generally referred to as 'squatters' because they were often illegal occupants of land.[7] Squatters had occupied the jungle fringes from the time of the first Chinese immigrants. Their numbers swelled with each recession in the economy and unemployment forced labourers to eke out a subsistence existence as best they could. Conversely, their numbers decreased once the economy revived and employment became plentiful. By the late 1940s, however, a unique combination of factors had resulted in an unprecedented number of squatters. Added to the exodus from the towns to the jungle fringes caused by the severe recession of the 1930s, was the dislocation of the Occupation during which many Chinese fled to remote areas in order to escape persecution by the Japanese. The uncertainties of the post-War years, added to the high prices they could get for their produce, persuaded most squatter families to stay where they were. In many families the men would go off in search of labouring work, returning to their holdings when employment was scarce. It was upon this pool of rural, self-sufficient Chinese, who had in the past received scant attention from the Government and who had developed a close relationship with the communists during the Occupation, that the guerrillas relied for much of their active support.

From his first assessment of the Emergency, Gurney had argued that something needed to be done so as to stop the Chinese squatters from co-operating with the guerrillas. Indeed, by early 1950, Gurney was telling the Federal Legislative Council that the squatters presented the country's 'most pressing problem.... There can be no question that upon its solution depends the end of the Emergency.'[8] Yet, despite reports from Gurney to the Colonial Office that the states appreciated the need for urgency and that resettlement schemes were 'going ahead in all states where they [were] necessary' and were 'meeting with a good and encouraging response', very little was being achieved. By the time of Briggs's arrival, only 18,500 squatters had been brought 'under control', and in a number of cases, resettlement had proved to be disastrous.[9]

Neither the Federal Administration nor the state governments were willing to take full responsibility for implementing a comprehensive resettlement programme. In September 1948, the Mentri Besar of each state had been asked to sit on a squatter committee with federal officers and report on the squatters and the prospects for resettlement. The report, which was produced in January 1949, was approved by the Federal Legislative Council and adopted by the Executive Council. However, Gurney felt that the implementation of the Squatter Committee's recommendations was largely a matter for the state and Straits Settlement governments. The latter were thus requested to prepare proposals based on an analysis of the squatters and to survey possible sites.[10] But lack of conviction about the feasibility of the resettlement policy, combined with the problem of raising adequate funds, dissuaded the states and Straits Settlement governments from proceeding beyond the planning stages. They seemed to concur with the assessment made in the *Report of the Committee to Investigate the Squatter Problem, 1949*, that resettlement 'could only be accomplished at considerable expense to the Government–an expense that the country could ill afford if it were multiplied by a large number of such operations on an extensive scale'.[11] Furthermore, it was argued that unless the policy was pursued on an extensive scale, the guerrillas would simply move to areas which had not been resettled and the problem would recur. So why start at all? Moreover, the Malay-dominated state governments, still very much on guard after their struggle over the constitutional division of power, were generally reluctant to hand over land, much of which was reserved for Malays, to Chinese squatters who were still considered foreigners. In the end, little was achieved.

Once Briggs arrived, he was able to inject a sense of direction and urgency into the resettlement programme. On 1 June 1950, the Federal Government took over responsibility for resettlement and the machinery for implementing the programme was put in place. In fact, the pace at which people were resettled was much greater than had originally been anticipated. For example, the plan for Johore estimated that with the experience that had been gained in synchronizing movements and land development, 500–1,000 families could be resettled each month. As it turned out, an average of just under 8,000 people per month were resettled in Johore between 1 June 1950 and 30 April 1951. Even Gurney was impressed: 'I recently spent two days in North Johore where the machine now works so quickly that a piece of virgin jungle becomes a settlement of 200 houses complete with roads, water and police posts and fencing in ten days.'[12] This pace was maintained as attention was switched to the other key states. During May 1951, for example, when the programme was in top gear, over 9,500 people were moved in Selangor, and over 23,000 in Perak. Moreover, it was originally estimated that fewer than 300,000 squatters were to be relocated. However, by December 1951, 385,000 people had been resettled; this figure was to reach over 570,000 squatters and landowners by the end of 1954.[13]

The prospect of resettlement was viewed with mixed feelings by the rural Chinese population. While there was widespread apprehension and many had to be forcibly moved, quite a few went willingly. They hoped that resettlement would enable them to escape being harassed by the army and the police as well as by the guerrillas, and allow them to obtain permanent title to some land. Added to this was the knowledge that those who moved first could get the best lots in the resettlement areas and might receive extra financial help from the Malayan Chinese Association. In the best resettlement centres, people could take advantage of the supply of clean drinking water, the mobile medical units, and the school for the children. Plots of land were made available to those who had farmed and the new roads made it much easier to market their fruits, vegetables, pork, and chicken. In some centres recreational facilities with a coffee shop were set up, and in one case the inhabitants, acting as shareholders, built a cinema.[14]

But such 'model' resettlement centres were very much the exception and most of the people who became caught in the resettlement machine found that their apprehensions were well founded. The actual process of moving was unpleasant and distressing. Invariably, immovable property–including buildings and crops and sometimes livestock–was destroyed so that they would not be of use to the guerrillas. The task of building a new home within a centre was not only hard work but very costly. Al-though each family received up to $100 as an allowance to assist in building their new home as well as a small subsistence allowance for about six months, these sums by no means compensated for the cost of materials needed or the loss of wages or income from their produce that resulted. Furthermore, the simultaneous resettle-ment of thousands of people naturally created a great demand for all types of building materials: with the Government failing to control supplies, the increased demand forced up prices. For a poor rural family, just reconstructing a liveable home entailed the outlay of a considerable sum of money.[15]

The speed with which resettlement took place meant that the process of creating the resettlement areas was 'a hurried one' that did not afford 'the opportunity for careful sociological and econ-omic surveys and planning which would normally precede so abrupt a disturbance of a long established pattern of rural life'.[16] When detailed plans were drawn up, they were usually ignored because of a lack of time, trained staff to interpret them, and the urgency of the situation. Putting the squatter inside a fence, and quickly, was all that seemed to matter. Sanitation and water needs were not always immediately satisfied. In some centres it proved impossible to provide for safe water supplies and the proper dis-posal of sewage. Medical officials were very concerned about the increased incidence of malaria, enteric fever, and dysentery, especially given the acute shortage of doctors and nurses.[17] Nor, indeed, were the squatters used to living in large communities, and social habits had to be adapted and restrictions accepted.

But probably the most important problem facing all who were resettled was that the move undermined their livelihood. Most critical was usually the loss of land. While squatters could be classi-fied as farmers or mine labourers or estate labourers and so on, almost every family, and most individuals, had more than one source of income and nearly all cultivated a piece of land. For instance, a squatter might tap rubber until midday and then look after his pigs or chickens and tend his vegetable plot in the after-noon. However, when they were resettled, many of these people were simply classified as wage labourers and not always assigned land that was equivalent in size to their previous plots. Even those who were officially designated as farmers often fared badly: com-pensation for the crops or livestock that were destroyed was paid later rather than on the spot, and the subsistence allowance was only $12 per person per month for five to seven months.[18] During this period the farmers were expected to coax their newly acquired land into production.

This task, however, invariably proved frustrating because the resettlement sites were chosen for reasons other than that they should be adjacent to plenty of defensible, fertile, agricultural land. For the Government, the primary concern was security. This meant that centres had to be located as far as possible from the jungle fringes so as to impede contact between the guerrillas and those being settled—preferably on sites such as hilltops or flat land where the guerrillas could not take advantage of an overlooking hillside, and near a main road so as to allow Government forces and administrators easy access. As a result, such factors as the fertility of the soil, the possibility of flooding, the ease of irrigation, and access to markets were not always fully explored. Shortly after resettlement had been completed, one observer wrote that in places in Perak and Selangor 'most of the villages are built on tin tailings which are almost uncultivable'. He went on to note that 'One goes to village after village in which the land surrounding the village allegedly for agricultural purposes is bare and untended.'[19] Where good land was available it was already being used for rubber or some other agricultural crop and was too expensive for the Government to buy in sufficient amounts. In addition, the state governments were loathe to alienate more land to the Chinese. Overall, then, as the Department of Agriculture noted in their report for 1950-1, there was a shortage of agricultural land in the resettlement areas. Inevitably, incomes from farming fell drastically. But it was not just their loss of land that caused resentment among the resettled squatter-farmers. Those that were given new plots of land had often to walk a considerable distance, and the transportation of produce and manure caused hardship and inconvenience. Furthermore, plots and livestock which were well outside the perimeter fence could not always be protected from predators and pests—human and otherwise.[20]

For those who gained their livelihood from working on rubber estates, smallholdings, or tin mines, the restrictions imposed by the 7.00 p.m. to 6.00 a.m. curfew, the long delays caused by security checks at the village gates, and the time consumed in travelling between the resettlement centres and their place of work limited their incomes and generated considerable antagonism towards officials. Moreover, because of the lack of land and the consequent restrictions on the supply of food, prices for pork, chicken, and even the most inferior vegetables increased markedly. The general cost of living, a chronic irritant in the years since the return of the British, once again became a major source of discontent.[21]

Added to all this, in June 1951 all existing and future resettlement areas were designated 'food restricted centres'. Under this law, all shopkeepers had to limit their stocks of restricted goods such as medicines, clothing, high energy foods, salt, pepper, and batteries; they had to open all tinned goods when they were sold; and they had to ensure that they sold goods only to people with valid identification cards. Settlers could not take food out to their place of work, and the movement by road of certain restricted goods was prohibited during curfew hours. Labourers found it very difficult to keep going from 6.00 a.m. or 6.30 a.m. until midafternoon, their normal work day. Productivity and, therefore, wages dropped off. The inconvenience, not to say indignity, of daily searches at the gate, the time lost in the mornings, and the problems of not being able to have a proper midday meal, all contributed to a bitterness and resentment within the resettlement centres.

Nor did the resettlement centres afford the squatters the security and protection they were seeking. Indeed, the centres became a key target for guerrilla attacks. Under such circumstances, actions of the special constables detailed to defend the resettlement areas were crucial. However, they were generally young, poorly trained, and without proper leadership. They were Malays and the Chinese squatters were not really surprised that they were unwilling to risk their lives to defend Chinese settlers whom they did not know and whom they generally distrusted. In many resettlement centres, there was considerable resentment that the Malay special constables were allowed to carry arms while the Chinese in the home guard were not. The Chinese also complained that the special constables took advantage of guerrilla attacks to fire into houses within the perimeter fence, sometimes with fatal results.[22] The shortage of barbed-wire meant that the perimeter fences themselves were very flimsy and of relatively little value. Of the 350 or so centres built by the end of 1951, only fifty-six had double fences, and only twenty-five had perimeter lighting as an added form of protection.[23] In addition to all these problems, the settlers still had to go outside the confines of the resettlement areas to tap the rubber or to tend their plots. At these times they were vulnerable to pressure from the guerrillas, or liable to be attacked by over-enthusiastic security forces. Even within the new settlements, people had to be very careful. On the one hand there were plenty of communist sympathizers ready to report them to the local Min Yuen or MRLA for co-operating with the police, while on the other hand the Special Branch had taken advantage of the resettlement process to install their own informers who could report on those who were aiding the communists. It was no wonder that so many of the new arrivals in the resettlement centres continued to feel insecure.

Further problems arose because of the lack of suitable recruits to act as Resettlement Supervisors (RS), Resettlement Officers (RO), and Assistant Resettlement Officers (ARO). When recruits could speak Chinese and understand the Chinese ways and culture, and when they took an active role in developing the amenities of the settlement and created a sense of community among the inhabitants, then resettlement worked well and people were generally happy. But this was all too rare. A major problem was that each month the number of experienced administrative officers assigned to resettlement work decreased because of sickness, retirement, and long leave.[24] Moreover, the Government found it very difficult to fill the positions that were created. For example, by the end of 1951, sixty-five RSs were needed but fewer than fifty had been signed on; similarly fewer than 300 of the required 350 AROs had been recruited. Inevitably, standards were lowered in order to fill as many of the vacancies as possible. Most of the RSs and ROs were recruited overseas and few could speak Chinese. Only six were of Chinese origin. On the other hand, practically all the AROs were Chinese; however, this made them the object of suspicion on all sides. They were not always trusted and given the proper guidance by their superiors; they had to face the hostility of the settlers, who had unreasonable expectations of what they could do; and they were an obvious target for the guerrillas. In the circumstances it was difficult for them to do an effective job.[25]

The task of these administrators was not made any easier by the failure of the Government to provide some of the basic services which were anticipated in the original resettlement plans. Much of the blame for this lay with the Public Works Department. With twenty vacancies for engineers unfilled, and with the proportion of experienced engineers to inexperienced assistant engineers or trainees dangerously low, important projects such as the provision of basic water, drainage, and sewage services in the resettlement centres fell seriously behind schedule. In fact, few settlements ever received the planned complement of drains and stand pipes. By the end of 1951, only just over 200 of the approximately 360 centres had schools, and most centres were without medical services.[26]

Hence, initially at least, there were very few benefits accruing to the rural Chinese population from their upheaval at the hands of the Government. Rather than enjoying the blessings of a sound administration and a wide variety of social services, it seemed to most of them that they were being placed behind the barbed-wire fences to make it easier for the police to screen, detain, and deport suspected communist sympathizers, and for the security forces to intimidate them. Resettlement, then, had the potential to create even more opposition to the Government and to swell the base of support for the MCP guerrillas. It is in this context that the consequences of the Korean War must be considered.

The Korean War Boom

On 25 June 1950, just a few weeks after the inception of the Briggs Plan, war broke out in Korea. The beginning of hostilities sent a ripple of apprehension throughout Malaya. Just as Europeans saw it as a prelude to a Russian strike into Western Europe, so those in the Federation and Singapore felt that Indo-China would be next on the list and Malaya not long after that. At the back of everyone's mind was the debacle of the fall of Malaya and Singapore in 1941-2, which was constantly analysed in the post-War period, and the prospects of another invasion through Thailand. Moreover, the War, especially the early success of North Korea and later the entry into the fray of the new Chinese Government, gave the impression of communism on the move. However, for Malayans there was a brilliant silver lining to this particular dark cloud. The possibility that the fighting might be extended to other parts of East and South-East Asia, coupled with an increased demand for strategic raw materials stimulated by stepped up military requirements and the competitive stockpiling of key commodities, produced a dramatic rise in the price of nearly all commodities. Prices for the two pillars of the Malayan economy—rubber and tin—were catapulted to record heights. The resulting boom had important consequences for the financial position of the Malayan Government as well as for the prosperity of Malayans in general. If not for the Korean War boom, the course of the Emergency would have been very different.

The Korean War could not have come at a more opportune time for the Malayan Government. In May 1950, the High Commissioner had predicted that even with a British Government contribution of about $25 million, the Malayan reserves would be exhausted by the end of the year.[27] The long-term future for both of Malaya's main revenue earners, rubber and tin, did not look promising. Prospecting for new tin deposits was curtailed by the Emergency, and rubber production was falling because of the ageing of the trees and the reluctance of tappers to work the more dangerous areas. Further, a study of Malaya's rubber industry for the Colonial Office predicted in 1948 that 'on any reasonable assumption the prospective demand for natural rubber over the next decade or so can be entirely, or almost entirely, satisfied from the four low-cost producing territories (the Netherland East Indies, Siam, Sarawak and French Indo-China) if their mature areas are fully tapped'.[28] To compound the problem the US Government was threatening to increase the production of synthetic rubber if natural rubber prices rose too high. In addition to all this, the Malayan Government faced the certainty of increased expenditure as resettlement got into full swing. Sir Henry Gurney's comments to the Federal Legislative Council that 'the solution of our difficulties and our future development in all fields is going to be concerned very closely with finance',[29] had a prophetic ring to it.

The price of rubber rose gradually but steadily during the second quarter of 1950. This was brought on by a number of factors, including the devaluation of sterling and the resurgence of the American economy after the slump of 1949. The price of rubber reached nearly $0.80 per pound for Rubber Smoked Sheet (RSS) No.1 in May 1950 up from an average of $0.40 per pound in 1949. However, this 'mini-boom', as it was called, was generally considered a temporary aberration which would be reversed in the very near future.[30] And, indeed, during the week ending 17 June, the 'phenomenal' prices dropped by $0.15 to $0.20 per pound.

Yet the prices recorded during the mini-boom were relatively low compared to the record prices induced by the Korean War. The price of rubber rose dramatically, doubling within a few months and ultimately reaching over $2.20 per pound in February 1951, before dropping again to an average $1.70 per pound for the year, or over four times the average price for 1949. The price of tin rose less quickly, but even so, in early 1951, it was over £1,300 per long ton on the London Market–a marked increase over the April 1950 price of £590. Tin prices would have gone much higher but for the American Government's decision, of 6 March 1951, to cease further purchases of tin until the price was reduced. Both rubber and tin attracted these inflated prices until well into 1952.[31]

These boom prices gave a great boost to the Government's revenue. The duty collected from the export of rubber rose from $28.1 million in 1949 to $89.3 million in 1950. The introduction of a new sliding scale tax to curb internal inflation and increase revenue netted the Government $214.1 million in 1951. The rise in the price of tin, allied to a steady increase in production and exports, doubled the duty received. And, as a result of the higher individual incomes and increased company profits during the boom years, income tax returns rose sharply, and the one-year lag for collection spread out the Government's boom revenues. These revenues unexpectedly and substantially swelled the Government's coffers. The estimate for total revenue in 1950 was put at $273.7 million; the sum actually received was $443.4 million. Similarly, the estimate for 1951 was $410.3 million while the sum actually received was $735.4 million. This major reversal in the country's fortunes meant that an accumulated deficit of $13.4 million shown against the General Revenue Balance and a Total Surplus Fund of only $40.4 million at the beginning of 1950 became, by the end of 1951, a General Revenue Balance surplus of $289.9 million and a Total Surplus Fund of $334.8 million.[32] It was this great increase in the prosperity of the country which prompted a Financial Secretary to tell the Federal Legislative Council that 'the financial fortunes of the Federation vary in direct proportion to the fortunes of our two main primary products, rubber and tin, and of these the more important is rubber. So close is this connection that it is probably not incorrect to say that "Malaya is as rubber does".'[33]

Increased revenue allowed for increased expenditure. There was little overall rise in the expenditure in 1950, but in 1951 expenditure was nearly $550 million or $200 million more than the 1950 figure. Those aspects of the Government most closely associated with the law and order approach to the Emergency were given priority. For example, the total spent on the police force went from $69 million and $73.5 million in 1949 and 1950 respectively to $138.4 million in 1951. Similarly, direct expenditure on the Emergency operations went from $82 million in 1949 to $101 million in 1950 and to $217 million in 1951. The spending on extraordinary non-recurrent public works projects increased dramatically from $13.9 million in 1950 to $34.3 million in 1951. The education and medical and health departments also experienced budget increases. And, of course, it was the revenue from the boom which supplied the funding needed to fuel the Government's new resettlement policy. By the end of 1951, over $40 million had been spent on resettlement compared with less than $2 million spent before the inception of the Briggs Plan.[34]

The Korean War boom saved the Government from having to institute debilitating restraint measures. Some help would no doubt have been forthcoming from the British Government, but, given the financial straits in which the Treasury found itself, it is unlikely that it would have been very substantial. And no other source of income could have approached that provided by the boom.[35] Indeed, had it not been for the boom, the Malayan Government would have found itself severely handcuffed by its financial problems, and its position could well have become untenable.

The economic boom brought on by the Korean War did not have a major impact on the resources available to the Malayan Government alone; it brought prosperity to all Malayans. It proved to be particularly fortuitous for the rural Chinese who were being resettled. Just when they were being forced to abandon their plots of land and had to face the prospect of imminent destitution, there was suddenly an insatiable demand for labour and extraordinarily high wages. The trade boom, which historically had always been the antidote to a burgeoning squatter population, thus provided not only employment and contract work for settlers but also considerable prosperity which mitigated against the distress and resentment caused by their forced relocation.

The first to benefit from the boom prices were the smallholders who sold their rubber at the prevailing market prices. Fieldworkers were hired as many smallholdings were given their first slashing and cleaning for years. The demand for tappers also increased substantially as more areas came under the knife. This produced a gradual shift away from the large European estates which found it difficult to offer competing wages because most of their rubber was sold on the basis of one year forward contracts. However, once these contracts expired and they could sell their rubber at the new prices, estates began to attract labour back with higher wage rates. In the tin industry, the expansion took place towards the end of 1950 with forty-one mines being reopened or started. Seven more were opened in 1951, and labour was in great demand.[36]

Prompted by this demand for labour, especially skilled labour, wages rose at a spectacular rate. Even the wages of the most lowly paid unskilled field-workers, who made up 20-25 per cent of estate workers, increased from $1.43 per day in the first quarter of 1950 to a record high of $2.90 per day in the second quarter of 1951. Daily-rated tappers could earn approximately $3.65 per day and piece-rate tappers approximately $4.35 per day during the palmy days of April-June 1951. The intense competition for labour led to the payment of substantial advances, often up to $500. In many instances, 'Asian' estate owners were willing either to pay three to four times the official rates on European estates or to contract out the tapping of areas prone to guerrilla attacks. Similarly, on small-holdings, systems of shared profits (bagi dua) proved to be highly remunerative for skilled tappers who could receive up to 70 per cent of production or profits.[37] In the tin industry, too, wages followed the upward trend of prices. Unskilled workers, such as dredge crewmen and engine drivers received much higher wages. Just as in the rubber industry, small operations operated on a profit-sharing system, and workers could earn very high incomes. More-over, the high wages paid to rubber and tin workers forced other industrial and commercial employers, as well as the Government, to grant substantial pay raises so as to stop labour deserting them altogether. Hence, despite the inflation which always accompanies commodity price booms, most Malayans experienced an increase in their 'real wage' and many did very well indeed.[38]

Signs of this new prosperity were everywhere, and stories of the money being made were legion. Holdings of 5-10 acres provided an excellent income for smallholders, some of whom were even said to drive their cars to collect the latex.[39] Scruffily dressed Chinese labourers carrying sacks of dollar notes on their backs, were reported frequenting the most respectable jewellers in Ipoh, Kuala Lumpur, and Johore Bahru. Radios and bicycles equipped with the latest gadgets could be seen in many of the resettlement centres and labour lines. The only complaint one Labour Depart-ment official heard during a visit to a mine area was regarding the poor radio reception from Peking.[40] Of course not everyone was like the Government clerk who was on a salary of $145 per month but who, with his son-in-law, had a contract for the supply of rubber which brought them in another $3,000 per month. Yet, as one MCS officer told a British audience, 'the general air of pros-perity in Malaya [had] to be seen to be believed'.[41] Another Euro-pean observer, perhaps exaggerating a little, declared that for the Chinese population, 'by far the most important event in recent years in their eyes is not the Emergency but the Korean War which produced a wave of prosperity in Malaya such as it had not known since 1940'.[42]

The boom also saved Malaya's rubber and tin companies. The low rubber prices of the post-War years, especially the slump in prices in mid-1949, together with the overall decline in production because of the ageing of the trees and the imposition of Emergency regulations, had meant that the more marginally profitable small-holdings were not tapped and that the less efficient estates were forced to cut back operations, reduce wages, and lay off workers. Equally, the low prices for tin, combined with the loans that had been taken out for rehabilitation, put many of the small, Chinese-owned tin workings deeply into debt. The Emergency imposed added hardships. Guerrillas slashed trees and damaged mining machinery as a means of extracting 'donations' from owners, managers, and workers. The constant threat of murder by the guerrillas that had to be endured by everyone who worked or lived on an estate or mine, reduced morale in both the rubber and tin industries and in some cases made recruits hard to obtain. In pre-boom years, capital flowed out of the country, morale among employees was very low, and faith in the economic and political future of the country were in short supply.

With the outbreak of the Korean War, this picture changed radically. Profits in the rubber industry, which had averaged below $0.07 per pound in 1948 and 1949, rose to over $0.37 per pound in 1950, and to over $0.53 per pound in 1951. As capital flowed back into the country, operations–such as replanting–got underway. Managers received healthy bonuses which, although not completely compensating for the constantly frayed nerves, made life a little easier and ensured that retirement, if it was not pre-empted by a bullet, would be well-endowed.[43] Moreover, the European companies used some of their revenue to fortify their estates and mines. In 1949, for instance, only $4 million had been spent on defence by European estates; during 1951, $16 million was spent. Dunlop, one of the major rubber plantation owners, alone spent well over $4 million on, among other things, seventy armoured cars and a number of highly trained European security officers.[44] Hence, although the boom made rubber production a prime target for the guerrillas, estates were able to step up their security arrangements.

However, for both the Government and the employees, the most important consequence of the increased profits received by the rubber and tin companies was their ability to regroup their labour in defensible areas. It has been estimated that some 650,000 people were regrouped: 510,000 on estates, 80,000 on mines, and 60,000 in other regroupment areas.[45] In a few cases, enhanced defence just meant the erection of a barbed-wire fence around the labour lines; more usually, dispersed homes had to be transferred to a central fortified area, or, as was often the case on smaller estates, concentrated at the factory or on nearby large estates. Relocation on tin mines was not usually so difficult because labourers were not as dispersed. The expense of regroupment was borne solely by the estates and mines and proved very costly for employers.[46] Had it been forced on them by the Government at a time of low prices, many rubber holdings, estates, tin mines, and dredging operations would have gone out of business or failed to comply with Government policy. Either consequence would have severely undermined the Government's counter-guerrilla campaign. The first would have led to widespread unemployment, the second would have allowed the guerrillas to rely on estate and mine labour once resettlement made access to squatter communities more difficult.

As was the case with resettlement, the quality of treatment afforded workers who were regrouped was mixed. The labour lines on some tin mines in Selangor, for example, were regrouped twice because of official reservations about the site chosen and because the managers were reluctant to provide more than the minimal housing requirements. The 'fortification' around some regroupment areas proved to be little more than a couple of strands of barbed-wire. Yet, in other instances, largely prompted by the intense competition for labour, good permanent accommodation was provided and the defensive measures included perimeter lighting and well-trained special constables. A few large European estates even went so far as to install community radios and basic medical and educational facilities. One estate, keen to attract Chinese squatters, set aside half an acre of land for each family to cultivate. An advantage for labourers living in the labour lines of the larger European estates was the greater security they offered. The presence of the special constables frightened off the guerrillas–the guerrillas could always 'visit' tappers as they were working on their task–and labourers were less likely to be harassed by prowling security forces.

The Korean War boom, then, proved to be a major and unexpected asset in the Government's campaign against the MCP. The Government gained much needed funding not just for its 'law and order' campaign but also–and just as importantly–for the massive resettlement programme. The general population of Malaya, par-

ticularly the rural Chinese squatters, whose fortunes were traditionally tied to the fluctuating prices of rubber and tin, were swept
along in a rolling tide of prosperity which benefited nearly everyone to a greater or lesser extent. And the rubber and tin industries
were provided with the incentive and the means to withstand the
threat posed by the MCP guerrillas. As General Sir Gerald Templer,
Gurney's successor as High Commissioner, commented in the
Federal Legislative Council a few years later, 'where courage pro-
vides the spirit of defence, economics provide the sinews and it is
only right that we should recognize also the great strain which the
Emergency has imposed upon the financial resources of these industries'. He went on to note: 'It is fortunate indeed that this occurred at a time when the prosperity of these industries has been
much greater than in preceding years.'[47]

Divisive Issues

While the Korean War boom nullified at least some of the ill will
caused by resettlement, a number of other contentious issues remained. Each of the main communities, the Malays, the Chinese,
the Indians, and Europeans had particular preoccupations. Some
of these proved difficult to reconcile and the Government was given
little rest as officials sought to address the dilemmas that arose.

From the point of view of the Chinese community, the Government was committing sins of commission and omission. Especially
vexing for male Chinese and their families were the Manpower
Regulations, which required young male residents of the Peninsula
to register with the Government for service in the police force and
which came into effect in February 1951. The labour shortages
generated by the boom made it exceedingly difficult for the Government to find recruits for the police.[48] What was essentially a
form of conscription was seen as one way around this problem. But
with so much money to be made in the booming economy, and with
the general respect for the security forces so low, few Chinese were
willing to comply with the new regulations. As a result, although
there was relatively little difficulty with the Malay and Indian con-
scripts, when the regulations came into operation, 6,000 Chinese
decamped to Singapore and several other thousand to China. Of
those Chinese who did report for service in the first few months,
over 95 per cent lodged appeals. In the end, fewer than 2,000 Chinese
were admitted into the police force under this programme.[49] Indeed, given the problems it caused, the benefits were meagre. The

policy was generally considered a 'fiasco', which not only undermined support for the Government among the Chinese community
but also increased 'anti-Chinese hostilities' among the non-Chinese
communities.[50]

For Chinese leaders, the issue of the Manpower Regulations was
inextricably linked to another crucial question, that of the citizenship laws. Tan Cheng Lock, in particular, argued that 'It would
be unfair in the extreme, and perhaps also illegal, if those who are
conscripted are at the same time considered aliens under the citizenship law.'[51] The citizenship provisions, which had been brought in
with the Federation Agreement, were viewed by the Chinese as far
too restrictive. Of the just over 3 million who qualified automatically for Federal citizenship, 2.5 million were Malays, 225,000 were
Indians, Pakistanis, or Ceylonese, and only 350,000 were Chinese.[52]
Citizenship by application could be obtained but this entailed providing proof of birth, or residence over a number of years, in the
Federation and a reasonable knowledge of the Malay or English
language. However, applicants, especially Chinese, had all sorts of
difficulty with the application process. Forms were in short supply,
they were difficult to fill in, clerks were said to place barriers in the
path of applicants, and applications were not processed. It was
claimed, for instance, that not only had the Trengganu Government not approved any of the applications made before 1 February
1951 but that it was also reluctant to inform people of the extension of the grace period to August 1951, during which the language requirements were waived. By the end of 1951, fewer than
290,000 Chinese had become citizens by application.[53]

A proposal to liberalize the citizenship laws was put forward in
April 1950 by a group which included leaders from each racial
community and which was known as the Communities Liaison
Committee. But this proposal was attacked by both Malays and
non-Malays. Indian and Chinese leaders argued strongly that the
principle of *jus soli* (citizenship as a right for those born in that country) should be applied. After much discussion, the Government
eventually drafted a bill which went as far as officials thought Malay
opinion would allow. But the bill itself came under attack, especially from Chinese leaders, and Gurney felt he could not press for it
to be placed immediately on the statute books. In July 1951, he put
the whole matter before another committee with the hope that some
consensus could be found. Thus, to the great disappointment of
the Chinese leaders with strong links to the Malayan Government,
although there was a considerable amount of discussion, there were

no changes in the citizenship laws.[54]

Even many of those Chinese who were citizens felt embittered by their situation. There was a great difference, they argued, between 'The King's Chinese', who had been born in the Straits Settlements, and the Malay subjects of the Rulers. Malays could join the Malayan Civil Service while non-Malays, except Europeans, were barred. Malay subjects of the Rulers were not liable to banishment while subjects of the King could be banished and deported. Furthermore, scholarships paid for by public funds went almost exclusively to Malays. As one strongly pro-British Chinese group told the Secretary of State for the Colonies, all this 'engendered a strong feeling of frustration in non-Malays'.[55]

Another issue which exercised the Chinese community was the failure of the Government to guarantee the integrity of the Chinese education system. Under pressure from all communities to improve the education system, and with the long-term view that there ought eventually to be a national system of education, the Government commissioned one investigation into Malay schools and another into Chinese schools. The result was two highly controversial documents. The Committee on Malay Education under the Chairmanship of L. J. Barnes proposed that all existing schools—not just Malay schools—be gradually transformed into National Schools in which all children would be taught in either English or Malay. Their report, which was published in early 1951, was widely criticized by Chinese and Indian leaders and in the Chinese-, Indian-, and even the English-language press. Both the Chinese and Indians viewed it as an attempt to 'Malayanize' their schools and undermine their language and culture.[56] The Fenn-Wu *Report on Chinese Education* came out in June 1951 and added fuel to the flames. It recommended, much to the annoyance of the Malays, that the Chinese school system be improved. Both reports were submitted to the Central Advisory Committee on Education which attempted to reconcile the competing viewpoints in the report it published in September 1951. Still under a cloud of conflicting, and at times, vitriolic criticisms, the whole matter was referred to a Special Committee of the Federal Legislative Council for the drafting of legislation. The main result of the whole process seemed to be to add to the growing list of people who viewed the Government with suspicion.

Two other policies continued to sour the Government's relations with the Chinese community. First, the position of the more than 10,000 Chinese and their dependants who were in detention camps began to cause problems. The ports in China started to re-

fuse to accept the shipment of detainees from Malaya and consequently shipping companies became reluctant to take on what they
considered to be a dangerous assignment. Alternative destinations
such as Christmas Island, North Borneo, and the Solomon Islands
Protectorate were explored but to no avail. One suggestion was
that the detainees be loaded on to amphibious landing equipment,
shipped across the South China Sea, and dumped on China's south
coast. In the meantime, the detainees, only some of whom were
communists or communist sympathizers, continued to languish in
the camps, and the doubtful legal position of their dependants—
many of the children had been born in Malaya—was perpetuated.[57]

Secondly, there were many complaints about the Government's
practice of imposing collective fines and strict curfews—sometimes
as long as twenty-two hours per day—on people in villages and areas
where the guerrillas were especially active. It was argued that it
was invariably the respectable inhabitants who ended up suffering
the most as the guilty soon disappeared. In order to highlight how
ridiculous it was to encumber a whole village or region just because
of the actions of a few who might not even live in the district, it was
suggested that a collective fine ought to be levied on the police after
five people were killed when a grenade exploded next door to the
Central Police Station in Georgetown, Penang. The general feeling
was that assigning guilt by proximity was a totally unfair policy for
the Government to adopt and that little of value resulted from the
use of either collective fines or curfews. Like the slow processing
and indecisive treatment of the detainees, these impositions only
served to create enemies for the Government.[58]

In their turn, Malay leaders still treated the Malayan Government with suspicion. The battle which had been fought over the constitutional arrangements continued to cast a shadow over the
Federal Government's relations with Malay political leaders, the
state governments, and the Rulers. Just as it was for the non-Malays,
the citizenship question was a key issue. Some Malay leaders in
Kedah and Perak, for example, claimed that the nationality proposals amounted to a delivery of Malaya to the Chinese. Moreover,
the Rulers expressed some disquiet that at least 50 per cent of the
Federal Legislative Council's Select Committee on Nationality,
to which Gurney had turned over the problem in July 1951, was
not Malay—although Gurney had agreed with the Rulers that all
Legislative Committees should be. They were, therefore, uneasy
about the eventual outcome.[59]

The general conditions of kampong life clearly preoccupied

Malays. The Government received numerous requests to upgrade services from roads and drainage culverts to medical and educational facilites. It was pointed out, for example, that there were no English language secondary schools in rural areas and, therefore, Malays had great difficulty in passing the School Certificate Examinations, the prerequisite for many Government jobs. In an open letter to Dato Onn in May 1950, Sir Henry Gurney admitted that the Emergency had diverted a lot of money which would otherwise have gone towards helping kampong development.[60] In an attempt to address Malay criticisms he created the Rural Industrial Development Authority (RIDA) with the hope that it might, as he noted privately to other officials, 'free the kampong Malays from their present economic slavery'.[61] Although money was put into a number of rural development programmes, RIDA appeared more to raise Malay expectations than to alleviate their problems.

Malay leaders also expressed their dissatisfaction with the way in which Malays were being employed in the counter-guerrilla campaign. Rather than use Malaya as 'a dumping ground for more and more expatriate officers', to use Dato Onn's words, it was argued that Malays should be promoted more quickly, especially in the police force, and moved into the senior ranks of the administration in greater numbers.[62] Strong pressure was exerted by all Malay leaders to have the Malay Regiment increased in size. This request, at least, was acknowledged in January 1951 when the British Government announced its decision to meet the capital cost of raising and equipping the Fifth and Sixth Battalions of the Regiment. Despite this, however, there were still Malays who argued that since the Government was not able to cope with the Chinese guerrillas, it was time that the Malays took the law into their own hands.[63] Against the background of the Maria Hertogh case, in which a Singapore court took away a child of Dutch parents from the Indonesian family who had adopted her after she had been abandoned, and the subsequent Muslim outpouring of emotion, this was a very disturbing threat.[64] It certainly could not be argued that the Malay community was solidly behind the colonial Government in its fight against the MCP.

The failure of the Government to take what were considered to be strong enough measures against the communist guerrillas was also a preoccupation of the European community. It irked many people, especially the ones who faced the threat from guerrilla activity on a daily basis, that the fighting was characterized as an 'emergency situation' rather than as a 'war'. The argument that industry in Malaya relied upon London insurance firms which covered their losses of stocks and equipment in riots and civilian activities in an emergency but not in a civil or international war was not completely persuasive. For many it seemed that although the communist offensive was officially thought to have been orchestrated at the February 1948 Democratic Youth Conference in Calcutta, and to be the work of aliens fighting on behalf of international communism, the colonial Government refused to accept that an 'external hostile attack' was involved because then Britain would have had to bear the full cost of the counter-insurgency campaign.[65] This failure to apply the appropriate label to what was going on in Malaya was, therefore, the source of considerable concern among Europeans.

A parallel issue in the minds of many European planters and their associations was the need to introduce martial law. From the beginning of the Emergency some planters had argued that the situation was out of the control of the civil and police authorities, and that the proclamation of martial law was the only hope left. Representative of planters' views was an editorial in the December 1950 issue of *The Planter*, which demanded that martial law be invoked. It was reproduced in nearly all the English-language newspapers and provoked widespread debate.[66] The Government considered martial law very seriously but, believing it would not necessarily aid its cause and might produce more harm than good, rejected it. A Colonial Office study noted the problems of using martial law in Palestine and the difficulty of finding military personnel to take over such functions as operating the court system. The overall conclusion was that the 'threat of the imposition of martial law can be a very useful weapon'; however, it would be 'better to continue the civilian administration using to the full the powers granted to the High Commission under the Emergency Regulations Ordinance, 1948'.[67] Both the High Commissioner and the Attorney-General reached similar conclusions.[68] Nevertheless, the persistent calls for stronger action by the Government were a clear indication of the lack of confidence among planters and others in the Government's ability to handle the recurring crises. Except for the boom in the economy, morale would have been at rock-bottom.

As it was, morale among Europeans working for the Federal Government and the state governments was extremely low. Home leave to the UK had been cut to 150 days for administrators and 120 days for police officers; expatriate allowances for schooling and other expenses were said to be low; there were no guarantees governing terms of service, security of tenure, or the exchange rate at which pensions would be paid; over 200 senior officers were on the waiting-list for living quarters, a wait which had been extended from three or four months to anywhere up to seven months. The problems were so severe that a meeting of the European Civil Servants Association of Malaya in February 1951 heard a speech by Gurney, in which he attempted to address these issues, and then promptly carried a motion by 400 votes to one which stated: 'This Meeting adopts the Annual Report but Members feel it their duty to impress upon the Government that the Members of this Association have lost confidence in the ability of the Malayan Administration to act justly towards expatriate officers.'[69] Essentially a motion of no confidence in the senior officials of the Government, it indicated the general sense of frustration which pervaded the administration. Some of the same issues were also being pursued by the Malayan Civil Servants Association. This dissension was not conducive to an efficient and whole-hearted prosecution of the Government's campaign against the MCP.

Nor were morale and confidence high within the police force. Past problems had not been rectified. The rank and file were still not receiving the training they needed, and too often they received no training at all. They were also led by inexperienced officers with little or no training. Furthermore, the rapidity with which the police force had expanded had produced many different categories and types of police and had become too complex an organization to be efficient in its assigned roles.[70] Equally debilitating were the squabbles that occupied the senior officers. The immense size of the police force and the attendant pressures on headquarters staff and senior personnel caused friction. Added ingredients were the clash of personalities, the continued antipathy between the expatriate officers trained in Malaya and those trained elsewhere, and the distance that had sprung up between headquarters staff and senior officers in the field. Resignations were submitted and retracted and senior officers were juggled around in order to try and find a mix that was acceptable to all.[71] The infighting clearly sapped the energies of senior officers and made it very difficult for them to carry out their assignments properly. One of the major consequences of this and the general confusion which permeated the police force was that the police continued to inflict on the population what Gurney delicately described as 'a number of discourtesies'.[72]

One bright spot for the Government was the arrival, in September

1950, of H. Carlton Greene as Head of Emergency Information Services. Prompted by Briggs's assessment after his initial tour of the country that the Government's propaganda was 'non-existent', the Secretary of State for the Colonies was able to persuade the British Broadcasting Corporation (BBC) to allow Greene to be seconded to the Malayan Government for a year. Greene was clearly struck by the opportunities that were being missed. For example, he found that the 'This is Communism' series on Radio Malaya was written by someone 'who lacked specialised knowledge of the subject and never related his talks to events in Malaya or China'. Greene reorganized the radio programming of Radio Malaya and, in order to bring radio to a wider audience, had community listening sets installed in various community centres and started Community Listening Programmes which were broadcast in Malay, Tamil, and four Chinese dialects. A big expansion of the Malayan Film Unit was initiated, and plans were made to double the number of mobile units equipped with public address systems and cinema projectors. Greater care was taken to make sure that the information given to the press was more detailed and that Chinese translations were made available.[73]

The most telling innovation made under Greene's auspices was the increased use of Surrendered Enemy Personnel (SEP) in the Government's propaganda campaigns. Instead of being prosecuted, the SEPs were put to work writing pamphlets and leaflets in their own handwriting which detailed the iniquities of the MCP and the generous treatment they had received at the hands of the Government. These pamphlets, which usually contained appropriate photographs, were then widely circulated. SEPs made lecture tours around areas in which they were well known, reiterating the points they had made in the leaflets. The best known and most effective of the SEPs was Lam Swee, the former Political Commissar of the Fourth Regiment of the MRLA in Johore. His pamphlet, *My Accusation*, was published and distributed by the Government in vast numbers; in August of 1951, he and C. C. Too of the Emergency Information Services Department, started the highly successful *New Path News* with a first run of 50,000 copies. Overall, then, Greene was able to set the Government's propaganda effort on a firm footing. But as Greene himself stated, 'propaganda is essentially an auxiliary weapon and cannot function in a vacuum'.[74] Against a background of a rising tide of violence, propaganda could not by itself regain the initiative for the Government.

Increasing the Pressure

During the second half of 1950 and throughout 1951, the MCP guerrillas and the Min Yuen stepped up their activities. The number of communist-instigated incidents reported by the Government rose from 1,442 in 1949 to 4,739 in 1950, and to 6,082 in 1951. Similarly, casualties inflicted on the security forces increased from 476 in 1949 to 889 and 1,195 in 1950 and 1951 respectively. Civilian casualties went from 694 in 1949 to 1,161 in 1950, and to 1,024 in 1951.[75] It was during this eighteen-month period, from June 1950 to the end of 1951, that the 'shooting war' reached its peak.

The events in both China and Korea greatly boosted morale among the ranks of the communists. With the Nationalist Government of Chiang Kai Shek forced to flee to Formosa, the MCP's ascendancy over the local Kuomintang organization was obvious to anyone in Malaya who still maintained a strong interest in the politics of their homeland. Moreover, the MCP, who were always alert to opportunities to show that the communist movement in Malaya was part of the world-wide and inexorable march of communism, gave great play to the early victories of North Korea and the relative success of the Chinese 'volunteers' in the Korean War. Details of the new Chinese Government's successes also appeared in the Chinese press. 'A new power is rising in China under the Communist Chinese. The Western nations no longer dare to look down on the new Chinese Government', trumpeted the *Nanyang Siang Pau*.[76] Clearly, the ability of the Chinese to hold their own against the combined might of the Western world was a source of considerable pride for large sections of the Chinese community.

But as the resettlement programme shifted into high gear towards the end of 1950, the MCP found that it could not just bask in the glory of the Chinese Government's victories. It had to face some immediate and major problems. The response of the MRLA units and the various local Min Yuen groups to resettlement was mixed. Instances were reported of attacks in which resettlement centres suffered serious damage and nearly all centres were the target of sniper fire. In Johore, the State Committee ordered an 'all-out intensification' of action, with guerrilla units instructed to give greater assistance to the Min Yuen.[77] Yet, as Humphrey has noted, at no time was there a co-ordinated, systematic attempt to destroy the resettlement centres and drive the squatters back into the countryside.[78] This may have been because the MCP thought that it might be able to turn resettlement to their advantage. A major propaganda campaign was mounted which emphasized the slum conditions of most settlements, the possibility of resettlement merely being a preliminary move before squatters were deported to China–as, indeed, had happened to some others before them–and the need to continue supporting the local Min Yuen as the best means of fighting the Colonial Government. There were reports that in some cases resettlement even facilitated the collection of subscriptions because of the ease with which members of the Min Yuen could visit everyone and because of the resentment that the move had engendered.[79]

Initially, resettlement appears to have had no adverse effect on the MCP's ability to attract new recruits. Indeed, resettlement seems to have increased sympathy for the communists. Moreover, the Manpower Regulations undoubtedly added more Chinese to the ranks of the MCP than to the police force. Certainly, there is every indication that the Min Yuen were active in most resettlement centres and that guerrilla units had all the recruits they could absorb. The problem was not so much getting people to join, but feeding them and keeping their morale up once they went 'inside'.

As the resettlement programme progressed, food became a greater and greater problem for the Min Yuen and the armed guerrilla units. Moved off their land and into the resettlement centres, the resettled squatters were no longer able to cultivate crops and raise pigs and chickens to the extent they once had. Just as the amount of food produced and shipped to market dropped, so the amount of food available to the communists declined dramatically. For example, the total weight of fresh vegetables moving from Johore to Singapore fell from 200 tons per month before resettlement to only 30 tons per month in 1951.[80] The Korean War boom also played a role here, for once squatters moved into the resettlement centres and were forced to look for sources of income other than from food production, they found it relatively easy to find employment on rubber estates or smallholdings, on mines, or in nearby towns. The numbers that returned to cultivation on any scale were greatly reduced.[81] As a result of the steadily decreasing sources of food among the squatters, the guerrillas had to break up their larger units of 100 and more into smaller groups. They also turned more and more to estate labourers as well as squatters in order to obtain supplies. However, as regrouping of estate and mine workers got underway, supplies, especially food, became more difficult to acquire. Stories of 'starving bandits' began to circulate.

It was under these circumstances that the Min Yuen, aided by the armed guerrilla units, began to resort increasingly to violence, extortion, and terrorist tactics. Attempts were made to disrupt the resettlement and food control programme, not just by direct attacks on resettlement centres but also by stopping buses and burning the identity cards of everyone on board. Without identity cards, settlers were vulnerable to increased attention from the police. The process of obtaining new cards was time-consuming and usually entangled the settler in the net of the sometimes corrupt bureaucracy. Individual settlers were visited while they went about their daily work on estates or smallholdings, and enough gruesome examples of what could befall those who did not co-operate with the Min Yuen or who worked for the Government were left in prominent places to instil fear in the Chinese population. Intimidation was also used to extract food and other supplies from Malays, who were normally not included in the massive resettlement campaign and whose kampongs were generally not protected. The mutual antagonism which had developed between Malays and Chinese during the weeks immediately after the Japanese surrender, and the almost totally Chinese composition of the MCP meant that the Malays were by no means willing helpers. However, faced with armed guerrilla groups, they, like the Chinese squatters, had little choice but to comply with the requests. For their part, the Chinese guerrillas were not keen to confront Malays and stir up retaliatory action by kampong youths—only their desperate need for food made them prepared to take the risk.

Although morale remained high within the MCP during 1950, by mid-1951 some questions were being raised about the overall strategy being pursued.[82] The problems of finding food created friction, with particularly dispiriting consequences for the units that had to trek from one area to another searching for new supplies. The prosperity created by the boom did not just distract attention from the MCP cause, it undermined one of the main appeals: trying to organize a revolution is not easy in times of full employment. And the increasing use of force produced a disillusionment among members and supporters which reduced the MCP's effectiveness. The terrorist tactics were viewed as making the MCP no better than the Government and seemed only to confirm the charges that Lam Swee had made from within the Party and was now making as he toured the country on behalf of the Government. Hence, while the MCP was not necessarily losing ground to the Government, it certainly was not making much headway.

Summary

Fear and resentment became the watchwords for 1951. Fear was pervasive because the shooting war had reached a new intensity. No one knew what area would be affected next or who would be the victims. The resentment was aimed at both the MCP for escalating their violent attacks, and at the Government for its inability to curb either the excesses of its own forces or the activities of the armed guerrillas and the Min Yuen. The one mitigating factor was the boom in the economy. Rather like the weather to an Englishman, the price of rubber became the main topic of conversation for the people of Malaya.

For the Chinese, especially the rural Chinese, Tan Cheng Lock's millstones began to grind finer and finer from mid-1950 onwards. Resettlement caused a great deal of hardship. The settlements themselves were often more akin to slums than to the 'model' centres that the planners had anticipated, and one of the major reasons for the whole programme, the provision of greater security for the population, had not materialized. Officials learned not to be surprised at the regular reports that guerrilla units were able to enter resettlement centres virtually at will.[83] The communists' use of violence mounted not only in the resettlement centres but also on the estates and smallholdings as they increasingly employed intimidation and propaganda in an effort to secure scarce supplies of food. Moreover, trapped within the new centres, the settlers became easy targets for police harassment and were forced to suffer numerous indignities in the name of a security they patently were not given. However, while the rural Chinese suffered the most because they were at the centre of the fighting, all Chinese felt somewhat vulnerable. Of the civilians who were killed by the MCP, more were Chinese than of any other racial community. Yet despite this, all Chinese were considered suspect by the security forces. Government protestations notwithstanding, for much of Malaya's rural population the guerrilla war was becoming decidedly more perilous.

For the Malays and the Indians, the guerrilla war was becoming a tiresome burden. Feelings ran high that although the Malays were doing all the fighting and dying to save the country from a Chinese guerrilla movement, the Chinese—the very people who were perpetuating the guerrilla war by supporting the communists—were benefiting from increased Government spending on land, clean drinking water, schools, and other services. Further, unease was growing among Indians and Malays about the Government's inability to protect them from those MCP guerrillas who, finding their former sources drying up, started to prey on first the Indian labour lines and then the Malay kampongs in order to obtain food and other supplies. Compounding this, the Government's failure to deal with the guerrilla problem did not encourage the Rulers and the senior officials in the state governments to relinquish more power to the Federal Government or to non-Malays in the form of more liberal citizenship laws or easier access to positions in the bureaucracy. In general, the Malay community's confidence in the Government remained low.

This was also true of the European community. Hard-pressed planters and miners were disheartened that the fighting, rather than abating as had been predicted by Gurney and other senior officials, was intensifying. There seemed to be no end in sight to the tensions and stresses created by the constant threat which lurked in the jungle only yards away. Among the European government officials morale was low. They felt that they were not being well treated by senior officials and they were certainly making no perceptible headway in the campaign against the communists. As Graham Greene noted in reflecting on his visit to Malaya in early 1951, 'there was defeat in the mind'.[84]

The one redeeming feature of this dark period was the economic boom. It was a most welcome tonic. The rubber and tin industries were given the resources to regenerate themselves. Incomes rose for nearly everyone–from European mine and plantation managers to contract tappers, estate field-workers, and government labourers. Increased revenue relieved the Government of one of its key restrictions in fighting the guerrillas. The boom gave the Government a much-needed respite as policies could be implemented without constant concern over finding the required funds. For the MCP, the advent of prosperity was a mixed blessing. It was able to benefit from the general increase in funds by making sure that 'subscription' rates rose appropriately, but the shortages of food created problems which even its increased funding could not resolve. Moreover, the high wages tended to distract people's attention away from the MCP's cause. Too many rubber tappers, complained one MCP propaganda pamphlet, were spending their money in cinemas, and drinking and gambling, and participating in other forms of the 'corrupted life' of capitalism.[85]

By well into 1951, then, it looked as if the Emergency had reached something of an impasse. Malayans appeared to be condemned to a chronic state of fairly intense guerrilla warfare for years to come. Certainly, few anticipated the change of fortune that the events of late 1951 were to set in train.

1. 'An Appreciation of the Military and Political Situation in Malaya as of 25 October 1950', CO 537/5975.

2. 'GHQ Far East Land Forces to Minister of Defence', 24 February 1950; Chiefs of Staff Committee, 'Situation in Malaya', 2 March 1950, and E. Shinwell, Minister of Defence to the Prime Minister, 7 March 1950, all in CO 537/5974.

3. 8 March 1950, CO 537/5974.

4. Transcript of an interview with W. C. S. Corry, mss. Ind Ocn S 215 (Rhodes House Library).

5. 'Federation Plan for the Elimination of the Communist Organisation and Armed Forces in Malaya', 24 May 1950, CO 537/5975, and Anthony Short, *The Communist Insurrection in Malaya 1948-1960* (London: Frederick Muller, 1975), pp. 234-41. Many people have since claimed credit for elements of the plan proposed by Briggs and there is little doubt that many of the ideas he put forward were circulating in Malaya well before his arrival. However, the value of Briggs's proposals lay in his ability to synthesize these ideas and to give a sense of direction to the Government's policies.

6. Short, *The Communist Insurrection*, p. 239.

7. See the discussions in Kernial Singh Sandhu, 'The Saga of the "Squatters" in Malaya: A Preliminary Survey of the Causes, Characteristics and Consequences of the Resettlement of Rural Dwellers during the Emergency between 1948 and 1960', *Journal of Southeast Asian History* 5 (March 1964), pp. 145-6, and Francis Kok-Wah Loh, 'Beyond the Tin Mines: The Political Economy of Chinese Squatter Farmers in the Kinta New Villages, Malaysia' (Ph.D. dissertation, Cornell University, 1980), pp. 34-67. See also Richard Stubbs, *Counter-Insurgency and the Economic Factor: The Impact of the Korean War Prices Boom on the Malayan Emergency*, Occasional Paper No. 19 (Singapore: Institute of Southeast Asian Studies, 1974), on which parts of this chapter are based.

8. *Proceedings of the Federal Legislative Council*, 3rd Session, 1950, p. 8. See also Gurney to MacDonald, 15 February 1950, CO 537/5974.

9. High Commissioner to Secretary of State for the Colonies, Despatch No. 3, 12 January 1950, CO 537/5974, and 'The Squatter Problem in the Federation of Malaya in 1950', *Papers laid before the Legislative Council*, 3rd Session, 1950, pp. B89-109.

10. See Federation of Malaya, 'Report of the Committee Appointed by His Excellency the High Commissioner to Investigate the Squatter Problem', 10 January 1949; 'The Squatter Problem in the Federation of Malaya in 1950', and High Commissioner to Secretary of State, Confidential Telegram No. 109, CO 537/4750.

11. The report was published by the Federation of Malaya on 10 January 1949. See pp. 2-3.

12. Gurney to Higham, 13 March 1951, CO 537/7270. See also 'The Squatter Problem in the Federation of Malaya in 1950', and 'Progress of Resettlement',

Office of the Director of Operations, June 1951, CO 537/7270. A copy of this document may also be found in the Tan Cheng Lock Private Papers, Item 170 (ANM).

13. See 'Progress of Resettlement', Office of the Director of Operations, June 1951, CO 537/7270; Federation of Malaya, *Progress Report on the Development Plan of the Federation of Malaya 1950-1952*, Kuala Lumpur, 1953, p. 61; *Proceedings of the Federal Legislative Council*, 6th Session, 1953, c. 756; Kernial Singh Sandhu, 'Emergency Resettlement in Malaya', *Malayan Journal of Tropical Geography* 18 (August 1964), p. 165; John Weldon Humphrey, 'Population Resettlement in Malaya' (Ph.D. dissertation, Northwestern University, 1971), pp. 118-21, and Stubbs, *Counter-Insurgency*, pp. 27-8.

14. See the rather glowing report in *The Times* (London), 15 March 1951, and 'Monthly Review of Chinese Affairs', August 1951, CO 537/7270.

15. See Sandhu, 'The Saga of the "Squatters"', p. 161; Department of Information, *Malaya Under the Emergency*, n.d., pp. 68-9; Humphrey, 'Population Resettlement', pp. 103 and 357, and Gordon P. Means, 'New Villages in Malaya', mimeograph (Hamilton, Ontario: Department of Political Science, McMaster University, n.d.), pp. 44-5. Rhoderick Dhu Renick Jr., 'The Emergency Regulations of Malaya: Causes and Effect', *Journal of Southeast Asian History* 6 (September 1965), p. 10, suggests that families received a cash grant of nearly $340 for building materials but gives no source.

16. General Sir Gerald Templer, High Commissioner, *Proceedings of the Federal Legislative Council*, 5th Session, 1953, p. 11.

17. See 'Medical Arrangements in New Villages', P/PM1, Chief Secretary 31/9 (ANM). Note was made of the Japanese experience of resettling 2,000 people near Bahau in 1943. Within a few months there was an epidemic of malaria with 1,200 cases in one month and 100 people were known to have died. A few months later there was an outbreak of Blackwater fever. It was no wonder people were scared of resettlement camps. Nor was it surprising that the communists were very active in the Bahau region. See also E. H. G. Dobby, 'Recent Settlement Changes in South Malaya', *Malayan Journal of Tropical Geography* 1 (October 1953), p. 6. Of course, in some instances the people who moved into the resettlement areas were already suffering from malnutrition, tuberculosis, or some other disease.

18. Sandhu, 'The Saga of the "Squatters"', p. 161.

19. William H. Newell, 'New Villages in Malaya', *The Economic Weekly*, 12 February 1955, p. 231. See also the discussion in Loh, 'Beyond the Tin Mines', pp. 118-27, and Paul Markandan, *The Problem of the New Villages in Malaya* (Singapore: Donald Moore, 1954), p. 9.

20. See 'Monthly Review of Chinese Affairs', April 1951, CO 537/7270. It was much easier to concentrate owners of pigs than the pigs themselves.

21. See 'Memorandum on the Subjects for Discussion with the High Commissioner by the Deputation to Wait on him on Thursday, June 21, 1951', CO 537/7265, and Stubbs, *Counter-Insurgency*, p. 31, for figures on the decrease in available food supplies.

22. 'Weekly Intelligence Summary', No. 31, 7 December 1950, CO 717/201, and 'Brief for the Secretary of State for a Meeting of the Malaya Committee, July 26, 1951', CO 537/7263.

23. *Proceedings of the Federal Legislative Council*, 'Resettlement and the Development of New Villages in the Federation of Malaya', Paper No. 33, 1952.

24. 'Memorandum by the O.A.G., Federation of Malaya in Connection with

General Briggs' Appreciation of the Military and Political Situation in Malaya as on October 26, 1950', CO 537/5975.

25. See Loh, 'Beyond the Tin Mines', pp. 137-9. It was widely assumed that the AROs were corrupt. See 'Notes of a Conference in Kuala Lumpur, August 22 and 23, 1951', CO 537/7254.

26. Public Works Department, by the Member for Public Works, 3 December 1951, briefs on 'Matters Likely to be Raised, Visit of the Secretary of State for the Colonies', P/PM1, Chief Secretary 438/B/51 (ANM); Humphrey, 'Population Resettlement', p. 211, and 'Resettlement', Legislative Council Paper No. 33, 1952.

27. High Commissioner to the Secretary of State for the Colonies, 17 May 1950, CO 717/200.

28. P. T. Bauer, *The Rubber Industry: A Study in Competition and Monopoly* (London: Longmans, 1948), p. 344.

29. *Proceedings of the Federal Legislative Council*, 1st Session, 1948, p. B537.

30. See 'Memorandum of the Penang Chamber of Commerce to the Secretary of State for the Colonies, May 30, 1950', CO 537/6090. Interestingly, the Malayan Government felt that this mini-boom was detrimental to their prosecution of the Emergency because the guerrillas were able to steal rubber and the higher prices allowed them to increase their income. Gurney felt a moderate fall in the price of rubber would aid the Government and asked if the British Government would sell 1,000-2,000 tons from its stockpile to bring this about. The British Government replied that the price was due to a technical position of the market and they would not interfere. See High Commissioner to the Secretary of State for the Colonies, 29 April 1950, and Secretary of State to Gurney, 6 May 1950, CO 537/5566.

31. For rubber and tin prices, see Colin Barlow, *The Natural Rubber Industry: Its Development, Technology and Economy in Malaysia* (Kuala Lumpur: Oxford University Press, 1978), pp. 440-3, and International Tin Study Group, *Tin 1950-51: A Review of the World Tin Industry* (The Hague: International Tin Study Group, 1951), p. 66.

32. See 'Report of the Director of Audit on the Accounts of the Federation of Malaya', 1950, p. 4, and 1951, p. 4 (ANM), and Department of Information, *Progress Report on the Development Plan of the Federation of Malaya, 1950-1952*, 1953, p. 19. Not knowing the way in which commodity prices might move in the forthcoming years, the Malayan Government's estimates were generally very conservative. The estimated price for rubber for 1950 was $0.47 per pound, and for 1951 $0.80 per pound. See R. L. Morris to J. R. Williams, 5 September 1950, CO 717/187.

33. *Proceedings of the Federal Legislative Council*, 6th Session, 1953, c. 800.

34. See Stubbs, *Counter-Insurgency*, pp. 12-18; High Commissioner to the Secretary of State for the Colonies, 26 May 1951, CO 537/7270, and Humphrey, 'Population Resettlement', Appendix E. The increased expenditure on the police allowed 353 European gazetted officers and 914 European non-gazetted officers to be brought to Malaya.

35. Stubbs, *Counter-Insurgency*, pp. 19-21.

36. *Federation of Malaya Annual Report*, 1950, p. 29, and *Monthly Statistics Bulletin*, July 1954, p. 36.

37. See Stubbs, *Counter-Insurgency*, p. 34; *Federation of Malaya Annual Report*, 1951, p. 36, and 1952, p. 37. The fact that rubber latex, which could not be traced, could be sold 'under the counter' for over $1.00 per pound led to a great deal of theft. Department of Labour, *Monthly Report*, July and August, 1950.

38. For a description of the tin industry in the boom years, see Siew Nim Chee,

Labour and Tin Mining in Malaya, Data Paper No. 7, Southeast Asia Program (Ithaca: Department of Far Eastern Studies, Cornell University, 1953). See also *Federation of Malaya Annual Report*, 1949, p. 17; 1950, p. 32, and 1951, pp. 36–7.

39. Judith Strauch, *Chinese Village Politics in the Malaysian State* (Cambridge, Mass: Harvard University Press, 1981), p. 68.

40. Department of Labour, *Monthly Report*, October 1950.

41. Dennis J. Duncanson, 'Impressions of Life in Malaya Today', *Journal of the Royal Central Asian Society* 38 (1951), p. 61. It was Duncanson who tells the story of the government clerk.

42. J. B. Perry Robinson, *Transformation in Malaya* (London: Secker and Warburg, 1956), p. 103.

43. This became popularly known as ending up in 'Devon or Heaven'. See, for example, *The Planter* 27 (October 1951), p. 448.

44. *The Times*, 16 September 1954.

45. Sandhu, 'Emergency Resettlement', p. 174.

46. 'Memorandum on the Cost of Regrouping', November 1951, P/PM1, Chief Secretary 438/B/51 (ANM).

47. *Proceedings of the Federal Legislative Council*, 6th Session, 1953, c. 25.

48. Gurney to Lloyd, 21 February 1951, CO 537/7262.

49. See note in the handwriting of Sir Henry Gurney found after his death, typed version, Tan Cheng Lock Papers, Item 144 (ANM), and *Federation of Malaya Annual Report*, 1951, p. 212. Rates of pay in the police force were relatively low but it was decided that they could not be higher than for the Malay Regiment.

50. Brian Stewart to Tan Cheng Lock, 2 January 1951, Tan Cheng Lock Papers, Item 144(i) (ANM).

51. *Straits Echo*, 24 January 1951.

52. *Federation of Malaya Annual Report*, 1950, p. 24. For detailed analyses of the citizenship regulations, see F. G. Carnell, 'Malayan Citizenship Legislation', *The International and Comparative Law Quarterly* 4th Series 1 (October 1952), pp. 504–18; J. M. Gullick, *Malaya* (London: Benn, 1964), pp. 237–43, and Purcell, *Malaya: Communist or Free?* (London: Gollancz, 1954).

53. *Federation of Malaya Annual Report*, 1952, p. 33. On the problems facing applicants, see *Sin Chew Jit Poh*, 30 July 1951, in 'Extracts from the Federation of Malaya', *Daily Press Summary, Vernacular Papers*, 30 July 1951; Department of Labour, *Monthly Report*, December 1949, and E. C. G. Barrett, 'The Meaning of Federal Citizenship', Chinese Affairs FM, 518/1325 (Federal Citizenship) (ANM). For the complaint about Trengganu, see B. T. W. Stewart to Chief Registration Officer FM, 22 May 1951, Chinese Affairs FM, 518/1325 (Federal Citizenship) (ANM).

54. The discussion prompted by the bill was initiated after Tan Cheng Lock drew up a memorandum which criticized the Government's proposals. He then had discussions with Gurney and MacDonald both of whom tried to dissuade him from opposing the Government's bill to amend the citizenship sections of the Federation Agreement. See Gurney to Tan Cheng Lock, 14 April 1951, Tan Cheng Lock Papers, not catalogued (ANM); Tan Cheng Lock to T. H. Tan, 2 June 1951, Tan Cheng Lock Papers TCL/V/121 (ISEAS), and Maxwell to Tan Cheng Lock, 16 May 1951, Tan Cheng Lock Papers, Item 102 (ANM).

55. Secretary of State's Meeting with the Straits Chinese British Association (Penang), 27 May 1950, CO 537/6090.

56. See Extracts from the Federation of Malaya, *Monthly Political Report*,

February 1951, CO 717/190. This file contains a great deal of information on Barnes and his Committee.

57. Executive Committee Minutes, 23 January 1951, CO 537/7273; the items on detention in CO 537/7274; Minutes of the 15th Conference (Federation/Singapore) held under the Chairmanship of His Excellency the Commissioner General for the UK in Southeast Asia, 7 June 1950, CO 537/5970, and Minutes of the 18th Conference of Rulers, 25 October 1951, P/PM1, Chief Secretary 501/51/5 (ANM).

58. See Department of Chinese Affairs, *Monthly Review*, February 1951 and March 1951, and *Singapore Standard*, 20 February 1951.

59. See the High Commissioner to the Secretary of State for the Colonies, 14 March 1951, CO 537/7341, and Minutes of the 18th Conference of Rulers, 24/25 October 1951, P/PM1, Chief Secretary 501/51/5 (ANM).

60. *Straits Times*, 25 May 1950.

61. 'Notes of a Meeting held at King's House, Kuala Lumpur, at 9.00 a. m. on June 3, 1950', CO 717/155.

62. Onn to Secretary of State for the Colonies, 1 November 1950, and the Secretary of State to Onn, 8 January 1951, CO 537/6020, and 'Notes of a Meeting between the Secretary of State for the Colonies and the UMNO', P/PM1, Chief Secretary 438/B/51 (ANM).

63. High Commissioner to Secretary of State for the Colonies, 14 March 1951, CO 537/7341

64. Short notes that the relations between the Colonial Government and an incalculable part of the Malay community had changed almost overnight because of the Hertogh case. Short, *The Communist Insurrection*, p. 252.

65. See the bitter debate over Britain's financial responsibilities in *Proceedings of the Federal Legislative Council*, 2nd Session, pp. 78-84.

66. See, for example, *Straits Times*, 21 January 1951. Other examples of calls for martial law include those by J. S. Ferguson, Chairman of the Central Perak Planting Association, *Straits Echo*, 10 March 1950; G. Treble, Chairman, Pahang Planters' Association, enclosed in W. C. Corry to Higham, 15 October 1950, CO 537/5999; the Selangor Planters, *Straits Echo*, 28 November 1950, and His Highness Tengku Abubaker Ibni Sultan Ibrahim, *Proceedings of the Federal Legislative Council*, 3rd Session, pp. 124-5.

67. See Joan A. Gaved, 'Draft Memorandum on the Implications of a Declaration of Martial Law', CO 537/4773.

68. Gurney's Minute of the 16th Meeting of the BDCC(FE) Annexure A, CO 537/4773. The view of the Attorney General, M. J. Hogan, is to be found in his minute on martial law in 'Visit of the Secretary of State for the Colonies, Briefs on matters likely to be raised', P/PM1, Chief Secretary 438/B/51 (ANM).

69. Minutes of the Annual General Meeting, The European Civil Servants Association of Malaya, 9 February 1951, and Minutes of the Meeting, 25 April 1951, CO 717/201. See also 'Personnel Matters, Visit of the Secretary of State for the Colonies, Briefs on matters likely to be raised', P/PM1, Chief Secretary 438/B/51 (ANM).

70. 'The Situation in the Federation of Malaya from the Point of View of the Director of Operations', 26 November 1951, CO 537/7263.

71. Letters of resignation and the various reviews of the situation undertaken by Briggs and others are to be found in CO 537/5973.

72. 'Notes of a meeting between the High Commissioner and leading members of commercial interests', 11 January 1951, CO 537/7262.

73. See 'Report on Emergency Information Services, September 1950–September 1951' by H. Carleton Greene, CO 537/7255. This may also be found in the Tan Cheng Lock Papers, Item 135 (ANM).

74. The usefulness of the SEPs helped Greene to persuade the Government to raise the amount given as rewards for information leading to the capture or killing of guerrillas. Ibid. See also Robinson, *Tranformation in Malaya*, pp. 47–53, and Short, *The Communist Insurrection*, pp. 416–21.

75. Department of Information, *Emergency Statistics for the Federation of Malaya Since June 1948*, 7/60/160 (Emerg) Appendix A. It should be noted that it is not clear in which category were put those people who were victims of the security forces but not clearly identified as communists.

76. Quoted in 'Political Report', December 1950, CO 537/6017B.

77. See 'Secret Abstract of Intelligence for February 14-28, 1951', CO 537/7300, and Department of Labour, *Monthly Report*, August and September 1951 (ANM).

78. Humphrey, 'Population Resettlement', p. 111. He argues that their failure to undertake such a campaign 'cost the Communists their last opportunity for victory' (p. 112).

79. 'Secret Abstract of Intelligence for May 16-31, 1951', CO 537/7270.

80. Dobby, 'Recent Settlement Changes', p. 6.

81. By 1952 the percentage of agriculturalists in the resettlement centres had dropped from 60 per cent to 27 per cent. See Sandhu, 'The Saga of the "Squatters"', p. 169.

82. The surrender rate during the last six months of 1950 was only 7.5 per month, the lowest rate for the first seven years of the Emergency. *Federation of Malaya Annual Report*, 1955, p. 4.

83. Humphrey, 'Population Resettlement', p. 122, and Graham Greene, *Ways of Escape* (Harmondsworth: Penguin, 1981), p. 120.

84. Greene, *Ways of Escape*. See also his 'Malaya, The Forgotten War', *Life*, 30 July 1951.

85. 'Extracts from the Minutes of the 29th Meeting of the Joint Information and Propaganda Committee held at Kuala Lumpur on June 1, 1951', CO 537/7288.

5
Changes at the Top

THE beginning of October 1951 brought two events which were to have a major impact on the course of the Emergency. Of most immediate consequence was the killing of the High Commissioner, Sir Henry Gurney, in a guerrilla ambush. This gave the newly elected Conservative Government in Britain an unwelcomed, but timely, opportunity both to reassess the overall strategy for fighting the MCP and to make changes among the key personnel who were responsible for putting these policies into effect. Of equal importance, although it took many months before Malayans recognized its significance, was the issuing by the MCP Central Committee of a set of lengthy directives of which the most crucial changed the emphasis of the Party's strategy. Less reliance was to be placed on the use of military tactics against the general population, and greater consideration was to be given to the development of the Party's organizational base among the masses. The military and the political were to be given equal prominence in the MCP's campaign. For Malaya's population, these two changes heralded the gradual introduction of a new phase in the country's guerrilla war.

Gurney's Death

On Saturday 6 October 1951, Sir Henry Gurney and his wife left Kuala Lumpur for a short holiday in the relatively cool climate of Fraser's Hill. At about 1.15 p.m., while the car in which they were being driven was passing through one of the narrowest points in the winding road up to the hill station, a guerrilla platoon hidden in the roadside jungle opened fire. For some unknown reason, Gurney got out of the car and moved towards the side of the road, only to be hit by a hail of bullets and fall into a drainage ditch. His wife and Private Secretary remained in the car and survived the attack unhurt.[1]

News of the High Commissioner's death cast a pall over the European community and, when combined with other events, appeared to signal the beginning of the unravelling of the Government's counter-guerrilla campaign. Less than three weeks after

Gurney was ambushed, a convoy in the same area suffered a similiar fate with sixteen killed and seventeen injured. And a few weeks later, MCP guerrillas mounted the highest number of attacks that had been recorded in a one-week period. The effectiveness of the resettlement programme was also being questioned. Towards the end of November, Mawai resettlement centre was closed down after a guerrilla attack, Bukit Changgang resettlement centre was ordered cleared and demolished, and there were a number of other centres which had to be closed because of the atrocious living conditions and inadequate security. Indeed, the whole of the Briggs Plan appeared to be in jeopardy because of the Government's failure to provide security to settlers. One report even went so far as to state that the resettlement camps were riddled with Min Yuen cells and had become 'hideouts and rest centres for bandits and the MRLA'.[2] To many, Gurney's murder was simply further evidence that the situation was getting worse and not, as the Government kept saying, better.

The killing of the High Commissioner also prompted a new wave of anti-Chinese feeling among the non-Chinese communities. Calls were made for stronger measures to be introduced against those who failed to lend their full support to the Government. Despite there being no evidence to suggest that any of them were involved in the ambush, the inhabitants of the closest Chinese village, Tras, were removed *en masse* because, it was said, they would not come forward with any information about the incident. In official circles there was talk of sequestering the property of all Chinese suspected of aiding the guerrillas.[3] In turn, this only served to heighten the Chinese feeling that they were ill-used, and that the Government misunderstood the nature of the guerrilla war.

The different perceptions of the causes of the Emergency were mirrored by the two different reactions of the Europeans and the Chinese to the circumstances in which Gurney died. The Europeans felt that Gurney had behaved with great distinction in an unfortunate situation. His action in getting out of the car and walking to the side of the road was interpreted as drawing the fire away from his wife and was cited as evidence of his courage and devotion. The callousness and brutality of the the Chinese guerrillas were universally deplored. On the other hand, many Chinese felt it was foolishness in the extreme for the man who was 'number one' in the country to allow himself to be trapped on what was obviously a dangerous road in an unarmoured car with flags flying, and with an inadequate guard. Given the prevailing state of lawlessness, he was virtually inviting an attack. Moreover, the general Chinese view was that he should not have stepped out of the car and left his wife alone.[4]

In part, no doubt, these perceptions of the way in which Gurney died were coloured by differing views of his performance as High Commissioner. For many Malayans, his appearance and manner had epitomized the traditional colonial style of Government. Despite the heat and humidity, he had invariably worn a suit, and when travelling he had sported a felt hat and a walking stick. In public he had tended to be reserved and aloof, his sartorial elegance accentuating the correctness and formality of his manner. In many ways he had looked just like the typical colonial official depicted in communist propaganda cartoons–a fact which had not been lost on the many who held grievances against the colonial regime. But for a population which placed a very high value on personal communications, the most damning criticism of Gurney was that he had been a remote, almost unknown, figure. He had tended to run the administration from his office, and when he had toured the country it had been mainly to visit the major centres in order to attend official functions, meet the sultans, address Rotary Club gatherings, or dine with leading businessmen. Only very rarely had he ventured into the more remote parts of the country to speak to those who were directly involved in the fighting. Many Chinese felt that Gurney had disliked and distrusted them. Overall, then, Gurney had had only limited success in inspiring among Malayans a loyalty towards the Malayan Government, and even less success in generating confidence in himself personally.

Within the European community, Gurney had been able to command respect because he was seen as a dedicated and extremely able administrator. Certainly few doubted his intelligence, his integrity, or his ability to exercise authority. Moreover, most Europeans had recognized that Gurney was tied to his office, not just because of a personal reticence about meeting people, but also because he was weighed down with extensive administrative duties. There was also a good deal of sympathy for the fact that Gurney had had to deal with a Labour Government in London. However, even among Europeans, Gurney had come in for criticism. He had been unable to develop a rapport with his officials, and he was widely viewed as being incapable of appreciating that low pay, difficult living conditions, and the feeling that their advice went unheeded had perpetuated low morale within the administrative and technical services. The general lack of urgency which pervaded the Malayan bureaucracy at all levels was also attributed to his low-key style. Nor, in the opinion of many within the wider European community, had Gurney been able to strike the necessary balance between making people aware of the nature and urgency of the threat from the guerrillas and reassuring them that the Government could maintain security and safeguard the general population. The course of the Emergency had worked against him. There were those who detected that from the middle of 1951 he had been running out of energy and initiative and seemed unsure of how next to proceed in prosecuting the Government's cause.

Gurney's death opened up a series of questions. Should the Government's strategy for fighting communism be changed? If so, how? How should responsibility for running the Emergency be assigned among senior officials? What type of person should be appointed to replace Gurney? Final responsibility for making these decisions rested with Oliver Lyttelton, the Secretary of State for the Colonies in the newly elected Conservative Government. It was on him that the spotlight now fell.

Lyttelton's Visit

The new Secretary of State for the Colonies placed a high priority on Malaya and its problems. Despite many other departmental issues which required urgent attention, he decided to make a trip to Malaya to assess the situation for himself. Before he left, he met a delegation of British businessmen with interests in Malaya, and was fully briefed by Colonial Office officials. His conclusion was that the Malayan Government was 'on the way to losing control of the country and soon'.[5] Lyttelton, accompanied by J. J. Paskin, Assistant Under-Secretary, A. M. MacKintosh, his Private Secretary, and Hugh Fraser, his Parliamentary Private Secretary, travelled out to Malaya in early December 1951. He quickly made it clear that he wanted to meet people rather than see things. He was especially keen to talk to small groups of key figures from the various communities in Malaya and hear their private and confidential opinions on all aspects of the Emergency and related matters. He later recorded his conclusion: 'The situation was far worse than I had imagined: it was appalling.'[6]

Lyttelton was told in graphic detail of the many shortcomings of the Government's machinery. The rift between Kuala Lumpur and the rest of the country was readily apparent. Officials of the state governments and those in the field saw Federal officials in the capital as chair-bound perfectionists, who appeared to be too scared to venture into the countryside to witness the practical diffi- culties of putting policies into effect. Federal Government officials based in Kuala Lumpur saw the state governments as obstruction- ist and only too ready to distort or delay Federal policy in order to protect local privileges and interests. Both views contained more than a kernel of truth. The lack of clearly defined spheres of re- sponsibility at the senior levels within the Federal Administration was obvious, as were the personal rivalries which accentuated this problem. The low morale among all sectors of the Malayan Gov- ernment, the shortage of trained technical, professional, and ad- ministrative staff, the chaotic state of affairs within the police force and the Home Guard, and the lack of Chinese-speaking personnel at every level and in all departments were made abundantly clear to the Secretary of State.

On a number of the other key issues, such as the way different communities should be treated, the need for harsher measures to be employed against suspected communist sympathizers, and the future political development of the country, Lyttelton was bom- barded with conflicting advice. On some of these issues, he had already formed an opinion. For example, he showed great under- standing of the plight of ordinary Malayans when he told a Euro- pean delegation who wanted severe punishments for those who paid protection money, that 'at the point of the gun you would pay rather than be murdered...and so would I and you know it'.[7] With regard to the political evolution of Malaya, Lyttelton had already made his thinking fairly clear before he left London. In a statement in the House of Commons, he noted that the Government's aim was to help 'the colonial territories to attain self-Government within the British Commonwealth'[8] and that in order for this to take place as rapidly as possible the Government was seeking 'to build up in each territory the institutions which its circumstances require'.[9] With particular respect to Malaya, he made the point to a delega- tion of businessmen that due attention had to be devoted to Asian claims for political and social advancements, and that the Asian population of Malaya must be given some incentive to fight com- munism.[10]

On other issues, however, Lyttelton sought out as many view- points as he could find. After travelling around the country talking with numerous people, and discussing what he heard with the three advisers who were travelling with him, he put together a six-point programme of action. In a broadcast which went over the air at

8.00 p.m. on 11 December, Lyttelton set out his main conclusions.[11] First, there would be overall direction of civil and military forces; secondly, the police would be reorganized and retrained; thirdly, there would be compulsory primary education so as to make it clear to everyone what they were fighting for; fourthly, a high measure of protection for the resettlement areas would be quickly achieved; fifthly, the Home Guard would be reorganized and larger numbers of Chinese would be enlisted, and sixthly, the great strain under which the Civil Service suffered would be tackled. He also promised armoured vehicles for the police and others who required them, an increase in the number of Malay- and Chinese-speaking Government officers, more appropriate weapons for planters and tin miners, and a review of the propaganda campaign. In a particularly intriguing passage, he made the point that 'We have to see that our philosophy opens up to the people of Malaya the prospect of a finer and freer life than that which our enemies are trying to instil.' Having set down the framework of a policy, Lyttelton now had to put in place the people and the administrative structure to execute his policy.

Making the personnel changes which Lyttelton saw as necessary was not as difficult as it might have been. Sir William Jenkin, Director of Intelligence, had submitted his resignation shortly after Gurney's death. General Sir Harold Briggs, who was neither in good health nor good spirits, had fulfilled his terms of contract and was anxious to leave.[12] He was persuaded to stay on until the beginning of December in order to brief Lyttelton personally, after which he departed for his home in Cyprus. Particularly fortunate from Lyttelton's point of view was the tendering of the resignation of Colonel W. N. Gray, the Commissioner of Police. This was hastily accepted. Gray quickly and quietly left the country without a word of explanation, making his departure almost as controversial as his time in office.[13] Moreover, Lyttelton felt that M. V. del Tufo, who had been Chief Secretary and had become Officer Administering the Government after Gurney's death, should be passed over for a top administrative position and, as a consequence, del Tufo decided to retire. In terms of the senior personnel, then, the new Secretary of State could start almost from scratch.

The key decision, of course, centred on the person to replace Gurney, and the powers he should be given. This was not an issue new to the Colonial Office. For instance, in late 1949, after he had made a tour of Hong Kong, Singapore, and the Federation of Malaya, the then Labour Parliamentary Under-Secretary of State for the

Colonies, David Rees-Williams, had made a strong case that the old conception of the Governor had gone with the changing situation and that what was needed was a person who had 'the time and the personality to get around among people, to hear different points of view, to discuss matters and so on'. In particular, although he did recognize that his position was constrained by his administrative responsibilities, Rees-Williams was critical of Gurney for not making enough outside contacts. For this reason he proposed that the duties of a Governor be divided into two: a Governor 'and in addition a Lieutenant Governor or Chief Secretary who [would] do the hard slogging administrative work'.[14] Undoubtedly, senior Colonial Office officials discussed such a division of responsibility with Lyttelton before he left for Malaya.

Lyttelton also found himself strongly advised by many groups to appoint a 'Supremo' or 'strong man'. One European woman stated that 'To us who are getting very disheartened the appointment of one strong man who would be prepared to give orders and see them carried out would be like a breath of fresh air as we battle with vaporous mists.'[15] A group of businessmen told Lyttelton they had in mind 'someone like Alexander', while a division of the UMNO sent a telegram to London urging that Earl Mountbatten be sent out to Malaya as Supremo.[16] However, perhaps the most influential recommendation, and one which tied in with the arguments of Rees-Williams, came from Briggs. As Director of Operations he had become frustrated and disillusioned by the lack of authority to deal with people like Gray, the Commissioner of Police, or the various military commanders. In his final assessment of the situation in Malaya, Briggs put forward four possible methods of conducting the campaign against the guerrillas. The fourth alternative he outlined, and clearly the one he himself favoured, argued for the appointment as High Commissioner and Commander-in-Chief of 'a serving or retired military leader of proved capacity, experience and national fame, e.g. Lord Alanbrook, Lord Ismay or Sir Archibald Nye, to direct the campaign in all its aspects'.[17] Briggs went on to suggest that this person should have complete executive authority over all services, civil and military, that he would need a military staff with a senior officer in charge, and a senior civil servant to relieve him of his day-to-day duties in civil administration. The first could be Deputy Director of Operations, the second Deputy High Commissioner.[18]

By the end of his tour in Malaya, Lyttelton had come to the conclusion that Briggs's advice should be followed. On his return to

London he reported to the Cabinet on the need to appoint a general as High Commissioner and Director of Operations, and the search for a suitable candidate began. After a number of senior military figures declined the position, Lieutenant-General Sir Gerald Templer, at that time General Officer Commanding-in-Chief Eastern Command, was chosen. On 10 January 1952, he was flown to Canada to be vetted by the Prime Minister, Sir Winston Churchill, who was in Ottawa presiding over a discussion of Commonwealth problems. Having decided that, indeed, Templer was the man for the job, Churchill told him to 'ask for power, go on asking for it and then never use it'.[19] This exhortation was probably unnecessary for, from the beginning, Templer was armed with some of the most comprehensive powers ever given a British colonial official.

Templer's New Broom

Templer's arrival in Malaya, in early February 1952, was greeted with mixed feelings. Although officially occupying a civilian position, he seemed to be most at home in his general's uniform. Those looking for evidence that 'firm action' was to be taken to deal with the Emergency welcomed this as a symbol of Templer's willingness to put the military in the driver's seat. Others, including Malcolm MacDonald and the editors of the *Straits Times*, were not happy with the appointment of a general, and a general with no previous experience of Malaya at that.[20] But of those with some understanding of the process by which Templer was appointed, essentially the European community and the Malayan élite, most were very impressed that here was a cabinet appointee, not just someone chosen by the Colonial Office, who had been interviewed and personally approved by Churchill himself. Equally important was the directive which Templer brought with him. It was widely believed to have emanated from the Prime Minister, and Templer gave it great prominence at his installation ceremony on 21 February.

The directive was, indeed, a significant document. It had originated in the depths of the Colonial Office as a rather rambling and lengthy text which repeated verbatim pertinent parts of the Federation Agreement and which stated in somewhat hopeful terms what was to be done for Malaya. In the hands of senior Colonial Office officials, this draft was severely pruned down to nine relatively short paragraphs. Officials in the War Office and the Prime Minister's Office were consulted as was Templer himself, yet despite the necessary compromises the directive became a surprisingly straightforward and forceful document.

Overall, the officials 'attempted to deal with the political matters in the first half of the document and to lead up to the necessity for forceful action to restore law and order in the second part of the document'.[21] Hence, the directive's first sentence stated: 'The policy of Her Majesty's Government in Great Britain is that Malaya should in due course become a fully self-governing nation.'[22] It then held out promises to each of the major communities in turn. For the Chinese and Indians, it was stated: 'To achieve a united Malayan nation there must be a common form of citizenship for all who regard the Federation or any part of it as their home and the object of their loyalty.' For the Malays, the point was made that they 'must be encouraged and assisted to play a full part in the economic life of the country so that the present uneven economic balance may be redressed'. And for the British, the directive contained the view that they had 'a mission to fulfil in the achievement of these objectives and that even after self-Government has been attained the British in Malaya will have a worthy and continuing part to play'. Yet while self-Government was to be the ultimate aim, it was also made clear that defeating 'communist terrorism' was to be Templer's 'primary task'. In order to achieve this, he was given the power to 'assume complete operational command over all the Armed Forces assigned to operations in the Federation' and 'to issue operational orders to their commanders without reference to the Commander-in-Chief, Far East'. The directive ended with the assurance that 'Her Majesty's Government will not lay aside their responsibilities in Malaya until they are satisfied that communist terrorism has been defeated and that the partnership of all communities which alone can lead to true and stable self-Government has been established.'[23]

Templer himself considered the directive to be crucial. Not long after he arrived he issued a General Circular to all Federal administrators which contained the directive and which stated that it was 'the duty of every officer to familiarise himself with its terms, and to work wholeheartedly for its fulfilment'.[24] In a similar vein, he told the Legislative Council that the directive was not just for him: 'I venture to suggest it is ours—yours and mine.'[25] Templer quoted from the directive on many occasions and, along with the statement that Lyttelton had broadcast to Malaya, it became the touchstone for his actions and his guide to policy-making.

Templer did not just bring with him new policy guidelines. He also brought new people to fill the top positions. Perhaps the most important appointment was that of Donald MacGillivray as Deputy High Commissioner. MacGillivray, who was relatively young at forty-five, had served in East Africa and Palestine and had been appointed Chief Secretary, Jamaica, in 1947. He was considered one of the ablest administrators in the Colonial Administrative Service. As Deputy High Commissioner, his task was to relieve Templer of many of the administrative chores which had so burdened Gurney. For example, he took over the day-to-day running of the Administration and, until a speaker was appointed in September 1953, presided over meetings of the Federal Legislative Council. Once MacGillivray had settled in, mastered the complexities of Malayan politics, and pulled together the strings of the Administration, he proved of invaluable help in shielding Templer from involvement in extraneous, minor, and time-consuming problems. Indeed, it was one of MacGillivray's major responsibilities to decide which matters should be referred to the High Commissioner for consideration. Fortunately for them both, the two got along very well and Templer had every confidence in MacGillivray's judgement. The establishment of the position of Deputy High Commissioner also abolished the bottleneck which had been created by the excessive responsibilities placed on the Chief Secretary.

The position of Deputy High Commissioner was, however, not created without some controversy. The Rulers and senior Malay politicians felt that a Malay should have been appointed to fill the post, or at the very least it should have been someone with a knowledge of Malaya.[26] There was also some sense of frustration among members of the MCS because they were being passed over for the top positions in the Malayan Government. Once it was realized, however, that Lyttelton had made up his mind and MacGillivray was his choice, the new Deputy High Commissioner was readily accepted by most with whom he had to work. Certainly, there was no repetition of the protests which had accompanied the installations of Gent and Gurney.

MacGillivray's counterpart in operational matters was General Sir Robert Lockhart, the Deputy Director of Operations. Not only did Lockhart have good military credentials, he had considerable experience with civil departments. For example, he had been Governor of the North West Frontier Province for the difficult period of the referendum, and was said by Field Marshal Sir William Slim, Chief of the General Staff, to have handled this lively political-military job admirably.[27] In this case, too, he and Templer got on reasonably well. Similarly, both Templer and Lockhart were on friendly terms with the GOC Malaya, first Major-General R. W. Urquhart, and later Major-General Sir Hugh Stockwell. Lyttelton was able to second as Commissioner of Police for one year A. E. Young, the Commissioner of Police for the City of London. He proved a great tonic for a police force whose morale was very low. He travelled extensively, saw a large number of people, and according to one of his contemporaries in the force, not only exuded confidence but also managed to inspire everyone around him with that confidence.[28] In the process, he became firm friends with Templer and greatly contributed to the generally harmonious relations which prevailed among senior officials.

Yet, during the first few months after his arrival it was not so much the Government's policies, nor the new team which was assembled to implement these policies, but Templer's personal style which attracted people's attention. A wiry, neat figure, Templer infused his every action with a seemingly boundless fund of nervous energy. He spoke directly and forcefully with a staccato brevity which emphasized the rasp of authority in his voice and his clear expectation that his orders would be promptly obeyed. He did everything with a military briskness and a sense of purpose: an explosive character, he neither spared himself nor allowed others to slacken from the tremendous pace he set.

Templer's military background was rather more diverse than might have been expected. In 1916, at the age of eighteen, he left the Royal Military College, Sandhurst, and was commissioned as a second lieutenant in the Royal Irish Fusiliers. He served on the European front, and from 1919 to 1921 fought against the Red Army in Persia and Mesopotamia. In the late 1930s, he experienced guerrilla warfare when he served in Palestine. His progress through the ranks was swift. In 1942, he was appointed a lieutenant-general, the youngest then in the British Army, and saw fighting in a number of arenas. However, it was his post-War appointments which were to stand Templer in particularly good stead. From May 1945 to April 1946, he was Director of Civil Affairs and Military Government for an area which included Belgium, a large part of Western Germany, and a small part of Holland. During a chaotic summer and a cold European winter, Templer was responsible for restoring a semblance of order to a vast area hit by the ravages of war. Above all, he had to ensure that as many people as possible were provided with the basic necessities of food, fuel, and housing. This was a tremendous task which he carried out with verve and efficiency.

It was also an experience which acquainted him with the practical problems of government and the importance of providing for the basic welfare of all individuals within a community. Later he became Director of Intelligence at the War Office and then Vice-Chief of the Imperial General Staff. These two posts gave him an appreciation of the importance of intelligence and how it could be effectively used, and a general understanding of how to get things done in the corridors of power. It was out of this set of experiences that Templer was able to establish basic principles from which to approach his new role as High Commissioner and Director of Operations.

Templer's reputation for getting things done and for not suffering fools gladly circulated within Malaya well before his arrival. It was said that he was impatient and determined and that he was liable to 'blow up' if he came across 'any inefficiency or dishonesty'.[29] It was rumoured, for example, that when he was Director of Civil Affairs and Military Government in Germany he had sent army clerks in Brussels, who had doubted the stories concerning the atrocities in the concentration camps, to the Bergen-Belsen camp to bury the corpses.[30] Once Templer arrived in Malaya it became clear that his reputation was well founded. In private conversations he was direct and his language was laced with invectives. At public meetings he spoke with a sharp, incisive voice, in a crisp forthright manner, echoing the traditions of the parade ground. After Templer's first address to the Federal Legislative Council, Dato Onn is reported to have stated that 'what he [Templer] was really saying was: "If anyone gets in my way he'll be trod on"'. Onn noted that this approach is 'exactly what we need'.[31]

One of Templer's primary concerns was to inject some urgency and energy into the Civil Service whose morale he himself later described as being 'in the gutter'.[32] Immediately after he arrived in Malaya, he introduced himself and outlined some of his preliminary views in a series of meetings with officials. For example, on the morning of 9 February, his first Saturday in Kuala Lumpur, he talked to all the Division One officers. It was a chance, as he said, for them to size him up. He talked about his interview with the Prime Minister and about the importance of the task that faced them, he invited ideas from anybody, read out the directive, and told them of his basic belief about putting policy into effect. He suggested that things might get worse before they got better but he accepted full responsibility for the ultimate outcome because he, for the first time, had the necessary powers. He also made it very clear what he expected of them. He wanted an end to red tape and buck passing. He told them that if mistakes were made he might 'do something very rude to the individual concerned' but that there would be no malice in his action. However, he went on, 'If someone below me fails to take action because he has not got the guts to take it, then I will take far more serious action against him; which is by no means the "all-clear" to any form of reckless, stupid or unconsidered action.'[33]

Yet, in attempting to shake the Administration out of its despondency, Templer did not forget that part of the problem lay in the poor conditions under which the civil servants had to work. Thus along with his refusal to accommodate all the normal civil service niceties and his willingness to roll heads when and where necessary, he did what he could to improve housing, increase pay, and generally upgrade the terms and conditions of employment within the Civil Service.[34] Moreover, he quickly realized that he could not get along without the Administration and to those who met his exacting standards he could be most friendly, co-operative, and helpful. He was also willing to change his mind and his plans quite radically if circumstances demanded it or if someone was able to convince him that change was needed.[35] Hence, while he ruffled a lot of feathers, he was widely respected, and there can be no doubt that the *Straits Times* was correct when it noted later: 'He invigorated the administration from the day he arrived.'[36]

News that Templer took his new role very seriously quickly spread beyond the Civil Service. It was duly noted that the new High Commissioner was setting a hectic pace: the lights in King's House, his official residence, were on well into the early hours of morning. He pointed out to a group of Europeans that communists did not go to parties or take afternoons off to play golf. A rumour circulated that one unfortunate official in a fairly remote corner of the Federation had been put on the next boat home after Templer had showed up on an unannounced visit and found him on the local golf course. Templer also had an armed guard wherever he went and had a wire fence put up around the grounds of King's House. Both were considered to be sensible, elementary precautions. It was generally felt that he was someone who meant business.

From the point of view of the mass of the population, what ultimately proved to be most impressive about Templer was his willingness to go out into the country, meet the ordinary people, and discuss their problems with them. He made his intentions clear on his arrival: 'I want to get to know people of all communities and classes so that I may better understand their thoughts and difficulties and hopes and so be better able to help them.'[37] By the beginning of June, he had visited every state in Malaya. In the first twelve months in office, he made forty-five tours. During his twenty-eight months as High Commissioner, he completed 122 tours of kampongs, New Villages, labour lines, mines, estates, and units of the security forces. Most of these tours lasted two or three days. Unlike Gurney, Templer tended to concentrate on the rural communities in the main arenas of the fight against communism. Often he was accompanied by his wife and between them they could 'blitz' an area. In all, he spent a third of his time away from his official residence. Indeed, Templer became famous for his surprise visits to schools, police posts, army units, shops, and coffee houses. Everyone was kept on their toes by the possibility of an appearance by the High Commissioner, and generally he was able to see things as they were rather than after careful preparation, prompted by a warning that His Excellency was on his way.

Templer's tours were impressive events. He was usually dressed in his army uniform and travelled in an armoured car or Churchill bullet-proof car. His cavalcade always included a strong army escort and made an impressive sight which was long remembered with awe by the people in the communities he visited. When he travelled by train on the newly reconstructed East Coast railway, there was a pilot train and the main armoured train followed by two armoured vehicles on rails. He was accompanied by a platoon of soldiers and armed railway guards. Overhead, an Auster aircraft patrolled the line ahead.[38] This show of strength was clearly not lost on Malayans. For example, Lucian Pye reports that most of the surrendered Chinese communists he interviewed in late 1952 'felt that generals played a decisive role at the highest level of politics'. He also makes the point that they assumed that 'skill in military affairs and the ability to command large numbers of men were valid indications of skill in political affairs'.[39] At each kampong or New Village (as the resettlement centres became known) he visited, he would inspect the Home Guard, the local police post, the school, and other features of note, and then gather the village leaders and other inhabitants under a tree, and through an interpreter give them a pep talk. He dished out compliments or criticisms depending on the circumstances. He would invite village leaders to state their grouses and try to clear up any minor points on the spot. After each of his tours, minutes would be sent out to state and district officials demanding action or information about grievances that had been aired or projects and people he had seen. At the bottom of each minute Templer would fill in the number of days the recipient had in which to remedy a problem and report back to him. Woe betide anyone who failed to meet this deadline.

Those who did not meet Templer personally heard about him through the media. He provided excellent copy and although, as he stated after leaving Malaya, he had always had 'a personal antipathy for the communications media', he enjoyed, as two very critical observers stated at the time, 'an excellent press'.[40] He met regularly with reporters and editors and took them along on his trips. They were able to record his 'tongue-lashing a town or village or order-ing on the spot electric lights or water to the pained surprise of the official responsible'.[41] His other activities were also well publicized, and he became a major topic of conversation, rivalling even the fluctuating price of rubber. Indeed, it would have been difficult not to know of his commanding presence in the Federation.

Underpinning all Templer's actions was his personal philos-ophy about how to conduct the counter-guerrilla campaign. Two aspects of this philosophy stood out. First, emphasizing a point originally made by Briggs, Templer believed that it was wrong to separate the peacetime activities of the Government from the Emerg-ency activities. He argued forcefully that 'you cannot divorce them unless you admit that the military side is the main thing which matters in the Emergency and that must be wrong–absolutely wrong'.[42] He was most insistent that all departments, no matter how far removed from the guerrilla war they thought themselves to be, had to be made to realize that the Emergency was their first concern. For Templer, the answer to defeating the communist guer-rillas lay in cultural, political, economic, and spiritual factors: the campaign as he envisaged it was to be all out and on all fronts.

Secondly, Templer considered the guerrilla war to be a battle for the hearts and minds of Malaya's population. The idea of the fight against communism being a battle for men's minds was asso-ciated with the Cold War, and it was obvious that Templer thought of Malaya as one of the key theatres in the confrontation with the Russians. However, it was also an approach which had gained cur-rency within Malaya, especially among those who knew the rural Chinese population, and it obviously struck a responsive chord in Templer when it was raised during his initial briefings. Just as im-portantly, it echoed a key part of Lyttelton's broadcast to Malayans. Within a very short time of his arrival in the region, Templer made the point that he could win the Emergency if he could get two-thirds of the people on his side. The way this was to be done, he later elaborated, was by persuading the people 'that there is another and far preferable way of life and system of beliefs than that expressed in the rule of force and the law of the jungle. This way of life is not the American way of life. It is not the British way of life. It must be the Malayan way of life.'[43] And, equally important, people were to be well treated and their grievances heard and when possible addressed. Templer's evident concern with the welfare of the general population marked a significant change in the direction of the Government's policy, one which was widely welcomed by all sections of Malayan society.

MCP Directives

During 1951, the MCP leadership came under considerable pressure to rethink its increasing emphasis on the use of violence and intimidation. First, the Government's resettlement policy was having a major impact on the relationship between the Min Yuen workers and the rural Chinese population. Some changes needed to be made in order to accommodate the new situation.[44] Secondly, the Government's propaganda effort was beginning to make a mark. In particular, the criticisms made by Lam Swee, an SEP who had formerly been a high-ranking member of the MCP, seem to have been very effective. He toured the resettlement centres giving speeches, and his pamphlet, *My Accusation*, was published by the Information Department in 1951 and given wide circulation. The MCP leaders were apparently especially stung by the charge that the liberation war was merely 'terrorism created by a few bandits'.[45] Thirdly, there were indications that the MCP leadership was being advised by international communist circles to study 'the rich experience of the Communist Party of China' and to modify their emphasis on a military solution.[46] Finally, although the guerrillas were not losing the war, there was no clear sign that victory was on the immediate horizon. As a result, MCP policy was becoming the target of internal and divisive criticism. Siew Lau, one of the chief critics of the Central Committee's policy, was eventually silenced by being executed, an act which in itself only further undermined morale and hastened the process of policy re-examination.

Meeting in late September and early October 1951, the Central Committee approved seven directives which were then issued to the Party. The directives, which ran to nearly 100 pages when translated into English, covered not just high strategy but also many aspects of the day-to-day life of members of the Party, the MRLA, and the various support organizations.[47] However, it was the first two directives, entitled respectively 'The Party's Achievements and Mistakes' and 'Struggle for Greater Victories in War', which provided the keys to understanding the shift in policy that was planned.

The first directive detailed the failures of the Party and of the Central Committee. It was admitted that mistakes had been made which amounted to 'left deviation'. These included establishing military bases before the supply problem had been solved, disregarding the interests of the masses by inflicting more harm on the local population than on the Government and its officials, and failing to distinguish between the 'big national bourgeoisie', who were implacably opposed to communism, and the 'medium national bourgeoisie', who were often fence-sitters and who could be won over to a broadly based united front.

The second directive set out the main lines of the new policy, and the remaining five directives fleshed out the details. The first of the seven urgent tasks of the Party was stated to be 'to expand and consolidate the mass organizations', particularly in the rural areas. In all circumstances, the measures used to continue the 'mass struggles against the enemy' had to meet the criterion that they 'should appear to be reasonable in the eyes of the masses'. The long-term aim of the policy was to develop a mass movement which had gone through 'organisational mobilization, ideological instruction' and had 'passed through the crucible of revolutionary training'. The primary emphasis, then, was to be placed on the work of the Min Yuen with the MRLA giving it support when necessary: a reversal of previous roles. The need to 'strive to develop the armed struggle' was still included as one of the seven urgent tasks for all Party comrades, but it had been relegated to second place. Where it was not needed to aid the Min Yuen, the MRLA was to be withdrawn to deep jungle to be retrained and held in reserve—ready for the time when the necessary popular base had been established and the armed struggle could be restored to centre stage.[48]

In order to avoid alienating possible sympathizers, specific instructions were given to cease certain activities. There was to be no more confiscation and burning of registration cards, slashing of rubber trees and damaging of tin mines, burning of labour barracks on British-owned estates, burning of public service vehicles, or sabotaging of other public services such as water supplies, electricity lines, or health care facilities. Moreover, nuisance raids and activities which might give an indication to the security forces as to where the Min Yuen were operating, were to be stopped.

Other instructions gave indications as to how the Party's base of support might be expanded. Malays and Indians were to be more actively recruited and Chinese cadres were ordered to cease treating them as inferiors; this was considered a form of 'nationalist deviation'. All elements of the national bourgeoisie, up to and including the 'medium national bourgeoisie', were to be won over where possible. To this end it was decreed that demands for subscriptions should be within the competence of the individual to pay, that the demands made by workers and tappers on small and medium estates had been extreme and that in the future the Party must hold the balance evenly between owners and tappers, and that tapping contractors and shareholders in bus companies could be sympathizers and should be treated as such, unless there was convincing evidence otherwise. Education and political activity were to be stepped up in the larger towns. Such organizations as the existing legal unions, the Home Guard, the Malay Regiment, the Civil Service, and the Malayan Chinese Association were to be penetrated and where possible the members won over. Where this was not possible the particular branch of the operation was to be rendered ineffective as an opponent of the Party.

Hence, while the MCP was certainly not abandoning the armed struggle, the 1951 directives introduced a decided shift in policy. The MRLA was to continue organizing battles, laying ambushes, and capturing arms, but this was to be done only when the military advantages accruing to the cause did not produce any unfavourable political and economic repercussions on the general public. In other words, the political and military considerations were given equal weight and the guerrilla war was to be conducted not just as a military campaign but as a struggle to win the support of the mass of the population.

Summary

The events of 1951 brought about a change in tack for both sides in the Emergency. Each came to the conclusion that its approach needed to be broadened, that heavy reliance on the use of violence and intimidation was counter-productive. On the Government's side, events eased the shift in policy. The murder of the High Commissioner, the advent of a new Government in London, and the resignations of most of the top officials in Kuala Lumpur allowed for a fairly wide-ranging review of the Government's position. In these circumstances, views which had been gaining momentum, within both the Colonial Office and Malaya, were given a good airing. Many of these ideas were incorporated into the broadcast to the country that was made by the new Secretary of State for the Colonies during his tour of Malaya, and became central to the policies of General Sir Gerald Templer when he was appointed High Commissioner and Director of Operations. On the MCP's side, the change in policy which was brought about by the issuing of the directives in September/October of 1951 was the result of months of internal debate and dissension. The new policy, of giving equal weight to the political and the military activities of the Party, was clearly designed to breathe new life into a flagging campaign.

While the long-term consequences of both the MCP and the Government's changes in policy were slow to emerge, one new ingredient manifested itself almost at once. From the time he set foot in Malaya, Templer was able to stamp his personality on the Emergency. He was, of course, aided in this by the almost complete turnover of senior personnel in the Malayan Government, as well as by the organizational changes which allowed him to hand over the administrative chores to his deputy and get out and meet people. He was able to inject urgency and energy into the Government's campaign and, perhaps surprisingly given his military background, to press for the fight against guerrillas to be fought on all fronts. Indeed, it may be considered ironic that it was the professional soldier rather than the professional administrator who grasped immediately that circumstances required the activities of the Government to be broadened and that the population had to be won over, not intimidated, if the guerrilla war was to be successfully prosecuted. In many ways, Templer acted more like a politician running hard for a second term in office than a general running a colony.

Hence, the MCP directives and the changes in policy and style that Templer introduced set the stage for the next three years of the Emergency. Both sides increasingly and with mixed success began to emphasize the need to gain the allegiance of the population. The battle for the hearts and minds of the people of Malaya was about to begin.

1. The most complete account of the ambush is to be found in Anthony Short, *The Communist Insurrection in Malaya 1948-1960* (London: Frederick Muller, 1975), pp. 303-5.

2. Hugh Fraser (Parliamentary Secretary to the Secretary of State for the Colonies), 'Papers on the Malayan Emergency', CO 1022/22. See also John Weldon Humphrey, 'Population Resettlement in Malaya' (Ph.D. dissertation, Northwestern University, 1971), pp. 121-3; Short, *The Communist Insurrection*, pp. 305-6; *Daily Telegraph*, 31 October 1951, and *The Times* (London), 1 November 1951.

3. See Short, *The Communist Insurrection*, p. 305, and 'Record of the Conference with the Mentri Mentri Besar, Resident Commissioner and the British Advisers on the Intensification of the Emergency Effort', CO 1022/148.

4. This point was first put to the author by C. C. Too in an interview, 30 January 1973, and later confirmed by other Malaysians.

5. See Viscount Chandos (Oliver Lyttelton), *The Memoirs of Lord Chandos* (London: Bodley Head, 1962), p. 362.

6. Ibid., p. 336. Papers dealing with Lyttelton's visit to Malaya may be found in P/PM1, Chief Secretary 438/51 (ANM).

7. Chandos, *Memoirs*, p. 367.

8. Secretary of State for the Colonies to the Prime Minister, 7 November 1951, CO 537/6696.

9. The statement of the Secretary of State for the Colonies in the House of Commons on 14 November 1951, CO 537/6696. He was specifically encouraged in this view of Malaya's future by both the Colonial Office and the Foreign Office. See CO 537/7263.

10. Draft memorandum of a meeting with the Secretary of State for the Colonies, 15 November 1951, CO 1022/39.

11. See P/PM1, Chief Secretary 438/W/51 (ANM). Progress on the points raised in the broadcast had to be detailed in monthly reports which the Malayan Government submitted to the Colonial Office.

12. Briggs's term of service was originally due to expire on 3 April 1951 but he had agreed to continue to the end of November. CO 537/7267.

13. The Colonial Office later acknowledged this piece of good fortune by noting that 'if Gray had not offered his resignation these plans might have been much more difficult since I am not aware of any grounds on which he could have been compelled to retire'. Secretary of State for the Colonies to the OAG, Federation of Malaya, 2 February 1952, High Commissioner Telegrams (ANM). See also Noel Barber, *The War of the Running Dogs: The Malayan Emergency, 1948-1960* (London: Fontana, 1972), p. 131.

14. See 'Report on a Short Tour of Hong Kong, Singapore and the Federation of Malaya October-November 1949'; 'Notes on a Conversation with Mr Rees-Williams on 18th November and Subsequent Days, O. H. Morris, 21 November 1949', and 'Notes on a Meeting with Mr Rees-Williams on Wednesday December 7, 1949', in CO 537/4870. Rees-Williams had a good understanding of Malaya having lived there before the Second World War.

15. Letter from an unknown European woman in Malaya to Viscountess Davidson enclosed with Viscountess Davidson to Lyttelton, 1 November 1951, CO 1022/1.

16. 'Memorandum of the Meeting with the Secretary of State for the Colonies, November 15, 1951', CO 1022/39, and UMNO, Tangkak division, to the Prime Minister, n.d., P/PESU 2 (ANM).

17. 'The Situation in the Federation of Malaya from the Point of View of the

Director of Operations, November 26, 1951', CO 537/7263.

18. Ibid. A pencilled note by a Colonial Office officer indicated that he also favoured this approach if the right man could be obtained. Both the European planting group and the MCA expressed their concern that Briggs had not been given the powers he needed. See *The Planter* 28 (December 1951), pp. 514-15, and the Tan Cheng Lock Papers, Item 169(i) (ANM).

19. Lord Moran, *Churchill: The Struggle for Survival 1940-1965* (Boston: Houghton Mifflin, 1966), p. 387, and John Cloake, *Templer Tiger of Malaya: The Life and Times of Field Marshal Sir Gerald Templer* (London: Harrap, 1985), pp. 203-6. See also *Time*, 15 December 1952, p. 24.

20. Short, *The Communist Insurrection*, p. 337.

21. See Minute by J. J. Paskin, 30 January 1952, CO 1022/102. This file contains the various drafts of the directive and the minutes which debate its exact wording.

22. It was at Templer's suggestion that the words 'in due course' were inserted by Lyttelton over the objection of the Permanent Under-Secretary. See CO 1022/102.

23. The text of the directive may be found in CO 1022/102; Victor Purcell, *Malaya: Communist or Free?* (London: Gollancz, 1954), pp. 86-7, and 'War in Malaya', *British Survey*, Main Series No. 39 (June 1952), appendix.

24. General Circular No. 4 of 1952 in P/PM1, Secretary to Government Y5 (ANM). The Information Services also put together a leaflet with a picture of Templer in his general's uniform on the front and the directive on the back. It was given wide distribution. In the original of any official correspondence, quotations from the directive were always underlined in red. See, for example, General Circular No. 5 of 1952, P/PM1, Chief Secretary 23/1 (ANM).

25. 19 March 1952, Leong Yew Koh Papers SP3/1/52 (ANM).

26. Chandos, *Memoirs*, p. 373.

27. Slim to Secretary of State for the Colonies, 24 July 1951, CO 537/7267.

28. Sir Kerr Bovell, mss. Brit Emp S 397 (Rhodes House Library).

29. See *Straits Times*, 19 January 1952; the observations of Captain Cyril Falls in a BBC overseas broadcast over Radio Malaya, 22 January 1952, and *The Observer* (London), 20 January 1952.

30. Humphrey, 'Population Resettlement', p. 125.

31. Transcript of 'War of the Running Dogs', Anglia Television, ITV (UK), 9 July 1974.

32. Ibid.

33. Because a mangled version appeared in the press, this portion of his speech was eventually circulated to all Administrative Officers throughout the Federation. See the verbatim record of Templer's speech to Division One officers, 9 February 1952, and the High Commissioner to all Mentri Mentri Besar, 20 February 1952, both in P/PM1, Secretary to Government Y5 (ANM).

34. An example of the 'head-rolling' stories which circulated may be found in *Time*, 15 December 1952, p. 26. Templer is reported to have told the Civil Service that 'If you don't make a decision and it's a mistake you'll be put on the next boat; if you make a decision and it happens to be a mistake you'll be put on the next boat, but somebody'll be there to see you off.'

35. W. C. S. Corry, tape and transcript of an interview, mss. Ind Ocn S 215 (Rhodes House Library).

36. *Straits Times*, 1 January 1954.

37. Government of the Federation of Malaya, Federal Government Press State-

ment, 7 February 1952, Department of Information, Kuala Lumpur.

38. 'Report by D. S. Armstrong, Canadian Trade Commission in Singapore, on a weekend with Templer', 17 July 1953, 18-9-36, Archives of the Department of External Affairs, Canada. See also Cloake, *Templer Tiger of Malaya*, p. 215.

39. Lucian Pye, *Guerrilla Communism in Malaya: Its Social and Political Meaning* (Princeton, NJ: Princeton University Press), p. 188.

40. Templer's comment comes from the BBC broadcast 'I remember', 12 December 1970, and the comments of the two critical observers are from 'Report on a visit to Malaya from 20 August-20 September 1952 at the invitation of the MCA by Purcell and Carnell', Tan Cheng Lock Papers TCL/VI/1, p. 125 (ISEAS).

41. *Malay Mail*, 30 July 1960.

42. Verbatim record of Templer's speech to Division One officers, 9 February 1952, P/PM1, Secretary to Government Y5 (ANM).

43. See *Proceedings of the Federal Legislative Council*, 5th Session, 19 March 1952. See also 'War in Malaya', *British Survey*, p. 15.

44. 'Weekly Intelligence Summary', No. 110, CO 1022/187.

45. See translation of a cyclostyled document entitled 'Workers express', Issue No. 6, 12 December 1951, CO 1022/249.

46. See Short, *The Communist Insurrection*, pp. 317-18; 'Monthly Emergency and Political Reports', No. 47, 15 November-15 December 1953, FO 371/111854, and captured MCP documents, CO 1022/187.

47. A copy and a precis of the directive as well as correspondence and other material may all be found in CO 1022/187.

48. The quotations and much of the rest of this and succeeding paragraphs are based on English translations and analyses of captured MCP documents to be found in CO 1022/157.

6
Beginning the Battle for the Hearts and Minds

BEGINNING in early 1952, the Malayan Government's policy was to put in place the major elements of what came to be known as the 'hearts and minds approach'. The aim was to persuade the people of Malaya to abandon the MCP by threatening to punish those who aided the guerrillas and, at the same time, holding out to those who supported the Government the promise of greater security and a better social, economic, and political environment than the communists could offer. It was felt that once the guerrillas were isolated from their base of support within the population, they would become easy prey for the security forces.

The Government was fortunate in pursuing this policy against a backdrop of a much reduced military threat from the guerrillas. As the September–October 1951 directives were disseminated throughout the Party, guerrilla-instigated incidents dropped dramatically from over 6,000 in 1951 to 3,700 in 1952 and 1,200 in 1953.[1] Not knowing about the directives until they were made public in December 1952, people generally credited the lull in activities to Sir Gerald Templer's new broom. Indeed, whereas at the end of 1951 the Government had been on the defensive and the MCP clearly in the ascendancy, by the end of 1952 the reduced number of incidents was broadly taken to mean that the positions were beginning to be reversed.

For the Government, despite their apparent success, progress was slow. It proved to be exceedingly difficult to change entrenched attitudes and habits, especially within the Administration and the security forces. Lack of trained manpower in virtually every aspect of the Administration, as well as the recession of 1953-4, undermined the full implementation of policies geared to severing the links between the people and the guerrillas. For the MCP, their change in strategy increased the burden on the Min Yuen and other organizations which worked among the various communities. The expansion of the organizational infrastructure that was necessary in order to undertake more political activity, confronted numerous difficulties, and the reduction in military activities did not immediately produce the expected benefits. Even once modifications were made to the 1951 policy, the MCP found it hard to regain the initiative. For the general population, although still wary of both the guerrillas and the security forces, the reduced intensity of the 'shooting war' was welcome. Yet within many of the resettlement centres, or 'New Villages' as Templer renamed them, fear was still endemic, and villagers continued to be harassed from all sides.

Retraining, Reorganization, and Expansion

In his broadcast to Malayans, Oliver Lyttelton had established as a priority the reorganization and retraining of the police and Home Guard. Templer immediately set about this task and simultaneously initiated a major expansion of the administrative arm of the Government to deliver the social services he saw as necessary to wean the people from the guerrillas.

The police force was in a particularly sad state. Hugh Fraser, Lyttelton's Parliamentary Private Secretary, who stayed on in Malaya after the Colonial Secretary's departure in order to prepare a detailed survey of the situation, reported that the longer he remained in Malaya, the less he was impressed by the morale and efficiency of the police. He noted that although there were some outstanding senior men in the force, for example, the Chief Police Officer (CPO) Kelantan ('of all places to put a good man'), the general level of leadership for such a large force was far too low. Fraser was particularly critical of the special constables, whom he described as badly officered, ill-trained, and poorly equipped— 'uniforms sometimes having to be provided by the man himself'.[2]

Templer gave his full support to the new Commissioner of Police, Colonel Arthur Young, and encouraged him to reorganize the administration and eliminate the inefficiencies in the system. Departmental duties were reassigned to give more responsibility to staff officers at Police Headquarters and to free the Commissioner from mundane administrative chores. This allowed Young to devote himself to directing and co-ordinating policy. The post of Deputy Commissioner of Police (Field) was created to link Federal Police Headquarters with the CPOs in the states and Straits Settlements. The change was intended to increase the exchange of information and encourage all members of the force to feel that they were participants in a more integrated organization. Training and retraining were given priority. The emphasis was shifted from the paramilitary function to ensuring that members of the force were properly trained in basic civil police duties. New training centres were established, staff recruited, and various types of courses put on for all levels of personnel. Particular attention was given to ensuring that special constables received a minimum level of training and were properly supervised.[3] As the 'shooting war' quietened down and the size of the police force stabilized, more members could be sent on training courses and very gradually the efficiency of the force increased.

Templer and Young were also very keen to foster better relations between the police and the public. Accordingly, late in 1952, it was decided to introduce 'Operation Service' in an attempt to emphasize that the police were servants of the people of Malaya and their job was to help and protect the members of all communities. Largely a public relations exercise, the results of Operation Service exceeded initial expectations. Because of the better training, and the new equipment sent out from Britain, as well as the reduction in both guerrilla-inspired incidents and the number of regular policemen and special constables killed by guerrillas, the police gained confidence in their own abilities, were less ill-disposed towards the general public, and less inclined to treat all Chinese as suspects.[4]

A number of groups among the general public gave Operation Service an excellent reception and were encouraged by the change in attitude it hoped to foster.[5] Even some in the Chinese community, finding themselves more secure and less subject to guerrilla intimidation, were more inclined to co-operate with the police.[6] Certainly, senior officials considered Operation Service enough of a success to extend the principle to other areas of Government. Despite this, however, it was some time before the overall effects of the exercise were much more than superficial.

The police force, which had numbered only 10,819 in 1947, had expanded nearly sevenfold by March 1953. Of its 71,000 members, 41,000 were special constables and 4,000 were extra police constables. By April 1954, the overall strength of the force had declined to under 54,000 and stabilized thereafter.[7] The better officers and men were retained and generally the overall quality of the force improved. However, the leadership of the force proved to be a problem. When Young left Malaya after serving for fourteen months, Templer appointed a Malaya-trained officer, W. L. R. Carbonnell, to be Commissioner of Police. Despite his relative youth, Carbonnell's appointment was generally applauded. One blight that continued to beset the police force was the shortage of Chinese in the rank and file and among the special constables. At no time did the Chinese members of the force exceed 2,000, and most of these were detectives. Thus the major barrier which separated the police from the mass of the Chinese community was perpetuated.

An important adjunct to the police force was the Home Guard. Like the police, it had expanded so quickly as to be considered generally ineffective by the time Templer arrived in Malaya. Although the Home Guard were expected to protect the resettled areas, the Government refused to arm them properly. Tan Cheng Lock, expressing the view of the Chinese community, described this policy as 'a half-hearted measure and a farce'.[8] To rectify matters, Major-General E. B. de Fonblanque, a retired British Army Officer, was made Inspector-General in April 1952, with instructions to build an organization which was independent of the police and capable of defending the rural population against guerrilla attacks. After careful consideration of the possibility that arms and ammunition might be lost to the guerrillas, Templer decided to take the risk and arm Home Guard units with shotguns. Indeed, he made an even more controversial decision: he agreed to implement the Kinta Valley Home Guard (KVHG) Scheme put forward by a leading Chinese politician, Leong Yew Koh. The proposal was that miners in the area would pay for a full-time armed Home Guard to provide security for the area.[9]

On balance, the Government's reform of the Home Guard paid off. Some arms were lost, primarily, as the Inspector-General explained, because the members of the Home Guard were usually young men—many in their teens—who were forced to follow public opinion in their village. If told by their elders to hand over their weapons to the guerrillas, they did so. Members of the Home Guard who tried to resist such pressure might go out tapping one day and never return. Home Guard morale, then, tended to reflect morale within the settlement.[10] Yet the loss of arms and ammunition was surprisingly limited. For example, only nine weapons were lost by the KVHG in the first two years of its existence.[11]

The benefits of the Home Guard were considerable. The Malay Home Guard of over 100,000 defended well over 2,000 settlements and even assisted the police and the army in some jungle operations. By the end of 1952, the Chinese Home Guard of over 50,000 had units in nearly every New Village; in 150 New Villages they were given full responsibility for the defence of their community.[12] The KVHG proved effective in turning the tables on the guerrillas despite internal divisions and indications that it may have been used to keep the work force on the tin mines in line.[13] In general, the Home Guard policy allowed the release of thousands of armed forces and police personnel for other assignments. Just as importantly, members of the Chinese community were impressed that Templer and his administration had, at long last, enough confidence in them to permit them to arm themselves for self-defence.

Despite the increased emphasis on divorcing the guerrillas from their base of support, it was still necessary to tackle the guerrillas in the jungle. The military continued to play a crucial role. By early 1952, the armed forces had reached nearly 30,000; over 22,000 were combat troops. The numbers remained at this level for the next four years. Gradually these troops were used more and more effectively. Fewer large-scale sweeps were employed, and small-scale operations, based on information supplied by the police, were more frequent. As a result, more contacts were made with guerrillas and the number of successes chalked up by the armed forces rose significantly.[14] Better equipment, such as the Sikorsky S55 helicopter, which allowed units to be transported between their base and the area of operations and for the speedy evacuation of casualties, improved morale and allowed a more efficient deployment of troops. From the viewpoint of the ordinary people in the rural areas, the changes were particularly welcome. When allied with the policy of resettlement and regrouping, they made chance encounters with troops prone to resorting to coercion and intimidation tactics much less likely.

A key to the success of any operation was intelligence. Templer, a former Director of Military Intelligence, recognized this and set about improving intelligence organizations. The second in command of Britain's MI5 was seconded for one year's term of duty to reorganize and expand the Special Branch within the police force. A Director of Intelligence was appointed to provide general information on such subjects as the MCP's strengths, weaknesses, and strategy, and the attitudes of various groups towards the communists. Indicative of the importance attached to the Director's role was his membership on the Director of Operations Committee. In addition, funds allocated to intelligence activities were increased, an Intelligence (Special Branch) training school was established, and other facilities generally improved.

Like the security side of the Malayan Government, the civil administration too needed to be reformed and expanded. The modification of the government's policy and the greater emphasis to be placed on delivering services, especially to the rural population, required an administrative capability that was obviously not yet in place. The altered strategy required a changed administrative structure.

Even before the Malayan Government could increase the size of its administration, it had to counter the erosion of its existing complement. Relatively low pay and poor conditions of service, most notably the terrible housing arrangements and concern over security of tenure with independence on the horizon, meant a steady loss of senior officials who chose to retire at fifty in the hope of obtaining civilian employment in Malaya or elsewhere. For example, of the sixty-three people filling the key senior jobs in 1948, only sixteen remained in December 1951. The high attrition rate undermined any sense of continuity that might have been built up and put a premium on experience. Additionally, it was exceedingly difficult to recruit good quality junior officials: technical and professional staff were in such short supply that in some departments one-third of the establishment positions were vacant, and many of the best personnel, who were on contracts, were so overworked and mistreated that they left Malaya after serving only one term. Templer responded by moving the question of increased expatriate pay from the 'tight-fisted' Legislative Council to a newly established Whitely Council system. The living and working conditions of officials were improved, and the Colonial Office was badgered to intensify its recruitment to all categories and levels. However, progress on all fronts was very slow.[15]

Nor did the recruiting of local personnel look much better in early 1952. Staffing the Malayan Administrative Service (MAS) had become an acute problem; the supply of candidates with the standard qualifications was insufficient to replace vacancies projected over the next ten years. To address the problem, qualifications to enter the MAS were lowered.[16] In addition, in November 1953, Templer persuaded the reluctant Rulers that the MCS, previously open only to British and Malay applicants, should admit non-Malays who had the necessary education and character. To assuage the Rulers' concern, recruits were to be admitted on the basis of one non-Malay for every four Malays. One year later, the policy had produced thirty-nine Malays but only five non-Malay applicants of sufficient quality to be admitted to the MCS.[17] Malayanization of the senior levels of the administration was accelerated somewhat, but the policy did not do as much as Templer had hoped to create links to the Chinese and Indian communities.

The most pressing need was for administrators at the state level and below who could speak Chinese and understand Chinese society and culture. The staff of the State and Settlement Secretaries for Chinese Affairs were still thin on the ground. For example, in April 1952, there were only eleven positions throughout the Federation compared to fifteen equivalent positions in pre-War Malaya. State governments, including the European officers, were most sceptical about what Secretaries for Chinese Affairs could do to help them and did not feel it necessary to provide them with more manpower or resources.[18] The DOs and Assistant District Officers (ADOs) were British or Malays who rarely spoke Chinese. The growing number of contract positions associated with resettlement included Emergency Administrative Officers, who essentially provided a secretariat service for the District War Executive Committees, as well as Resettlement Supervisors, Resettlement Officers, and Assistant Resettlement Officers, who all dealt directly with the issues arising from resettlement. However, there were grave shortages of suitable candidates for all positions, not everyone spoke Chinese, and these officers had no formal link to the administrative hub of the area, the district office.

These deficiencies were tackled in two ways. First, a major search was launched for missionaries who had worked in China and left when the Chinese Communist Party took power, and who might be persuaded to come to Malaya and work as Resettlement Officers. The search was conducted against the advice of the Colonial Office who claimed to have done all it could to secure applicants through the normal channels. However, pressed by various European organizations, most notably the Negri Sembilan Planters' Association, Templer arranged for Dawson, an energetic ex-China missionary and Resettlement Supervisor, to go to the United Kingdom to beat the bushes. Aided by a Chinese-speaking MCS officer, R. G. K. Thompson, on leave in Britain at the time, Dawson managed to generate a good deal of interest. His personal contacts, enthusiasm, and assurance based on firsthand knowledge that the situation was not nearly so black as the press had painted, were rewarded by a number of private applications and the commitment by missionary societies, such as the China Inland Mission, to expand their work in Malaya. Overall, Dawson's visit was most successful, and led to a small but steady stream of missionary workers being sent out to the New Villages.[19]

Secondly, a scheme for the appointment of Chinese Affairs Officers which had been first introduced in May 1950 but which had not achieved anticipated results, was upgraded. It was recognized that combating the spread of communism within the New Villages required more personal contact with the people: this could only be achieved effectively through the employment of adequate Chinese field staff. The new proposal, then, was to attract both the necessary quality and quantity of candidates by providing a pensionable career scheme rather than contract positions. The idea was that these Chinese Affairs Officers (CAOs) and Assistant Chinese Affairs Officers (ACAOs) would be members of a Federal Service and that one CAO was to be placed in every district in the Federation with a substantial Chinese population. Each officer was to be responsible to the DO and would constitute his main liaison with the Chinese in his district.[20]

By early 1954, there were only fifty-four CAOs and thirty-one ACAOs. The large number of vacancies reflected the difficulty of finding enough Chinese with the requisite Chinese and English language qualifications. The CAOs performed a variety of tasks associated with the Chinese community. Much of their work entailed ensuring that village councils and committees ran smoothly. In essence, they acted as Assistant District Officers, although the state governments were opposed to designating them as such for fear that it would be interpreted as a sign that the political position of Malays was being challenged. In part because of this attitude and the general uncertainty over their status, the CAOs tended to be treated by everyone, including Resettlement Supervisors, as glorified Assistant Resettlement Officers. This downgrading of their position and the failure of DOs to give them the anticipated responsibility and authority caused a great deal of dissatisfaction among CAOs and ACAOs and severely undermined their effectiveness. In some cases, the state Secretary for Chinese Affairs was able to intervene and advise DOs on how to make the best use of their new officials. Where the CAOs were given responsibility and allowed to exercise their initiative, they were able to forge useful links between the Government and the Chinese villagers. However, this ideal was often slow to emerge.[21]

One major weakness that continued to dog the Government was corruption. The Attorney-General noted in a memorandum on the subject that allegations of corruption in the civil service were fairly general and were causing public anxiety throughout the country.[22] Opportunities for corruption were legion. For example, government officials and the police in New Villages were known to borrow money from individual villagers and not repay them, or to buy goods from a village shop on credit and not settle their account before being transferred to a new position. Most corruption arose out of the widespread use of 'delaying tactics'. A lorry full of fish or perishable fruit or vegetables which might be destined for the morning market in Singapore had to cross the causeway before the evening curfew stranded it for the night, making it late and increasing the risk of the load going bad. At any of the many police road-blocks, it could be legitimately and disastrously delayed so 'coffee' or 'tea money' often changed hands. Similar delays were to be expected at district offices and government departments which dealt directly with the public. Bribes to lubricate the system had become an accepted part of many government transactions.[23]

Part of the problem was that as the Government extended its administrative net over the population, more and more people who had never dealt with any government before, and some of whom were illiterate, now had to cope with government officials, government forms, and government regulations. Many assumed that 'paying' for government services was the normal practice; they were rarely disabused of this view by the many petition writers and intermediaries whom they hired to help them through the bureaucratic maze.[24] For their part, junior government servants, particularly clerks, found the 'tips' a necessary part of their income, given the high cost of living and their relatively low pay. For instance, a report prepared for the High Commissioner pointed out that one reason for the debt-ridden position of the Asian staff was that they had to 'spend large sums of money on medical attention for themselves and their families'.[25] Moreover, the system of paying the wages and salaries of government employees once a month inevitably led to requests for credit in shops, which in turn increased costs and debts.

To counter corruption, the Government launched a publicity and education campaign, changed the rules of evidence in bribery cases, and tried to ensure that opportunities for corruption were reduced to a minimum. These measures, however, did not prove to be as effective as they might have been primarily because, as a Commission which inquired into this question noted, the senior officers of the administration did 'not regard the prevention of corruption as a matter with which they should be concerned'.[26] This 'defeatist' attitude and lack of leadership made corruption impossible to eradicate. They not only reduced efficiency in the administration but also produced a certain amount of cynicism within the general public.

During the first two years of the Templer administration, although there were concerns with the rapidly rising cost of the Emergency and the declining price of rubber, money was not a major

constraint in reorganizing, retraining, and expanding various aspects
of the administration. The Korean War boom had solved the Government's financial problems. The Government's total revenue
had risen from $235.5 million in 1948 to $725.4 million in 1951,
and even in the 'recession' years of 1953 and 1954, revenues had
remained around $620 million. The boom had created a large surplus
of revenue over expenditure in each of the three years 1950, 1951,
and 1952, and Templer was quite prepared to dip into these reserves to fund the administrative reforms he thought necessary.
For example, the total cost of 'Defence, Police and Emergency'
rose from $82 million in 1949 to a peak of $287 million in 1952 and
$296 million in 1953. This represented a 350 per cent increase in
Emergency expenditure–a notable asset in the fight against the
communists.[27]

The recession of 1953 and 1954 did force the Government to
cut back on the numbers in the police and the Home Guard, and
to curtail the expansion of the Malay Regiment. There were complaints about understaffing, but in many ways the retrenchment
allowed for a much-needed period of consolidation, even pruning,
and did not affect the Government's campaign too severely. The
pressures produced by the recession clearly demonstrated the importance of the boom years in fuelling the growth of the military,
the police, and the administration. Templer himself stated at the
time that a main weapon in the past four years has been the ability
derived from a large Federal income to carry through rapidly the
resettlement programme, the sevenfold expansion of the police
and the raising of 240,000 Home Guards and of four more battalions
of the Malay Regiment'.[28]

Templer's attempt to limit the abuses inflicted on the general
public and to create a more efficient and effective police, military,
and administrative structure, which could put into effect the hearts
and minds strategy, had mixed results. While considerable progress in achieving these goals was made from the beginning of 1952
onwards, in many cases the problems to be overcome were so fundamental that their elimination required much time and even then
was not assured. It is within this context that the Government's
hearts and minds approach has to be assessed.

The Stick

As the Malayan Government's hearts and minds approach slowly
took shape, it became clear that the strategy entailed the use of both

the stick and the carrot. Initially at least, the stick appeared to be given more public prominence; however, the balance shifted as the strategy evolved.

Templer's most publicized use of the stick came only two months after his arrival in Malaya. In early April 1952, twelve men, including the ADO for the area, were ambushed and killed near Tanjong Malim. The ADO was Michael Codner, one of the heroes of the famous 'Wooden Horse' escape from a German prison camp during the Second World War. The incident, therefore, received a great deal of publicity in both Malaya and Britain. Retribution was swift. Templer arrived in the town, addressed about 300 elders using his own brand of vitriolic language, imposed a twenty-two hour curfew, and reduced the rice rations from five katis per head per week to three katis for adults and two and a half for children.[29] This sort of punishment had been inflicted on communities before, but not in so dramatic a fashion and with such fanfare. What was also new was the circulation of questionnaires in which residents were instructed to write what they knew of the communists. The questionnaires were then collected in a special box which was later opened by Templer. A number of suspects were subsequently arrested, although it was never made clear if this was the result of information gleaned from the questionnaires or from other sources. After more than a week, the curfew was lifted and the rice ration returned to normal. The town was said to be co-operating with the Government.

In the next few months, similar measures were taken against towns and villages in, or near, which major incidents took place. Added to the curfews and the reduction in rice rations was the imposition of a collective fine. For example, an incident at Pusing prompted a curfew, the closing of shops for forty-four days, and a collective $40,000 fine.[30] On another occasion, in August 1952, after a Chinese ARO was killed in a coffee shop in the small village of Permatang Tinggi and the villagers refused to provide any information about the incident, all sixty-two residents–men, women, and children–were sent to detention camps and the village destroyed.[31]

Templer's actions received a mixed reception. In Britain, they provoked a wave of criticism in Parliament, in the press, and in telegrams and letters to the Prime Minister and the Colonial Secretary. Why was Templer punishing innocent people? Were collective punishments really achieving any results? And perhaps most pertinently, could the Government guarantee the security of villagers who gave information?[32] In Malaya, these criticisms were muted.

Groups, mainly within the European community, loudly applauded his actions which did as much to assuage their demands for summary justice and to boost their morale as anything else Templer achieved in his first year as High Commissioner. Certainly, Templer was never attacked for being soft on the 'fence-sitters' nor was he constantly assailed with demands for the introduction of martial law as Gurney had been.

It is difficult to assess how the New Villagers judged the policy. Humphrey, for example, argues that the 'threat of a fine, extended curfew, reduced rice ration or (almost equally feared) a lecture from Templer' had the effect of improving 'both the quantity and the quality of the information' given by the villagers to the government officials.[33] However, some of the more extreme measures were discarded by Templer presumably because they were judged ineffective or counter-productive. Indeed, the removal of Permatang Tinggi's sixty-two inhabitants was the only case of collective detention after Templer became High Commissioner,[34] and in 1953 the regulation allowing for mass detention and deportation, Emergency Regulation 17D, was rescinded. Templer also made sure that the numbers held in detention camps, as well as the numbers deported, steadily declined. As only a very small number of people detained under Emergency Regulations were charged in court, the detention camps were a source of considerable frustration: this change in policy, therefore, addressed a major grievance within the Chinese community.[35]

The harshness and unpredictability of some of the treatment meted out to New Villagers did drive people to help the communists. Demonstrations against the long curfews were not unknown. A particular target of resentment were the identification parades in which SEPs or local informers hidden from view pointed out 'collaborators' as a whole village was paraded before them. It is said some of those so arrested were never heard of again. As late as 1955, villagers were still reported as being arrested in their homes in the middle of the night.[36]

Perhaps the most effective stick wielded by the Government was food control. This policy was made possible by a combination of the fact that Malaya did not produce enough rice for its population, and the resettlement programme which allowed for strict supervision of the distribution of food and other essentials such as clothes and medicine. The initial food control policies were developed in 1951, but they too often backfired. As the Chairman of the Johore State War Committee reported, they had 'a harmful effect on the good-will and co-operation of the public out of all proportion to the effect on the bandit supply problem'.[37] Under Templer, the food control mechanisms were systematically refined. Strict controls covering the movement of goods throughout the entire country were enforced. The curfew restricted the legal use of roads to daylight hours, road and rail traffic were subject to inspections, and there were spot checks. Those who were transporting goods without a permit were liable to heavy fines and long jail terms. Village shops had to account for all stocks and sales, cans of food were punctured at the time of sale in order to ensure their immediate use, and villagers were searched as they left for work in the mornings. In areas where special food denial operations were undertaken, teams of administrators were moved in to tighten up the controls even further. In some New Villages, central cooking facilities were built, after which no uncooked rice was sold. This allowed rice to be stored under direct supervision of officials and meant that cooked rice, which spoils in a few hours, could not be smuggled out of the New Village and stored for use by the communist guerrillas.[38]

The refinements to the food denial operations made them more and more effective. But some supplies still inevitably reached the guerrillas as the complete monitoring of the movement of restricted goods was beyond the capability of the local police and administrative personnel. For example, in the New Villages, large numbers gathered at the gates in the early morning to get out to their work once the curfew terminated. Usually only a few random searches were made because a riot would have been provoked if the few special constables were to take the time to search every individual every morning. The initial shortage of female searchers made it impossible to stop women and young girls from smuggling food and other supplies out of the New Village. But the controls did cause the supplies reaching the guerrillas to dwindle sufficiently to make their mere survival more difficult. Moreover, while there remained individuals willing to help the communists and risk being caught because of their family or friendship ties, their personal grievances against the Government, or because of intimidation, the system of food control gave other villagers an excuse for not aiding the guerrillas. As Harry Miller, a journalist for the *Straits Times* has said, the policy answered the Chinese request to 'do something to us which will enable us to tell the Communists that we really cannot help them anymore, otherwise we shall be punished by you'.[39]

The use of the really big stick, a full-scale food denial operation, was reserved for those areas in which guerrillas were known to be operating and clearly being supported by the local population. In such instances, the area became the focus for the concentrated activities of the army, the police, and civilian officials, and co-ordinated by the District War Executive Committee. Central cooking stations were set up, or only one or two licensed shops were left open, and strict rationing imposed with the daily amount barely enough for people to live on. Special teams were brought in, and anyone leaving or entering the New Villages was thoroughly searched. These restrictions were usually kept in place until results were achieved—sometimes as long as a year.

Food control and especially food denial operations were very unpopular. The restrictions placed on the individual were onerous, and the ability of New Villagers to earn a decent income was greatly hampered. Rubber tappers who had to wait for the end of the curfew at 6 a.m., go through a time-consuming search, and then walk to work, found that they arrived so late that the latex would not run properly, so that their yields and their incomes were reduced. Workers, and students who went to schools in nearby towns, could not take a midday meal with them, making it difficult for them to keep up their energy levels for work in the afternoon.[40] Chinese who worked in the jungle logging timber were not allowed to ensure their personal safety by leaving food for the gods in the jungle. Similarly, villagers were prohibited from taking food to the cemeteries as offerings to the dead in celebration of *Qing Ming* or All Soul's Day.[41] And, of course, restrictions were placed on the cultivation of food outside a New Village's perimeter fence.

Overall, then, the use of highly publicized punishments such as extended curfews and the food denial operations, did begin to drive a wedge between the guerrillas and the New Villagers. However, some of the harsher measures were counter-productive, and the use of the stick only perpetuated the general level of antipathy towards the Government that had traditionally existed among the rural Chinese. It was to try to minimize the effects of this antipathy and, if possible, to woo the rural Chinese population away from the communists that the carrot, in the form of the development of the New Villages, was introduced.

The Carrot

Almost immediately after being installed as High Commissioner, Templer turned his attention to resettlement. To encourage the new settlers to become 'ordinary citizens' as quickly as possible, he decreed that the 'resettlement camps' and 'resettlement areas' were to be known as 'New Villages'. The provision of services and amenities in the New Villages was no longer to be referred to as 'after-care' but as 'development'. Templer created a senior post, New Village Liaison Officer, and appointed J. L. H. Davis, whose knowledge of the rural Chinese from his days in Force 136 and after the War in the Labour Department, was a major asset. The Government's overall objective was made clear in a Federal Legislative Council Paper produced in May 1952: 'The New Villages mean in effect a new life for the people who dwell in them and it is imperative that this new life should, after the initial disturbance of moving, be more attractive than the old.'[42]

The foundations of this better life were to be not only freedom from fear but also access to a number of basic services. By March 1953, the attributes necessary for a New Village to be described as properly settled had been defined. They were: a modicum of agricultural land and the granting of long-term land titles, an adequate water supply, a reasonably well-functioning village committee, a school which could accommodate at least a majority of the children, a village community centre, roads of passable standards and with side drains, reasonable conditions of sanitation and public health, a place of worship, trees along the main street and *padang*, an effective perimeter fence, a flourishing Home Guard, a reasonably friendly feeling towards the Government and the police, and the beginning of certain activities such as the Scouts, Cubs, and Girl Guides.[43] The extent to which each of the well over 500 villages met the criteria varied considerably. A few villages could have been considered properly settled by late 1952. But for most villages, these criteria set out goals which were to take many years to achieve. Indeed, some villages never did come close to being properly settled in the Government's terms.

One major obstacle was the poor performance of the Public Works Department (PWD). A small committee, asked by Templer to inquire into the implementation of the Government's policy, stated that 'of all the Government Departments, we feel that the PWD is the one that is playing the least effective part in the States and Settlements in Emergency work'.[44] In part this was because of the great difficulty the PWD had in recruiting and keeping engineers and the fact that it was consequently understaffed and overworked. But it was also because of the reluctance of senior officials in the Department to consider the existence of a State of Emergency as sufficient reason for relaxing their standards. This proved particularly frustrating in the New Villages. To speed along the necessary work, construction was done by Chinese contractors under the supervision of the DO or the RS. The results were mixed and varied according to the village site, the experience and conscientiousness of the contractors, and the experience and workload of the DO or RS. If the basic infrastructure, such as the roads and drains, the perimeter fence, the water supply, and the sanitation facilities were badly built, then it was often very difficult to get the money to rebuild or repair them. Too many New Villages, especially in Johore, where the first wave of resettlement had taken place, had been badly planned and poorly built, and thus got off to a bad start. It took a long time to resolve these early problems.

Education was a vital ingredient in the life of all New Villages. The Chinese valued education, and the overwhelmingly Chinese population of the New Villages placed a high priority on setting up Chinese-language schools. Initially, the Malayan Chinese Association donated money to help build new schools, but they found it impossible to satisfy the many requests they received for funds.[45] Government assistance was gradually increased as officials began to appreciate the key role education played in the fight against communism. By early 1952, New Village schools received $1,400 towards the construction of each new classroom, $1,500 for each teacher's quarters, and an initial grant of $10 per pupil towards the cost of books, furniture, and equipment.[46] Despite this help, progress was slow; fewer than half the 500 or so New Villages had schools by the end of 1952.[47] However, the Federal and state governments increased their overall spending on education during the next two years and the 1954 'Annual Report on Education' was able to claim that no New Village with a population of more than 400 was beyond easy walking distance of a school.[48]

The major barrier to the development of schools within the New Villages was less the lack of facilities as the shortage of teachers.[49] Teaching jobs were readily available in the towns and were more attractive. In the New Villages the living conditions were poorer, the pay and status lower, the social life more restricted, and the threat of simultaneous pressure from the Min Yuen and government officials constant. To counter the possible ill-effects of having disenchanted and frustrated teachers in the New Village schools, and to recruit more teachers to accommodate the rising demand for schooling, the Government introduced in late 1952 a new salary grant-in-aid scheme. This raised the status of teachers and gave them higher salaries and more security. By the end of 1954, every eligible Chinese primary school had accepted the salary contribution provided for in the grant-in-aid scheme.[50] Surprisingly popular were the short courses for teachers of Chinese and English from the New Village schools.

Despite these efforts, all children in the New Villages did not receive an education. In early 1952, the enrolment in New Village schools was just under 40,000 or about 39 per cent of the population of primary school age (six to twelve years old). By 1954, the new facilities and increased number of teachers allowed about 60 per cent of the New Villages' primary school-age population to attend school.[51] Although this was clearly an advance over 1952, and especially over pre-resettlement days when very few Chinese squatter children attended school, there was still plenty of room for improvement.

The funding schemes paved the way for greater intervention by the Government in schools in the New Villages and elsewhere. The ROs exercised control over the selection of members for the school management committee or the education committee of the Local Council. But even more importantly, all non-Government operated schools and their managers and teachers had to be registered with the Registrar of Schools in their state or settlement. If a school was not registered or was struck from the register, then it could not operate. Teachers and school managers were also strictly controlled by the Registrar. An added benefit of such control over the schools was that, after establishing a committee to oversee the revision of Chinese school textbooks, the Government was able, in 1953, to begin introducing texts with a more Malayan orientation. While all this was encouraging for the Government, schools nevertheless continued to be a key factor in the persistent support for the communists. Moreover, a severe shortage of Chinese-speaking school inspectors left much of what transpired in Chinese-language schools outside the ken of the Government long after these reforms were introduced.

In many ways, the development of health services in the New Villages followed the same pattern as the development of educational facilities. In early 1952, the New Villages were described by the Malayan Branch of the British Medical Association as posing 'a new risk to public health, threatening epidemics which may endanger not only the areas themselves but also the adjacent populations'.[52] Concern was also expressed over the 'gross inadequacy of medical services in the resettlement areas'.[53] Apparently, some personnel from travelling dispensaries were unwilling to travel in known 'bad areas'. In July 1952, the Deputy Director of Operations reported that many New Villages had never seen travelling dispensaries. Even in the larger centres, to which New Villagers who lived close by went for medical attention, the shortage of trained medical staff was acute, and some hospital employees expected to be bribed by the public for their services.[54]

In response to the general demand for better health care and to the obvious needs of the New Villagers, and aided by the increased revenue from the Korean War boom, spending on health and medical facilities rose steadily. The combined expenditure of both the Federal and state governments went from $24.8 million in 1950 to $43.6 million in 1952, and to $49.4 million in 1954.[55] The number of static dispensaries, most of which were in New Villages, rose from thirty-two at the end of 1951 to 172 at the end of 1954. In addition, during the same period, over 500 infant welfare centres and sub-clinics were established and the number of mobile dispensaries rose from twenty-nine to seventy-five. Staff to fill these facilities were obtained both by increasing the salaries and benefits paid to doctors and nurses, and by setting up rural health training centres. Valuable help was also forthcoming from twenty-six St. John Ambulance and thirty Red Cross teams recruited from Britain and Australia, which toured rural areas, dividing their time between the New Villages and Malay kampongs.[56] Less visible, although often very effective, were a number of public health programmes which dealt with problems of sanitation, typhoid, smallpox inoculation, and malaria control. Despite this effort, however, medical and health services were slow to reach many New Villages: even by as late as 1958, 21 per cent received no direct medical services at all.[57]

The Government was anxious to develop acceptable social organizations and a general sense of community in the New Villages as an antidote to communist organizational activities. Community centres were built in most New Villages, many of which doubled as the school in the smaller villages, and acted as the focus of social activity. The most successful ones in the larger villages contained a canteen or coffee shop, and a communal radio. Church and missionary workers performed social welfare functions in some villages; the MCA funded sports teams, most notably basketball, in the larger villages; and Boy Scout and Boys Brigade groups were sponsored by the Government. In most New Villages, there was a Women's Institute which provided a forum for giving demonstrations in child-care techniques, health information programmes, and instructions in cooking and sewing.⁵⁸ As with other aspects of the Government's attempts to develop the New Villages, the extent to which these activities took root and became an integral part of village life varied tremendously. In time, however, many of the New Villages did develop a sense of identity and community.

The protection afforded New Villages slowly improved with the evolution of the Home Guard and the training of police and special constables. Yet many New Villages remained very insecure. For example, only seventeen of the 180 villages for which the Director of Operations' criteria stipulated that perimeter lighting was needed to maintain security, had received it by the end of 1952. Progress was equally slow in subsequent years. Despite the reduced use of intimidation tactics by the Min Yuen and the MRLA after the 1951 MCP directive percolated down through the ranks, villagers remained subject to, and fearful of, the local Min Yuen members present in nearly every New Village. Just as importantly, New Villagers and estate labourers in regroupment areas had to leave the relative protection of the New Villages or labour lines daily to work in the rubber estates or smallholdings. This made them continually vulnerable to guerrilla pressure and whatever safety was afforded by the New Villages was of little help.

The safety of New Villagers was threatened not only by the guerrillas, but also by special constables overstepping their authority. As one official report stated, in characteristically euphemistic fashion, Chinese and Indian workers had, as an 'unavoidable consequence' of the continual pressure from, and extortion by the guerrillas, 'suffered counter-pressure from the Police and Military and... become the object of their suspicion'.⁵⁹ It took some time to modify the old habits of treating all New Villagers as if they were communists.⁶⁰ And even with the marked decrease in MCP guerrilla-inspired incidents, it was a long time—many years in parts of Johore and Perak—before New Villagers began to feel that the New Villages were the safe havens they wished for.

The most important factor in making for a 'properly settled' village was a sound economic base. The dislocation of the first years of resettlement ended when the general shortage of labour caused by the Korean War boom created ample opportunities for New Villagers to provide for their families. Agriculturalists deprived of their land by forced resettlement were able to find work on rubber smallholdings and Asian-owned estates and tin mines. Even the large European-owned estates, previously somewhat reluctant to hire Chinese labourers and tappers, were happy to have these new pools of labour close by. Indeed, these additional casual labourers were doubly welcome because they had their own homes and employers did not have to house and feed them.[61] Cases of unemployment were scarce and generally only temporary. Wages were high; many were making a lot of money on a *bagi dua* or shared profits basis on small estates, smallholdings, or Asian-owned tin mines; and prosperity was widespread. Hence, the combined effect of resettlement and the boom was to convert many of the former rural Chinese farmers into wage earners and to make the economic stability of the New Villages dependent upon the international prices of rubber and tin.[62]

The problems posed by this metamorphosis became apparent during 1952 as the boom petered out. First, the London offices of the large European estates ordered their managers to cut costs and dispense with as much labour as possible. Although most managers were reluctant to take such drastic action, it appeared that large-scale unemployment was just around the corner.[63] Secondly, as the international price of rubber continued to decline during 1953, a number of small Asian estates considered it uneconomical to tap their rubber and thus laid off workers. With less land being cultivated, food production had declined and food prices had risen. During the boom years, the relatively high incomes enjoyed by most people had meant that inflation in high food prices had not caused too many problems, but as wages were reduced, according to the sliding scales tied to the price of rubber, high food prices once again became a major concern. And finally, the likelihood of New Villagers being put out of work highlighted the very limited amount of land that was available in the New Villages for cultivation. With this traditional means of weathering a recession in short supply, the prospects both for the development of the New Villages and the Government's strategy of winning the hearts and minds of the villagers dimmed considerably.

Government officials did recognize the urgency of providing more land to the villagers. The 1952 Federal Legislative Council Paper on the New Villages stated that 'further agricultural land has to be acquired' and that much remained 'to be done in providing the settler with facilities for creating a stable economic environment for himself'.[64] In his 1953 budget speech to the Federal Legislative Council, Templer noted that the provision of agricultural land was among the first priorities for developing the New Villages. The Government's goal was to ensure that families which depended on farming for their income had three acres of land, and families which depended on wages for their income had half an acre of land.[65]

The Federal Government, however, found it difficult to implement this policy. A major hurdle was the cost of buying suitable land. For security reasons, the New Villages had been located near main roads and thus were invariably surrounded by valuable estate or smallholding land which the owners were reluctant to sell except for a handsome sum. Up to 1954, $3.4 million had been spent on acquiring land; a further $10 million was believed necessary to complete the policy.[66] And this was only to cover a more limited goal of half an acre per family. Indeed, W. C. S. Corry, in his 1954 report on the New Villages, felt that even the amount of land still due to be acquired was 'unrealistically large and the whole question [merited] re-examination'.[67] A further complicating factor was the attitude of the Malay-dominated state governments which exercised constitutional jurisdiction over land. Having seen the large amount of money and attention being lavished on the New Villages and the rural Chinese, whom they considered to be responsible for the lawlessness and upheaval, and being frustrated by the lack of attention given to rural Malays, the state governments were very reluctant to alienate more crown land for New Village agriculture.

The recession of 1953 and 1954 did not produce the massive, widespread unemployment many had feared. The Government still employed large numbers of people in the Federation Army, the police, the civil administration, and the Home Guard. The urban areas, which had expanded markedly over the preceding few years, were employing more people as businesses, which had been given a boost by the Korean War boom, were consolidated. Most rubber estates sold their rubber on the basis of a yearly forward contract so that the full impact of the lowest rubber prices was avoided by some managers and minimized by others. Estates continued to make a profit; the bulk of their labour force was retained; and indeed, there was still a demand for labour, especially for skilled tappers, on estates in the more remote areas.[68] Generally, Chinese labour moved from the smallholdings and smaller estates, which had attracted workers by offering high wages and which ceased to be worked as the price of rubber dropped, to relieve the shortage of labour on the larger estates. In addition, the significant drop in the cost of living during 1953 and 1954 compensated to some degree for the lower wages most workers received.[69]

But what the Member for Economic Affairs called the 'remarkable resilience in the major industries'[70] in the face of recession should not be overestimated. The official figures for the number of labourers employed declined from 505,000 in 1952 to 467,400 in 1954. The largest decrease in employment was among Chinese labourers whose numbers dropped from 185,300 in 1952 to 160,300 in 1954. These figures did not include employment statistics for smallholdings of under 25 acres which represented a considerable portion of the industry and from which many Chinese had earned their income on a profit-sharing basis.[71] However, it was clear that the hardest hit were the tin mining areas, particularly the Kinta Valley of Perak, where, as the Labour Department Annual Report for 1953 noted, 'considerable unemployment existed at the end of the year'.[72] Loh, in his study of the Kinta region, notes that in 1953 in one New Village near Kampar, 'it was estimated that 50 per cent of all adults and 30 per cent of all male adults were unemployed'.[73] Other areas fared better, although there were pockets of unemployment throughout the country.

Equally frustrating, and far more pervasive, was the incidence of underemployment. Faced with the recession, some employers tended to put workers on short-time employment rather than decrease the number of employees. They hoped thereby to keep their employees around for when the economy picked up and they once again had to compete for the short supply of skilled labour. Other employers simply closed down and waited for better times. Those in or near the main urban centres who found themselves unemployed looked for work as casual labourers, hawkers, or trishaw operators. Many males left the more remote New Villages and travelled the country in search of casual work. Some returned to cultivation to supplement family incomes, but the limited amount of suitable land caused a good deal of resentment.[74] An intrepid few resorted to the traditional ploy of illegal cultivation, but this was actively discouraged by government officials.

The recession's overall impact on Malayans, and especially on the New Villagers, was mixed. In areas where estates could absorb any unemployment or where agricultural land had been made available, the disruption to people's lives was minimal. In other areas the recession caused considerable hardship. As one observer argued at the time, it was the economic insecurity of settlers in the New Villages which was largely responsible for their indifference and often hostility towards the Government.[75] It should also be noted that the Malayan Christian Council's survey makes the point that the availability of work was the primary factor conducive to a stable New Village community.[76] Where unemployment was a problem, the Government's task of winning people's hearts and minds was clearly exceedingly difficult.

Until 1952, the Malayan Government had directed its energies and activities at the Chinese population. This was because well over 90 per cent of the MCP, the guerrilla units, and the Min Yuen were Chinese and relied heavily on the rural Chinese for their support. From 1952 onwards, this began to change. Forced by the resettlement programme to abandon some of their old haunts and sources of supply, the guerrillas increasingly turned to Malay and aborigine communities in search of food and other necessities.

The Malays did not welcome this development. Racial and religious differences had meant that a relatively small number of Malays had supported the communists. Indeed, many Malays were openly antagonistic to the guerrillas. Humphrey notes that 'accounts of Malay villagers hacking to death armed guerrillas who had intruded into their kampongs were far from uncommon'.[77] The one major exception to this anti-MCP feeling among Malays was in Pahang where atrocious conditions among the poverty-stricken riverine kampongs and the Government's neglect enabled a Malay guerrilla leader, Wan Ali, to form the Tenth (Malay) Regiment. This group, however, was crushed in a determined campaign by a volunteer unit made up of local kampong guards, and by early 1950 it had ceased to operate.[78] There were subsequently very few incidents of Malays actively supporting the guerrilla cause.

Hence, when the guerrillas started to seek food and supplies from the more remote kampongs, they invariably used violence and intimidation to get what they needed from unsympathetic and often hostile Malays. During 1952, it became apparent to the authorities that the success of the food denial programme required extension of the Briggs Plan to the most exposed Malay kampongs. In the past, the Government had been reluctant to resettle Malays for fear of alienating their most important supporters. Malays were rarely squatters, as most Chinese had been, having inherited their land or acquired it through the Malay system of land ownership. They were very keen to continue living on or near their holdings, and officials, who were becoming more and more conscious of the high cost of relocating people, were sympathetic.[79] Some Malays were moved to New Villages where a separate section was usually set aside specifically for them. It was hoped this would avoid some of the major irritants—such as the presence of pig sties—which might provoke interracial ill will. In the main, however, those Malays who were most subject to guerrilla pressure were regrouped in such a way as to minimize possible hardships. Many of these regrouping areas did not even have a perimeter fence: a well-organized Home Guard unit usually proved sufficient to deter the communists from preying on the newly consolidated kampongs.

The Malays were not just concerned with security; they also wished to benefit from the services being extended to the New Villages. Complaints about the inaccessibility of kampongs and the lack of medical and educational facilities had been directed towards the Government even before the advent of the New Village development programme.[80] As money was poured into these essentially Chinese communities, Malay leaders demanded equal treatment. The Government had originally responded to these requests by setting up, in August 1950, the Rural and Industrial Development Authority (RIDA) as a department of the Government under the Malay leader, Dato Onn. Initially, RIDA proved very ineffectual because of the severe shortage of trained development officers and the lack of co-operation from the state governments which arose because of the rivalry between Dato Onn and the traditional Malay state leaders. Indeed, RIDA came under a good deal of criticism from all quarters.[81]

Templer was not slow in recognizing the importance of ensuring that Malays did not become too disillusioned with the Government. In addition, improving the economic lot of Malays was one of the key points in the British Government's directive. He therefore set up and chaired a committee which examined possible measures to improve the conditions of life in the average Malay kampong. The committee investigated the need to build more roads to allow outside benefits to be delivered to the kampongs. Roads would make the tasks of the St. John Ambulance and Red Cross medical teams, which were instructed to spend half their time in predominantly Malay areas, much easier. Templer increased RIDA's budget for 1953 to $8 million, and on 1 January 1954, RIDA was made a quasi-governmental corporation to give it more flexibility and independence. These actions helped to give the Malays a sense that their grievances were recognized, even if not nearly as much was being done to redress them as most desired.[82]

As the Malays were gradually regrouped and it became more difficult for the communist organizations to use them as a source of food, the guerrillas turned their attention to the *orang asli* or aborigines of the deep jungle. Communist contacts with aborigine groups developed during the Japanese Occupation were renewed and expanded from late 1950 onwards as acquiring food supplies became the communists' major preoccupation. Early Government attempts to counter these links, by removing the aborigines from the jungle and resettling them, proved disastrous. Diseases previously unknown to the jungle people caused numerous deaths, and many of those who survived found the confinement too much and lapsed into the trance-like behaviour of the severely depressed. The major beneficiaries were the guerrillas. Their promises to protect the aborigine community from the *orang puteh* (the white man), their knowledge of aborigine culture and languages, and, in particular, their appreciation of the crucial role of a group's headman, persuaded a number of aborigine communities that the communists would be useful allies. The guerrillas, in turn, were able to use the aborigines as guides, messengers, cultivators, and sources of information on the movement of the Government's security forces.[83]

During 1952, the full significance of the aborigines to the course of the Emergency became apparent when estimates of their numbers were revised upwards from the 34,000 recorded in the 1947 census to between 68,000 and 100,000.[84] Under Templer, the Government re-examined its whole approach. Rather than opt for resettlement, it decided to construct a series of 'forts' to which nearby aborigines could come and go as they pleased. It was hoped that the forts would give protection to those who were being dominated by the communists through coercion, and would at the same time provide medical services and supplies. However, progress was very slow and towards the end of 1953, as the role of the aborigines in providing food for the guerrillas became more crucial, Templer placed the Department on an Emergency footing. The Federal Government took over full responsibility for the aborigines; Richard Noone, an anthropologist with extensive knowledge of Malaya's aborigines, was made head of the Department of Aborigines, and the staff was expanded to enable more field teams to be sent out to make contact with aborigines under communist influence. This campaign was rather more successful. Official estimates, which were perhaps a little optimistic, were that of the 6,000 or so aborigines under varying degrees of communist control at the end of December 1953, 3,500 had been brought under the Government's influence by the end of December 1954.[85]

In September 1953, the Government made an important addition to its hearts and minds strategy. Templer declared 221 square miles of Malacca a 'white area'. In this area, many of the most irksome Emergency regulations, including food controls, curfews, limited hours for business, and restrictions on the movement of goods and people, were lifted. The only major regulations not affected were those which required residents to remain in the New Villages or regroupment areas, and to maintain the defences of the village, including a skeletal Home Guard unit.[86] By the time Templer left Malaya in mid-1954, there were 'white areas' containing over 1,300,000 people along much of Malaya's coastline. In October 1954, after discussion among senior officials and state representatives, and with the experience of the past year of virtually no incidents in the 'white areas', it was decided to relax the qualifications for declaring an area white. It was felt that the benefits and the psychological advantages gained by the Government would outweigh the risks.[87] There can be no doubt that the steady spread of these deregulated areas across Malaya was a major incentive for the people to co-operate with the Government.

Propaganda and Psychological Warfare

As the hearts and minds strategy evolved, the contributions that could be made by a well-organized propaganda offensive became obvious. If people were to accept the strategy, its intent and benefits had to be explained. Moreover, it was hoped that an information campaign which was tied to an improvement in the living conditions of the rural population, and especially the New Villagers, would persuade more guerrillas that a better life could be led outside the jungle than in it. In a number of ways, then, the propaganda programme overlapped with the psychological war being waged against the guerrillas. As with so many other aspects of the Government's campaign, both the propaganda and psychological warfare efforts developed in fits and starts.

Initially, at least, the most important channel for government propaganda was the printed word. From the beginning of the Emergency, the Information Services Department had put out fortnightly Malay and Tamil vernacular papers. A little later, some Chinese papers were started up by the Department, the *Farmers' News* being the most widely circulated. In 1951, the total of all weekly and periodical publications printed by the Government exceeded five million copies.[88] A particularly important addition to this battery of publications was the *New Path News*, a monthly paper started by two psychological warfare specialists, C. C. Too and Lam Swee. By the end of 1952, this influential paper had a monthly circulation of 70,000.[89] Of course, the distribution of these publications was crucial to their overall impact on public opinion. Chinese newspapers were very much a part of the local Chinese coffee shop scene and were read by successive customers, some sections being read aloud for the benefit of everyone. Similarly, the Malay tradition of reading a newspaper aloud boosted its effective circulation. In the New Villages, the Government was willing to help fund the building of community centres so that they could be used as a distribution point for government-sponsored publications. There were even some reading rooms and information centres built in a few rural kampongs and New Villages. By 1953, the half million copies of the thirteen monthly government publications were receiving a fairly wide circulation.[90]

By the end of 1951, the Government had come to realize that radio was an alternative source of information to the printed word. Revenues from the Korean War boom were used to expand programming and to purchase new equipment. The most important programming innovation was the creation of the Community Listening Service. This provided broadcasts in Malay, Chinese, and Tamil on such subjects as health, agriculture, infant welfare, language instruction, and civics, as well as various forms of entertainment and plenty of news and features. Newly trained local staff were sent out to all parts of the Federation and by the end of 1952, broadcasts had been made from every state and Settlement. Moreover, by 1953, the Federation had its own studios, offices, and transmitting stations, and no longer had to rely on Singapore for these facilities. This move, of course, now gave the Malayan Government full control over programming arrangements.[91]

The Government was especially fortunate that these developments coincided with the phenomenal increase in the number of radios and the rapid expansion of the listening audience. It is paradoxical that while broadcasting holds such potential for reaching a large proportion of the illiterate population of a society, it is this very group, who because of the lack of funds to acquire a radio, are often the last to benefit from this channel of communication. For the Malayans, it was the Korean War boom that changed all this. High wages allowed many labourers to buy small luxury items such as radios. The boom also enabled estate and mine owners, as well as the Government, to install radios in regroupment areas and New Villages. In 1949, only 35,000 listeners' licences were issued; by 1953, this figure had risen to 110,800. Similarly, the number of schools with radio receivers jumped from 265 in 1948 to 1,364 by the end of 1953. The most dramatic increase was in the use of 'community receivers'. In 1949, there were only thirty-two such sets but by the end of 1952 there were over 1,400 in use in kampongs, New Villages, mines, and estates around the country. In the words of one official statement, 'radio reached into the rural areas and for the first time became an important medium of information, education and entertainment for the isolated population which hitherto had been largely outside its range'.[92]

In the post-War period, Malayans were among the most avid film-goers in the world.[93] The newsreel, and the one or two short films that preceded every feature film, gave the Government ample opportunity to extol the virtues of its policies and denounce the evils of communism. But as in so many other areas, little advantage was taken of this opportunity until the revenue from the Korean War boom made funds available. Even then the Malayan Film Unit, which had been in existence since 1946, took some time to gear up to the potential of the medium. And, indeed, the potential was considerable. In 1952, there were 155 commercial cinemas in Malaya and more opening all the time. But perhaps even more important for their primary audience were the mobile film units which could reach people in the rural areas where the communists were most active and public co-operation most necessary. At the beginning of 1951, there were only sixteen mobile film units; by 1954, there were ninety government-operated units serving one million people each month. In combination with plays and speeches by SEPs, they made a significant contribution to the Government's propaganda campaign.[94]

Like most other departments, the main problem facing the Information Services was a severe shortage of skilled manpower. The numbers of Chinese and Chinese-speaking European officers were limited, and not all were skilful propagandists. Even the use that could be made of SEPs was limited; few were as effective as Lam Swee. Hence, although a good deal of propaganda and psychological warfare material was produced, its quality varied considerably. For example, much of the Department's material was produced first in English, and then translated into Chinese, Malay, or Tamil; the inevitable result was that Europeans were impressed by the message while Chinese, Malays, and Tamils were left nonplussed. This problem was compounded when the Information Services were reorganized in 1952.[95] An *ad hoc* advisory group, asked by Templer in early 1953 to report on the implementation of government policy, singled out the new Department of Information Services because so many of the people they talked to mentioned its failings. They felt that the newly recruited expatriate officers in the states and Settlements were 'unlikely for a very considerable time to be able to understand the hearts and minds of the people'.[96] They particularly noted the impact of the reorganization on the morale of the Asian officers. And, indeed, some Chinese officers became so frustrated by the turn of events that they resigned, thus weakening the Department even further.[97]

Because the information programme was also an integral part of the psychological war being waged by the Government against the guerrillas, the conduct of the one affected the other. This was most noticeable in the campaign to induce guerrillas to surrender. As the most cost-effective way of reducing the guerrilla threat, it was considered a primary goal of the psychological war.[98] During late 1952 and 1953, the surrender rate was high in the wake of the reversal of fortunes that followed Templer's first year in office; however, it was not sustained. Lower surrender rates came about because of the communist successes in Indo-China and tighter MCP discipline, and also because it took some time for the Government to weaken the guerrilla's morale.[99]

An early assessment by a group of SEPs indicated a wide range of commitment to the communist cause among the guerrillas. There was a core group whom it would be difficult to persuade to surrender because they had either a strong commitment to communism and its goals, or had achieved a degree of power within the MCP which they could not obtain elsewhere. Past experience suggested that others might be induced to surrender by exploiting their doubts about such things as the wisdom of having left their homes, families and friends, the brutal treatment occasionally inflicted on innocent people, and the uncaring behaviour of some of their leaders.[100]

There were two main impediments to the members of the MRLA surrendering. First, they feared disciplinary action if discovered to be even considering surrendering. Harsh punishments, including in a few extreme cases the death sentence, had been meted out to those found in possession of Government surrender leaflets or other propaganda material. Secondly, they feared their treatment by the Government. MCP propaganda emphasized that they would either be shot on sight by the security forces, or if captured, tortured and hanged. This fear was reinforced by the actions of the security forces and the Government's policies in the first few years of the Emergency.

At its best, the Government's psychological warfare campaign demonstrated to guerrillas why they should surrender, how they could do so safely, and how they could benefit financially. The most effective vehicles were leaflets which were dropped by the thousand, and 'voice aircraft' which circled over the jungle canopy and broadcast to nearby guerrilla groups through loud-speakers. Particularly successful were campaigns which employed leaflets or broadcasts to address specific local grievances or relay a message from a family member of a guerrilla, or a recently surrendered comrade, calling on specific individuals to give themselves up.

An equally important ingredient in the psychological war was the rewards programme. Rewards were given for either bringing in a guerrilla–dead or alive–or for information which led to the capture or killing of a guerrilla.[101] The Government's propaganda material emphasized that surrendered guerrillas could take advantage of this programme. While the morality of these 'bribes' can be and was questioned, their effectiveness was not disputed.

The success of the propaganda and psychological warfare campaigns varied considerably from region to region. Often the results depended on the energy, imagination, and understanding of the guerrilla mentality exhibited by the local officer in charge. Moreover, propaganda could not by itself win the war; it was only as effective as the other elements in the Government's strategy. The influence of propaganda on the general population and the MCP guerrillas, therefore, fluctuated as the Government's own overall credibility in an area waxed and waned.

Legislative Issues

While much of the hearts and minds approach concentrated on the local level and especially on the New Villages, there were some issues which primarily occupied the attention of Malaya's community leaders. These issues were usually associated with specific policies which needed legislative action and because they often pitted the Government against the local élites, and therefore aroused anti-Government feelings, they acted as a drag on the implementation of the hearts and minds strategy.

One of the most important questions concerned the right to be a citizen of Malaya. This had been a contentious issue in the years immediately after the British return to Malaya, and despite British hopes had not been resolved with the proclamation of the Federation of Malaya Agreement. Gurney had clearly grossly underestimated the strength of feeling on this matter in his first address to the Federal Legislative Council when he said: 'I can find no desire in any quarter to amend the Federation Agreement in any respect.'[102]

Eventually, prompted by the persistent arguments of the non-Malays that their legitimate rights had been sacrificed, the proposals of the unofficial–but highly influential–Communities Liaison Committee, and the failure of the Government's first citizenship bill to attract a consensus, he had set up a select committee of the Legislative Council in July 1951 to review the whole question.[103]

This committee reported to the Legislative Council in March 1952, just a few weeks after Templer took over as High Commissioner. In May 1952, the new Citizenship Bill, based on the committee's recommendations, was debated and passed by the Federal Legislative Council, and on 15 September 1952, after each state had passed its own Nationality Laws, both the Federation of Malaya Agreement (Amendment) Ordinance and the State Nationality Laws came into effect.[104] The complex new laws went part way to satisfying the demands of the non-Malays. Of particular importance was the introduction of what the Attorney-General termed the 'delayed *jus soli*'.[105] This referred to the criteria for citizenship by which anyone born in the Federation who had a parent who was born in the Federation automatically became a subject of the sultan of the state in which he was born and, consequently, a citizen of the Federation. The criteria for citizenship by application were also modified with respect to the residency requirements although, unlike the 1948 stipulations, an applicant was required to renounce the exercise of any other citizenship (excepting the citizenship of the United Kingdom and Colonies) and take an oath of allegiance.[106]

Despite some criticisms, which mainly centred around the problem of state nationality creating disunity, and the legal problems of those who could not gain citizenship, the legislation was fairly well received.[107] The Malays, some reluctantly, accepted the necessity of encouraging the loyalty of all residents of Malaya. Non-Malays viewed the amendments to the Federation Agreement as too limited, but agreed to them as a step towards the goal of the adoption of the principle of *jus soli*. It was officially estimated that as a result of the new laws, 2,727,000 Malays and Orang Asli, 1,157,000 Chinese, and 222,000 Indians automatically became state nationals and citizens.[108] However, the importance of this newly acquired status was not immediately appreciated by those outside the élites of the main racial communities. Perhaps somewhat frustrated by this turn of events, given all the anguish which had been caused by trying to satisfy all the different interests, Templer noted in November 1953 that 'among all those people who recently attended a civics course in Penang for New Villagers from Province Wellesley, not one knew whether or not he was a Federal Citizen'.[109]

The most controversial issue was education. The special committee appointed in 1951 to recommend legislation reported in 1952. Its major recommendations were incorporated into the Education Ordinance 1952 and passed by the Legislative Council in October of that year.[110] At the heart of the legislation was the transformation of the existing schools into National Schools, in which the children of all races would be given a free education in either English or Malay. Facilities were also to be provided for instruction in Kuo Yu (the Chinese national language) and Tamil where parents of fifteen pupils requested it in any one school. While some Malays and Europeans welcomed the legislation as a step towards national integration, other Malays disliked the introduction of national streams into vernacular schools. Most bitterly opposed, however, were the Chinese and Indian community leaders. They felt that the Ordinance amounted to an attempt to undermine Chinese and Indian culture by limiting the use of Kuo Yu and Tamil as teaching languages. The Malayan Chinese Association (MCA)–the main organization representing the Chinese in Malaya–dispatched detailed briefs to King's House criticizing the legislation and recommending drastic changes. The Chinese press also reacted strongly to what was thought to be an attack on a fundamental facet of Chinese life.[111] In the end, however, it was not so much this barrage of criticism as the reduced revenues of 1953 and 1954, as well as the chronic shortage of teachers, which forced the Government to shelve the National Schools programme.

Chinese leaders were also upset by a number of other pieces of legislation passed by the Legislative Council. The Immigration Control Ordinance of November 1952, which decreed that non-citizens born in the Federation who left Malaya temporarily could not return without the permission of the Controller of Immigration, was considered to be blatant discrimination against the Chinese community, and particularly worried Chinese businessmen who travelled extensively.[112] The Registration and Licensing of Business Bill was also thought to be discriminatory by the Chinese business community. The Bill was designed to raise 50 per cent of the money for the Education Development Fund by taxing businesses in such a way as to require each partner to pay a licensing fee which was related to the overall capital assets of the business. Chinese leaders argued that money for education should come out of general revenue and that the legislation discriminated against small businesses with large numbers of partners. Perhaps most galling of all for the

Chinese political leaders was the introduction by their arch political rival, the Minister of Home Affairs, Dato Onn, of a ban on all
lotteries run by political parties. This severely curtailed the welfare work of the MCA in the New Villages and limited the MCA's
ability to establish grassroots links with the mass of the Chinese.[113]
Sir Gerald Templer, despite repeated representation, refused to
change either piece of legislation. The result was to perpetuate
some of the old tensions between the Chinese élite and the Government.

But it must be pointed out that, compared with Gurney, Templer's relations with the élite of all racial communities were fairly
good. This was not simply because of the reduced guerrilla threat–
although this, of course, helped considerably–but also because of
Templer's willingness to listen to people and to require his officials
to travel and talk with community representatives. One example of
Templer's astuteness was his decision to appoint David Gray, at
that time Secretary for Chinese Affairs, as Acting Chief Secretary
for a short period in 1953-4. For the first time, a Chinese-speaking
MCS officer occupied a key post. The appointment assured the
Chinese that their interests would be represented at the highest
levels and it returned to the Chinese Affairs Department much of
the 'face' it had lost in the post-War period. In general, just as the
Government had mixed success in wooing the hearts and minds of
the general population of Malaya, so its relations with the various
élite groups were akin to a roller-coaster ride with all its ups and
downs.

The MCP on the Defensive

In early 1952, the guerrilla forces were in good shape. While casualties were relatively high, replacements were readily available.
Official figures, which undoubtedly underestimated the strength
of the guerrillas, suggested there were just under 6,000 guerrillas,
10,000-15,000 regular workers, and about ten times as many active
adherents of one sort or another.[114] Gradually, over the next five
years, the MCP lost the initiative it had gained in the early years of
the Emergency. Much of the MRLA was forced into deep jungle,
the MCP headquarters were removed to the Thai border region,
and both the general support for the MCP and the numbers of guerrillas began to decline.

The strategy outlined in the October 1951 directives, which put
equal emphasis on political and military activities, did not provide

the successes that the MCP leadership had hoped for. On the political side, it proved much easier to issue directives than to restructure the Party organization to implement them. Eventually, however, attempts were mounted to organize more cells in New Villages, to infiltrate Home Guard units and village councils, and to gain support among Chinese students, especially those in Chinese middle schools. In some of the major centres, MCP members resorted to pre-Emergency tactics. They worked through front organizations which attracted supporters by emphasizing patriotism and the growing stature of the new China. Overall, the results were mixed, with the best headway being made among students.

On the military side, the lull in guerrilla activity following the dissemination of the directives, caused concern because of the detrimental effect the inactivity had on the morale of the MRLA units and the boost it gave to the Government's cause. Indeed, in October 1952, while not explicitly criticizing their 1951 directives, the MCP leadership issued new orders which instructed the MRLA to spend less time on jungle cultivation and more on aggressive military action. They were also told not to worry too much about the repercussions such actions might have on the masses.[115] However, the MRLA units faced two problems which significantly undermined their ability to regain their military effectiveness.

First, dwindling food supplies proved debilitating and demoralizing. While food was still being obtained from the New Villages, the Government's food control measures, and in some areas the increasing reluctance of New Villagers to co-operate with the Min Yuen, were causing serious logistical problems. In areas where Government forces could concentrate their efforts, food became especially scarce. Growing food in the jungle was not as easy as had been anticipated. From the air the security forces soon spotted the neat rows in suspicious looking clearings that were characteristic of early guerrilla attempts at jungle market gardening. Even adopting the techniques employed by the *orang asli* was not the answer. Although their cultivated patches could not easily be detected from the air, they did not allow for the growing of the amount of food required by the MRLA. In some places the guerrillas were forced to buy their food on the open market. This was costly, and with the 1953-4 economic slump reducing their income, the MRLA leaders had to deduct between $25 and $35 for food out of the approximately $38 per month paid to each guerrilla.[116] Even with these measures, some captured and surrendered guerrillas came out of the jungle malnourished. Inevitably, there were incidents of friction and recrimination between the MRLA and the Min Yuen over the distribution of food.[117]

Secondly, the possibility of infiltration by Government agents became a preoccupation of the guerrilla leaders. The fear of a repetition of Lai Tek's treachery, the suspicion that the security forces were placing informers in the New Villages, and the heightened incidents of betrayal sparked by the rewards programme combined to spread mistrust within the MRLA. Subsequent attempts to maintain strict control over the rank and file within guerrilla units, and the occasional execution of Party members and supporters suspected of being 'politically unreliable' eroded people's confidence in the MCP and its cause.[118] In addition, scarce propaganda resources had to be shifted away from wooing the general population to shoring up the morale of Party members and supporters.

The MCP's change in strategy neither forestalled problems that were overtaking the military campaign nor brought about the hoped for surge in popular support. Forced by the food shortages to operate in small units of between three and fifteen, and relatively isolated from the MCP headquarters which had been moved to a more secure base across the Thai border, it was almost impossible to sustain a co-ordinated military attack on the Government. This problem was magnified by the increasing difficulty the Party faced in trying to find suitable recruits. As a consequence, the guerrilla force shrank, as did the areas which it controlled.[119] And with the Min Yuen becoming increasingly concerned with the survival of the guerrilla units and themselves, it was not easy to expand their proselytizing activities among the general population. Yet, for all these problems, the MCP remained a potent force. At the end of 1954, they still had about 4,000 guerrillas in the jungle, and were intent on rebuilding their support organizations among the Malayan population.

Summary

During the three years from the beginning of 1952 to the beginning of 1955, there was a decided shift in the course of the Emergency. For the first time, the Government was able to seize the overall initiative and force the MCP guerrillas back on to the defensive. Yet the swing towards the Government was neither pervasive nor decisive; indeed, it was most uneven.

In a few areas, resettlement had gone well and the development of the New Villages progressed steadily. The buildings and trained personnel for the delivery of social services were put in place, and employment and agricultural land were available. Villagers were able to use the strict control exercised by the security forces as an excuse for not aiding the guerrillas. Confidence in the Government increased, and a few people were willing to provide information on the local Min Yuen members and guerrilla movements. Using this information, the security forces were able to disrupt the activities of the guerrillas and reduce their effectiveness. This, in turn, induced more people to co-operate with Government officials. As the security forces gained the ascendancy at the local level, surrendered or captured guerrillas provided even more valuable information, and gradually an area became free of active guerrillas and could be declared 'white'.

However, in many places it took a long time before this somewhat idealized picture was even nearly replicated. More often than not, either resettlement had not gone well or development was extremely slow. In parts of Johore, for example, where the resettlement programme had been implemented with no real planning, the process had simply produced concentrated slums. In the Kinta Valley in Perak, the problem was a lack of land and a secure economic base on which the New Villagers could depend for their livelihood. In many areas–usually the more remote–the promised social services were slow to materialize. These delays made it very difficult for the Government to break the long-standing links between the villagers and the MCP. Gradually, however, as the pool of trained manpower was increased, and the social services introduced into more villages, and as the security forces were reorganized and retrained and their food control operations refined, the Government was able to extend its control over the rural population.

On the Government's side, much of the credit for what success was achieved during this period was attributed to Templer. He was certainly fortunate in inheriting from Briggs, Gurney, and Lyttelton a workable plan for the prosecution of the counter-guerrilla campaign. He was also able to exploit the massive accumulation of funds built up in the Government's coffers as a result of the Korean War boom. Nevertheless, Templer did make a significant personal contribution to the Government's cause. By using the powers of his dual appointment and his strong personality, he gave a 'tremendous lift to morale throughout the Federation and imbued the Security Forces and civil administration with a new spirit and a will to win'.[120] Tan Cheng Lock, the leader of the MCA, who had clashed with Templer on more than one occasion, told the 1954 Annual General

Meeting of the MCA that Templer was 'a true soldier-statesman who had filled the needs and demands of the critical hour in Malaya'.[121] Certainly Templer had provided much-needed leadership, and in the process, given form and substance to the hearts and minds strategy.

But it must be borne in mind that not only did the Government gain ground, the MCP lost it. At least part of the reason for the change in the fortunes of the two sides lay in the new policy set out in the 1951 directives. The lull in guerrilla-initiated incidents in 1952 gave the security forces the breather they needed to reorganize and retrain, and greatly boosted their morale. Moreover, the problems faced by the guerrilla units in securing food and guarding against infiltration, and the length of time it took Party members to reorient themselves to rebuilding their organizational support among the 'masses', as well as the Party's failure to expand its base of support into the Malay and Indian communities, made it difficult for them to return to the offensive on a broad scale.

Despite all this, the situation remained in a state of flux. Both MacGillivray and Templer were at pains to underline their assessment that 'the end of communist terrorism in Malaya is by no means in sight'.[122] There was a good deal of concern expressed in official circles that once Templer stepped down as High Commissioner, the Government's momentum would be lost. It was decided that the date on which Templer would hand over to MacGillivray would be announced nearly six months in advance to allow the people of Malaya to become accustomed to the idea of a new administration and to ensure a smooth transfer of power.[123]

When he took over as High Commissioner in mid-1954, MacGillivray (now Sir Donald) declared that a stalemate had been reached. He pointed out that over the preceding twelve months, the rate of incidents and of casualties had continued more or less unchanged and that the surrender rate, far from improving, had declined almost to the vanishing point.[124] Like Templer before him, he was especially concerned with the increased emphasis that the MCP was placing on expanding its organizational base. MacGillivray was pessimistic about major advances in the Government's campaign being made in the near future. It was in these circumstances that the rising tide of political activity became so important.

1. See Department of Information, *Emergency Statistics for the Federation of Malaya Since June 1948*, 7/60/160 (Emerg), 1960, Appendix H.

2. Hugh Fraser, 'Papers on the Malayan Emergency', CO 1022/22.

3. In addition to receiving cash benefits and benefits in kind upon leaving the force after a specified period, many special constables were given courses in civic responsibilities, vocational training, and reading, writing, and arithmetic so as to equip them to enter civilian life when their term of duty was up. *Proceedings of the Federal Legislative Council*, 6th Session, cc. 29-30.

4. The number of regular police killed fell from 116 in 1951 to 65 in 1952 and 10 in 1953. The number of special constables killed dropped from 217 in 1951 to 134 in 1952 and 34 in 1953. Department of Information, *Emergency Statistics for the Federation of Malaya*, Appendix H.

5. Public support for Operation Service was encouraged by such diverse sources as *The Planter*, 29 January 1953, and *Melayu Raya*, 9 March 1953, translated in Colony of Singapore, *Daily Digest of Non-English Press*, No. 54/53.

6. The number of civilians killed dropped from 533 in 1951 to 343 in 1952 and 85 in 1953. See Department of Information, *Emergency Statistics for the Federation of Malaya*, Appendix H.

7. See P/PM1 Secretary to Government 32 (4/7), and Department of Information, *Communist Banditry in Malaya: The Emergency, June 1948-June 1951*, p. 120.

8. *Straits Times*, 9 February l952.

9. For details of the Kinta Valley Home Guard Scheme, see *Federation of Malaya Annual Report*, 1952, p. 14; Leong Yew Koh Papers, Box 8, SP 3, and Business SP 3/1/4 (ANM), and CO 1022/36.

10. See the interview in *Straits Times*, 26 February 1955. During Christmas week 1954, six Home Guard commanders were killed.

11. See High Commissioner's Press Conference, 26 May 1954, Department of Information, 5/54/193 (HC).

12. By the end of 1954, the number in the Home Guard which had reached over 250,000 in 1953 was around 170,000. Federation of Malaya, *Annual Report*, 1954, p. 409, and P/PM1, Secretary to Government 32(4/7) (ANM).

13. See Chinese Affairs, September, 1952, CO 1022/36, and Leong Yew Koh Papers, Business SP 3/1/4 (ANM).

14. See Richard Clutterbuck, *The Long, Long War: Counterinsurgency in Malaya and Vietnam* (New York: Praeger, 1966), p. 54; J. B. Oldfield, *The Green Howards in Malaya, 1949-52* (Aldershot: Gale and Polden, 1953), p. 191; R. W. Komer, *The Malayan Emergency in Retrospect: Organization of a Successful Counterinsurgency Effort* (Santa Monica: Rand, February 1972), pp. 49-51, and Anthony Short, *The Communist Insurrection in Malaya 1948-1960* (London: Frederick Muller, 1975), pp. 368-9.

15. These issues are covered in P/PM1, Chief Secretary 438/13/51 (ANM); Fraser's Report, 'Papers on the Malayan Emergency', CO 1022/22, and 'Notes of a Meeting on Malayan Subjects', 23 June 1952, CO 1022/492.

16. 'Monthly Administrative Report' for April 1952, CO 1022/449.

17. See *Proceedings of the Federal Legislative Council*, 5th Session, p. 473; CO 1022/107, and CO 1022/110.

18. The SCA's work in fact covered everything to do with the Chinese community, including acting as Chairman of the Chinese Advisory Board, Registrar of Societies, and New Village development work. See the list in Chinese Affairs 1530 (ANM). See also Deputy Secretary for Chinese Affairs, Federation of Malaya, to

Chief Secretary, Federation of Malaya, 29 April 1952, Chinese Affairs 1495 (ANM).

19. See the minutes and documents on Dawson's visit in P/PM1, Chief Secretary 31/8 (ANM), and CO 1022/378.

20. See Acting Chief Secretary to all Mentri Mentri Besar and Resident Commissioner, 8 March 1952, Chinese Affairs FM 1648 (ANM); CO 1022/449, and Fraser's Report, CO 1022/22.

21. See the Reports of the State SCAs in Chinese Affairs FM 1648 (ANM) and the President of the Chinese Affairs Association, Federation of Malaya, to Secretary for Chinese Affairs, Federation of Malaya, 6 January 1955, Chinese Affairs FM 1635 (ANM).

22. See 'Corruption', 24 May 1952, Executive Council Paper No. 16/13/52, Leong Yew Koh Papers SP 3/3/24 (ANM).

23. See Gordon P. Means, 'New Villages in Malaya', mimeograph (Hamilton, Ontario: Department of Political Science, McMaster University, n.d.), p. 84; Francis Kok-Wah Loh, 'Beyond the Tin Mines: The Political Economy of Chinese Squatter Farmers in the Kinta New Villages, Malaysia' (Ph.D. dissertation, Cornell University, 1980), p. 139; Minutes of the 9th Meeting of the Chinese Advisory Board, Perak, 17 March 1955, p. 3 (ANM), and 'War in Malaya', British Survey Main Series, No. 39, June 1952, p. 20.

24. Federation of Malaya, Commission of Enquiry into Matters Affecting the Integrity of the Public Service (Kuala Lumpur: Government Printer, 1955), p. 59.

25. Memorandum by R. H. Oakley, J. L. H. Davis, and J. A. Cradock, 12 February 1953, P/PM1, Chief Secretary 11/7 (ANM).

26. Commission of Enquiry, p. 15. See also Chinese Affairs FM 1440 (ANM), and P/PM1, Chief Secretary 102/5 (ANM).

27. See Richard Stubbs, Counter-Insurgency and the Economic Factor: The Impact of the Korean War Prices Boom on the Malayan Emergency, Occasional Paper No. 19 (Singapore: Institute of Southeast Asian Studies, 1974), pp. 4-24. The cost of police alone in 1952 and again in 1953 was $173 million. See P/PM1, Secretary to Government 32 (4/2) (ANM).

28. See Director of Operations, The Protection of Estates and Mines, 1953.

29. Short, The Communist Insurrection, p. 340; John Weldon Humphrey, 'Population Resettlement in Malaya' (Ph.D. dissertation, Northwestern University, 1971), pp. 129-30; High Commissioner to Secretary of State, 26 May 1952, CO 1022/56, and also papers in CO 1022/54. Fears were expressed by one authority that the reduction in the intake of calories would cause problems for mothers and children. See CO 1022/55. A kati equals one and one-third pounds. The curfew was normally from 7.00 p.m. to 6.00 a.m.

30. Loh, 'Beyond the Tin Mines', p. 129; Department of Information, Malaya Under the Emergency, n.d. pp. 30-3.

31. See CO 1022/56, and The Times (London), 28 August 1952.

32. See, for example, Manchester Guardian, 26 August 1952; The Times (London), 28 August 1952, and the letters and telegrams in CO 1022/56. A reply to this last point was given by a Malayan Security Officer who argued that those who gave information could be removed to another part of the Federation. Manchester Guardian, 10 September 1952.

33. Humphrey, 'Population Resettlement', p. 131. Judith Strauch reports that informants in one new village felt that 'effective "passification" resulted more from the stick than from the carrot'. See Judith Strauch, Chinese Village Politics in the Malaysian State (Cambridge, Mass: Harvard University Press, 1981), p. 72.

34. This compares with 19 cases of collective detention involving over 10,000 people between January 1949 and November 1951. See CO 1022/132, and 'Detention and Deportation During the Emergency in the Federation of Malaya', *Proceedings of the Federal Legislative Council*, Paper No. 24, 1953, p. 17.

35. *Proceedings of the Federal Legislative Council*, Paper No. 24, 1953, pp. 6–14. By December 1953 only 822 were in detention camps. See 'Monthly Administrative Report', December 1953, CO 1022/450; and High Commissioner to Secretary of State for the Colonies, 29 July 1952, CO 1022/132.

36. Loh, 'Beyond the Tin Mines', pp. 130–1.

37. 'Report to the Director of Operations, November 20, 1951', CO 1022/22.

38. See the description of food control in Rhoderick Dhu Renick, Jr., 'The Emergency Regulations of Malaya: Causes and Effect', *Journal of Southeast Asian History* 6 (September 1965), pp. 28–31, and R. W. Komer, *The Malayan Emergency in Retrospect: Organization of a Successful Counterinsurgency Effort* (Santa Monica: Rand, February 1972), pp. 58–61.

39. Harry Miller, *Menace in Malaya* (London: Harrap, 1954), p. 189.

40. Department of Labour, *Annual Report*, 1954, p. 38.

41. Loh, 'Beyond the Tin Mines', p. 133.

42. 'Resettlement and the Development of New Villages in the Federation of Malaya 1952', *Proceedings of the Federal Legislative Council*, Paper No. 33.

43. See High Commissioner to Secretary of State, 16 March 1953, CO 1022/29.

44. Memorandum, 12 February 1953, P/PM1, Chief Secretary 11/7 (ANM).

45. Where they could, the MCA granted $800 per classroom and $300 per teacher's quarters. See MCA (Perak Branch) Report, for the year ending 30 June 1953, Leong Yew Koh Papers, Box 8 SP 3 (ANM). When the MCA lottery was prohibited in 1953, the MCA's ability to fund New Village schools was greatly reduced.

46. 'Resettlement and Development', *Proceedings of the Federal Legislative Council*, 1952. These grants were not intended to cover the full costs. In many cases, buildings could not have been completed without financial assistance from the local branch of the MCA.

47. Loh, 'Beyond the Tin Mines', p. 116, citing Federation of Malaya, *Social Services in the Federation of Malaya* (London: Central Office of Information, Research Division, 1954), p. 32.

48. Although Federal spending on education declined from 1952 to 1954, state spending increased by a greater amount. Combined spending increased from $72.2 million in 1952 to $77.4 million in 1953, and to $80.8 million in 1954. See Stubbs, *Counter-Insurgency*, p. 16.

49. Although it was particularly so in the New Villages, this was also true for all types of schools. For instance, there was only one qualified teacher for every ninety-two pupils in English language secondary schools. Memorandum from the Director of Education, Executive Council Paper, No. 14/18/52, Leong Yew Koh Papers SP 3/2/96 (ANM).

50. Department of Education, *Annual Report*, 1954, p. 21. Teacher training facilities were developed in Kirby, near Liverpool, England, as well as in Malaya.

51. This is the calculation of Means, 'New Villages in Malaya', p. 155. For 1952 figures, see 'Resettlement and Development', *Proceedings of the Federal Legislative Council*, Paper No. 33, 1952. Overall estimates by the High Commissioner were that 42 per cent of all primary school age children were attending school. Statement to the Press by Templer, 19 June 1952, CO 1022/492. An interesting development

was the expansion of adult literacy classes sponsored mainly by the MCA. For 1954 figures, see International Bank for Reconstruction and Development, *The Economic Development of Malaya* (Singapore: Government Printer, 1955), p. 442.

52. *Straits Budget*, 17 April 1952.

53. Ibid. See also CO 1022/3

54. Memorandum, 12 February 1953, P/PM1, Chief Secretary 11/7 (ANM), and Minutes of Director of Operations' Committees, 17/52 and 23/52, P/PM1, Chief Secretary 31/9 (ANM).

55. Stubbs, *Counter-Insurgency*, p. 16.

56. See Means, 'New Villages in Malaya', pp. 131-2; P/PM1, Chief Secretary 31/9, Chief Secretary 31/13 (ANM); P/PM1, Secretary to Government 67/1 (ANM), and CO 1022/31.

57. Malayan Christian Council, 'A Survey of the New Villages in Malaya', mimeograph (Kuala Lumpur: revised version, 1959) cited in Loh, 'Beyond the Tin Mines', p. 115, and Humphrey, 'Population Resettlement', p. 223. The Red Cross and St. John Ambulance only maintained teams in the field during the early and mid-1950s.

58. Means, 'New Villages in Malaya', p. 134.

59. Department of Labour, *Annual Report*, 1953, p. 17.

60. See Minutes of the 9th Meeting of the Chinese Advisory Board, Perak, 17 March 1955, in which complaints about the conduct of the police were put forward. Leong Yew Koh Papers SP 3 (ANM).

61. Department of Labour, *Monthly Report*, October 1952, p. 2. The Incorporated Society of Planters, which held examinations for its members in Malay and Tamil, decided that there were so many Chinese being employed on estates they ought to set up examinations in Hakka, Cantonese, and Hokkien. See General-Secretary, The Incorporated Society of Planters to Secretary for Chinese Affairs, Federation of Malaya, 16 August 1952, Chinese Affairs 1441 (ANM).

62. By 1952 the percentage of agriculturalists in the New Villages had dropped from 60 per cent to 27 per cent. See Kernial Singh Sandhu, 'The Saga of the "Squatters" in Malaya: A Preliminary Survey of the Causes, Characteristics and Consequences of the Resettlement of Rural Dwellers during the Emergency between 1948 and 1960', *Journal of Southeast Asian History* 5 (March 1964), p. 169. See also Means, 'New Villages in Malaya', p. 110.

63. Department of Labour, *Monthly Report*, August 1952, p. 2.

64. 'Resettlement and the Development of New Villages in the Federation of Malaya', 1952, *Proceedings of the Federal Legislative Council*, Paper No. 33.

65. Ibid.

66. W. C. S. Corry, *A General Survey of New Villages, A Report to His Excellency Sir Donald MacGillivray, High Commissioner of the Federation of Malaya* (Kuala Lumpur: Government Printer, 1954), and Federal Press Statement, Department of Information 10/53/232 (Lands), CO 1022/29.

67. Quoted in Loh, 'Beyond the Tin Mines', p. 122. There were over 100,000 families involved. Thus over 100,000 acres would have been required under the old scheme and over 50,000 under the new. Corry estimates that the Government had made available 47,800 acres of agricultural land (p. 24) but it is not clear on what basis he makes this estimate. Other admittedly fragmentary evidence suggests that the amount was much lower. See, for example, the 'Bimonthly Progress Report' from the Member for Lands, Mines and Communication on the alienation of land as of 30 September 1953 in P/PM1, Secretary to Government 67/1

(ANM). In Negri Sembilan, only 1,851 acres of the estimated 5,184 that were needed were available and in Johore, only 4,658 acres of the 9,897 needed were available. And this is on the basis of a half acre per family. See P/PM1 Secretary to Government, 67/1 (ANM). Nor is it clear how good this land was. A correspondent in *The Economic Weekly* says that in parts of Malaya the agricultural lands were based on tin tailings and 'almost uncultivable'. See William H. Newall, 'New Villages in Malaya', *The Economic Weekly*, 12 February 1955.

68. On profits, see R. Ma, 'Company Profits and Prices in the Rubber Industry in Malaya, 1947-58', *The Malayan Economic* Review, 4 October 1959, p. 4. Company net profits averaged 10.8 cents per pound and 17.4 cents in 1953 and 1954 compared to 6.6 and 6.9 cents per pound in 1948 and 1949. On the demand for labour on estates, see 'Memorandum from the Member for Economic Affairs, Effects of the Fall in the Price of Rubber and Tin', CO 1022/462. It is interesting to note that in constant 1981 US dollars, the price of rubber in 1953 and 1954 averaged more than the price of rubber in any year since 1963. These years were considered recessionary years only because of the preceding boom years. See World Bank/FAO, *Commodity Trade and Price Trends*, 1982/3.

69. Department of Labour, *Annual Report*, 1954, pp. 91 and 95, and 1953, p. 7. The estimated adult male working population (aged 15-54 years) rose very little: from 1.3 million in 1947 to between 1.38 million and 1.4 million in 1951. There was a chronic labour shortage in the post-War years. *Federation of Malaya Annual Report*, 1957, pp. 39-40.

70. 'Memorandum from the Member for Economic Affairs, Effects of the Fall in the Price of Rubber and Tin', CO 1022/462.

71. For Malaya-wide statistics, see *Federation of Malaya Annual Report*, 1954, pp. 32-3, and 1953, p. 20.

72. Department of Labour, *Annual Report*, 1953, p. 18.

73. Loh, 'Beyond the Tin Mines', p. 125. The Department of Labour, *Annual Report*, 1954, p. 18, states that at the beginning of January 1954 some 16,000 people in the New Villages reported themselves to be unemployed. However, the data collection techniques were not very sophisticated. DOs and ROs were asked to keep a check on the numbers who reported themselves to be unemployed.

74. See Chairman of Pauh New Village School, Perlis, to President of the MCA, 16 March 1954, Leong Yew Koh Papers SP 3, Box 9 (ANM). Also see Loh, 'Beyond the Tin Mines', pp. 124-5, for his comments on the failure of Corry, in his influential report, to appreciate the land hunger problem of New Villagers. There is no evidence that Corry visited many New Villages. Humphrey, 'Population Resettlement', p. 157, says Corry based his report on files and statistics at Federal Headquarters.

75. Paul Markandan, *The Problem of the New Villages in Malaya* (Singapore: Donald Moore, 1954), pp. 12 and 17.

76. Malayan Christian Council, 'A Survey', p. 5, cited in Humphrey, 'Population Resettlement', p. 228.

77. Humphrey, 'Population Resettlement', p. 151.

78. Short, *The Communist Insurrection*, pp. 209-10.

79. Resettlement costs averaged $500 per family. See High Commissioner to Secretary of State for the Colonies, 4 April 1953, CO 1022/29.

80. See, for example, Malay representatives on the Perak State Council to Sir Hylton Poynton, Colonial Office, 2 June 1950, CO 717/205.

81. See *The Times* (London), 20 March 1952; *Warta Negara*, 22 November 1952, and the *Majlis*, 27 November 1952, in Department of Information, *Fortnight-*

ly Press Digest, 22/52, 30 November 1952; CO 1022/253, and CO 1022/465.

82. *Proceedings of the Federal Legislative Council*, 6th Session, cc. 17-18, and 'Report on the Implementation of Government Policy', 12 February 1953, P/PM1, Chief Secretary 11/7 (ANM).

83. Sandhu, 'The Saga of the "Squatters"', p. 167, and Short, *The Communist Insurrection*, pp. 442-5. Documents captured by the Government in Kelantan in June 1954 give an indication of the relationship between the guerrillas and the aborigines. See 'Monthly Emergency and Political Report', 18 July-15 August 1954, No. 55, FO 371/111855.

84. The 1952 estimate was made by P. D. R. Williams-Hunt, the Protector of Aborigines, in *An Introduction to the Malayan Aborigines* (Kuala Lumpur: Government Press, 1952), p. 1. This booklet was made available to those who dealt with the aborigines.

85. *Federation of Malaya Annual Report*, 1954, p. 254. The story of the work of the two brothers Pat and Richard Noone among the aborigines is told in Dennis Holman, *Noone of the Ulu* (London: Heinemann, 1958), and Richard Noone, *Rape of the Dream People* (London: Hutchinson, 1972). Noone replaced John Blacking who was fired after two weeks because he disagreed with the Government's method of winning over the aborigines. See *Straits Budget*, 3 December 1953, for Blacking's views, and High Commissioner to the Secretary of State for the Colonies, 14 December 1953, CO 1022/475, for the Government's views.

86. See *Proceedings of the Federal Legislative Council*, 6th Session, c. 745; Rhoderick Dhu Renick Jr., 'The Emergency Regulations of Malaya: Causes and Effect', *Journal of Southeast Asian History* 6 (September 1965), p. 32; Humphrey, 'Population Resettlement', pp. 165-8, and B. T. W. Stewart to the Editor, *Far Eastern Economic Review*, 19 December 1985.

87. The figures at Templer's departure were given in Sir Gerald Templer's Press Conference, 26 May 1954, Department of Information, 5/54/193 (HC). The declaration of the first 'white areas' was interpreted by the Chinese-language paper, *Nanyang Siang Pau*, 8 September 1953, as a prelude to the end of the Emergency. See Colony of Singapore, Public Relations Office, *Daily Digest of Non-English Press*, No. 201/53, p. 8.

88. See *Federation of Malaya Annual Report*, 1948, p. 112; 1949, p. 126; 1950, p. 142, and 1951, p. 180.

89. *Federation of Malaya Annual Report*, 1952, p. 286, and 'Report on Emergency, Information Services, September 1950-September 1951' by Hugh Carleton Greene, CO 537/7255. For copies of this report, see Tan Cheng Lock Papers, Item 167(i) (ANM), where it is claimed the October 1952 issue of *New Path News* had a circulation of 110,000 copies.

90. See *Federation of Malaya Annual Report*, 1953, p. 318, and 1954, p. 378, and Norton Ginsburg and Robert F. Chester Jr., *Malaya* (Seattle: University of Washington, 1958), p. 171.

91. See Department of Broadcasting, *Annual Report*, 1952, pp. 289-91, and 1953, p. 322.

92. *Federation of Malaya Annual Report*, 1951, pp. 181-2. See also Federation of Malaya, *Monthly Statistics Bulletin*, 1949-53 (Kuala Lumpur: Government Printer, n.d.); *Federation of Malaya Annual Report*, 1952, p. 290, and 1953, p. 322.

93. In Kuala Lumpur in 1948, there was a weekly attendance of about 100,000 persons, and this was in an urban area of only 176,000 population. See

UNESCO, *Report of the Commission on Technical Needs in Press, Film and Radio* (Paris: UNESCO, 1948), Vol. 2, p. 272.

94. *Federation of Malaya Annual Report*, 1953, pp. 313-14.

95. This was done in response to the highly critical comments of Fraser in his report, 'Papers on the Malayan Emergency', CO 1022/22.

96. See 'Report on the Implementation of Government Policy', 12 February 1953, P/PM1, Chief Secretary 11/7 (ANM).

97. C. C. Too, later Director of Psychological Warfare, was one of those who resigned. Interviews 1973 and 1982. After this the *New Path News* suffered major production problems.

98. Komer, *The Malayan Emergency in Retrospect*, p. 71.

99. Surrender figures are to be found in CO 1022/49. For example, in January 1953, thirty-nine surrendered; by May 1953 this figure had fallen to fourteen.

100. See 'Memorandum to OC CID Selangor on a Meeting of Surrendered Enemy Personnel', 18 December 1949, Hugh T. Pagden Papers SP7/2 (ANM).

101. Such rewards were not a new feature of Malaya's society. For example, before the Emergency, in March 1947, police paid $30,000 for information received 'which led to the discovery of a large dump of illicit arms'. *Straits Times*, 6 March 1947. These rewards varied according to the rank of the guerrilla involved, but even the amount for a member of the rank and file of the MRLA was a relatively large sum by any standard and a major stimulus to giving information to the police. Komer, *The Malayan Emergency in Retrospect*, pp. 72-5.

102. *Proceedings of the Federal Legislative Council*, 1st Session, p. B524.

103. On the views of non-Malays, see Tan Cheng Lock, 'A Chinese View of Malaya', in David R. Rees-Williams, Tan Cheng Lock, S. S. Awberry, and F. W. Dalley, *Three Reports on the Malayan Problem* (New York: International Secretariat, Institute of Pacific Relations), 1949, p. 18, and *Jananayakam* (a Kuala Lumpur Tamil Daily), 15 November 1948, English translation in Tan Cheng Lock Papers, Item 173 (ANM). For opposition to the original Bill based on the Community Liaison Committee's proposals, see 'Apa Khabar', *Straits Echo*, 20 May 1950; *Tiger Standard* (Singapore) 28 July 1950, and the correspondence between Tan Cheng Lock and Malcolm MacDonald, Sir Henry Gurney, T. H. Tan, and Sir George Maxwell in the Tan Cheng Lock Papers, Item 102 and uncatalogued (ANM) and TCL/V/121 (ISEAS). The Rulers are also reported to have rejected the Government's initial proposals. See *Straits Echo*, 16 September 1950 and *Straits Times*, 11 January 1951.

104. Some of the major points of contention that had to be resolved by the committee are listed in Attorney-General to Chief Secretary, 26 November 1951, P/PM1, Chief Secretary 438/3/51 (ANM).

105. *Proceedings of the Federal Legislative Council*, 5th Session, p. 174. *Jus soli* refers to the right of those born in a country to be automatically given the citizenship of that country.

106. For details of the citizenship regulations introduced by the Federation of Malaya Agreement (Amendment) Ordinance, see Victor Purcell, *Malaya: Communist or Free?* (London: Gollancz, 1954), pp. 218-20.

107. *Proceedings of the Federal Legislative Council*, 5th Session, pp. 167-73.

108. These figures are for 30 June 1953. Only 203 direct citizenships and 38,334 citizenships through state nationality were acquired by registration or naturalization up to 13 December 1953. *Federation of Malaya Annual Report*, 1953, pp. 15-16.

109. *Proceedings of the Federal Legislative Council*, 6th Session, c. 10.

110. Federation of Malaya, *Report of the Special Committee Appointed on the 20th Day of September, 1951 to Recommend Legislation to Cover all Aspects of Education Policy for the Federation of Malaya* (Kuala Lumpur: Government Printer, 1952); Federation of Malaya, *Education Ordinance* (Kuala Lumpur: Government Printer, 1952).

111. See the correspondence in Tan Cheng Lock Papers, Chinese Education No. 2 (ANM); 'Memorandum on Chinese Education in the Federation of Malaya', 21 March 1954, Tan Cheng Lock Papers TCL/XIII/25 (ISEAS), and the translations of articles in the Chinese Press in Colony of Singapore, Public Relations Office, *Daily Digest of Non-English Press*, 20 October 1952, No. 40; 30 October 1952, No. 49, and 27 July 1953, 167/53. See also the Department of Education, *Annual Report*, 1955, pp. 20-2; and CO 1022/285, and CO 1022/286.

112. See 'Memorandum' in Tan Cheng Lock Papers, Box 1, No. 65 (ANM), and Purcell, *Malaya*, pp. 116-17.

113. The lotteries question is discussed in Gordon P. Means, *Malaysian Politics* (London: Hodder and Stoughton, 1976), pp. 137-9. The importance of the lotteries to the MCA social welfare programme is noted in Tan Cheng Lock to Sir Gerald Templer, 15 May 1953, Tan Cheng Lock Papers TCL/XIV/60 (ISEAS).

114. No. 44, Foreign Office, 'Intel', 21 February 1952, CO 1022/2. Short, *The Communist Insurrection*, p. 472, puts the figure at 8,000 in 1951. Renick, 'The Emergency Regulations', p. 4, says the Min Yuen numbered 15,000-25,000.

115. See 'Monthly Emergency and Political Report', 15 January-15 February 1954. The 'Monthly Emergency Political Report', 15 May-15 June 1954 reported that captured MCP pamphlets called for 'active courageous attacks against sentry posts, special constable posts and home guard posts', FO 371/111854.

116. See *The Times* (London), 20 February 1952 and 'Monthly Emergency and Political Report', 15 September-15 October 1954, FO 371/111845. The MCP's total expenditure for 1952 was believed to be $7,500,000. The Government estimated that the MCP's reserves at the end of 1953 were in the region of $300,000 and that the bulk of their expenditure went to maintaining the guerrillas in the jungle. 'MCP Finances', Paper by the Combined Intelligence Staff, 27 November 1953, CO 1022/187.

117. For example, this occurred in 1954 in South Johore. See 'Monthly Emergency and Political Report', 15 January-15 February 1954, FO 371/111845.

118. On the question of executions within the MCP ranks, see the Governor of Singapore to Secretary of State for the Colonies, 26 August 1953, CO 1022/249; *Manchester Guardian*, 4 May 1954, and 'Monthly Emergency and Political Report', 15 April-15 May 1954, FO 371/111845.

119. This point was mentioned in a number of Party documents issued in 1954. See 'Monthly Emergency and Political Report', 15 April-15 May 1954; 15 August-15 September 1954, and 15 September-15 October 1954, FO 371/111845.

120. This is the assessment of senior military officers towards the end of 1952. See 'An Appreciation of the Situation in Malaya', 22 September 1952, WO 216/561.

121. Tan Cheng Lock Papers, Item 177 (ANM).

122. MacGillivray to Lloyd, 17 June 1953, and Templer to Lyttelton, 16 June 1953, CO 1022/98.

123. Churchill was unsure about replacing Templer with MacGillivray. He minuted, 'Are we sure that MacGillivray can fill the gap?' and insisted on seeing MacGillivray personally before agreeing to his appointment as the new High Commissioner. Prime Minister's Personal Minute, 16 November 1953 and 21 November

1953, CO 1022/98. Templer was confident that MacGillivray could do the job, although he recognized that MacGillivray minimized his own qualities. See Templer to Lyttelton, 16 June 1953, CO 1022/98. At the request of the Colonial Office, Templer stayed on a few months longer than his original two-year term. See WO 258/130.

124. These views were expressed in a discussion with Foreign Office and Colonial Office officials in London. See Minute by W. O. Allen, 27 July 1954, FO 371/111855. At this meeting, MacGillivray suggested that overtures might be made 'to the Chinese Government in an attempt to settle the question of Malaya'.

7
The Political Ingredient

IN a guerrilla war, as in any essentially political battle, political organizations that can mobilize support have a significant role to play.
For the Malayan colonial administration, however, the benefits that
might accrue from encouraging the development of political organizations had to be weighed against what were considered to be the
many problems that such a policy was bound to create. Certainly in
the early years of the Emergency, the general consensus within the
Malayan Government was that local politicians and political parties
should not be allowed to interfere with the primary objective of restoring law and order. From the beginning of the Emergency, then,
senior officials in Kuala Lumpur were reluctant to open up the political process and did so only gradually after some prodding by the
Colonial Office and in the face of mounting pressure from local politicians.

During the years immediately following the Second World War,
political activity blossomed. The events of the War had acted as a
catalyst on the political life of South-East Asia and much of Malaya's
educated population was caught up in the general ferment. The social
and economic turmoil, the influence on events in China, India, and
Indonesia, and the bungling attempts of the British and Malayan
Governments to set the ground rules for political development in
the Peninsula, prompted considerable political activity. All communities and all parts of the political spectrum were represented,
and there appeared to be the beginnings of a fascinating, intense,
and many-sided political contest.[1]

With the declaration of the Emergency and the subsequent enforced polarization of allegiances, the political landscape changed
drastically. A month after the Emergency Regulations were prom-
ulgated, the MCP and its front organizations were declared illegal.
Organizations such as the Malayan Democratic Union which favoured non-violent opposition to the colonial regime, went into
voluntary dissolution. Leaders of the radical Malay nationalist
groups were either detained or closely watched by the authorities.
It was almost impossible for all those who wished to advocate either
independence or socialism, but who did not wish to be associated

with the MCP, to continue their political activities.[2]

Once the dust had settled, it became clear that only two groups were viewed by the Government as sufficiently responsible to be encouraged to play a significant role in Malayan politics. The moderate Malay nationalists, including the Rulers and the Malay élite, had demonstrated their political strength in the wake of the introduction of the Malayan Union, and the Government obviously felt that it could not afford to alienate them once again. Indeed, senior colonial officials had been persuaded that the political rights of the Malays were to be enhanced and safeguarded and generally looked on the moderate Malay leaders as their main allies. Hence, the United Malays National Organization (UMNO), which had organized the protest against the Malayan Union and negotiated the Federation Agreement on behalf of the Malays, was allowed to continue its work unaffected by the declaration of the Emergency. The leaders of the conservative Chinese business community, who were either anti-communist because of their pro-Koumintang leanings, or pro-British because of their English-language education, were another group on whom senior officials felt they could call for support against the MCP. However, there was no one organization which united all the different factions within the Chinese community and with whom senior officials were willing to work.

This problem was solved in February 1949 with the inauguration of the Malayan Chinese Association (MCA). Various people, including Yong Shook Lin, Khoo Teik Ee, H. S. Lee, Tan Cheng Lock, and Leong Yew Koh, have been credited with originating the idea of the MCA; however, it also needs to be pointed out that the High Commissioner, Sir Henry Gurney, played a key role. Well before the dinner on 15 December 1948 at Yong Shook Lin's house, during which the decision was taken to form the MCA, Gurney wrote to a colleague in the Colonial Office indicating his intention to attend the dinner and to propose to the heads of the Chinese members of the Legislative Council that the time had come 'for them to start a "Malayan Citizens' Party"'.[3] Gurney's sponsorship clearly signalled that the MCA was expected to play an important part in the Government's anti-guerrilla campaign.

Treading Water

The primary concern of the Colonial Government was for the MCA and the UMNO to aid the Government in defeating communism and returning law and order to Malaya. However, at least initially, the MCA and the UMNO found this to be an almost impossible task. It was not just that the Government itself was unpopular but that both the MCA and the UMNO had too many problems of their own to be effective.

Initially, the MCA was a group of leaders in search of followers. In building their organization from the top down the MCA leaders encountered a number of major problems. First, they had difficulty reaching a consensus on the goals of the Association. Each of the main factions represented at the inaugural meeting had its own ideas of the direction that the MCA should take. Some felt it should promote justice for the Chinese in Malaya, others that it should help mobilize support for Chiang Kai Shek's Government, and still others that it should undertake social welfare and relief work among the rural Chinese.[4] Perhaps the one objective on which they could all agree was that the Government be made fully aware of the concerns of the Chinese business community. None of these goals, however, meshed with the views of the Government. This became evident even before the inauguration of the MCA. When Gurney was shown a draft of the constitution at the end of January 1949, he found that the prime purpose for which he had thought the Association was to be created–'to assist the Government in the restoration of law and order'–had been omitted from the list of objectives. Indeed, there was no mention, as he had suggested, of the Association mobilizing the Chinese community 'to collaborate with the Government'.[5] Efforts to get the MCA to correct these omissions were unsuccessful. As a result, relations between the MCA and senior colonial officials were, from the beginning, complicated by suspicion on both sides.

Secondly, attempts by the MCA leaders to develop a base of support among the wider Chinese community were limited. Many of the MCA members were still preoccupied with trying to re-establish their businesses in the wake of the Occupation. Those who were willing to devote some time to the Association tended to get caught up in the personal rivalries that occupied so many of the leading figures.[6] Of the urban business-oriented members, few volunteered to brave the dangers of trying to aid the scattered Chinese squatter families that inhabited the jungle fringes. Moreover, with the exception of Johore, the MCA had difficulty raising the money to fund schemes that might have helped the squatters and gained supporters for the Association.[7] Even after the Korean War boom enabled the MCA to elicit substantial contributions from its members, and there was a steady flow of money coming in from the lottery established by the Association, it was still difficult to get MCA members to visit the resettlement centres and help harassed Chinese settlers. As Leong Yew Koh, one of the few MCA leaders who tried to do something for the rural Chinese, noted in a letter to Tan Cheng Lock in 1951, 'It is a heart-breaking job to persuade members of our Association to have close contacts with the people.'[8]

Thirdly, in order to gain acceptance by the general Chinese population, the MCA leaders had to demonstrate their influence with the Government and their ability to extract concessions that would materially benefit the Chinese communities. But government officials, especially at the lower levels, were not willing to co-operate with the MCA. Language barriers were largely to blame: Government officials were unable to speak Chinese and local MCA officials often unable to speak either English or Malay. This lack of communication invariably fuelled the popular suspicion among European and Malay administrators that all Chinese were sympathetic towards the communists and that the wisest course of action was to distrust them all without favour. The MCA officials were not usually pro-communist, but neither were they very keen to be too closely associated with the Government. This was in part because of the Government's policies and some of the attitudes and practices of the police and the army, and in part because of the fear of MCP reprisals if they were seen to be too friendly towards the colonial administration. In this respect the many incidents in which MCA officials were killed or injured, and especially the attack on Tan Cheng Lock while he was addressing an MCA meeting in Ipoh in April 1949, had a salutory effect on all MCA officials.[9]

By the end of 1951, the MCA leaders had become frustrated by the Government's unwillingness to place any confidence in them. At a meeting in late October 1951, shortly after Gurney's death, they argued strongly that in order to mobilize the Chinese population they needed to be given positions of real influence, if not power. They pointed out that the Government's general failure to co-operate with them had produced a loss of face, which in turn, had reduced their prestige and effectiveness among the Chinese population. These points were reiterated at a meeting with the Secretary of State for the Colonies, Oliver Lyttelton, when he arrived in Malaya in December 1951.[10] In essence, the MCA had found it very difficult to act as a viable counter to the MCP while they were allowed only a very minor role in Malaya's political process.

But the Government was unwilling to give the MCA a greater role until the Association demonstrated that it represented the

Chinese community. With only 160,000–200,000 members by the end of 1951, the MCA was unable to make such a claim, even if it had wanted to.[11] Senior government officials quickly became disenchanted. The Commissioner of Police, Colonel Gray, noted after the MCA had been in existence for only six months that the Association, which had promised so much, had produced so little, particularly in the way of information.[12] Sir Henry Gurney, too, seems to have been discouraged by what he considered to be the failure of the MCA. He noted in a memorandum written shortly before his death in October 1951 that he was very disappointed that the Association had not become more representative of the Chinese community as a whole and that it had failed to instil in the rural Chinese an appreciation of the Government's cause.[13]

The prospects for the MCA, therefore, looked bleak. On both sides the vital element of trust was missing.[14] The MCA was caught in a vicious circle. It could not mobilize Chinese grassroots support until the Government gave its leaders some powers, yet the Government was unwilling to hand over these powers until the MCA had demonstrated that it fully represented the Chinese community.

By contrast the UMNO, in the first few years of the Emergency, was already a fully fledged and successful organization. However, like the MCA, it too was plagued by internal policy disputes. At the centre of this debate was the UMNO's President, Dato Onn bin Jaafar. A mercurial and impulsive individual Dato Onn was widely respected. His ability to mobilize the Malays against the Malayan Union, and the UMNO's success in forcing the British Government to back down and negotiate the Federation Agreement, made him a powerful force in Malayan politics. Among the Malays he was widely thought to be the only person who could hold together the disparate groups that had originally joined forces to form the UMNO. Among senior government officials, Onn's pre-eminent position as the most powerful local politician was readily acknowledged, although there were some misgivings about his unpredictable temperament—at one time virulently anti-British, at the next charming and solicitous of British opinion.[15] However, any concerns that officials harboured about Onn's judgement were generally set aside because of the need to maintain Malay support in the Government's fight against the communists.

Onn himself appeared to be caught between the two currents of his distrust of the British as the colonial power and the architects of the Malayan Union, and his sense that he needed to maintain their support if he was to inherit their mantle of power. Having been a staunch advocate of Malay rights during the battle to overturn the Malayan Union, Onn began, not long after the promulgation of the Federation Agreement, to advocate the necessity of Malays recognizing the political rights of non-Malays. He was encouraged in this course of action by the view of senior government officials that inter-communal harmony and the emergence of a non-communal governing party would be prerequisites to any future moves towards self-government. In conjunction with Malcolm MacDonald, Onn brought together an informal group of community leaders known as the Communities Liaison Committee.[16] It was hoped that this could be the vehicle for developing a consensus among the various communal groups. After lengthy negotiations, a set of recommendations were drawn up which sought to accommodate some of the changes in the politically crucial criteria for citizenship. Onn's subsequent attempts to educate the Malay community into accepting the non-Malay requests for reform brought the issue of UMNO's role in Malayan politics to a head.

The first crisis came in June 1950 when Dato Onn resigned over the refusal of a special General Assembly of the UMNO to endorse the Communities Liaison Committee's proposals for changes in the citizenship laws. The resignation left the UMNO in disarray and, although many disagreed with Onn's policy, the general feeling was that the Organization needed his leadership. Hence in August 1950, after repeated appeals by various sections of the UMNO, Onn was re-elected to, and accepted, his former post as President. The Communities Liaison Committee's proposals also obtained the approval of the Organization.

But Onn's victory had a price. Over the next year his leadership came under greater scrutiny and his critics became more vocal. The Rulers and the conservative elements of the Malay élite worried that Onn was challenging their traditional role as leaders of the Malays. Malay newspaper articles attacked Onn for acting more like a representative of the Malayan Government than the President of the UMNO. Many felt that his assumption of the head of the Rural and Industrial Development Authority (RIDA) and his appointment to the Federal Legislative Council deprived him of the necessary time to travel the Peninsula talking with the UMNO members and testing their mood. He was said to have lost touch with the rank and file and no longer to represent properly Malay grievances to the Government. In particular, his lack of action over what was widely considered among Malays to be an anti-Malay/Muslim decision by the Singapore High Court in the Nadra or Maria

Hertog case caused resentment. The UMNO leaders were frustrated by the way in which Onn made every issue a personal matter and refused to discuss questions on their merits.[17]

Even with his support melting away, Onn decided to press for the conversion of the UMNO into a non-communal party. However, he failed in his attempts to get members to agree to change the name from the United Malays National Organization to the racially all-embracing United Malayan National Organization. Unable to gain the collective support of the UMNO for his non-communal policies, but convinced that the majority of the UMNO's leaders as well as the kampong Malays would go with him, he left the Organization, and on 16 September 1951 he founded the multiracial Independence of Malaya Party (IMP).

Onn's attempts to impose his will on an unresponsive UMNO membership had a debilitating effect on the Organization's cohesiveness and, thus, on its capacity to mobilize fully and to co-ordinate active Malay support for the Government's fight against the communists. Nor did the creation of the IMP help the Government's cause. The move left the UMNO divided and with an inexperienced leadership. Moreover, while the new party was applauded by some, it was treated warily by many communal leaders who were unsure of how it would be viewed among the general population. Initially at least, rather like the MCA, the IMP attracted more leaders than rank and file supporters, and the leaders were generally only those who were personally committed to Onn. Certainly Onn's popularity among Malays appeared to wane rapidly after he left the UMNO.[18]

Opening up the Political Process

While the two political parties were preoccupied with resolving their internal differences, the Malayan Government was being advised by the Colonial Office, at the behest of Labour Government Ministers, to live up to the wording of the Federation Agreement and start Malaya down the long road to self-government.[19] In Malaya, such promptings were treated with some scepticism. In 1948, even Dato Onn was talking about self-government in twenty-five years. A few months later Onn had revised his assessment downwards but he was still thinking in terms of a gestation period of fifteen years.[20] Members of the traditional Malay élite and the European community felt that all mention of self-government should be shelved until the communist threat had been overcome. Perhaps inevitably, then, the Malayan Government's policy towards opening up the political process evolved slowly.

The Government's first foray into the realm of political reform came with the introduction of the 'Member System' in April 1951.[21] The idea had first been broached by a senior Colonial Office official who, in a letter to Gurney, noted that the African colonies were experimenting with a system whereby non-official members of the Legislative Councils–usually referred to as 'unofficials' in Malaya, these were non-Government representatives appointed by the High Commissioner to represent various interest groups such as communal, business, or labour organizations–were appointed to supervise departments and answer for them in the Legislative Council.[22] Eventually, a Malayan version of the Member System was developed although its implementation was delayed, first, by the need to proceed in step with similar changes in Singapore, and then by Dato Onn's unwillingness to allow the changes to proceed until he had been given the Home Affairs portfolio.[23] But if Gurney had hoped that the Member System would establish links between the Government and the supporters of the two major political organizations and give their supporters greater access to the Federal Administration, he was to be disappointed. A few months after being installed as Members, the Malay appointees left the UMNO, and, following Dato Onn's lead, became founders of the IMP. They thus moved from a party with grassroots support to one with none. Moreover, the Chinese appointee, Dr Lee Tiang Keng, although an *ex officio* member of the MCA by virtue of his seat on the Federal Legislative Council, was certainly not its most active or senior official. Hence, while the introduction of the Member System did demonstrate the Malayan Government's willingness to open up the political process and give Malayan politicians administrative experience, it did little to extend the popularity of the political organizations or to further the Government's fight against the guerrillas.

The most important factor in the development of Malaya's political parties was the advent of municipal and state elections. Beginning in December 1951, these elections provided the political parties with the incentive to expand their base of support. The spur to action was the prospect that eventually the most successful party would take over the reins of the Federal Administration. The resulting dramatic rise in the level of political activity also signalled a turning point in the impact the political parties were to have on the course of the Emergency.

Following on from the British Labour Government's general

policy of encouraging political development in the colonies, it was decided, after the constitutional furore had died down, that Malayans should be introduced to elections gradually: first at the local level, then the state, and finally at the federal level. After much uncertainty, discussion and delay, the necessary legislation was passed and plans were drawn up for municipal elections in the major urban centres. The first elections were held in George Town, Penang, on 1 December 1951. Registration during May and June went well, with a carnival atmosphere being generated on the last two nights. Coloured lights were strung up around the Town Hall porch, election films alternated with Laurel and Hardy films, and the Municipal Band put on concerts. In the next few months, political meetings in Penang's parks and open spaces were well attended and 'any new arrival to the town must have been instantly aware that elections were about to take place'.[24] Election day saw a turn-out of over 72 per cent of those registered. After the 'disappointment, disillusionment and even bitterness' produced by post-War conditions, Government officials found the enthusiasm of the participants in the election process particularly gratifying.[25]

The first local elections of national consequence were the Kuala Lumpur Municipal Council elections of February 1952. Here the parties vying for country-wide support, the UMNO, the MCA, and the IMP first clashed. It was also in this election that the UMNO and the MCA first joined forces to counter the electoral threat of Onn's IMP. The decision by local leaders of both parties to combine the MCA's electoral strength and funds with the UMNO's organizational strength was prompted by personal animosity towards Onn, and by a recognition that this was the only way to defeat his IMP. The move proved to be as successful as it was unexpected. Predictions of an IMP sweep were confounded. The new partnership won nine of the twelve seats leaving the IMP with only two seats, and an independent with one.[26]

While the partnership between the MCA and the UMNO was initially considered only an *ad hoc*, local arrangement, its very success prompted the leaders of both organizations to consider its perpetuation on a peninsula-wide basis. Directly after the Kuala Lumpur elections, therefore, Colonel H. S. Lee of the MCA and Tunku Abdul Rahman, the recently elected President of the UMNO, began a series of talks which led to expanded co-operation between the two parties.[27] They faced some major obstacles. Members of the MCA and the UMNO found themselves at odds in the Federal Legislative Council over such issues as educational policy, citizenship reforms, and immigration regulations. Relations were also soured by the visit of two British academics, Victor Purcell and Francis Carnell, who had been invited to visit the Federation by the MCA and, over the objections of the UMNO officials, asked to prepare a report on the Chinese in Malaya. Both men were considered unabashedly pro-Chinese, and Purcell in particular, who had served for many years in the MCS and had been adviser on Chinese affairs in the post-War period, was critical of what he saw as the pro-Malay policies of the Malayan Administration. Not only did the visit in August 1952 cause friction but also, once he returned to England, Purcell produced a series of controversial articles and a book. These contained bitter attacks on Templer and his overall approach to countering the MCP and to moving Malaya towards independence, and clearly had the potential to cause a rift between the MCA and the UMNO.[28]

Yet a working relationship did develop. Both sides saw too many advantages to continuing the arrangement for it to be jettisoned. First, the key leaders involved were united by their fear and distrust of Dato Onn and they were all encouraged by this new-found way of challenging his seemingly dominant position in Malayan politics. Secondly, both sides quickly appreciated the advantages of maintaining the communal identity of their organizations while at the same time combining forces at the polls. Thirdly, all political leaders were well aware of the Colonial Secretary's admonition that independence would be granted only when the various races in Malaya had demonstrated that they were united.[29] Finally, the dramatic successes of the UMNO–MCA partnership at the polls convinced all but the most ardent communalists that the arrangement was worth continuing.

The electoral successes of the UMNO–MCA partnership were impressive by any yardstick. In the municipal elections in six of Malaya's major centres during December 1952, they won twenty-six of the thirty-seven seats contested, including a convincing sweep in Johore Bahru, Dato Onn's home town. Over the next two and a half years, the UMNO–MCA Alliance, as it became officially known in 1953, went from strength to strength, winning 226 of the 268 municipal and town council seats up for election.[30] State elections, which had been discussed as early as 1950, were delayed by difficulties in getting all states to agree on the ground rules, and by the obvious fears of the traditional Malay élite, who were members of the state councils by appointment and generally supporters of Dato Onn, that they would be replaced by the UMNO–MCA Alliance candidates.[31] And, indeed, when the first state and settlement council elections took place in late 1954 and early 1955, their fears proved to be justified.

Each electoral success increased support for the UMNO and the MCA within their respective communities, and this in turn boosted their electoral prospects. Within the UMNO, Onn's successor as President, Tunku Abdul Rahman, became a particularly effective campaigner. His past, strong and well-known 'Malaya for the Malays' stand gave him impeccable Malay nationalist credentials and made him relatively immune from criticism of his decision to co-operate with the MCA. Indeed, his electoral success, personal charm, and appeal as a prince with a populist message, made him an increasingly formidable political figure in the Malay community. The Tunku, as he was widely known, toured the country ensuring that the UMNO's grassroots organization was not neglected. He sought out the various local rural leaders and gained their support before visiting the kampongs in their area. In this way, he was able to incorporate the existing kampong social and political structures into the UMNO hierarchy, thereby ensuring for the Organization good and continued leadership at the local level. He found the organizing a time-consuming and arduous task: 'Sometimes I am away from the office for months on end. At most I am here about 7 days in the month. My duty is to make contact with the kampong people who are the backbone of the UMNO at this moment.'[32] The reward for his hard work came at the polls.

The MCA also began to adapt to its new role as a successful political party. During early 1952, Tan Cheng Lock reorganized the Association. Determined to make it 'a strong and effective force throughout the country', he recruited a small full-time staff to run the central office, encouraged the revitalization of state and district branch offices, and created an 'Inner Cabinet' which was to expedite the work of the Association. The result was a distinct improvement in the organizational capacity and efficiency of the MCA. At the same time, more MCA members were starting to develop contacts with the New Villagers. In Malacca, for instance, a scheme by which MCA members 'adopted' New Villages proved successful, and became a model for other such programmes, notably in Perak and Selangor.[33] The MCA's work in helping the new settlers was greatly assisted by the increased donations made by members who had grown wealthy during the Korean War boom and by the revenues received from the MCA-run lotteries. Altogether, nearly $4 million was spent by the MCA on subsidizing the building of houses, the erection and maintenance of school buildings, the provision of such amenities as piped water, dispensaries and recreational facilities, the payment of the salaries of teachers and health teams, and the formation of Home Guard units.[34] This and the Association's extensive welfare work gained for the MCA leaders kudos among the Chinese, who equated it with traditional norms of community leadership, and the respect of Government officials, who viewed it as helping to confront the communist threat.

The MCA's success at the polls gave the Association a credibility it had previouly lacked. The leaders of the Alliance were now in a position to begin wielding political power. This fact was underlined for the Chinese community when Templer, recognizing the Alliance's electoral success, made Colonel H. S. Lee Member for Railways and Ports, and Dr Ismail bin Dato Abdul Rahman Member for Lands, Mines and Communications. Gradually the MCA leaders were able to convert their new political power into a network of relationships which linked them, via state-level leaders, to local Chinese community leaders. It was an arrangement which benefited all parties. With their new positions of power, as well as their access to the Administration and the increasingly important Malay political élite, the English-speaking national leaders of the MCA were able, as Heng Pek Koon has put it, 'to dispense political and economic patronage to their clients in the State Branches of the party'.[35] In return, the Chinese-speaking state leaders, through their economic hold over the Chinese traders and retailers in the New Villages and small towns of the Peninsula, were able to mobilize local-level political support for the MCA. Generally, everyone felt comfortable operating in a structure which, while accommodating itself to the political changes underway in Malayan society, still echoed the traditional structures of the pre-War Malayan Chinese community.[36]

The other political parties were unable to duplicate the success of the UMNO-MCA Alliance. This in most part was because of the difficulties they faced in creating a grassroots organizational base and resolving internal divisions. However, the activities of these organizations–the IMP and its major component, the Malayan Indian Congress (MIC), the Pan-Malayan Labour Party, the Perak National Party, a group led by Dato Panglima Bukit Gantang which had broken away from the UMNO, and the Perak Progressive Party–had the effect of heightening people's awareness of the expanding role of local politicians. Moreover, the competition among the parties stimulated them to greater efforts in order to attract public support. Certainly the fight between the IMP-led group of organizations that sponsored the 'National Conference' and the coalition of organizations led by the UMNO–MCA Alliance that held the 'National Convention' aroused a great deal of public interest.[37]

This increase in party political activity had important consequences for the course of the Emergency. Just when the MCP's October 1951 directive was being put into effect, and greater emphasis was being placed on rebuilding the Party's organizational base and intensifying its political campaign against the Government, the emerging political parties were starting to provide alternative channels for people to express their grievances and aspirations. The MCP's task was thus made much more difficult, and to some extent the Government's original hopes for the MCA and the UMNO began to be realized. Yet this turn of events was not necessarily as senior government officials had anticipated. Part of the general appeal of the UMNO–MCA Alliance and the reason for its growing effectiveness in countering the MCP was its criticism of the Administration's policies and its leaders' call for the early introduction of self-government.

Village Councils

Another element in the Government's policy of developing a 'parish pump' approach to democracy, or 'self-government from the ground up', was instituted with the passage of the Local Councils Ordinance in 1952.[38] To some extent, the creation of local councils was simply an extension of what had already developed on an *ad hoc* basis over the preceding years. At the outbreak of the Emergency, a number of rural communities had set up village committees in an attempt to establish a liaison with the Government. These groups had had very little success and were usually dismantled during the dislocation caused by resettlement. With resettlement, however, came a concerted effort by ROs to establish village committees. First started in Johore, they were intended to provide a link between the local district administrator and the settlers. Usually, members of the village committees were appointed by the officer in charge of the village or chosen in an informal election from among the recognized leaders within the community.[39] With the advent of the Local Councils Ordinance, these village committees were gradually converted to councils and allowed to impose taxes, rates, and fees, and pass by-laws with respect to health measures, educa-

tional facilities, public markets, community centres, and the maintenance of streets and roads.

Not all local councils were a success. The main problem was that
the villagers had little appreciation of the role of a village council.
Preoccupied with making a living and keeping out of the way of
the security forces and the communists, most villagers saw little
advantage in getting involved in an institution whose practical
value was not immediately apparent. As a consequence, many councils found it difficult to collect fees, and few New Villages that were
administered by councils were solvent in their early years. Inefficiencies also plagued the councils as elected members and the small
council staff struggled with the problems of drawing up and implementing programmes and managing budgets. In some cases
these problems were compounded by the lack of a common Chinese
dialect among the council members and by the need to provide an
informal English translation for government officials who attended
the meeting but could not speak the local dialect.

Nor did the elections to the village councils initially meet the
hopes of senior government officials. Much depended, as with other
aspects of the councils, on the enthusiasm, industry, and imagination of the local officials. Candidates were sometimes difficult to
find. Usually the ROs or CAOs had to persuade a number of acknowledged village leaders to stand for election. When approached
directly in this way most accepted because they did not wish to
incur the displeasure of officials by refusing them. The turn-out
of eligible voters—those who were over twenty-one years of age and
normally resident in the village—was sometimes very poor. However, if, during the run-up to the election, the process was fully
explained by officials and election day itself well publicized and
made into a festive occasion, then a good deal of enthusiasm among
the villagers could be generated. In a few instances, the zeal of inexperienced Chinese AROs got the better of them; in one case every
eligible male voter stood as a candidate, and in another thirty-one
of 153 eligible voters stood for seven seats. In some cases, the proper
voting procedures were not followed or not properly explained to
the voters. For example, problems arose with maintaining secrecy
and checking the eligibility of voters. A few voters marked crosses
against the names of all candidates, not wishing to offend any of
them, and one woman was reported not to have voted for anyone
because they were all either too old to be her sons or too young to
be her husband.[40]

Despite these obstacles, federal and state government officials continued to establish more and more village councils. By mid-1954, 142 of the 410 New Villages had local councils, and by the end of 1955 over half had set up councils.[41] Overall, the results were mixed. W. C. S. Corry in his 1954 report on the New Villages characterized the committees and councils in Selangor, Negri Sembilan, and Pahang as having 'achieved less than mediocre success', but suggested that in the key states of Johore and Perak they had generally worked well.[42]

The contribution of village committees and councils to both the Government's fight against the guerrillas and the development of a capacity for self-government should not be exaggerated, but neither should it be ignored. They were, in some cases, an effective liaison between the villages and state and federal officials, as well as a means by which grievances could be aired. They were also a useful adjunct to hard-pressed state administrative structures, and served to extend administrative control over the villages, thereby acting as vital counters to the influence of the communist Min Yuen cells. Moreover, the educational value of the councils should not be overlooked. The experience of operating a council, combined with the civics courses which were conducted throughout the Peninsula for councillors and others from the New Villages, resulted in a greater appreciation by villagers of how to run their own affairs within the context of the changing political and administrative structures. Finally, although the political parties as such played little or no part in council elections, some of the prominent village leaders were both MCA members and members of their village councils. This gave them experience and status, both of which proved valuable in getting the vote out for the MCA in state and federal elections.

The 1955 Federal Election

The initial climax to the gradual opening up of the political process came with the first federal election in July 1955. Despite the many obvious misgivings harboured by senior colonial officials about the timing, the number of seats to be contested, and the advisability of handing over some of their powers to the machinations of Malayan politicians, the 1955 election proved to be a major asset in undermining the MCP's cause.

During early 1953, the UMNO-MCA leaders began a campaign to persuade Templer that a federal election should be held in 1954. They had little to lose and much to gain by advocating such a policy.

Their representation in the Federal Legislative Council was less than that of their main opponent, the IMP, and thus their overall influence on policy was limited. Moreover, the success of the combined efforts of the UMNO and the MCA in the municipal elections was considered a good indication of probable successes when the electoral process was extended. However, Templer was reluctant to alter the electoral programme he had initially planned which called for federal elections in 1956 or 1957.[43] He did, nevertheless, see the merit of a full discussion of the question of federal elections, and in July 1953 appointed a Legislative Council committee to examine the issue.

While the committee was deliberating, the major protagonists set out their positions. Dato Onn and his supporters in the IMP–and later the Parti Negara–held a series of meetings of the 'National Conference', out of which came a call for caution and a delay in the introduction of elections. In response, the UMNO–MCA Alliance held meetings of the 'National Convention' which prepared a much more radical blueprint for federal elections. The report of the Legislative Council committee in February 1954 reflected the two viewpoints. The majority report of Onn and his supporters on the committee favoured less than 50 per cent of elected seats and a 'proper' date (presumably 1956 or later) for elections. The minority report of the UMNO–MCA Alliance members of the committee proposed a three-fifths elected majority and November 1954 as the date for the elections.[44] In two meetings between Templer and the Rulers, whose concurrence was needed for any amendment to the Federation Agreement, a compromise was set out which the Government hoped would gain the acceptance of all parties. Alliance demands were acceded to on a number of fronts: government servants would be allowed to stand as candidates, the election was promised for the earliest practicable date in 1955, and provision was made for fifty-two elected members in a Council of ninety-nine.

It was on this last matter of the size of the elected majority within the Council that the Alliance balked. Their leaders insisted on sixty out of 100 elected seats, arguing that an elected majority-government would be impossible otherwise and that a new government would be subjected to the whims of minority groups within the Council. A delegation led by Tunku Abdul Rahman flew to London and attempted to persuade the Secretary of State for the Colonies, Oliver Lyttelton, of the need to accommodate them on this final point. They were politely but firmly told that there would be no change. The British and Malayan Governments felt that they had gone far enough. They had, with some difficulty, persuaded the Rulers, whose advisers were generally in Onn's camp, to accept the compromise, and could not expect them to move any further towards the Alliance's position. There may also have been a fear that if the larger elected majority in the Legislative Council was accepted as a precedent for the Executive Council, then this key decision-making body might no longer be within the control of the senior colonial administrators. The Alliance's response was to organize a mass boycott by the UMNO and the MCA members of all federal executive and legislative councils, state and settlement councils, municipal councils, and town boards. Just over two weeks after the beginning of the boycott, the impasse was broken when MacGillivray, who had only a few weeks earlier taken over from Templer as High Commissioner, agreed that he would consult with the leader or leaders of the majority among the elected members in appointing the five seats reserved for special interests not otherwise represented in the Council.[45]

The boycott, despite criticisms even from within the UMNO-MCA Alliance, was clearly a success. Although initially there was some confusion, it was well supported and organized. The crowds which turned out to support the boycott were impressive, and most of the Malay-, Chinese-, and Tamil-language press supported the Alliance's stand. Even an internal government report noted that 'on the whole it must be admitted that the Alliance has effectively shown its strength throughout the Federation'.[46] The Alliance leaders had shown they were willing to stand up to the British colonial administration at the risk of being dismissed from their positions of power and possibly being imprisoned.[47] Finally, the boycott stimulated, and tied the Alliance irrevocably to the growing sense of Malayan nationalism. Certainly it firmly established the UMNO-MCA coalition as the pre-eminent force in Malayan politics.

The Alliance was able to carry the political momentum gained from the boycott into the federal election campaign of 1955. Their leaders were given a clear indication that they were on the right tack when, in October 1954, the Alliance won 75 per cent of the votes and all sixteen seats contested in the Johore state elections and 80 per cent of the votes and all fifteen seats contested in Trengganu.[48] As the federal election approached, two issues were given prominence by the Alliance leaders. They were insistent that an early date be set for independence and shouts of 'Merdeka'–meaning 'freedom' or 'independence'–became the rallying call at all Alliance meetings and demonstrations. Tunku Abdul Rahman also proposed an amnesty for the communist guerrillas. This was done in the face of objections from the Director of Operations, but was generally welcomed by Malayans as an indication that an Alliance government might produce an early end to the Emergency.[49] There were, of course, problems to be overcome. Tunku Abdul Rahman was privately very critical of the MCA leaders' failure to put election campaigning ahead of their business interests; the Malayan Indian Congress (MIC), representing the third major racial bloc in Malaya, had to be absorbed into the coalition; the Alliance National Council found that reaching agreement on party policy was not always easy, and the distribution of seats among the Alliance members caused a great deal of anguish with, at one point, the MCA threatening to quit the coalition. However, all these complications were eventually smoothed over and the Alliance leaders went into the election with confidence.

Their confidence was well placed. By mid-1955, there were a number of active political parties. These included the radical Malaya Youth Congress, which decided not to nominate candidates; the religiously motivated Pan-Malayan Islamic Party (PMIP); and the increasingly left-wing, though fragmented, Pan-Malayan Labour Party. But no other party was as well organized nor as closely associated with the rise of Malayan nationalism as the Alliance. Its major rival, Onn's Parti Negara, was really no match because it was too closely associated with the colonial administration. After the votes had been counted, the UMNO-MCA-MIC Alliance had won fifty-one of the fifty-two seats contested, with the PMIP taking the remaining seat in an overwhelmingly Malay constituency in Perak.

The impact of the federal election on the Emergency should not be overstated. Of those registered to vote, only 11.2 per cent were Chinese. Only one in four adult Chinese who had been eligible to vote had registered to do so.[50] Whether this was due to a lack of interest, a feeling of ineffectiveness, or for some other reason, the election clearly did not serve to bring as many Chinese as might have been expected into the orbit of the emerging party political structure.

Yet the election was significant in a number of ways. First, the election campaign had allowed the Government to be attacked and anti-British sentiment to be voiced without the critics being associated in any way with the communists. With the growing vitality of legally sanctioned political life in Malaya, many who might otherwise have joined the MCP could now turn to a wide range of political parties in order to express their fears and aspirations. Secondly, the enthusiasm that the election generated within the Malay community added to the difficulties which the MCP faced in their attempts to develop political support among Malays. Finally, the Alliance's successful fight for self-government and the prospect of early independence which came with their victory undercut a major aspect of the appeal of the MCP's original programme. For many politically active Malayans the MCP was becoming increasingly irrelevant.

Summary

During the first three and a half years of the Emergency, then, the influence of local political organizations on the course of the guerrilla war was minimal. This was in part because of the internal problems which beset the two leading political organizations, the UMNO and the MCA. It was also in part because the Government was unwilling to allow these organizations a larger role, fearing that any change in the political process might interfere with the restoration of law and order and detract from finding a solution to what the Government saw as the major problem of weeding out the 'communist agitators' and 'criminal elements'. Senior administrators did expect the UMNO and the MCA to muster support for the Government among the general population; however, they were generally unwilling to reciprocate by giving these organizations the necessary political power to develop their political networks and build up widespread grassroots support.

The introduction of elections brought about a marked change in the political life of the Peninsula. It encouraged the development of a fairly wide range of competing political parties. But most importantly, it gave one political party—the UMNO–MCA Alliance—the opportunity to establish itself in a pivotal position in Malayan politics. By 1955, the Alliance's success in the elections had given the party access to power; its battles with the Government over a number of policy matters, including the fight over the introduction of federal elections, had gained its leaders a well-deserved reputation as opponents of the continuation of colonial rule and champions of Malayan nationalism. Hence, when the MCP members attempted to carry out the instructions contained in the October 1951 directive by giving equal weight to political and military activities, they were confronted by the growing influence of Malaya's political parties. Communist political organizers found that they no longer enjoyed a monopoly on personal contact with Malayans who could now look to others to represent their grievances and right wrongs. Indeed, for most of the politically aware, it was the Alliance's leaders who were responsible for self-government and promises of early independence for Malayans–not the MCP. The opening up of the political process and, in particular the success of the Alliance in the July 1955 election, helped to put the MCP back on the defensive and set the stage for the winding down of the Emergency.

1. This chapter relies in part on the author's, 'The United Malays National Organization, the Malayan Chinese Association and the Early Years of the Malayan Emergency', *Journal of Southeast Asian Studies* 10 (March 1979).

2. See Yeo Kim Wah, 'Study of Three Early Political Parties in Singapore, 1945-1955', *Journal of Southeast Asian History* 10 (March 1969); Gerald de Cruz to the Editor, *Journal of Southeast Asian Studies* 1 (March 1970), p. 125; *The Times* (London), 24 July 1948 and 26 July 1948, and Gordon P. Means, *Malaysian Politics* (London: Hodder and Stoughton, 1976), p. 119.

3. Gurney to J. J. Paskin, 10 December 1948, CO 537/3758. For accounts of the origins of the MCA, see 'Extracts from the Pan Malayan Review', 2 March 1949, CO 537/4761; K. G. Tregonning, 'Tan Cheng Lock: A Malayan Nationalist', *Journal of Southeast Asian Studies* 10 (March 1979), p. 59; Margaret Roff, 'The Malayan Chinese Association', *Journal of Southeast Asian History* 6 (September 1965), pp. 40-2; Soh Eng Lim, 'Tan Cheng Lock: His Leadership of the Malayan Chinese', *Journal of Southeast Asian History* 1 (March 1960), p. 45; Means, *Malaysian Politics*, pp. 116 and 120, and Heng Pek Koon, 'The Social and Ideological Origins of the Malayan Chinese Association', *Journal of Southeast Asian Studies* 14 (September 1983), pp. 293-4.

4. Heng, 'The Social and Ideological Origins,' pp. 294-5 and 303-6, and Roff, 'The Malayan Chinese Association', p. 42.

5. MCA leaders argued that the word 'collaborate' was reminiscent of the Occupation. See 'Extracts from the Pan Malayan Review', February and March 1949, CO 537/4761.

6. The appointment of Tan Cheng Lock as head of the MCA was generally seen as a compromise between two stronger rivals and bitter opponents, Yong Shook Lin and H. S. Lee. There were fears that Tan Cheng Lock inclined 'too much to the left through reading too many books' but it was promised that he would be kept on the right road. See 'Extracts from the Federation of Malaya, Political Report', March 1949, and Gurney to Paskin, 4 April 1949, CO 537/4761. See also the material in CO 717/205.

7. Kernial Singh Sandhu, 'Emergency Resettlement in Malaya', *Malayan Journal of Tropical Geography* 18 (August 1964), p. 162.

8. Leong Yew Koh to Tan Cheng Lock, 15 October 1951, Tan Cheng Lock Papers TCL/XV/64a (ISEAS).

9. Tan Cheng Lock gained a good deal of publicity and sympathy from the incident. His famous bedside message–'Do not be afraid. Go ahead with the aims of

the MCA'–was widely quoted. His return to Malacca from Ipoh was something of a triumphal procession. But Government reports suggest that his family tried to persuade him to give up MCA activities and Tan Cheng Lock himself thought that the MCP would try again. He decided, however, that he was too involved in the MCA to withdraw his services. See 'Pan Malayan Review', 14 April 1949 and 25 May 1949, and 'Review of Chinese Affairs', April 1949, CO 537/4761.

10. 'Note of a Meeting held at King's House', 28 October 1951, CO 1022/148; King's House, 2 December 1951, P/PM1, Chief Secretary 438/B/51 (ANM), and Tan Cheng Lock Papers TCL/III/271 (ISEAS).

11. These figures come from Soh Eng Lim, 'Tan Cheng Lock', p. 46, and Department of Information, *Communist Banditry in Malaya: The Emergency, June 1948–June 1951*, n.d., p. 17.

12. *Straits Echo*, 6 August 1949. See also Department of Information, *Communist Banditry*, p. 28.

13. Tan Cheng Lock Papers, Item 144 (ANM). Gurney also felt that MCA leaders were too preoccupied making money from the boom in rubber and tin prices and were losing their influence over the Chinese community. See Gurney to Higham, 13 June 1951, CO 537/7303.

14. This forced the Commissioner-General, Malcolm MacDonald, to remark at a meeting shortly after Gurney's death that he hoped that the MCA would not wait until there was evidence of 100 per cent trust at all levels but that they should get on with the collection of funds for the establishment of their organization on a firmer basis in all states and settlements and down to district levels. Tan Cheng Lock Papers, Item 144 (ANM). Dato Tan Cheng Lock noted at the time that 'The whole tragedy has been that Government and officialdom do not trust the Chinese and think the Malayan Chinese have an idea to make Malaya a province of China.' Tan Cheng Lock to Sir George Maxwell, 18 December 1951, Tan Cheng Lock Papers TCL/V/232 (ISEAS).

15. Gurney referred to Onn as a Jekyll and Hyde character and complained that in the first two years of the Emergency he had difficulty dealing with Onn because of his proximity to the Commissioner-General, Malcolm MacDonald. Onn was Mentri Besar, Johore, and was based in Johore Bahru where MacDonald had his official residence. In turn, Onn was suspicious of Gurney in part because of the High Commissioner's sponsorship of the MCA. See Gurney to Higham, 17 March 1949, CO 537/4790.

16. The original group of Malay and Chinese leaders was known as the Malay-Chinese Goodwill Committee. The name was changed when other community leaders were included in the deliberations. For a review of the activities of the Committee, see Means, *Malaysian Politics*, pp. 122-4; Mohd. Noordin Sopiee, 'The Communities Liaison Committee and Post-War Communal Relations in Malaya: A Historical Sourcebook', mimeograph (Kuala Lumpur: University of Malaya, n.d.); 'Political Report', September 1949, CO 537/4790, and Khong Kim Hoong, *Merdeka! British Rule and the Struggle for Independence in Malaya, 1945-1957* (Petaling Jaya, Malaysia: Institute for Social Analysis, 1984), pp. 156-9. For an interesting critical discussion of the activities of the Communities Liaison Committee, see *Indian Daily Mail*, 27, 28, and 29 September 1949.

17. In particular, the Rulers opposed a proposal put forward by Onn for a Malay Deputy High Commissioner. See Ishak bin Tadin, 'Dato Onn and Malay Nationalism 1946-1951', *Journal of Southeast Asian History* 1 (March 1960), pp. 73-4, and the material in CO 537/4784. For the newspaper attacks, see in particular the *Utusan*

Melayu during the latter half of 1950 and the reports in the *Straits Echo*, 27 May 1950 and 23 October 1950. See also CO 537/4790 for critiques of Onn's leadership.

18. Most of the Community Liaison Committee participants moved over to the IMP. MacDonald has stated since the event that he advised Onn to move cautiously but that Onn was keen to go ahead with the new party. See 'Transcript of an Interview with Malcolm MacDonald', PR 27 (ANM).

19. See, for example, Rees-Williams to J. B. Williams, 27 May 1948, CO 537/3746, and Rees-Williams' minute of 12 September 1949, CO 537/4790.

20. See 'Notes of a Conversation with Mr Rees-Williams', 21 November 1949, CO 537/3746.

21. In 1950, Gurney had suggested to Onn that the UMNO hold an election among its members for the six Federal Legislative Council seats that he was willing to make available but Onn turned the idea down and it was eventually superseded by the Member System. See Minute High Commissioner to Chief Secretary, 19 May 1950, and 'Reports of Proceedings of the Eleventh Meeting of Rulers', 24 and 25 May 1950, P/PM1, Chief Secretary 331/50.

22. Draft of Lloyd to Gurney, 3 January 1949, CO 537/3746.

23. The six original 'unofficials' appointed as Members were: Dato Onn bin Ja'afar, Home Affairs; Tengku Jaacob Ibni Sultan Abdul Hamid, Agriculture and Forestry; Dato Mahmud bin Mat, Lands and Communications; Dr Lee Tiang Keng, Health, and M. J. O. Mead, Works and Housing. See *The Times* (London), 14 March 1951. It should be noted that the revenue from the Korean War boom made it easier for the High Commissioner to agree to inexperienced individuals taking on key spending departments. The progress of the Member System may be followed in High Commissioner to Secretary of State for the Colonies, 12 January 1952, CO 537/6026; Minutes of the 15th (Federation/Singapore) Commissioner-General's Conference, 7 June 1950, CO 537/5970 or P/PM1, Chief Secretary 331/50; Dato Onn to Gurney, 6 January 1951, and Gurney to Higham, 17 January 1951, CO 537/7297.

24. See Federation of Malaya, A. S. M. Hawkins, *Report on the Introduction of Elections in the Municipality of George Town, Penang 1951* (Kuala Lumpur: Government Printer, 27 December 1953).

25. Ibid. Elected were six Radicals, one Labour, one UMNO, and one Independent.

26. The MCA won six seats and the UMNO three seats. See R. K. Vasil, *Politics in a Plural Society: A Study of Non-Communal Political Parties in West Malaysia* (Kuala Lumpur: Oxford University Press, 1971), pp. 10-11 and 56-60, and Means, *Malaysian Politics*, pp. 132-4.

27. See H. S. Lee to Tan Cheng Lock, 18 February 1952 and 22 February 1952, Tan Cheng Lock Papers TCL/IX/33 and 35 (ISEAS), and Tan Cheng Lock to Sir George Maxwell, 11 March 1952, Tan Cheng Lock Papers TCL/V/261 (ISEAS).

28. Victor Purcell's best-known analysis of the Emergency was his book, *Malaya: Communist or Free?* As befitted the leading scholar on the Chinese in South-East Asia, the text of the book provided a useful insight into the historical context to the guerrilla war. However, his view of the Emergency and the progress towards independence were clearly influenced by his deep distrust of Templer. His views were reinforced by the shouting match he had with Templer during his visit to Malaya. See Means, *Malaysian Politics*, p. 135, and John Cloake, *Templer Tiger of Malaya: The Life of Field Marshal Sir Gerald Templer* (London: Harrap, 1985), pp. 307-9. For a discussion of Purcell's criticisms, see Anthony Short, *The Communist Insur-*

rection in Malaya 1948-1960 (London: Frederick Muller, 1975), pp. 379-87.

29. See 'Notes of a Meeting Between the Secretary of State for the Colonies and the UMNO', P/PM1, Chief Secretary 438/B/51. This point was acknowledged by Tunku Abdul Rahman in an address to the National Convention, 23 August 1953, UMNO Files No. 7, UMNO/SG No. G 12/1954 (ANM).

30. *The Economist*, 25 June 1955, p. 1139. In 1954 alone the Alliance won eighty-two of eighty-six seats. See 'Report to 7th Annual General Committee', 15 January 1955, in Leong Yew Koh Papers SP 3/7/22 (ANM).

31. Gurney considered getting the mechanisms for state elections in train in early 1950. See Gurney to Higham, 1 March 1950, CO 537/6026. Much of the negotiations over the introduction of state elections are reported in P/PM1, Chief Secretary 19/9 (ANM).

32. Tunku Abdul Rahman Putra to M. A. Hamid, Muslim University, India, 22 June 1953, UMNO Files, UMNO/SG 35/53 (ANM).

33. See Tan Cheng Lock Papers TCL/III/274 (ISEAS); Tan Cheng Lock Papers, Item 144(i) and Item 175 (ANM), and Leong Yew Koh Papers, Item 16 (ANM).

34. See Kernial Singh Sandhu, 'The Saga of the "Squatters" in Malaya: A Preliminary Survey of the Causes, Characteristics and Consequences of the Resettlement of Rural Dwellers during the Emergency between 1948 and 1960', *Journal of Southeast Asian History* 5 (March 1964), p. 120; 6th Annual Meeting of the MCA, Leong Yew Koh Papers, File 43 (ANM), and Gordon P. Means, 'New Villages in Malaya' (Hamilton, Ontario: Department of Political Science, McMaster University, n.d.), p 173.

35. Heng, 'The Social and Ideological Origins', p. 300.

36. Wang Gungwu, 'Chinese Politics in Malaya', *The China Quarterly* 43 (July-September 1970), pp. 4-5 and 19-21, has called it 'a brilliant marriage' of the 'hard-headed and realistic majority of the Chinese who are concerned with the indirect politics of trade and community associations', to the connections of the small group of Babas, British Straits Chinese, and Malayan nationalists, who had a traditional loyalty to Malaya. It brought together, he argued, a type of organization familiar to the former but led by the latter.

37. See Vasil, *Politics in a Plural Society*, pp. 76-7 and 82-3, and Means, *Malaysian Politics*, Ch. 10.

38. See Renick, 'The Emergency Regulations', p. 36, and Means, 'New Villages in Malaya', pp. 90-2.

39. See, for example, Judith Strauch, *Chinese Village Politics in the Malaysian State* (Cambridge, Mass: Harvard University Press, 1981), pp. 69-70.

40. See Lee Moke Sang (General-Secretary, Pan-Malayan Labour Party), 'Elections in Salak South New Village', and reports by the SCA Johore on local council elections, Chinese Affairs 1633 (ANM).

41. See Federation of Malaya, W. C. S. Corry, *A General Survey of New Villages, A Report to His Excellency Sir Donald MacGillivray, High Commissioner of the Federation of Malaya* (Kuala Lumpur: Government Printer, 1954), p. 38, and Means, 'New Villages in Malaya', p. 92.

42. Corry, *A General Survey of New Villages*, p. 40. Of the 142 New Villages with local councils in 1954, sixty-eight were in Johore and forty were in Perak, p. 38.

43. Templer to Tunku Abdul Rahman, 30 October 1953, UMNO Files, UMNO/ SG No. 7/1953 (ANM). Although the High Commissioner foresaw federal elections by 1957, contemporary government records do not corroborate Lucian W. Pye's recollection in 'Five Years to Freedom: Sir Gerald Templer's Part in Building a

Nation', *The Round Table* 278 (April 1980), pp. 149-53, that Templer went to Malaya 'under orders to bring the country to independence in five years'.

44. Federation of Malaya, *Report of the Committee Appointed to Examine the Question of Elections to the Federal Legislative Council* (Kuala Lumpur: Government Printer, 1954), pp. 7-8 and 23-4. See also the Minutes of the Federal Elections Committee, 21 January 1954, UMNO Files UMNO/YPD, 15/1954 (ANM). UMNO-MCA correspondence on this issue may be found in Leong Yew Koh Papers SP 3, File No. 69 (ANM).

45. Much of the correspondence among Alliance leaders on the negotiations with Lyttelton and the boycott is to be found in Leong Yew Koh Papers SP 3 (ANM). The Malayan Government's position may be gleaned from 'Monthly Emergency and Political Reports' for 1954, FO 371/111854.

46. 'Monthly Emergency and Political Reports' for 1954, FO 371/111854.

47. Tunku Abdul Rahman thought imprisonment was a possibility although there is no evidence that it was seriously considered by the Government. See Harry Miller, *Prince and Premier* (London: Harrap, 1959), p. 145.

48. See Leong Yew Koh Papers SP 3/7/22, and FO 371/111854.

49. See the Director of Operations' comments at the Conference of Mentri Mentri Besar, Resident Commissioners and British Advisers, 30 May 1955, P/PM1, Chief Secretary 3/2 18 (ANM).

50. See K. J. Ratnam, *Communalism and the Political Process in Malaya* (Kuala Lumpur: University of Malaya Press, 1965), p. 187, who also notes that 'about 75 per cent of the Chinese and Indian Federal citizens were under twenty years of age, hence ineligible to register as electors'.

8

The Final Years

By the end of 1955 there were a number of indications that the tide of the Emergency was running in the Government's favour. The estimated strength of the guerrillas was down to 3,000, a marked decline from the 8,000-10,000 guerrilla force of the early 1950s. The number of 'contacts' with the guerrillas initiated by the security forces consistently outnumbered the 'incidents' initiated by the guerrillas. For a growing number of Malayans, the Emergency regulations were, for all practical purposes, a thing of the past as more and more regions of the Peninsula were designated 'white areas'. And the net yearly outflow of Chinese from Malaya, a factor which had been a consistent feature of the post-War years, had become a noticeable net inflow. Chinese who had the right of residence in the Federation were returning as confidence in the country's future was being restored.[1]

Yet there could be no complacency on the part of the Government. The MCP guerrillas were by no means a beaten foe and the possibility of a relapse and a resurgence of sympathy for the communist cause could not be ignored. For their part, the communists had to try to adapt to the changing circumstances, search out any weaknesses in the Government's strategy, and gradually rebuild their organization.

The Political Battle

With the success of the Alliance in the federal election, the prospect of independence for Malaya in the very near future and the Government's ascendancy in the 'shooting war', the MCP began to seek other ways to achieve their objectives. A number of factors encouraged MCP leaders to rethink their strategy: first, a reassessment was advocated at a meeting of leaders of communist and workers' parties of the British Commonwealth, held in London in April 1954; secondly, an important cue was provided by Chou En Lai's conciliatory line towards colonialism at the Bandung conference in Indonesia in April 1955; and, thirdly, a general discussion was taking place in communist circles about the benefits of adopting a strategy of 'peaceful co-existence'.[2]

As a result of this change of emphasis, the MCP leadership developed two related initiatives. First, Chin Peng, the MCP leader, offered to negotiate an end to the Emergency. His first offer was made a few weeks before the federal election and was renewed shortly after the new Alliance Government was installed. Secondly, on 22 December 1955, the Party issued a communique in which it detailed changes in the Party's organization and set out a new programme. The major feature of the reorganization was the elevation of a number of Malays and Indians to positions within the Party's Central Committee so as to present a multiracial image to Malayans. The MCP's new 'minimum programme' attempted to appeal to as many Malayans as possible and bore an uncanny resemblance to the Alliance's own election manifesto. For instance, the Party called for an end to the fighting on just and reasonable terms, for a fully elected Malayan Assembly, and for the strengthening of national unity around the theme of a Malayan nationality.[3]

For their part, the new Alliance Government was somewhat uncertain about the MCP's overtures. They too wanted a quick end to the Emergency but were wary of the MCP's motives. The new Chief Minister, Tunku Abdul Rahman, favoured offering an amnesty to the guerrillas as the best means of bringing the Emergency to an end. He was prepared to meet Chin Peng in order to explain the terms of the amnesty, which he introduced in September 1955, and to listen to the MCP's views. After some preliminary negotiations, during which representatives of both sides made the necessary arrangements, it was agreed to meet in the small town of Baling not far from Malaya's border with Thailand.

The Baling talks were held on 28 and 29 December 1955. Chin Peng led the MCP delegation which also included Chen Tien, the head of the Party's Central Propaganda Department, and Abdul Rashid bin Mydin, a representative of the Malay Nationalist Party. The Government's delegation was made up of Tunku Abdul Rahman, David Marshall, Singapore's new Chief Minister, and Tan Cheng Lock, President of the MCA. No European government official was at the negotiating table. The ensuing discussions revealed that the MCP had two key objectives. The first was to leave the jungle without giving the appearance of surrendering. The communists were prepared to lay down their arms but they would not submit to the terms of the amnesty which required that they be detained and investigated until it was determined that they genuinely intended to be loyal to the Government of Malaya and give up their communist activities. Secondly, Chin Peng insisted that the MCP be recognized as a legitimate political party and that members be allowed to put the Party's ideology and programme before the voters at election time. Tunku Abdul Rahman could not agree to either of these conditions. He had been well briefed by government officials and was fully cognizant of the potential problems should he acquiesce to such proposals. During the meeting, he also became convinced of the impossibility of communism co-existing with what he considered to be the Malayan way of life. With Tunku Abdul Rahman unwilling to change his position and Chin Peng not empowered to accept the terms of the amnesty, the negotiations broke down. The only positive outcome of the talks was an agreement signed by both sides which stated that as soon as the Federal Government obtained complete control of internal security and local armed forces, the MCP would end hostilities, lay down its arms, and disband its armies.[4]

Public reaction to the Baling talks was mixed. Many Malays as well as most of the British community were relieved that the MCP was not to be legalized. However, within the Chinese community, and especially in the Chinese press, there was more sympathy for the view that the MCP's requests were fairly moderate and that it would probably have been worthwhile striking a deal with Chin Peng in order to end the Emergency. In Kuala Lumpur, the Malayan Film Unit's newsreel of the Baling talks drew large crowds of Chinese, and Chin Peng was applauded when he appeared on the screen.[5] The disappointment generated by the failure of the Baling talks and, indeed, by the poor results of the amnesty meant that there was continued pressure on the Government to seek a political short-cut to end the Emergency. However, the two obstacles which had derailed the Baling talks remained and, while occasional overtures were made–including a direct letter from Chin Peng to Tunku Abdul Rahman shortly after Independence at the end of August 1957–no more talks were held. The MCP leadership continued to be defiant: it would not surrender nor would it disband the Party. It claimed that the maintenance of British and Commonwealth troops in Malaya after Independence was proof that the Federal Government had not obtained complete control over internal security and, therefore, the Party did not have to fulfil their part of the Baling agreement. The Government, on the other hand, saw little value in a repetition of the Baling talks and, perhaps more importantly, was becoming increasingly sure of ultimate victory.

Denied an overt role in Malayan politics, the MCP continued its covert activities. Special emphasis was placed on using Chinese schools to organize support. New Village schools and Chinese middle schools had long been recruiting grounds for the MCP and the importance of working among students had been a constant theme of the Party's pronouncements from the October 1951 directive onwards. This was reaffirmed once again and raised to a new level of significance in June 1956 when a directive was issued stating that 'the work of winning support from school children and organizing them to struggle is more important than military activity'.[6]

Indeed, Chinese-language schools continued to provide fertile ground for the MCP for a number of reasons. First, the massive increase in enrolment in Chinese-medium schools put a strain on both human and physical resources. From 151,000 in 1953, the numbers in Chinese schools rose to 277,500 in 1955 and 392,000 in 1957.[7] The result was a chronic shortage of teachers, and those who were brought in to fill the breach were sometimes sympathetic to the communists or the target of communist intimidation. Added to this, the large size of the schools in the major centres often made discipline difficult to enforce, while enabling communist ideas to be circulated more readily. In some schools, the curriculum and books used continued to perpetuate racial chauvinism and anti-British sentiment: despite Government efforts, new textbooks to complement a curriculum which emphasized Malayan values could not be produced fast enough to keep up with the rising enrolment.

Secondly, a number of concerns among Chinese students were used by communist sympathizers to their advantage. In many schools, and especially in the New Village schools, there were still large numbers of over-age pupils. Denied access to an education during the Japanese Occupation and the early post-War period, many young Chinese, particularly in the rural areas, were receiving their schooling well past the normal age. In classes where the ages of pupils could range from six to twenty, the difficulties of keeping all the students interested in the material and maintaining discipline were acute. Further, those who were able to obtain a sound education found it extremely difficult to go on to university. The authorities did their best to prevent students who had been to university in China–the traditional finale to a Chinese-language education–from returning to Malaya. And the vast majority of those who had been taught in Chinese-medium schools found that their English was not good enough to get into English-language universities and colleges, even if their families could afford to send them.

Finally, there was the chronic fear in the Chinese community that the Government was intent on undermining Chinese education. This became an important rallying point for students and an issue that the communists tried to use to enlist student support. Most of the criticism of the Government's policy was focused on a report prepared by a committee of the Federal Legislation chaired by the Minister of Education, Abdul Razak. The report was published in 1956 and passed by the Legislature in March 1956. The 'Razak Plan', as it was popularly known, appeared to the Chinese community to favour the Malays and limit opportunities for those with a Chinese-language education. Interestingly, among senior community leaders, this perceived attack on the Chinese education system was associated with the general decline in traditional Chinese social structures and family life; it raised their fears that younger generations might look to communism to provide a more inspiring social order.[8] From the MCP's point of view, the Razak Plan created organizational problems for it limited access for over-age students to the school system, and it had been the older students upon whom communist organizers had relied for spreading their ideas and gathering support.[9] The Party, therefore, had an additional reason to oppose the Alliance Government's new educational policies.

At its most successful, primarily in Singapore, the MCP was able to build on the discontent in Chinese schools and develop an organizational framework. Using recruiting techniques that had been successful in the months preceding the Emergency, Party members began by forming school committees with representatives from all standards—or years—in the school. These were followed by other organizations such as old boys' associations, literary societies, singing and theatrical clubs, and sporting associations. Gradually these groups were steered in the direction of Mao Tse-tung's 'Hsueh Hsih' or 'study for action', and emphasis was placed on the groups' members developing a 'collective life'. In Singapore, the student groups were able to mount a series of demonstrations, some of which became full-blown riots.[10] At times, notably in November 1956, the Singapore Government's ability to maintain order was severely tested. However, although these student organizations were an important part of the MCP's political offensive in Singapore, they were not nearly as effective in the Federation. While demonstrations by Chinese students in Penang, Kuala Lumpur, Seremban, and Ipoh proved to be major irritants for the Government, student organizations in the Federation were nevertheless unable to fulfil the MCP's hopes of mobilizing significant support for the Party.

Indeed, it proved impossible for the MCP to mount any sustained political campaign in the face of the tidal wave of enthusiasm that was generated by the prospect of Independence. The negotiations with the British in London; the deliberations of the Reid Commission, which was established to advise on the drawing up of the new constitution; and the preparations for Merdeka Day caught the imagination of much of the politically aware sections of Malaya's population, as well as many who were simply swept along by the general air of pride and accomplishment which engulfed the country. There were, of course, disagreements over issues such as the place of the Rulers in an independent Malaya, Malayanization of the administration, and the rights to be given to each racial community. But on the whole, the march towards Independence went remarkably smoothly, given the possibilities for recrimination and division which were to be found in Malayan society. Hence, when the new flag of the Federation of Malaya was slowly raised over 'Merdeka' Stadium on 31 August 1957, as a symbol of the transfer of sovereignty from the British, the prevalent view was that there was little justification for the MCP to continue its military offensive. The communists could no longer claim to be waging a struggle of national resistance.

Certainly, many of those who were sympathetic to the communists were no longer prepared to take to the jungle; they saw future battles taking place at the polls. In the Federation, the Labour Party and the coalition which it headed, the Socialist Front, became the organizations towards which most who had some sympathy for the communists gravitated. As Stenson has pointed out, from 1958 onwards it was the Labour Party which was 'the main instrument of the MCP's switch from guerrilla warfare to the use of legal political parties'.[11] But the Labour Party and the Socialist Front were not the only political parties by which Malayans, especially disaffected Chinese, could fight established government policy. Even the MCA had developed a more radical wing which appeared to be gaining support. And with more non-Malays able to become citizens, and thus eligible to vote under the provisions of the 1957 Constitution, there appeared to be a good possibility that the dominant position of the UMNO within the Alliance Party, as well as the Alliance Party's dominant position in Malayan politics, could be challenged. There seemed to be every chance that the existing political structure could allow for the expression of all viewpoints and accommodate most hopes and ambitions. The Alliance Party gained a convincing victory at the 1959 elections, winning seventy-four of the 104 federal seats. Their percentage of the popular vote was, however, substantially reduced–from 81.7 per cent in 1955 to 51.8 per cent in 1959. This fact, together with the success of the opposition parties in some state and municipal elections, was enough to suggest that the Alliance might become vulnerable in the future.[12]

At the local level, interest in party politics had grown apace. By 1958, there were few New Villages where branches of one political party or another had not been organized, and the general level of participation in party meetings and at polls had increased appreciably. In many New Villages, the main combatants were the MCA and the Socialist Front, and the resulting battles–usually fought on local rather than national issues–were often intense.[13]

In Singapore, the traditional centre for communist activity in the region, the argument that a return to 'peaceful agitation' might lead to power was even more compelling than in the Federation. Up to 1953, the colonial administration in Singapore had for the most part been able to nullify the work of the communist organizations, which essentially saw themselves as aiding the guerrillas in the jungle. From 1953 onwards, however, the communists paid more attention to local organizations, emphasizing, in particular, work in schools and key trade unions. Most importantly, the People's Action Party (PAP), which was founded in 1954 and over which the communists were able to gain a good measure of influence, emerged as an increasingly popular political party. With the organizational means gradually being built up and advantage being taken of such issues as the compulsory registration for conscription contained in the National Service Ordinance, the communists could feel, with some justification, that they were well placed to capitalize on the opportunities that might arise out of future elections and the move to full self-government. Indeed, the communists became key players in the political skirmishes which took place from the mid-1950s to the early 1960s. Their battles for power, first with David Marshall's combined Labour and Alliance Party administration and then with Lee Kuan Yew's faction of the PAP, were a central feature of both Singapore's struggle for self-government and, after self-government had been attained in 1959, the struggle over the direction the country should take. For communist sympathizers in Singapore, and even in adjacent parts of the Federation, the increasingly dubious appeal of the armed struggle as an approach to power was no match for the excitement, intrigue, and potential for participation in its many forms, which was to be found in Singapore's partisan political life.

Overall, then, the MCP's decision to reorientate its strategy was a response, not just to cues from the British Communist Party and the Governments of China and the Soviet Union, but also to the political events unfolding in Malaya and Singapore. As communist sympathizers became aware of the potential for action which the blossoming of legitimate political activity created, fewer of them were prepared to back what was widely seen as a losing cause and go into the jungle to replace guerrillas who had been killed, captured, or surrendered. The armed struggle was, therefore, running out of its essential fuels—popular support, recruits, supplies, and information.

Economic Developments

Just as political events were forcing the MCP back on to the defensive, so economic developments were allowing the Government to attack from high ground. During the last half of the 1950s, the fluctuating but generally high international price of natural rubber brought prosperity to Malaya. With the exception of 1958, the average price for each year stayed above the $1.00 per pound mark, and in two years, 1955 and 1960, the price at times approached $1.50 per pound. This general level of prosperity generated a high level of government revenue, especially when compared to the pre-Korean War boom years. New tax laws, introduced in 1957, provided the basis for a rise in revenue: the $730 million in total domestic revenue in 1955 rose to $1,029 million in 1960.[14]

By continuing the colonial administration's traditional, conservative approach to budgeting, an ordinary budget surplus of $342 million was accumulated between 1955 and 1960, and the increased revenue allowed for a steady increase in expenditure. The cost of 'Emergency, Defence and Security' rose from $211 million in 1955 to a peak of $233 million in 1958; spending on civil works more than doubled; and spending on education and medical, health, and social welfare grew substantially.[15] Increased expenditure by the Government was particularly important in rounding out the services provided to the New Villages. By 1959, virtually every New Village had a school. This meant that 'tens of thousands of children whose previous isolation would have surely doomed them to illiteracy and an uncertain future, were able to secure at least some schooling in the New Village'.[16] Moreover, 10 per cent of New Villages had static clinics, 67 per cent were served by mobile clinics, and a number of others had access to facilities in nearby towns or cities.[17] This basic level of medical care, as well as the safe supplies of drinking water, sanitation facilities, and malarial control measures, ensured a relatively healthy New Village population. Overall, enough money and administrative resources had been pumped into the New Villages so that, by Independence, 80-85 per cent of all the New Villages had come close to meeting the objectives set out in the Government's 1953 directive for a 'properly settled New Village'.[18] This point was underlined in the years after the end of the Emergency when, although people were allowed to live wherever they chose, few New Villages were abandoned and residents only left their village if forced to do so in order to seek employment.

The prosperity which boosted the Government's revenues also helped to raise the real income of most workers. The cost of living remained relatively constant, apart from a minor increase in 1957 which was followed by an equal decrease a year later. On the other hand, wage rates crept up gradually. For example, the average basic earnings for rubber tappers on large European-owned estates, not normally known for their generosity, rose from $75.42 per month in August 1955 to $81.00 per month two years later.[19] For workers in white areas, increased employment opportunities came from the easing of restrictions and the freedom of movement which allowed previously unworkable rubber estates and smallholdings and logging areas to be opened up. In a number of areas of the Peninsula, there was full employment and at times even a slight shortage of labour.

One development which proved to be particularly fortuitous for the Government was the rapid urbanization of Malaya's Chinese population. The initial impetus for rural Chinese to move into nearby towns was the search for greater security. Later, resettlement and the rapid expansion of some New Villages close to the main urban centres, as well as the development of new sites to serve the urban overflow, all accelerated the process. Large dormitory towns of over 15,000 people—Petaling Jaya, Jinjang, Guntang, and Pasir Pinji—sprang up seemingly overnight. Between 1947 and 1957, Raub grew fivefold, Kuantan threefold, and numerous centres such as Klang, Johore Bahru, Butterworth, Kluang, Betong, Segamat, Sungei Siput, and Kulim doubled their populations. Over the same period, Kuala Lumpur grew from 176,000 people to a city of 316,000; George Town's population increased from 189,000 to 235,000 and Ipoh's from 80,000 to 125,000. By 1957, 73 per cent of the Chinese population were living in urban areas of 1,000 people or more–including the larger New Villages–as compared to only 43 per cent in 1947.[20] This increased concentration of the population in the main centres of the Federation certainly made it much easier for the security forces to provide protection against guerrillas who were essentially jungle-based.

Urbanization also made available employment opportunities, amenities, and services not only to those in the towns, but also to the 222 New Villages (representing 37.5 per cent of a total of 592 New Villages) which lay within a 15-mile radius of centres containing 10,000 or more residents. In the main centres, the number of jobs in secondary industries grew rapidly. For example, excluding factories connected with oil palm and rubber estates, almost 85 per cent of the factories in Selangor were to be found in and around Kuala Lumpur. Similarly, pineapple canneries, sawmills, rubber shoe factories, two large biscuit factories, and a number of furniture-making factories had been built in or near Johore Bahru. Other centres had grown with the expansion of the government bureaucracy, which were needed to administer the increased services and support the expansion of the security services. The New Village populations were generally provided with transportation by the rapidly growing bus companies, which between 1950 and 1953 alone doubled their number of employees, or in a few cases by the improving local railway service. And, of course, there was always the bicycle.[21]

Yet not every part of the country was reached either by prosperity or by government services. Indeed, it is quite clear that in those areas where the population continued to harbour grievances over inadequate services, lack of employment, and insufficient agricultural land, the Government had its greatest difficulty overcoming the remaining communist guerrillas. For example, in Perak in 1959, nearly one-third of all New Villages had no medical services; after 1956, the restrictions on the production of tin under the International Tin Agreement reduced the numbers employed in the industry by 50 per cent; and because many New Villages had been built on old tin tailings, good agricultural land was extremely scarce.[22] The social and economic problems provided fertile ground for the communists and, indeed, the Emergency regulations stayed in force in much of northern Perak until July 1960 when the Emergency was declared to have come to an end. In other parts of the Federation, too, notably in Kedah, Johore, and parts of Pahang, similar problems arose.

At the heart of the difficulties experienced by many of the more remote New Villages was their lack of an economic base. New Villages with growing populations and limited employment opportunities required greater amounts of agricultural land to provide alternative sources of income. However, the Federal Government continued to balk at making funds available to buy nearby private lands, while state governments maintained their reluctance to alienate additional state land to non-Malays. New Villagers in some states even encountered difficulty in persuading local officials to grant them title at a reasonable price to land they had originally been allocated during resettlement. Villages in which there was a severe shortage of land and a scarcity of employment had, as an IBRD mission recorded, 'no economic future'.[23] This view was reinforced by Major-General Fonblanque, the Inspector-General of the Home Guard, who in his tours of the country observed 'too many New Villages in which living conditions [were] such as to produce a borderline existence'.[24] The inhabitants of these villages either had to suffer the degradations of a limited income or send members of the family off to seek employment elsewhere. Either course of action tended to breed frustration and resentment. And when these problems were compounded by grievances associated with the original settlement site–grievances such as flooding, poor drainage, or infertile soil–then the communist organizations' task of maintaining a base in the population was that much easier.

Overall, then, the moderate prosperity that Malaya enjoyed during the second half of the 1950s helped the Government. It increased revenues and enabled services to be extended and at least some people's grievances to be addressed. It also helped to create employment opportunities in many areas of the Peninsula. These benefits, however, did not penetrate to all parts of the country. Where economic and social grievances were most keenly felt and distrust of the Government continued, the Min Yuen and other communist organizations were able to maintain their support and the guerrillas were able to continue operating.

The Shooting War

As the political and economic turn of events further undermined the MCP guerrillas' base of support and severely restricted their ability to secure recruits and supplies, the nature of the shooting war began to change. Aware of their increasing vulnerability, the guerrillas tended to curtail activities which might bring them into contact with security forces or make it easier for government intelligence officers to pin-point their camps and identify local political organizations. Many guerrilla units had withdrawn into the relative safety of the deep jungle where they lived in camps alongside aborigine communities. Other units remained in the jungle near the areas which were traditional strongholds and where economic and social grievances continued to provide them with popular support. In addition, by the end of 1955, it was the committed and obdurate hard core of the guerrilla force who were doing the fighting. All these factors made the security forces' task of dislodging the guerrillas from the jungle extremely difficult.

But the security forces had a number of advantages which allowed them to maintain pressure on the guerrillas. First, as the white areas expanded and the Home Guard units and the special constables became better trained and more reliable, the Government no longer had to spread its forces so thinly across the Peninsula–it could concentrate its eighteen or nineteen operational battalions in strategic areas. Moreover, the police, Home Guard, and special constables provided not only static defence but also nearly 1,000 jungle squads.[25] The Government's overall plan was to split the MCP organization in two by creating a white area belt across the middle of the Peninsula from the Pahang coast to Malacca. Once this was achieved the security forces were then to work their way north and south on a district by district basis. They were to attack the 'static District and Branch organizations on which the Malayan Communist Party hierarchy and offensive platoons [relied] for their supply'.[26] The Government's ability to concentrate its forces played an important part in the campaign to whittle away the guerrillas' stamping ground–a campaign that was slower than anticipated but nevertheless eventually successful.

Secondly, with the increasing number of government successes in the jungle as well as in the political realm, and with the security forces' growing capacity to provide protection and to offer large amounts of money to informers, quality intelligence about the guerrillas and their movements became more readily available. Information was channelled through members of the Home Guard, CAOs and ACAOs, or other officials. The Special Branch found itself better able to recruit agents who could infiltrate the MCP's local political organizations and on occasion even guerrilla units. Members of communist organizations were also 'turned' as they were made aware that their activities were known to the police. In addition, guerrillas who had surrendered continued to be good sources of reliable information.

Thirdly, by 1956, food denial operations had become a reasonably effective means of flushing out the guerrillas. Where conditions warranted, the many and pervasive restrictions on the movement and distribution of key goods such as food and medicine were relaxed or partially lifted. In areas where guerrillas were known to be active, the screws were tightened even further. An important innovation was the establishment of the Emergency Food Denial Organization headed by M. C. ff. Sheppard. As British Adviser in Negri Sembilan, Sheppard had developed a form of food control called 'Central Cooking of Rice'. Under this scheme, all rice for a particular village or group of villages was cooked in a central location; this enabled the commercial buying and selling of all uncooked rice to be prohibited and the normally meagre Emergency rice ration to be increased. Sheppard immediately took his show on the road moving from district to district as operations were mounted against specific groups of guerrillas. Once in top gear, the Emergency Food Denial Organization was cooking for as many as 50,000 people in centrally located and well-guarded kitchens around the country.[27] And the prospect of food regulations being lifted was an important incentive in getting the villagers to co-operate with the security forces.

Fourthly, by 1956, the Government had built up an impressive propaganda machine. Personnel from the Information Services Department were an integral part of the selective operations carried out against the MCP's district-level organizations. Their task was to go in and prepare the local population for the impending operation and, where possible, to gather information on MCP activities. Both in these specific campaigns and in the overall propaganda effort that was mounted across the country, a variety of techniques were employed. Civics courses were put on for teachers, community and youth leaders, and others from 'black areas'. In the last few years of the Emergency, around 11,000 attended these courses each year. Live shows, which usually included sketches, talks by surrendered guerrillas, and perhaps a performance by a drama troupe, were always well received. Films were popular and, by 1956 the Malayan Film Unit was producing colour documentaries on the Emergency. In 1958, there were ninety mobile information vans and four boats touring the country and reaching about one million people per month. A wide range of popular monthly and weekly publications in each of the main languages–Malay, Chinese, English, and Tamil–continued to be written by the Information Services Department and distributed throughout the Federation.

The value of radio as an instrument of propaganda grew steadily as the number of community listening sets gradually increased and the moderate levels of prosperity enabled more and more families to buy their own radios. An added boost to the propaganda effort was the formation of 'Good Citizens' committees in various centres across the country. First started in Selangor, and quickly promoted by both Tunku Abdul Rahman and MacGillivray, these committees held anti-communist rallies in an attempt to show the guerrillas that the population had turned against them. In one incident, 300 Kluang residents 'invaded' the jungle and, in a march that lasted from dawn to dusk and covered twelve miles, called on the guerrillas to surrender.[28]

Finally, the psychological war that had been waged against the guerrillas had, by 1956, intensified immeasurably. For example, ninety million leaflets were printed and distributed in 1956. Twenty million of these announced the result of the Baling talks and the end of the amnesty, and a further ten million reminded guerrillas of the coming of Independence and the Government's continuing commitment to defeating communism. Moreover, the number of guerrillas left in the jungle had been so reduced and the information gathered by the intelligence services so extensive that it was possible to drop leaflets which had personal messages on them for one particular guerrilla known to be in that area. Even more disconcerting from a guerrilla's point of view was for him to hear his name, and even an appeal to surrender from his mother, wife, or friend, being broadcast from an aircraft flying only a few thousand feet above his head. In 1956 over 600 separate voice messages were recorded and more than 2,200 flights were made by aircraft broadcasting these messages to the guerrillas in the jungle below.[29] It was perhaps not surprising, then, that it proved difficult for the MCP leadership to maintain a reasonable level of morale in the face of both this onslaught as well as the turn of events in the political and military realms.

It should not, however, be assumed that the Government had things all its own way. Apart from complaints about the social and economic conditions, the Government was faced with a number of other difficulties in bringing the Emergency to a speedy conclusion. The most serious of these stemmed from the imposition of the Emergency restrictions on the general population. Unless the security forces were careful, the extremely strict controls, which circumscribed the daily lives of the inhabitants of the 'black areas', could—as they had in the past—cause much resentment and bitterness. Although an extreme case, some idea of the hardships and indignities which New Village inhabitants had to suffer can be gleaned from the inquiry into the incidents which took place at Semenyith in the Kajang district of Selangor: the booths and trucks in which women had to undress and be searched allowed people outside to see in; searchers treated people roughly and threw their clothes on the ground or outside the booths; a shortage of searchers, especially female searchers, led to long delays; and police were quick to use force in attempting to control the large crowds which formed at the village gates prior to the 6.00 a.m. ending of the curfew.[30]

Such issues as arose at Semenyith usually surfaced when an operation against guerrillas required stricter searches, greater use of road blocks, centrally cooked rice, and an extension of the curfew hours. Closing the administrative and military vice on a district in order to force the guerrillas and the members of the Min Yuen organization to show their hand always entailed the risk of so enraging previously uncommitted villagers that they sided with the communists. Compounding this was the problem of the police and the armed forces acting arbitrarily, detaining people without proper cause, and abusing suspects.[31] Tan Siew Sin spoke of this problem in the Federal Legislative Council when he noted that the livelihood of New Villagers was insecure, that they were liable to arrest at any time, and that they were 'sometimes, perhaps more often than people realise, subject to gross indignities by the Security Forces'.[32] While he was speaking in the debate on the Malayan Constitutional Conference and was, no doubt in part, using the plight of some New Villagers and the fear of their turning to communism as a means of trying to win more concessions for the Chinese in the battle over the distribution of rights in the new constitutional framework, he was also making it clear that as in the past repressive measures were liable to backfire.

A miscellany of other problems also beset the Government. Weaning the aborigines away from the guerrillas whom they were supplying with food and information was a slow process. The last 250 or so aborigines who supported guerrillas in the deep jungle in Perak and central Pahang, were only gradually persuaded to go to the Government's jungle forts to seek protection. Labour Department officials found that the temporary accommodation which had been built on some small- and medium-sized estates at the time of regroupment was quickly deteriorating. While those labourers on estates in the white areas were allowed to move back to the old labour lines, a number of employers in parts of the country still under strict Emergency regulations had to be prodded into improving conditions in the regroupment areas so as not to present the communists with an issue around which they could muster support.[33] The growing influence of secret societies drained away valuable police manpower as a special section in each police contingent was established to combat their activities.[34] There were also, perhaps inevitably, disruptions and inefficiencies which resulted from the rapid Malayanization of the senior ranks of the administration as expatriate officers took early retirement after Independence.[35] And, finally, 'Emergency fatigue' became a factor. With people growing tired of the Emergency regulations and complacency setting in as the Government pushed the guerrillas further and further on to the defensive, the lax implementation of controls allowed food and other supplies to find their way from the white areas, and in particular from the major centres such as Kuala Lumpur, to the communists' political organizations, and on to the guerrillas.[36]

Yet, despite all these problems, the advantages which had gradually accrued to the Government took their toll on the communists, and the security forces eventually prevailed. The breakthrough came in the immediate post-Independence period. During the months following the 31 August 1957 celebrations, a series of mass surrenders brought about an almost complete collapse of the communist guerrilla army. Before this, the surrender rate had fluctuated around the 200-a-year mark, with the previous high point being 372 in 1953. By contrast, in 1956—a very disappointing year for the Government—only 134 guerrillas gave themselves up. This was mainly because the prospects of the Baling talks and then the possibility of further negotiations between the two sides encouraged guerrillas to believe that a settlement would soon be reached and that there would, therefore, be no need to take the risks involved in surrendering. However, prompted by the news that 'Merdeka' had been celebrated by all communities, by the accumulated pressure of the intensified food control measures, the presence of massive and concentrated formations of the security forces, and by the growing realization that the struggle was hopeless, over 500 guerrillas surrendered during 1958.[37] These surrenders made it possible for the Government to declare the whole of the state of Johore and half of Perak white areas. For the MCP, the loss of nearly one-third of the guerrilla army and the resulting information acquired by the security forces proved to be near fatal blows. And with no new recruits to fill the gaping holes left behind in their organization, the MCP could only order a retreat and attempt to pick up the pieces.

During the next eighteen months, the Government was engaged in a mopping-up operation. For the great majority of Malayans, the Emergency had become a relatively remote issue which impinged on their lives mainly through media accounts of the exploits of the security forces and the jungle squads. In 1959, there were four major and eight minor incidents compared to 2,333 major incidents and 3,749 minor incidents at the height of the Emergency in 1951. Only one member of the security forces and three civilians were killed that year, and in 1960 there were no civilian or security force casualties attributable to MCP guerrilla action.[38] On 31 July 1960, the Government declared an end to the Emergency. The newly passed Internal Security Act provided the necessary regulations imposing restrictions on the areas adjacent to the Thailand-Malaya border where guerrilla activity might occur. The 'Victory Parade' in front of the Secretariat building in Kuala Lumpur in the early morning of 1 August developed something of a carnival atmosphere; the bitterness and frustrations of the dark days of the late 1940s seemed a long way away.

The armed forces of the MCP had been reduced to less than 100 guerrillas scattered across Peninsular Malaya, and 400-500 guerrillas, including Chin Peng and his headquarters staff, who were based in the Betong salient, a finger of Thai territory which pokes down into northern Malaya. During the next ten years, although communism could claim a small number of adherents throughout the Peninsula, the MCP's guerrilla units confined themselves to a few skirmishes along the Thai border. They were not a major presence in the country. Somewhat surprisingly, relatively little was heard of the MCP during 'Confrontation', when the Malaysian armed forces were preoccupied with threats from the North Borneo National Army and the communists in Sarawak, both purportedly sponsored by the Indonesian Government. The North Kalimantan Communist Party—or the Clandestine Communist organization as the Sarawak Government called them—remained in operation even after the end of 'Confrontation'. It was not until 1974, after a series of surrenders and defections—prompted by Chief Minister Rahman Yaakub's offer of amnesty—had left it totally ineffective, that the threat posed by the communists in Sarawak virtually withered away. Although the Malaysian Government found some evidence of communists at work in the May 1969 race riots in Peninsular Malaysia, the MCP was evidently in no position to take advantage of the turmoil, and little was heard from them as the Government hastened to return the country to an even keel. During the mid-

1970s, there was a resurgence of communist guerrilla activity in the Peninsula, especially in the urban areas. This was sparked by a number of factors: competition among three factions of the Malayan Communist Party–the original group and two splinter groups, the MCP (Revolutionary Faction) and the MCP (Marxist-Leninist Faction); frustrations caused by a marked downturn in the Malaysian economy; discontent over the Government's pro-Malay policies, and the success of communism in nearby Vietnam, Laos, and Cambodia. But the guerrilla actions petered out as the economy bounced back in the late 1970s and as the Government adapted its security and social policies to meet the new challenge.[39]

Indeed, the communist movement in Malaya/Malaysia never really recovered from its defeat in the twelve-year long Emergency. Nor has it been able to surmount the problems posed by being thought of within the Malay community as a predominantly Chinese organization. By the mid-1980s there were approximately 2,000 communist guerrillas based on the Thai side of the Thailand–Malaysia border and a very much smaller number in Sarawak. Most importantly, neither group had been able to develop substantial support among the general population. And while there is always the possibility that the MCP could once again pose a major threat to the Government, it is more likely that communism will remain a persistent though minor irritant which becomes more troublesome when the Malaysian economy is in recession and less so when the economy is strong. Certainly, the Malaysian Government has the resources to be able to keep the MCP in check, especially if it keeps in mind the major tenets of the 'hearts and mind' approach so successfully put into operation during the Emergency.

Summary

For the last five years of the Emergency, the Government had the whip hand. The political and economic turn of events was in their favour and they were able to stage a formidable military and psychological warfare campaign.

Perhaps the most interesting question, then, is why it took so long for the Government to bring the Emergency to a close, given that they had so many advantages. Part of the answer lies in the MCP's shift in strategy. With the guerrilla units becoming more preoccupied with survival than with mounting a sustained offensive, the MCP leadership chose to put greater emphasis on political work among the general population and less emphasis on military activities. This made the guerrillas, who in the past had proved to be very difficult to track down, an even more elusive target for the security forces. A second reason why it took so long for the Government to clear Peninsular Malaya of MCP guerrillas was that some of the reasons for the guerrillas' early successes lingered on. Poor economic and social conditions in a number of New Villages, especially the more remote ones, continued to produce grievances, frustrations, and bitterness upon which support for the guerrillas could be sustained. In places, these problems were compounded by the occasionally harsh and arbitrary treatment meted out by the police and military units, and by the inequalities of the strict food control measures.

In the long term, however, the Government's strategy prevailed. Support for the guerrillas was gradually reduced as a result of both the Government's ability to take advantage of some good fortune, as well as its political, economic, social, and security policies. The Min Yuen and the other political organizations were themselves being whittled away and could not act as the lifeline to the population that the guerrillas needed. This affected the guerrillas in two ways: first, they became more vulnerable as they were forced to take risks in order to search out food and other vital supplies; secondly, as the guerrilla numbers were reduced, there was no one to replace them. Hence, although it took a relatively long time to remove the last 2,500 or so guerrillas from the jungle, in the end the Government could claim a complete victory.

1. For estimates of guerrilla strength, see Anthony Short, *The Communist Insurrection in Malaya 1948-1960* (London: Frederick Muller, 1975), p. 472. See Department of Information, *Emergency Statistics for the Federation of Malaya Since June 1948* (7/60/160 [Emerg]), 1960 for 'contacts' and 'incidents'. And see Federation of Malaya, H. Fell, *1957 Population Census*, Report No 14 (Kuala Lumpur: Department of Statistics, 1960), p. 17 for net inflow/outflow numbers.

2. Interview with C. C. Too, May 1982; *Straits Times*, 14 May 1956; Short, *The Communist Insurrection*, pp. 459-60; J. H. Brimmell, *Communism in South East Asia: A Political Analysis* (London: Oxford University Press, 1959), pp. 279-93, and Charles B. McLane, *Soviet Strategies in Southeast Asia: An Exploration of Eastern Policy under Lenin and Stalin* (Princeton, NJ: Princeton University Press, 1966), pp. 464-73.

3. Brimmell, *Communism in South East Asia*, pp. 333-4.

4. See Federation of Malaya, *Report by the Chief Minister of the Federation on the Baling Talks* (Kuala Lumpur: Government Printer, May 1956) for a detailed report of the meeting and a copy of the amnesty. For the thinking of the Special

Branch on Chin Peng's proposals, see Harry Miller, *Jungle War in Malaya: The Campaign against Communism, 1948-60* (London: Arthur Barker, 1972), pp. 161-3. A dress rehearsal of the meeting was staged in order to anticipate Chin Peng's tactics. See Noel Barber, *The War of the Running Dogs: The Malayan Emergency, 1948-1960* (London: Fontana, 1972), p. 212, and interview with C. C. Too, May 1982. For Tunku Abdul Rahman's thoughts on Chin Peng, see mss. Ind Ocn S 232 (Rhodes House Library), and Harry Miller, *Prince and Premier* (London: Harrap, 1959), pp. 192-3.

5. *Straits Times*, 6 January 1956.

6. Colony of Singapore, *Singapore Chinese Middle School Students' Union* (Singapore: Government Printing Office, No. Cmd. 53 of 1956), p. 1.

7. Department of Education, *Annual Report*, 1954, 1955, and 1957.

8. See Minute, Acting Secretary for Chinese Affairs to the High Commissioner, 12 April 1955, P/PM1, Chief Secretary 102/66 (ANM).

9. William Shaw, *Tun Razak: His Life and Times* (Kuala Lumpur: Longman, 1976), pp. 103-5.

10. See Colony of Singapore, *Singapore Chinese Middle School Students' Union*, pp. 8-10; Gordon P. Means, 'New Villages in Malaya', mimeograph (Hamilton, Ontario: Department of Political Science, McMaster University, n.d.), pp. 159-62; Gordon P. Means, *Malaysian Politics* (London: Hodder and Stoughton, 1976), pp. 223-7, and Richard Clutterbuck, *Riot and Revolution in Singapore and Malaya 1945-1963* (London: Faber and Faber, 1973), pp. 84-92.

11. M. R. Stenson, *Class, Race and Colonialism in West Malaysia: The Indian Case* (Vancouver: University of British Columbia Press), p. 186. See also Short, *The Communist Insurrection*, p. 491, for the observation of one surrendered guerrilla that 'the People's Progressive Party that was centred in Ipoh was directing its political activities on similar lines to those of the MCP. The difference was only in the name.'

12. See Means, *Malaysian Politics*, pp. 250-3, and K. J. Ratnam, *Communalism and the Political Process in Malaya* (Kuala Lumpur: University of Malaya Press, 1965), pp. 200-8. The vulnerability of the Alliance Party in urban Chinese areas was underscored when the People's Progressive Party won control of the Ipoh Town Council in 1961. See Francis Kok-Wah Loh, 'Beyond the Tin Mines: The Political Economy of Chinese Squatter Farmers in the Kinta New Villages' (Ph.D. dissertation, Cornell University, 1980), pp. 193-206.

13. Ray Nyce, *Chinese New Villages in Malaya: A Community Study* (Kuala Lumpur: Malaysian Sociological Research Institute, 1973), pp. 136-55.

14. *Federation of Malaysia Annual Report*, 1963 (Kuala Lumpur: Government Printer, 1964), pp. 291-2. For rubber prices, see Colin Barlow, *The Natural Rubber Industry: Its Developments, Technology and Economy in Malaysia* (Kuala Lumpur: Oxford University Press, 1978), pp. 440-1.

15. *Federation of Malaysia Annual Report*, 1963, p. 292.

16. John Weldon Humphrey, 'Population Resettlement in Malaya' (Ph.D. dissertation, Northwestern University, 1971), p. 271.

17. Ibid., pp. 223-4 and 299-341, where the Malayan Christian Council's report, 'The New Villages in Malaya' (Kuala Lumpur: 1958), is cited.

18. Means, 'New Villages in Malaya', p. 169.

19. Ministry of Labour and Social Welfare, *Annual Report*, 1957 (Government Printer, Kuala Lumpur, 1957), p. 7.

20. Fell, *1957 Population Census*, pp. 8 and 11.

21. Ibid., and Humphrey, 'Population Resettlement', pp. 192-6. The number of employees in the bus companies rose from 3,175 in 1950 to 6,320 in 1953, and 8,290 in 1959. See Department of Labour, *Annual Report*, 1954, p. 69 and 1959, p. 52.

22. Statistics for medical services are from Humphrey, 'Population Resettlement', pp. 299-341, who cites the Malayan Christian Council's 'The New Villages in Malaya'. See also Loh, 'Beyond the Tin Mines', p. 115. Three of the villages without medical services had populations of over 2,000 and a fourth had a population of 5,000. Many of these New Villages were in the Bantang Padang region of Perak in the south-east corner of the state. Employment statistics in the tin mines are from Department of Labour, *Annual Report*, 1956 and 1959.

23. *Straits Times*, 5 January 1956.

24. *Straits Times*, 5 January 1956. See *Straits Times*, 2 December 1955, for a review of the IBRD Mission's analysis. Lack of suitable, inexpensive agricultural land was most noticeable in the most populous states of Perak, Selangor, and Johore. Each of these states had 'black areas' until near the end of the Emergency.

25. Short, *The Communist Insurrection*, p. 480.

26. Director of Operations, 'Review of the Emergency Situation in Malaya at the end of 1956', cited in ibid., p. 477. See also Clutterbuck, *Riot and Revolution*, pp. 227-8.

27. See Tan Sri Dato Mubin Sheppard, *Taman Budiman: Memoirs of an Unorthodox Civil Servant* (Kuala Lumpur: Heinemann, 1979), pp. 202-4, 212, and 218-21.

28. See Department of Information, *Annual Report*, 1956 and 1958; *Federation of Malaya Annual Report*, 1957; Department of Information, *Role of Information Services in the Emergency* (7/60/160 [Emerg]), 31 July 1960; R. W. Komer, *The Malayan Emergency in Retrospect: Organization of a Successful Counterinsurgency Effort* (Santa Monica: Rand, February 1972), p. 70, and 'Quarterly Report from Members of the Executive Council to the Secretary of State for the Colonies', P/PM1, Secretary to the Government 67/9 (ANM).

29. See Department of Information, *Some Notes on Psychological Warfare* (7/60/160 [Emerg]), 31 July 1960, and Komer, *The Malayan Emergency in Retrospect*, p. 72.

30. See Federation of Malaya, Selangor State Information Officer, *Report on the Semenyith Inquiry*, n.d., and J. B. Thompson, *Report on the Conduct of Food Searches at Semenyith* (Kuala Lumpur: Government Printer, 1956).

31. See, for example, New Villager to Leong Yew Koh, 29 June 1957, Leong Yew Koh Papers SP 3/18 (ANM).

32. *Proceedings of the Federal Legislative Council*, 14 March 1956, cited and discussed in Loh, 'Beyond the Tin Mines', pp. 151-2.

33. Department of Labour, *Annual Report*, 1956, p. 30.

34. Wilfred Blythe, *The Impact of Chinese Secret Societies in Malaya: A Historical Study* (London: Oxford University Press, 1969), p. 478.

35. See Robert O. Tilman, *Bureaucratic Transition in Malaya* (Durham, NC: Duke University Press, 1964), pp. 77-81.

36. See, for example, *Malay Mail*, 20 March 1956, cited in Means, 'New Villages in Malaya', pp. 74-5.

37. Department of Information, *Emergency Statistics for the Federation of Malaya Since June 1948* (7/60/160 [Emerg]), Appendix H.

38. Ibid.

39. See Richard Stubbs, 'Peninsula Malaysia: The 'New Emergency''', *Pacific Affairs* 50 (Summer 1977), pp. 249-62.

9
Conclusion

The Course of the Emergency

FROM its declaration in June 1948 to its close at the end of July 1960, the Malayan Emergency wound a tortuous course. By reviewing not just the military and administrative aspects of the guerrilla war, but also the social, economic, and political aspects, and by focusing on the shifting sympathies of the general population, it has been possible to plot the changing fortunes of the Malayan Government and the Malayan Communist Party and to gain some understanding of why the Government won and the guerrillas lost.

The immediate cause of the Emergency is clear and relatively simple. In order to adopt a strategy of 'armed struggle', the MCP decided to take to the jungle. Its reasons for doing so were, however, more complicated. In the immediate post-War period, the Central Committee of the MCP was controlled by those who favoured a moderate policy of 'peaceful agitation'. Gradually, as events unfolded, this group lost its grip on the Committee and a more radical faction took over. First, Lai Tek, the main proponent of the peaceful agitation policy and the Secretary-General of the Party, was unmasked as a traitor. Not only did this remove a key figure from the deliberations but it also tainted the policies he had advocated. Secondly, the news from the February 1948 Calcutta Conference that the new Cominform policy encouraged the use of violence as one means of fighting imperialism gave the radical group the ideological justification it needed for pursuing a policy of armed struggle. Thirdly, the actions of the British Government, not only of reversing itself over the introduction of constitutionally entrenched political equality for all races but also of using every means at its disposal to counter the peaceful agitation approach of the MCP, gave the Party's radical group plenty of ammunition with which to argue that the old strategy had failed and that a new, more aggressive one was called for. Fourthly, for the many Chinese MCP members who still followed events in their homeland with a keen interest, the success of the Chinese Communist Party in the war against the Kuomintang Government was a powerful incentive to adopt a similar strategy. And finally, the widespread dissatisfaction with the Government, not just over its political manoeuvrings but more importantly because of the disastrous economic conditions prevailing at the time, must have persuaded some Central Committee members that they could mobilize the masses in a fight for national independence.

Although the MCP's Central Committee decided to take up arms against British rule at its May 1948 meeting it had little control over the initiation of guerrilla activities. Rather, it appears that the escalation of violence in May and June 1948 was the work of a small number of radical guerrilla units who had developed an autonomy in the uncertain months after Lai Tek disappeared. The fact that these guerrilla units jumped the gun and that the Government was forced by the strength of the outcry from the European community to introduce at short notice the Emergency regulations caught the MCP leadership offguard. With only half its membership fully mobilized, some key people had to scramble to avoid the police and a few were arrested. There can be no doubt that, as far as the MCP's leadership was concerned, the guerrilla war against the British went off at half cock. And yet, despite the disorganized way in which the MCP's offensive began, the guerrillas were soon able to expand their numbers and to enjoy at least the passive support of a substantial portion of the Chinese community.

The success of the guerrillas in the first few years of the Emergency was as much a consequence of the Government's misguided strategy as it was a result of the MCP's efforts. Encouraged by both the traditional philosophy of the colonial regime and the Malayan Security Service's assessment of events, the Government responded to the increased guerrilla activity as if it were simply a criminal rather than a political problem. The threat was seen as coming from a conspiracy by armed agitators who had to be eliminated if law and order were to be restored. The Government had little appreciation of either the strength of support for the guerrillas within the Chinese community or of how guerrilla warfare was conducted, and hence of what counter-measures would be appropriate. Indeed, the emphasis on restoring law and order and adopting a 'coercion and enforcement' approach proved counter-productive. The indiscriminate way in which the security forces used their superior fire-power to shoot on sight anyone vaguely suspected of being a guerrilla or communist sympathizer, the burning of homes, and the threat of detention and deportation faced by those who had been connected with the communists or their front organizations drove many in the Chinese community to support the MCP as the only means of defending themselves, their families, and their friends against the actions of the Government. The security forces too often appeared to be at war with the people, especially the Chinese population, and too frequently behaved more like an army of occupation than the protectors of a civilian population. Similarly, the increasing brutality of the police force and the many incidents of corruption created more sympathy for the communists and additional criticisms of the Government.

There were a number of other reasons why the Government received little active support from Malayans. Most people were preoccupied with the meagre daily ration of rice and the exorbitant prices of nearly all foodstuffs. Compounding this problem were the low wages which employers, seemingly with the connivance of the Government, were intent on maintaining. Large sections of the rural population without a link to the administration considered the Government to be either irrelevant or a distant object of distrust. Indeed, for the majority of rural Chinese who most of all wanted to be left in peace, it was the MCP not the Government to whom they turned if they needed help. This was simply because members of the Party were known to them personally, were close at hand, and were Chinese.

Although the MCP gained recruits both for the guerrilla army and the Min Yuen—their crucial political support group—they were not really in a position to take full advantage of the widespread distrust of the Government. First, during the weeks after the Occupation, the MCP had rooted out collaborators, many of whom were thought to be Malays. This, plus the Chinese chauvinism which characterized the behaviour of some communist guerrilla units, had led to racial clashes and the MCP being considered as 'the Chinese Party'. The MCP was consequently viewed with grave suspicion by nearly all Malays and many Indians. Secondly, because the British and the Japanese, aided by Lai Tek, had been able to eliminate so many from the top echelon of the MCP's leadership, the Party suffered from a severe shortage of good leaders and administrators. It thus took a considerable amount of time to get both the guerrilla army and the Min Yuen on to a firm operational footing. Thirdly, the inexperienced MCP leadership appeared uncertain about the strategy they should pursue. Initially they adopted a policy of wooing support but later put a much greater emphasis on the military aspects of the struggle. Not unlike the Government's campaign, this approach tended to alienate more people from the communists' cause than it attracted to it. Overall, however, it was clearly the guerrillas who were gaining the ascendancy and the Government who were put decidedly on the defensive.

It was the boom in the economy caused by the rising demand for rubber and tin during the Korean War which gave the Government the respite it so desperately needed. The boom produced full employment, high wages, and a doubling of the Government's revenue. It is testimony to the deep distrust with which the Government was viewed as well as to the high level of support for the communist guerrillas that the MCP's revolution was not swept away by the wave of prosperity which engulfed the country. However, the boom simply stabilized the position of the two sides by providing for an uneasy stalemate which gave little hope to the bulk of the population caught in the middle of the fighting. The Korean War boom also made possible the massive resettlement programme introduced by the Government in mid-1950. Without the substantial increase in revenue, the Government could not have sustained either the pace or the scale of the programme that was implemented. And without the high wages that could be obtained on the rubber estates and tin mines, those Chinese squatter farmers forced to leave their land would have become destitute, and the resettlement centres would have undoubtedly been turned into pro-communist strongholds.

The opportunity that the boom gave the Government to rethink its policies and alter the balance of popular support amongst the general public was not fully utilized until a spate of changes in key personnel came about in late 1951 and early 1952. The killing by a guerrilla unit of the High Commissioner, Sir Henry Gurney, in October 1951 and the installation of a newly elected Conservative Government in Britain brought about a thorough review of the Malayan Government's approach to fighting the communists. It was clear that attempting to restore law and order–and at the same time the political, social, and economic *status quo*–by means of a coercion and enforcement policy offered little hope of defeating the guerrillas. The coercion and enforcement approach might ensure that the British did not lose, but neither did it give them any hope of winning.

As the review progressed, an alternative approach which emphasized gaining the support of the population took shape gradually. The principles embodied in the new policy were not new. Sir Thomas Lloyd of the Colonial Office, for example, had written in August 1948 that the Malayan Government needed to have 'a programme which commands not merely the acquiescence of the people of the country but their enthusiastic support'. He also asked Malayan officials: 'Are there any further measures which we can take to mobilize Chinese support behind us more effectively than hitherto?'[1] In Malaya a number of officials with an extensive knowledge of the Chinese community had emphasized from the beginning that the Government needed to actively seek out Chinese support.[2] As the limitations of the old policy became evident more and more people were persuaded of the benefits that could accrue from an approach which wooed the people of Malaya, especially the Chinese, away from the MCP. During their tour of Malaya in December 1951, Oliver Lyttelton, the new Secretary of State for the Colonies, and his advisers sketched out some of the elements of the new policy. Later, General Sir Gerald Templer, the new High Commissioner, after a thorough briefing in London and a review of the situation in Malaya, developed and implemented what became known as the 'hearts and minds' approach.

There were a number of aspects to this new strategy. First, the New Villages—as the resettlement centres came to be called—were developed and most were provided with supplies of clean water, schools, community centres, basic medical care, some agricultural land, and often a few other additional services and amenities. Secondly, elections were introduced in some villages and municipalities and later extended to the state and federal levels. Thirdly, increased protection was provided through both the establishment of a Home Guard drawn from the local community and the retraining of the members of the police force engaged in static defence of the villages and kampongs. Training emphasized the need to help Malayans rather than abuse them. Fourthly, in addition to the general restrictions that were imposed on everyone, very strict controls on all foodstuffs and other essential supplies were introduced in selected areas as a means of depriving guerrillas of vital supplies. Fifthly, severe penalties continued to be imposed on those caught, or suspected of, aiding the communist organizations. These penalties varied from lengthy curfews for unco-operative villages to detention, life imprisonment, and even the death penalty—used only rarely in later years—for individuals. Sixthly, in areas that were considered to be free of guerrilla activity—those known as white areas—most of the Emergency regulations were suspended so that inhabitants could enjoy a normal existence. Seventhly, a major propaganda offensive was mounted; this included the distribution of millions of leaflets and news-sheets, tours by mobile film units, speeches by surrendered guerrillas, and the expansion of the country's broadcasting service. And, finally, with better information coming in from a more sympathetic population, a reorganized intelligence organization, and the use of small patrols, the army and the police jungle units had become more effective in seeking out guerrillas. Now it was the army who could mount ambushes, make use of intelligence on guerrilla movements, and force the guerrillas and armed elements of the Min Yuen on to the defensive.

While these ingredients characterized the hearts and minds approach in its ideal form, the transition period from the old to the new policy was a fairly lengthy one. It took time for the training to become effective and for the members of the security forces to become accustomed to the idea that they were meant to help, not intimidate, the general public. And in the New Villages of a few regions, most notably in Perak and Johore, some of the promised services and amenities did not materialize—and those that did were often not up to standard. Where grievances were not addressed, the guerrillas usually found enough supporters to supply them with food, medicines, and other essentials so that they could maintain a minimum level of operations. The guerrillas were also able to take advantage of the aborigines in the deep jungle; some guerrilla units came to depend on them for their survival. For the Government, weaning the aborigines away from the communist influence proved to be a difficult task.

Despite the Government's efforts, then, the 'hearts and minds' approach was still being refined and improved well after the first federal elections in 1955. Indeed, in some areas it was never fully implemented. Nor should it be thought that this approach totally won over the population. Rather, the result was more to neutralize the key sectors of the population—the rural Chinese and especially the New Villagers—and to make it impossible for the guerrillas to rely on them for recruits and supplies. Without these critical ingredients, the communist revolution gradually withered away and the few communists who remained became increasingly vulnerable to the operations of the security forces.

An important boost to the implementation of the 'hearts and minds' approach came with a crucial change in the MCP's strategy. In late 1951, at roughly the same time that the British were reassessing their own approach, the MCP's Central Committee issued new directives in which greater emphasis was to be placed on the political work of the Min Yuen, with the military struggle being downgraded. This switch to a policy of building up the MCP's political base required a reorganization of the Party, the MRLA, and the Min Yuen, and while this was taking place the guerrillas began to lose the initiative. The reduction in guerrilla-initiated incidents which accompanied the change in strategy coincided with the arrival of Templer and the beginning of the 'hearts and minds' strategy. The boost this gave to the Government's morale and the impact it had on public opinion in Malaya worked in the Government's favour. Moreover, the lull in guerrilla activity made it easier for the Government to develop the infrastructure within the New Villages and train and deploy the security forces. The result was an expanded administrative network, a more effective police force, and consequently a greater ablility to regulate the daily lives of much of the population. The general wish of the New Villagers to be left alone so that they could live as peaceful and prosperous a life as possible now started working to the Government's advantage. By the time the MCP was in a better organizational position to mount a sustained political campaign, it had been forced on to the defensive, while the rising tide of government-sanctioned political activity had swept away any hope the communists might have had of building a significant base of popular support. The continuing antagonism of the Malays, the general apathy of the Indians, and the growing neutrality of the Chinese made it ultimately impossible for the communist guerrillas to continue their fight within Malaya.

The strategy adopted by the MCP raises an interesting and important question about which side was responsible for the final outcome of the Emergency. Was it the case, as Humphrey and others have concluded, that 'the British did not win the Emergency so much as the Malayan Communist Party lost it'?[3] Humphrey is particularly critical of the 'ineptitude and doctrinal myopia' of the MCP leadership, a criticism confirmed by this study and which seems to have come about primarily because of the elimination of any capable leaders during Lai Tek's treacherous association with the Party. As a result, Humphrey argues, the MCP attempted to win a quick military victory rather than adopt Mao Tse Tung's policy of waging a protracted struggle; they maintained the Chinese character of the Party and failed to reach out and appeal to the other races; they did not foresee, until it was too late, how vulnerable they would become because of the dependence of the guerrilla units on food supplies from the populated centres; they failed to appreciate fully the immediate concerns of the Chinese population, and, finally, they did not find a way to counter successfully the Government's resettlement programme.[4] Certainly, Humphrey's case is persuasive.

And yet the Government, too, could have found a way to lose: indeed, it seemed as if they were intent on doing so during the first few years of the Emergency. By employing a strategy of coercion and enforcement, they alienated much of the Chinese population and generated a good deal of sympathy for the MCP. However, the Government must be credited for rethinking its policy and gradually adopting a strategy which addressed at least some of the grievances of not only the Chinese but other sections of the population as well. As a consequence, it was able to neutralize sympathy for the MCP within the Chinese population and win crucial support among all communities for the evolving political system. If both sides had adopted short-sighted, counter-productive strategies which gave no chance of achieving a comprehensive victory, then the result would undoubtedly have been a stalemate, a chronic state of fluctuating civil violence which could have continued for years. Indeed, a victory for the MCP could have come about only if its leaders had avoided most of the mistakes detailed by Humphrey and if the Government had not been able to revise and implement its strategy. In actual fact, overthrowing a government is no easy matter: while there can be no doubt that a guerrilla movement can hasten the process, much depends on a government's own ineptitude. In sum, then, although the MCP's problems were clearly a contributing factor, there is a strong argument to be made that the Malayan Government was in large measure responsible for its own success.

The Lessons of the Malayan Emergency

The eventual success of the Malayan Government has raised the question of whether it is possible to derive lessons from the Emergency which could be applied to the conduct of other counter-guerrilla campaigns. This, of course, was a major topic of debate during the war in South Vietnam. And because guerrilla wars have continued not only in South-East Asia but also in many other regions of the world, the question remains an intriguing and important one.

Various scholars have expressed serious reservations about trying to generalize from the Malayan Government's success.[5] They argue that there were a number of aspects to the Emergency which worked to the Government's advantage and which are so unlikely to be duplicated elsewhere that no lessons may be usefully drawn from the experience. The aspects of the Emergency they allude to can be grouped around three main points. First, the MCP had some major obstacles to overcome. Their base of support was effectively confined to the Chinese community which constituted less than 40 per cent of the total population. This allowed the Government to concentrate its counter-guerrilla efforts on that one sector of Malayan society. Nor could the guerrillas count on any outside material aid being provided by sympathetic governments. The geography of Peninsular Malaya and Britain's control of Singapore meant that the MCP had to fight a relatively self-sufficient campaign with only the narrow Thai border providing a land route to the outside world and a sanctuary for rest and recuperation. Moreover, partly as a consequence of this lack of an outside supply of weapons, the fire-power of the MCP was said to be severely limited.

Secondly, the British were able to take full advantage of their position as a colonial power. The British colonial administration already had within its ranks a number of people with a knowledge and understanding of the different racial communities in Malaya. It was also possible for senior colonial officials to redress some of the major grievances held by various sectors of the population by introducing social, economic, and political reforms–changes which a less autonomous, locally based government might not have had the political will to undertake. And, of course, by negotiating Independence with a locally elected government of which they approved, the British were able to ensure continued good relations with Malaya and at the same time undercut the appeal of the MCP.

Finally, the British were lucky. Although they would no doubt wish to argue that their foresight in inserting Lai Tek into the MCP in the 1930s led eventually to the dearth of good strategists among the Party's leaders, there was certainly an element of luck in the way in which the Malayan Government benefited from the inexperience of the communist leadership and especially from the reduction in guerrilla activity produced by the 1951 policy directive. But clearly, for the British and the Malayan Governments, the best piece of unexpected good fortune was the prosperity generated by the Korean War. Indeed, the price of natural rubber on the international market during the 1950s was the best for any decade from the boom years of the First World War right up to the present. This prosperity made resettlement possible and financed much of Templer's hearts and minds strategy. Without the Korean War boom and the general economic buoyancy of the period, the Malayan Government's task would have been many times more difficult.

Essentially, these points emphasize that each guerrilla war has its own unique characteristics and, as a consequence, particular policies and the way in which they were implemented in one arena cannot necessarily be transferred to another. A number of the themes in this study underscore this argument. The tactics adopted by each side in a guerrilla war must take into consideration the unique circumstances of each society in which such a war is waged. And yet, as the extensive theoretical literature on the principles of waging a guerrilla war suggests, all rural guerrilla wars have some basic features in common. With this in mind, it would seem possible to review the Malayan Emergency in order to draw general conclusions about the philosophy underpinning a successful counter-guerrilla campaign.

First, a number of points may be raised about the Malayan Government's initial response to the guerrilla campaign. In many ways, their reaction was typical of most governments facing a fairly well-supported guerrilla movement. Failing to appreciate either the extent of the grievances which had developed within the general population, or the resulting strength of the opposition to their administration and policies, the Malayan Government saw the guerrilla threat as a conspiracy by a relatively small group of 'criminals'.[6] The guerrillas were viewed as the cause of the Government's problem rather than as a symptom of fundamental social, economic, political, and cultural ills to be found within Malayan society. As a result, the Government focused all its attention on the communists' guerrilla army in an attempt to eradicate it as quickly as possible. What was perceived to be a military threat induced a primarily military response. Almost as a reflex action, the use of force to challenge law and order was answered by a reciprocal use of force on the part of the army and police.

Such a strategy is, at first glance, appealing. If the guerrillas are not supported by a significant section of the population, as was the case for example in Che Guevara's effort to mount a guerrilla campaign in Bolivia in 1966-7, it is possible to eliminate the threat before it gains any momentum. Moreover, it is probably the best strategy for ensuring that the Government does not lose the war; the military ought to be able to make sure that control is maintained over a minimum portion of the country including the major urban centres. Certainly, this was the case in Malaya where, as Short has pointed out, the Malayan Government 'continued to govern'.[7]

And yet, such a 'not lose' approach–which in this study has been labelled a 'coercion and enforcement' strategy–virtually guarantees that the government employing it cannot win a guerrilla war in which they are confronted by an already well-supported guerrilla army. The use of coercion, repression, and enforcement terror in making the costs to individuals of supporting or joining the guerrillas widely appreciated and in bringing pressure to bear directly on the guerrillas themselves tends to produce more sympathy and more recruits for the guerrilla organization. This is what happened in Malaya where the indiscriminate shooting of rural Chinese squatters fleeing army patrols, the burning of rural homes, and the brutal treatment meted out by the police, all served to swell the ranks of both the guerrilla army and the communists' political-support organizations. The just over 2,000 guerrillas in late 1948 had become a guerrilla army of well over 8,000 by the end of 1951.

Similar policies have produced similar results in other wars. For example, in the Philippines in the late 1940s, the Government introduced its 'iron fist' policy which was based on President Roxas's view that the only way to fight force was to use superior force.[8] The result was that most Hukbalahap guerrillas and their supporters became rebels, 'not through the urging of others but out of anger, revenge and a desire to protect themselves against the Philippines Constabulary and civilian guards'.[9] Between 1946 and 1950, the Huk rebellion expanded rapidly with the number of recruits far outstripping the weapons, ammunition, and supplies available. In the second Vietnam War, too, the use of a coercion and enforcement strategy fuelled the Vietcong's campaign. Philippe Devillers, for example, has observed that in 1958 a certain 'sequence of events became almost classical: denunciation, encirclement of villages, searches and raids, arrest of suspects, plundering, interrogations enlivened by torture (even of innocent people), deportation and "regrouping" of populations suspected of intelligence with the rebels'.[10] Thompson makes the point that the Vietcong were able to turn the South Vietnam Government's reflex, retaliatory action to their advantage. The guerrillas would fire a few shots from a village before they themselves disappeared. This invariably induced a government or American response which then did their work for the guerrillas, with the result that 'people who were previously innocent and uncommitted peasants are then likely to be turned into willing Vietcong'.[11]

The key problem, then, for any government facing a well-supported guerrilla army is that there will always be recruits ready to take the place of those captured, injured, or killed. Indeed, because it leads to the alienation of large sections of the population, the use

of a coercion and enforcement strategy tends to ensure that this
is the case. It is rather like bailing out a dinghy with a large hole
in it; the bailing cannot solve the problem especially if the very act
of bailing rocks the boat so much that more water keeps pouring
in. At best, because a sense of fatigue can sometimes result in a
temporary lull in the war, a coercion and enforcement policy can
produce an uneasy and fluctuating stalemate; at worst it can lead
to a devastating war of attrition which slowly undermines government morale and may even lead to the government's collapse.

Secondly, a number of points may be raised about the difficulty
of changing over from a coercion and enforcement strategy, which
seems most likely to avoid defeat, to a hearts and minds strategy,
which is most likely to bring about victory or the elimination of
civil violence and the permanent restoration of stability. These
two approaches should not be considered in terms of a dichotomy
but rather as two poles of a continuum. Any counter-guerrilla campaign will contain elements of both strategies although one will
usually predominate. Getting any government to change its policies
is always a major task. The egos and careers of senior politicians, military officers, and administrators become tied to particular policies.
Political interests become entrenched, institutional roles become
fixed, and the bureaucratic ramparts are manned in order to repel
invaders. Governments even begin to believe their own propaganda.
The tendency is for most governments to assume that their inability to reduce the guerrilla threat is not so much a failure of policy
as a failure of implementation. Usually, the problem is seen as a
need for more resources, more fire-power, and a more rigorous
application of the policy. Rather like the horse in George Orwell's
Animal Farm, the answer to all problems seems to be to work harder.
But unless the initial coercion and enforcement policy is exchanged
for a predominantly hearts and minds approach, doubling the
effort–as Thompson has commented with respect to US policy in
Vietnam–only squares the error.[12]

The experience of the Emergency suggests that the best, if not
the only chance for a change in policy, comes with a change in the
senior personnel responsible for conducting the counter-guerrilla
campaign. However, the people taking over must have not only the
ability to implement the substantial reforms needed to move the policy in the direction of a hearts and minds approach, but also the
resources and the will to do so. The will to carry through new policies
is especially important because it takes so long to bring about the
required changes. Government leaders must ensure that the lengthy

process of retraining the armed forces and the police results in an understanding that the government's security forces are engaged not so much in a war against the enemy as a battle to win over the people. An expanded administrative capability is also needed in order to address local grievances by delivering programmes to satisfy people's basic needs and at the same time extend control over the general population. This is, however, easier said than done because finding enough people who are qualified to act as local administrators is no easy task. And, of course, a strengthened intelligence network is required to allow the increased flow of information from the population to be passed along to the army and the police.

But the most severe obstacle facing government leaders in implementing a hearts and minds strategy is the need to engineer a redistribution of political and economic power. A major shift in attitude is necessary. The belief that the restoration of law and order must come before the pursuit of justice for the aggrieved must give way to the key assumption of the hearts and minds approach that grievances should be redressed so as to restore order and political stability. Redressing the grievances which have persuaded people to support the guerrillas may necessitate the implementation of programmes which provide–or at least give promise of providing–for such innovations as fair elections at the local as well as the national level, removal of power from the hands of the military, land reform, fairer wages for labourers, and so forth. In other words, those who are themselves the targets of guerrilla attacks must give up some of their political and economic power to the very people whom they blame for the prevailing violence and lawlessness. The difficulty of doing this results in governments trying short-cuts or superficial reforms, such as using the army to extend administrative control or introducing elections which are irrelevant to the real distribution of power. Even if some reforms are attempted, it is quite possible that the coercion and enforcement approach will remain predominant.

Finally, a number of points can be made about the implementation of a hearts and minds strategy. As the key elements of such a strategy are put in place, the general population can gradually be weaned away from the guerrillas. Some may be persuaded by the mere promise of reforms made by someone in whom they have come to trust. This was the case for Templer in Malaya and Magsaysay in the Philippines. Others will be persuaded by having the military placed under civilian authority, tighter reigns put on their activities, and reforms introduced which increase people's general sense of security. Still others will need their economic, political, and social grievances tended to. Guerrilla wars are usually complex and messy affairs and successful guerrilla movements can gain support from many different groups for many varied reasons. This, of course, underscores Templer's point that counter-guerrilla campaigns must be fought on all fronts and include all the normal activities of any government. It is interesting to note that Templer commented in November 1952, less than a year after his arrival in Malaya, 'The shooting side of the business is only 25% of the trouble and the other 75% lies in getting the people of this country behind us.'[13]

While Templer argued for the need to get the people of the country behind the Government and while the importance of 'winning' hearts and minds has generally been emphasized, it may only be necessary to neutralize most of the key groups from which the guerrillas draw their support. As long as the government is able to gain some level of support from part of the population and the rest are neutral, supporting neither one side nor the other, then the guerrillas will find it more difficult to replace lost comrades with new recruits and to secure money, weapons, food, and other essential supplies. The guerrillas' numbers will shrink and they will become more and more concerned with survival and less able to conduct operations. Moreover, as sympathy for the government grows and as people see that support for the government as the best way of restoring peace and order to their lives, more and more reliable information about the guerrillas and their supporters will become available, the army and police will be able to act with more discrimination, and there will be less chance of their operations alienating people.

But the ability of either side to take advantage of a neutral population lies in the extent to which they have been able to extend administrative control to all parts of the country. Eqbal Ahmed has argued that 'Once a revolutionary movement enters the guerrilla phase, its major task is to outadminister the established authority.'[14] In a similar vein, Bernard Fall has argued that 'When a country is being subverted it is not being outfought, it is being out-administered. Subversion is literally administration with a minus sign in front.'[15] In Malaya, it was the Malayan Government who eventually outadministered the MCP. Indeed, it is only through an extensive and reasonably efficient administrative structure that the basic needs of the population may be catered to and grievances redressed. The importance of developing a sound administration to the successful pursuit of a hearts and minds campaign cannot be exaggerated.

If these are the lessons to be learnt from the Malayan Government's policies during the Emergency, what can be learnt from the MCP's policies? In many ways the lessons are similar. While in the first few months of the Emergency, the MCP tried to woo key sectors of the Chinese population, from 1949 to 1951 it adopted an essentially military-style campaign and resorted more and more to the use of a coercion and enforcement strategy. Rather than heeding the advice of the major theorists of guerrilla warfare and preparing for a 'protracted struggle', it tried for an early decisive victory. By the time the Party had realized its mistake and put its organizational and political work on an equal footing with the military campaign, the Party found it difficult to regain the offensive. Moreover, the MCP leadership failed to analyse properly its own weakness and the strengths of the Malayan Government. All of this suggests that members of revolutionary movements can learn as much as governing administrations from the success of the Malayan Government. As Sun Tzu has said: 'Know your enemy and know yourself; in a hundred battles you will never be in peril.'[16]

Malaya after the Emergency

Since the Emergency, Malaya–or Malaysia as it became known in 1963 when Peninsular Malaysia was joined by Sabah, Sarawak, and Singapore–has prospered. Apart from the hiatus caused by the May 1969 race riots, the country has benefited from a remarkable degree of political stability. In good part as a consequence of this stability, the economy has performed well. Real Gross Domestic Product has consistently grown by about 7 per cent per year, and Malaysia's per capita income places it only behind Singapore and oil-rich Brunei in South-East Asia. Much of Malaysia's development has been influenced by what happened during the Emergency. Clearly the years 1948-60 were formative ones for Malaysia.

First, the Emergency helped set the course of the country's political institutions. The demands of fighting a co-ordinated counter-guerrilla campaign contributed to the development of Malaya's (and subsequently Malaysia's) highly centralized federal system. The strong and heartfelt assertions of states' rights, which came to the fore after the Malayan Union was replaced by the negotiated Federation Agreement in 1948, eventually had to be toned down as the necessity for co-operation became evident to all.[17] Particularly important was Templer's ability to obtain the states' co-operation once it was realized that he was gaining ground against the communists. Compounding these initial centralizing tendencies were the emergence of the Alliance Party as a dominant force at both the federal and state levels and the extensive federal powers which, in part at least because of the continuing needs of the Emergency, were incorporated into Malaya's constitution at Independence in 1957.

The Emergency also, of course, paved the way for the development of the Alliance and especially of its senior partner, the UMNO. Fearful of anyone who might be remotely connected with the communists, the Government initially allowed only right-of-centre parties to participate in legally sanctioned political activities. Having gained power, the UMNO and its allies in the Alliance–the MCA and the MIC–skilfully used their position to maintain their dominance of Malayan–and then Malaysian–politics. Intriguingly, the Alliance has combined an essentially conservative philosophy with a willingness to intervene in the economic and social life of the country. This is in large measure a result of the demonstration effect of a philosophically highly conservative British administration successfully intervening in every facet of the Peninsula's life in order to implement its hearts and minds strategy.

Secondly, once the Emergency was over, the Malayan–and later the Malaysian–Government inherited a substantial security apparatus. The ranks of the police and the locally manned regiments had grown markedly during the first few years of the Emergency and, therefore, although the police force was pruned on occasion, the strength of the security forces was maintained at a relatively high level. Since the Emergency, both the police and the armed forces have remained sizeable organizations. Moreover, the Special Branch has retained much of its efficiency as an intelligence-gathering agency. Backing this impressive institutional power has been the Internal Security Act, which replaced the Emergency regulations in 1960 and which was drawn up in such a way as to ensure that the Government had all the legal power it might require to repel any future communist threat. The extensive powers of the Government under the Internal Security Act, as well as some of the operations of the security forces, have been criticized both within Malaysia and internationally. However, one beneficial consequence of the Emergency in this respect is that in the end the primary responsibility for security was given to the police while at the same time the armed forces were placed firmly under civilian control. Despite their size and their crucial role in the Emergency and later in the 'Confrontation' with Indonesia, Malaya's/Malaysia's armed forces have stayed out of politics–an unusual state of affairs for any developing country, especially for one that has fought a guerrilla war.[18]

Thirdly, the Emergency radically changed the social and economic landscape of rural Malaya. At the heart of this change was the resettlement of over 500,000 people, mainly rural Chinese peasants. By the end of the Emergency in 1960, only a few of the more than 500 New Villages had been abandoned and Malaya's settlement patterns had been irrevocably altered. With the average New Villages containing over 1,100 people and the New Villages in Johore, Perak, and Selangor averaging over 1,500 people, Malaya had become one of the most urbanized countries in Asia.[19] Along with this urbanization came a change in the economic base of the rural Chinese. From a mainly agricultural population, which also worked as day labourers on rubber estates and smallholdings and on tin mines, the majority of New Villagers became labourers who also worked small plots of land. Except where the proximity of a major urban centre gave New Villagers alternative employment opportunities, this transformation made the rural Chinese reliant on the prosperity of the rubber and tin industries and sowed the seeds of the problems which were to emerge, especially in the more remote New Villages, from the late 1960s onwards as the international prices of natural rubber and tin steadily declined.

Fourthly, the Emergency left a legacy of racial distrust. The Malayan Government felt that resettlement would be more likely to succeed if each centre was, as far as possible, occupied by a single race. This practice accentuated the geographic racial divisions which had characterized the Peninsula since the mid-nineteenth century. Resettlement also caused resentment among Malays because the social services delivered to the rural population benefited the mainly Chinese population of the New Villages to a far greater extent than the Malays who lived in less concentrated, and thus less easily serviced, kampongs. And of course, underlying the relationship between the racial communities in Malaya was the fact that the members of the MCP and their supporters were primarily Chinese while the members of the security forces were mainly Malays. The country was fortunate that the multiracial Alliance Party was able to dissipate much of the racial tension which built up during the Emergency.[20]

Finally, the Emergency set the stage for the implementation of Malaya's/Malaysia's later development plans. By 1960, because of the strategic requirements of their counter-guerrilla campaign, the Government had put a great deal of money into expanding the country's economic infrastructure. The benefits of this expansion became fully evident in the 1960s. For example, roads and railways, which had been improved so as to give the security forces easy access to New Villages and other strategic areas, opened up new rubber growing areas, allowed rubber and other export crops to be moved to the main centres more easily, and linked the growing major urban centres to pools of labour in nearby New Villages. Along with the expansion of the economic infrastructure, the Emergency produced a massive increase in the size of the civil administration. This forced growth in administrative capacity came about in part because of the arguments made by Briggs that the Government needed to reassert its administrative authority in all regions of the Peninsula, and in part because of the administrative requirements of the hearts and minds approach, particularly the delivery of services to the New Villages. From an overall total of 48,000 administrative employees at the federal, state, and municipal levels in 1948, the number climbed to 140,000 in 1959.[21] The importance of this administrative expansion to the execution of the country's development plans cannot be underestimated.

The Emergency also had an impact on the country's education system. Because of the MCP's ability to penetrate the Chinese schools, the Government started to take over and fund all schools so as to exercise greater control over the teachers and the curriculum. The schools became a vital battleground in the fight for the allegiance of Malaya's youth. As a consequence, the financial resources allocated to the education system rose from $34 million in 1950 to $78 million in 1955, and to $135 million in 1958; the number of schools—especially English-language and vocational and professional schools—increased rapidly; and the number of students more than doubled between 1950 and 1958.[22] This produced a relatively well-educated labour force and a pool of educated people who could be recruited into the civil service. As a consequence of the availability of at least a minimum number of suitably educated personnel, the loss of British administrators who chose to retire after Independence and the acceleration of the Malayanization of the bureaucracy in the late 1950s and early 1960s were not as debilitating as they might otherwise have been.

But perhaps most interesting of all are the echoes of the conduct of the Emergency which are to be found in the way in which the Ministry of National and Rural Development put into effect Malaya's/

Malaysia's development plans. The 'Red Book', the operations room, and all the devices for ensuring that the plans were executed were derived from the experience of the Emergency. Indeed, Tun Abdul Razak simply appropriated the approach he had supervised as Minister of Defence during the late 1950s and adapted it to the operations of the new Ministry of National and Rural Development when he took it over in October 1959. Even Razak's technique of turning up in districts unannounced, making decisions on the spot, and publicly praising and berating his officials was based on the means Templer had employed to inject energy into the counter-guerrilla campaign. Razak was clearly keen to emulate Templer's success.[23]

The Emergency years, then, are crucial to understanding modern Malaysia. Many of Malaysia's developments over the last quarter-century have their roots in the turbulent twelve years from 1948 to 1960. The Emergency, and especially the reversal of policy which came about in 1952, have cast a long shadow over many areas of Malaysian life. But perhaps most importantly, the course of the Emergency—and particularly the abandonment of a coercion and enforcement approach in favour of a hearts and minds approach—paved the way for a relatively peaceful and prosperous aftermath to the fighting, a legacy which few guerrilla wars have bequeathed their participants.

1. T. I. K. Lloyd to Sir Alexander Newbolt, 23 August 1948, CO 537/3758.
2. See, for example, Hugh T. Pagden, 'Unrest in Malaya', para. 116, CO 537/3757
3. John Weldon Humphrey, 'Population Resettlement in Malaya' (Ph.D. dissertation, Northwestern University, 1971), p. 173. See also Francis Kok-Wah Loh, 'Beyond the Tin Mines: The Political Economy of Chinese Squatter Farmers in the Kinta New Villages, Malaysia' (Ph.D. dissertation, Cornell University, 1980), p. 152.
4. Humphrey, 'Population Resettlement', pp. 173-8.
5. See, for example, Robert O. Tilman, 'The Non-Lessons of the Malayan Emergency', Asian Survey 6 (August 1966); Bernard Fall, The Two Vietnams (New York: Praeger, 1967), pp. 340 and 342, and Anthony Short, 'The Malayan Emergency', in Ronald Haycock, ed., Regular Armies and Insurgency (London: Croom Helm, 1979), pp. 65-6.
6. See Royal United Services Institution, Lessons from the Vietnam War: Report of a Seminar held at the Royal United Services Institute on Wednesday, 12 February 1969 (London: RUSI, 1969), p. 4, for the comments of M. Elliott-Bateman on this issue.
7. Anthony Short, The Communist Insurrection in Malaya 1948-1960 (London: Frederick Mueller, 1975), p. 499.

8. Benedict J. Kerkvliet, *The Huk Rebellion: A Study of Peasant Revolt in the Philippines* (Berkeley: University of California Press, 1977), pp. 189-98.

9. Ibid., p. 205, and also p. 253.

10. Philippe Devillers, 'Ngo Dinh Diem and the Struggle for Reunification', in Marvin E. Gettleman, *Vietnam: History, Documents, and Opinions on a Major World Crisis* (Harmondsworth, Middlesex: Penguin, 1965), pp. 232-5, cited in Geoffrey Fairbairn, *Revolutionary Guerrilla Warfare: The Countryside Version* (Harmondsworth, Middlesex: Penguin, 1974), pp. 216-17.

11. Robert Thompson, *No Exit From Vietnam* (London: Chatto and Windus, 1969), p. 41.

12. Ibid., p. 89.

13. John Cloake, *Templer Tiger of Malaya: The Life of Field Marshal Sir Gerald Templer* (London: Harrap, 1985), p. 262.

14. Eqbal Ahmed, 'Revolutionary War and Counter-Insurgency', *Journal of International Affairs* 25 (No. 1, 1971), p. 8.

15. Bernard Fall, 'The Theory and Practice of Insurgency and Counter Insurgency', in M. Smith and C. Johns, eds., *American Defense Policy* (Baltimore: Johns Hopkins Press, 1965), p. 277, cited in O. P. Dwivedi and J. Nef, *Public Administration and Development* 2 (1982), p. 60.

16. Sun Tzu, *The Art of War*, translated by Samuel B. Griffith (London: Oxford University Press, 1971), p. 84.

17. See Zakaria Haji Ahmad and Kernial Singh Sandhu, 'The Malayan Emergency: Event Writ Large', in Kernial Singh Sandhu and Paul Wheatley, eds., *Melaka: The Transformation of A Malayan Capital c.1400-1980*, 2 vols. (Kuala Lumpur: Oxford University Press, 1983), Vol. 1, pp. 402-3.

18. Ibid., pp. 406-9. It should be noted that because Britain and other Commonwealth countries provided and controlled a significant portion of the armed forces in Malaya, the Malayan army did not have the sense of power or the expectation of power that armed forces in say Vietnam or the Philippines obviously had. On the coercive powers of the Government, see Simon Barraclough, 'The Dynamics of Coercion in the Malaysian Political Process', *Modern Asian Studies* 19 (October 1985).

19. Humphrey, 'Population Resettlement', p. 200.

20. Ibid., 286-9.

21. See Department of Labour, *Monthly Report*, June 1948, and Ministry of Labour, *Annual Report* for 1959. By 1965 the civil administration in West Malaysia had grown to about 228,000 and Milton Esman has noted that by 'international standards this was a high figure comparable to such countries as the United Kingdom and Denmark'. See *Administration and Development in Malaysia: Institution Building and Reform in a Plural Society* (Ithaca: Cornell University Press, 1972), pp. 70-1.

22. *Federation of Malaysia Annual Report*, 1963 and 1964.

23. See W. C. S. Corry, Tape and Transcript of an Interview, Malayan Civil Service, 1923-53, British Adviser, Pahang 1948-53, mss. Ind Ocn S 215 (Rhodes House Library), and Gayl D. Ness, *Bureaucracy and Rural Development in Malaysia: A Study of Complex Organizations in Stimulating Economic Development in New States* (Berkeley: University of California Press, 1967), pp. 142-221; William Shaw, *Tun Razak: His Life and Times* (Kuala Lumpur: Longman, 1976), pp. 128-37, and Esman, *Administration and Development in Malaysia*, pp. 216-26.

Select Bibliography

Unpublished Official Records

THE main sources in the Public Record Office, London (Kew), are the Cabinet Papers Series (CAB) 128, 129, 130, and 131; the Colonial Office Records Series (CO) 717, 537, 825, and 1022; the Foreign Office Records Series (FO) 371, and the War Office Records Series (WO) 216. The main sources in the Arkib Negara Malaysia (National Archives of Malaysia), Kuala Lumpur, are the Prime Minister's Department Files, especially the Secretary to the Government and Chief Secretary Files; Federal Secretariat Files; Malayan Union Secretariat Files; Chinese Affairs (Federation of Malaya) Files, and Labour Department Files.

Published Official Records

(A) United Kingdom

Parliamentary Debates (Commons), 5th Series, 1948-54.
An Economic Survey of the Colonial Territories, London: HMSO, 1955.

(B) Malayan Union/Federation of Malaya/ Federation of Malaysia

Anatomy of Communist Propaganda, 1950-1953, Kuala Lumpur: Government Printer, 1954.

Awberry, M. S. S. and Dalley, F. W., *Labour and Trade Union Organization in the Federation of Malaya and Singapore*, Kuala Lumpur: Government Printer, 1948.

Barrett, E. C. G., *Report of the Registration of Residents for the Year 1949*, Kuala Lumpur: Registration Office, 1949.

Central Advisory Committee on Education: Report on the Barnes Report on Malay Education and the Fenn-Wu Report on Chinese Education, Kuala Lumpur: Government Printer, 1951.

Commission of Enquiry into Matters Affecting the Integrity of the Public Service, Kuala Lumpur: Government Printer, 1955.

Communist Banditry in Malaya: Extracts from Speeches by The High Commissioner, Sir Henry Gurney, October 1948 to December 1949, Kuala Lumpur: Government Printer, n.d.

Communist Threat to the Federation of Malaya, Kuala Lumpur: Government Printer, 1959.

Conduct of the Anti-Terrorist Operations in Malaya, Kuala Lumpur: Government Printer, 1958.

Corry, W. C. S., *A General Survey of New Villages, A Report to His Excellency Sir Donald MacGillivray, High Commissioner of the Federation of Malaya*, Kuala Lumpur: Government Printer, 1954.

Department of Broadcasting, *Annual Report*, 1953 and 1954.

Department of Chinese Affairs, *Annual Report*, 1947 and 1948.

———, *Monthly Review*, 1951.

Department of Education, *Annual Report*, 1946-50, 1952-5, and 1957.

Department of Information, *Annual Report*, 1947, 1949, 1956, and 1958.

———, *Communist Banditry on Malaya: The Emergency, June 1948-June 1951*, n.d.

———, *Communist Terrorism in Malaya: The Emergency, June 1948-June 1952*, n.d.

———, *Emergency Statistics for the Federation of Malaya Since June 1948* (7/60/160 [Emerg]), 1960.

———, *Role of Information Services in the Emergency* (7/60/160 [Emerg]) 31 July 1960.

———, *Fortnightly Press Digest*, various dates.

———, *Malaya Under the Emergency*, n.d.

———, *Progress Report on the Development Plan of the Federation of Malaya, 1950-1952*, 1953.

Department of Labour, *Annual Report*, 1946-9 and 1953-7.

———, *Monthly Report*, various months between June 1947 and December 1960.

Department of Public Relations, *Anatomy of Communist Propaganda, July 1948 to December 1949*, December 1949.

Department of Public Works, *Annual Report*, 1946-9 and 1954-60.

Director of Operations, *The Protection of Estates and Mines*, 1953.

Draft Development Plan of the Federation of Malaya, Kuala Lumpur: Government Printer, 1950.

Education Ordinance, Kuala Lumpur: Government Printer, 1952.

Emergency Regulations Ordinance, Kuala Lumpur: Government Printer, 1953.

Establishment, Organization and Supervision of Local Authorities in the Federation of Malaya, Kuala Lumpur: Government Printer, 1953.

Federation of Malaya Annual Report, 1948-61, Kuala Lumpur: Government Printer.

Federation of Malaysia Annual Report, 1963 and 1964, Kuala Lumpur: Government Printer.

Fell, H., *1957 Population Census*, Report No. 14, Kuala Lumpur: Department of Statistics, 1960.

Final Report by the Joint Wages Commission, Kuala Lumpur: Government Printer, 1948

Handbook to Malaya and the Emergency, Kuala Lumpur: Government Printer, 1955.

Hawkins, A. S. M., *Report on the Introduction of Elections in the Municipality of George Town, Penang 1951*, Kuala Lumpur: Government Printer, 27 December 1953.

Interim Report on Wages by the Joint Wages Commission, Kuala Lumpur: Government Printer, 29 July 1947.

Malayan Union Annual Report, Kuala Lumpur: Government Printer, 1947.

Ministry of Labour, *Annual Report*, 1958-61.

Monthly Statistics Bulletin, Kuala Lumpur: Government Printer, various months between July 1952 and July 1957.

Police Force, *Annual Report*, 1949, 1955, 1957, and 1958.

Proceedings of the Federal Legislative Council, 1948-57.

Report by the Chief Minister of the Federation of Malaysia on the Baling Talks, Kuala Lumpur: Government Printer, 1956.

Report of the Committee Appointed by His Excellency the High Commissioner to Investigate the Squatter Problem, Kuala Lumpur: Government Printer, 1949.

Report of the Committee Appointed to Examine the Question of Elections to the Federal Legislative Council, Kuala Lumpur: Government Printer, 1954.

Report of the Committee on the Malayanization of the Government Service, Kuala Lumpur: Government Printer, 1954.

Report of the Financial Review Committee, Kuala Lumpur: Government Printer, 1947.

Report of the Mission of Inquiry into the Rubber Industry of Malaya, Kuala Lumpur: Government Printer, 1954.

Report of the Police Mission to Malaya, Kuala Lumpur: Government Printer, 1950.

Report of the Special Committee Appointed on the 20th Day of September, 1951 to Recommend Legislation to Cover all Aspects of Education Policy for the Federation of Malaya, Kuala Lumpur: Government Printer, 1952.

Report on Chinese Education, Kuala Lumpur: Government Printer, 1951.

Report on Malay Education, Kuala Lumpur: Government Printer, 1951.

Selangor State Information Officer, *Report on the Semenyith Inquiry*, n.d.

Thompson, J. B., *Report on the Conduct of Food Searches at Semenyith*, Kuala Lumpur: Government Printer, 1956.

Tufo, M. V. del, *Malaya: Report on the 1947 Census of Population*, London: HMSO, 1949.

Williams-Hunt, P. D. R., *An Introduction to the Malayan Aborigines*, Kuala Lumpur: Government Press, 1952.

(C) Colony of Singapore

Public Relations Office, *Daily Digest of Non-English Press*, 1952-4.

Singapore Chinese Middle School Students' Union, Singapore: Government Printing Office, No. Cmd. 53 of 1956.

Books and Published Papers

Allen, Charles, ed., *Tales from the South China Seas: Images of the British in South-East Asia in the Twentieth Century*, London: Futura, 1983.

Allen, J. de V., *The Malayan Union*, New Haven: Yale University Press, 1967.

Arasaratnam, Sinnappah, *Indians in Malaysia and Singapore*, Kuala Lumpur: Oxford University Press, 1970.

Barber, Noel, *The War of the Running Dogs: The Malayan Emergency, 1948-1960*, London: Fontana, 1972; first published as *The War of the Running Dogs: How Malaya Defeated the Communist Guerrillas, 1948-60*, London: Collins, 1971.

Barlow, Colin, *The Natural Rubber Industry: Its Development, Technology and Economy in Malaysia*, Kuala Lumpur: Oxford University Press, 1978.

Barraclough, Simon, 'The Dynamics of Coercion in the Malaysian Political Process', *Modern Asian Studies* 19 (October 1985).

Bartlett, Vernon, *Report from Malaya*, London: Verschoyle, 1954.

Bauer, P. T., *The Rubber Industry: A Study in Competition and Monopoly*, London: Longmans, 1948.

Blythe, Wilfred, *The Impact of Chinese Secret Societies in Malaya: A Historical Study*, London: Oxford University Press, 1969.

Brimmell, J. H., *Communism in South East Asia: A Political Analysis*, London: Oxford University Press, 1959.

Campbell, Arthur, *Jungle Green*, Boston: Little Brown and Co., 1954.

Carnell, F. G., 'British Policy in Malaya', *Political Quarterly* 23 (1952).

———, 'Communalism and Communism in Malaya', *Pacific Affairs* 26 (June 1953).

———, 'Malayan Citizenship Legislation', *The International and Comparative Law Quarterly* 4th Series 1 (October 1952).

Chandos, Viscount (Oliver Lyttelton), *The Memoirs of Lord Chandos*, London: Bodley Head, 1962.

Chapman, F. Spencer, *The Jungle Is Neutral*, London: Chatto and Windus, 1949.

Cheah Boon Kheng, *Red Star Over Malaya: Resistance and Social Conflict During and After the Japanese Occupation 1941-1946*, Singapore: Singapore University Press, 1983.

———, *The Masked Comrades: A Study of the Communist United Front in Malaya, 1945-1948*, Singapore: Times Books International, 1979.

Chin Kee Onn, *Malaya Upside Down*, Singapore: Jitts, 1946.

Clarkson, James D., *The Cultural Ecology of a Chinese Village: Cameron Highlands, Malaysia*, Chicago: Department of Geography, University of Chicago, 1968.

Cleaveland, Norman, *Bang! Bang! in Ampang: Dredging Tin During Malaya's Emergency*, San Pedro, California: Symcon, 1973.

Cloake, John, *Templer Tiger of Malaya: The Life of Field Marshal Sir Gerald Templer*, London: Harrap, 1985.

Clutterbuck, Richard, 'Reviews: Insurrection in Malaya', *Modern Asian Studies* 11 (1977).

———, *Riot and Revolution in Singapore and Malaya 1945-1963*, London: Faber and Faber, 1973.

———, *The Long, Long War: Counterinsurgency in Malaya and Vietnam*, New York: Praeger, 1966.

Cruz, Gerald de, *Facing Facts in Malaya*, London: The Union of Democratic Control, 1952.

Dobby, E. H. G., 'Recent Settlement Changes in South Malaya', *Malayan Journal of Tropical Geography* 1 (October 1953).

Donnison, F. S. V., *British Military Administration in the Far East*, London: HMSO, 1956.

Duncanson, Dennis J., 'Impressions of Life in Malaya Today', *Journal of the Royal Central Asian Society* 38 (1951).

Dwivedi, O. P. and Nef, J., 'Crises and Continuities in Development Theory and Administration: First and Third World Perspectives', *Public Administration and Development* 2 (1982).

Eqbal Ahmed, 'Revolutionary War and Counter-Insurgency', *Journal of International Affairs* 25 (No. 1, 1971).

Esman, Milton, *Administration and Development in Malaysia: Institution Building and Reform in a Plural Society*, Ithaca: Cornell University Press, 1972.

Fairbairn, Geoffrey, *Revolutionary Guerrilla Warfare: The Countryside Version*, Harmondsworth, Middlesex: Penguin, 1974.

Fall, Bernard, *The Two Vietnams*, New York: Praeger, 1967.

Foster, G. M., 'Peasant Society and the Image of the Limited Good,' *American Anthropologist* 62 (April 1965).

Furse, Ralph, *Aucuparius*, London: Oxford University Press, 1962.

Galula, David, *Counterinsurgency Warfare: Theory and Practice*, New York: Praeger, 1964.

Gamba, Charles, *The Origins of Trade Unionism in Malaya: A Study in Colonial Labour Unrest*, Singapore: Donald Moore for Eastern Universities Press, 1962.

Ginsburg, Norton and Chester, Robert F. Jr., *Malaya*, Seattle: University of Washington, 1958.

Girling, John L. S., *America and the Third World: Revolution and Intervention*, London: Routledge and Kegan Paul, 1980.

Greene, Graham, 'Malaya, The Forgotten War', *Life*, 30 July 1951.

———, *Ways of Escape*, Harmondsworth: Penguin, 1981.

Griffith, Samuel B., ed., trans., *Mao Tse-tung on Guerrilla Warfare*, New York: Praeger, 1961.

Guevara, Che, *Guerrilla Warfare*, New York: Vintage Books, 1961.

Gullick, J. M., *Malaya*, London: Benn, 1964.

Gurr, Ted, *Why Men Rebel*, Princeton, NJ: Princeton University Press, 1970.

Gwee Hock Aun, *The Emergency in Malaya*, Penang, Malaysia: Sinaran Brothers, 1966.

Han Suyin, ... *And the Rain My Drink*, St. Albans: Panther, 1973; first published London: Jonathan Cape, 1956.

Hanrahan, Gene Z., *The Communist Struggle in Malaya*, Kuala Lumpur: University of Malaya Press, 1971; first published New York: Institute of Pacific Relations, 1954.

Heng Pek Koon, 'The Social and Ideological Origins of the Malayan Chinese Association', *Journal of Southeast Asian Studies* 14 (September 1983).

Heussler, Robert, *British Rule in Malaya: The Malayan Civil Service and Its Predecessors, 1867-1942*, Westport, Connecticut: Greenwood Press, 1981.

———, *Yesterday's Rulers: The Making of the British Colonial Service*, Syracuse, NY: Syracuse University Press, 1963.

Holman, Dennis, *Noone of the Ulu*, London: Heinemann, 1958; reprinted Singapore: Oxford University Press, 1984.

Horowitz, Donald L., *Ethnic Groups in Conflict*, Berkeley: University of California Press, 1985.

Huntington, Samuel, *Political Order and Changing Societies*, New Haven: Yale University Press, 1968.

International Bank for Reconstruction and Development, *The Economic Development of Malaya*, Singapore: Government Printer, 1955.

International Tin Study Group, *Tin 1950-51: A Review of the World Tin Industry*, The Hague: International Tin Study Group, 1951.

Ishak bin Tadin, 'Dato Onn and Malay Nationalism 1946-51', *Journal of Southeast Asian History* 1 (March 1960).

Johnson, Chalmers, *Revolutionary Change*, Boston: Little Brown and Co., 1969.

Jones, S. W., *Public Administration in Malaya*, London: Oxford University Press, 1953.

Kerkvliet, Benedict J., *The Huk Rebellion: A Study of Peasant Revolt in the Philippines*, Berkeley: University of California Press, 1977.

Khong Kim Hoong, *Merdeka! British Rule and the Struggle for Independence in Malaya, 1945-1957*, Petaling Jaya, Malaysia: Institute for Social Analysis, 1984.

Komer, R. W., *The Malayan Emergency in Retrospect: Organization of a Successful Counterinsurgency Effort*, Santa Monica: Rand, February 1972.

Lawrence, T. E., 'Guerrilla–Science of Guerrilla Warfare', *Encyclopaedia Britannica*, 14th edn., Vol. 10.

Lee Ting Hui, *The Communist Organisation in Singapore: Its Techniques of Manpower Mobilization and Management, 1948-1960*, Field Report Series No. 12, Singapore: Institute of Southeast Asian Studies, August 1976.

Leites, Nathan and Wolf, Charles Jr., *Rebellion and Authority: An Analytic Essay on Insurgency Conflicts*, Chicago: Markham, 1970.

McLane, Charles B., *Soviet Strategies in Southeast Asia: An Exploration of Eastern Policy under Lenin and Stalin*, Princeton, NJ: Princeton University Press, 1966.

McVey, R. T., *The Calcutta Conference and the South-east Asian Uprisings*, Interim Report Series, Modern Indonesia Project, Ithaca: Cornell University Press, 1958.

Ma, R., 'Company Profits and Prices in the Rubber Industry in Malaya, 1947-58', *The Malayan Economic Review* 4 (October 1959).

Markandan, Paul, *The Problem of the New Villages in Malaya*, Singapore: Donald Moore, 1954.

Means, Gordon P., *Malaysian Politics*, London: Hodder and Stoughton, 1976.

Mao Tse Tung, *Selected Military Writings*, 2 vols., Peking: Foreign Language Press, 1966.

Miller, Harry, *Jungle War in Malaya: The Campaign against Communism, 1948-60*, London: Arthur Barker, 1972.

_____, *Menace in Malaya*, London: Harrap, 1954.

_____, *Prince and Premier*, London: Harrap, 1959.

Mills, Lennox A., *Malaya: A Political and Economic Appraisal*, Minneapolis: University of Minnesota Press, 1958.

Moran, Lord, *Churchill: The Struggle for Survival 1940-1965*, Boston: Houghton Mifflin, 1966.

Ness, Gayl D., *Bureaucracy and Rural Development in Malaysia: A Study of Complex Organizations in Stimulating Economic Development in New States*, Berkeley: University of California Press, 1967.

Newell, William H., 'New Villages in Malaya', *The Economic Weekly* (12 February 1955).

_____, *Treacherous River: A Study of Rural Chinese in North Malaya*, Kuala Lumpur: University of Malaya Press, 1962.

Noone, Richard, *Rape of the Dream People*, London: Hutchinson, 1972.

Nyce, Ray, *Chinese New Villages in Malaya: A Community Study*, Kuala Lumpur: Malaysian Sociological Research Institute, 1973.

O'Ballance, Edgar, *Malaya: The Communist Insurgent War, 1948-1960*, London: Faber and Faber, 1966.

Oldfield, J. B., *The Green Howards in Malaya, 1949-52*, Aldershot: Gale and Polden, 1953.

Ovendale, Ritchie, 'Britain, the United States and the Cold War in Southeast Asia', *International Affairs* 58 (Summer 1982).

Paret, Peter and Shy, John W., *Guerrillas in the 1960s*, New York: Praeger, 1962.

Pollitt, Harry, *Malaya: Stop the War*, London: Communist Party Publications, 1952.

Popkin, Samuel P., *The Rational Peasant: The Political Economy of Rural Society in Vietnam*, Berkeley: University of California Press, 1979.

Purcell, Victor, *Malaya: Communist or Free?*, London: Gollancz, 1954.
———, *Malaysia*, New York: Walker and Co., 1965.
———, *The Chinese in Malaya*, 2nd edn., Kuala Lumpur: Oxford University Press, 1967; first published London: Oxford University Press, 1948.
———, *The Chinese in Southeast Asia*, 2nd edn., Kuala Lumpur: Oxford University Press, 1965; first published London: Oxford University Press, 1951.
Pye, Lucian, *Guerrilla Communism in Malaya: Its Social and Political Meaning*, Princeton, NJ: Princeton University Press, 1956.
———, *Lessons from the Malayan Struggle Against Communism*, Cambridge, Mass: Center for International Studies, Massachusetts Institute of Technology, 17 Februrary 1957.
Ratnam, K. J., *Communalism and the Political Process in Malaya*, Kuala Lumpur: University of Malaya Press, 1965.
Renick, Rhoderick Dhu, Jr., 'The Emergency Regulations of Malaya: Causes and Effect', *Journal of Southeast Asian History* 6 (September 1965).
Robinson, J. B. Perry, *Transformation in Malaya*, London: Secker and Warburg, 1956.
Roff, Margaret, 'The Malayan Chinese Association, 1948-1965', *Journal of Southeast Asian History* 6 (September 1965).
Roff, W. R., *The Origins of Malay Nationalism*, New Haven: Yale University Press, 1967.
Royal United Services Institution, *Lessons from the Vietnam War: Report of a Seminar held at the Royal United Services Institution on Wednesday, 12 February 1969*, London: RUSI, 1969.
Rudner, Martin, 'Financial Policies in Post-War Malaya: The Fiscal and Monetary Measures of Liberation and Reconstruction', *Journal of Imperial and Commonwealth History* 3 (May 1975).
———, 'The Draft Development Plan of the Federation of Malaya 1950-1955', *Journal of Southeast Asian Studies* 3 (March 1972).
———, 'The Malayan Post-War Rice Crisis: An Episode in Colonial Agricultural Policy', *Kajian Ekonomi Malaysia* 12 (June 1975).
———, 'The Organization of the British Military Administration in Malaya 1946-48', *Journal of Southeast Asian History* 9 (March 1968).
———, 'The Political Structure of the Malayan Union', *Journal of the Malaysian Branch, Royal Asiatic Society* 53 (Part 1, 1970).
Sandhu, Kernial Singh, 'Emergency Resettlement in Malaya', *Malayan Journal of Tropical Geography* 18 (August 1964).
———, 'The Saga of the "Squatters" in Malaya: A Preliminary Survey of the Causes, Characteristics and Consequences of the Resettlement of Rural Dwellers during the Emergency between 1948 and 1960', *Journal of Southeast Asian History* 5 (March 1964).
Scott, James C., *Political Ideology in Malaysia: Reality and the Beliefs of an Elite*, New Haven: Yale University Press, 1968.

———, *The Moral Economy of the Peasant: Rebellion and Subsistence in Southeast Asia*, New Haven: Yale University Press, 1976.

Shaw, William, *Tun Razak: His Life and Times*, Kuala Lumpur: Longman, 1976.

Sheppard, Tan Sri Dato Mubin, *Taman Budiman: Memoirs of an Unorthodox Civil Servant*, Kuala Lumpur: Heinemann, 1979.

Short, Anthony, 'Communism and the Emergency', in Wang Gungwu, ed., *Malaysia: A Survey*, New York: Praeger, 1964.

———, *The Communist Insurrection in Malaya 1948-1960*, London: Frederick Muller, 1975.

———, 'The Malayan Emergency', in Ronald Haycock, ed., *Regular Armies and Insurgency*, London: Croom Helm, 1979.

Siew Nim Chee, *Labour and Tin Mining in Malaya*, Data Paper No. 7, Southeast Asia Program, Ithaca: Department of Far Eastern Studies, Cornell University, 1953.

Silcock, T. H., *Dilemma in Malaya*, London: Fabian Publications and Gollancz, 1949.

Silcock, T. H., and Ungku Abdul Aziz, 'Nationalism in Malaya', in William L. Holland, ed., *Asian Nationalism and the West*, New York: MacMillan, 1953.

Skocpol, Theda, *States and Social Revolutions: A Comparative Analysis of France, Russia, and China*, Cambridge: Cambridge University Press, 1979.

Soh Eng Lim, 'Tan Cheng Lock: His Leadership of the Malayan Chinese', *Journal of Southeast Asian History* 1 (March 1960).

Stenson, M. R., *Class, Race and Colonialism in West Malaysia: The Indian Case*, Vancouver: University of British Columbia Press, 1980.

———, *Industrial Conflict in Malaya: Prelude to the Communist Revolt of 1948*, London: Oxford University Press, 1970.

———, 'The Ethnic and Urban Bases of Communist Revolt in Malaya', in John Wilson Lewis, ed., *Peasant Rebellion and Communist Revolution in Asia*, Stanford, California: Stanford University Press, 1974.

Stockwell, A. J., *British Policy And Malay Politics During The Malayan Union Experiment, 1942-1948*, Kuala Lumpur: Malayan Branch of the Royal Asiatic Society, Monograph No. 8, 1979.

———, 'Colonial Planning During World War II: The Case of Malaya', *Journal of Imperial and Commonwealth History* 2 (May 1974).

———, 'Insurgency and Decolonization During the Malayan Emergency', *Journal of Commonwealth and Comparative Politics* 25 (March 1987).

Stogdill, Ralph M., *Handbook of Leadership*, New York: The Free Press, 1974.

Strauch, Judith, *Chinese Village Politics in the Malaysian State*, Cambridge, Mass: Harvard University Press, 1981.

Stubbs, Richard, *Counter-Insurgency and the Economic Factor: The Impact of the Korean War Prices Boom on the Malayan Emergency*, Occasional Paper No. 19, Singapore: Institute of Southeast Asian Studies, 1974.

———, 'Peninsula Malaysia: The "New Emergency"', *Pacific Affairs* 50 (Summer 1977).

———, 'The United Malays National Organization, the Malayan Chinese Association and the Early Years of the Malayan Emergency', *Journal of Southeast Asian Studies* 10 (March 1979).

Tan Cheng Lock, 'A Chinese View of Malaya', in David R. Rees-Williams, Tan Cheng Lock, S. S. Awberry, and F. W. Dalley, *Three Reports on the Malayan Problem*, New York: International Secretariat, Institute of Pacific Relations, 1949.

Tan, T. H., *The Prince and I*, Singapore: Sam Boyd Enterprise/Mini Media, 1979.

Thompson, Robert, *Defeating Communist Insurgency: Experiences from Malaya and Vietnam*, London: Chatto and Windus, 1966.

———, *No Exit From Vietnam*, London: Chatto and Windus, 1969.

———, *Revolutionary Warfare in World Strategy, 1945-1969*, London: Secker and Warburg, 1970.

Thornton, Thomas Perry, 'Terror as a Weapon of Political Agitation', in H. Eckstein, ed., *Internal War: Problems and Approaches*, New York: The Free Press, 1964.

Tilly, Charles, *From Mobilization to Revolution*, Reading, Mass: Addison Wesley, 1978.

Tilman, Robert O., *Bureaucratic Transition in Malaya*, Durham, NC: Duke University Press, 1964.

———, 'The Non-Lessons of the Malayan Emergency', *Asian Survey* 6 (August 1966).

Tregonning, K. G., 'Tan Cheng Lock: A Malayan Nationalist', *Journal of Southeast Asian Studies* 10 (March 1979).

UNESCO, *Report of the Commission on Technical Needs in Press, Film and Radio*, Paris: UNESCO, 1948.

Vasil, R. K., *Politics in a Plural Society: A Study of Non-Communal Political Parties in West Malaysia*, Kuala Lumpur: Oxford University Press, 1971.

Wang Gungwu, 'Chinese Politics in Malaya', *The China Quarterly* 43 (July-September 1970).

'War in Malaya', *British Survey*, Main Series No. 39 (June 1952).

Wilson, H. E., *The Klang Strikes of 1941: Labour and Capital in Colonial Malaya*, Research Notes and Discussion Paper No. 25, Singapore: Institute of Southeast Asian Studies, 1981.

Winstedt, Richard O., 'What's Wrong in Malaya', *The Spectator*, 16 July 1948.

Yeo Kim Wah, 'Study of Three Early Political Parties in Singapore, 1945-1955', *Journal of Southeast Asian History* 10 (March 1969).

———, 'The Anti-Federation Movement in Malaya, 1946-48', *Journal of Southeast Asian Studies* 4 (March 1973).

Zakaria Haji Ahmad and Sandhu, Kernial Singh, 'The Malayan Emergency: Event Writ Large', in Kernial Singh Sandhu and Paul Wheatley, eds., *Melaka: The Transformation of a Malayan Capital c.1400–1980*, 2 vols., Kuala Lumpur: Oxford University Press, 1983.

Unpublished Private Papers and Interview Transcripts

(A) Arkib Negara Malaysia (ANM) (Kuala Lumpur)

Aziz bin Ishak. Press Clippings.
Leong Yew Koh. Papers.
MacDonald, Malcolm. Oral History Transcript.
Maxwell, Sir George. Papers.
Pagden, Hugh T. Papers.
Tan Cheng Lock. Papers.
United Malays National Organization Headquarters. Papers.

(B) Institute of Southeast Asian Studies (ISEAS) (Singapore)

Tan Cheng Lock. Papers.

(C) Rhodes House Library (Oxford)

Barnard, H. J. Note.
Blythe, W. L. Papers.
Bovell, Sir Kerr. Papers.
Corry, W. C. S. Interview Transcript.
Dodewell, G. C. Diary.
Horne, W. D. Papers.

(D) Royal Commonwealth Society Library (London)

British Association of Malaya. Papers.
Haynes, A. S. Papers.

(E) University of Malaya Library (Kuala Lumpur)

Tan, Dato Sir Cheng Lock. A Collection of Correspondence.

Daily Newspapers, Weeklies, and Monthlies

Indian Daily Mail (Malaya).
Malay Mail (Malaya).
Manchester Guardian (UK).
Morning Star (UK).
Singapore Standard (Singapore).
Straits Budget (Malaya).
Straits Echo (Malaya).

Straits Times (Malaya).
Sunday Gazette (Malaya).
The Economist (UK).
The Financial Times (UK).
The Observer (UK).
The People (UK).
The Planter (Malaya).
The Spectator (UK).
The Times (UK).
Tiger Standard (Singapore).
Time (New York).

Unpublished Theses and Papers

Humphrey, John Weldon, 'Population Resettlement in Malaya', Ph.D. dissertation, Northwestern University, 1971.

Loh, Francis Kok-Wah, 'Beyond the Tin Mines: The Political Economy of Chinese Squatter Farmers in the Kinta New Villages, Malaysia', Ph.D. dissertation, Cornell University, 1980.

Means, Gordon P., 'New Villages in Malaya', mimeograph, Hamilton, Ontario: Department of Political Science, McMaster University, n.d.

Mohd. Noordin Sopiee, 'The Communities Liason Committee and Post-War Communal Relations in Malaya: A Historical Sourcebook', mimeograph, Kuala Lumpur: University of Malaya Library, n.d.

Park, Bum-Joon Lee, 'The British Experience of Counterinsurgency in Malaya: The Emergency, 1948-1960', Ph.D. dissertation, The American University, 1965.

Stubbs, Richard, 'Political Leadership, Colonial Government and the Malayan Emergency', Ph.D. dissertation, University of Alberta, 1975.

Zakaria Haji Ahmad, 'Police Forces and Their Political Roles in Southeast Asia: A Preliminary Assessment and Overview', mimeograph, MIT/National University of Malaysia, n.d.

————, 'Political Violence in Malaysia: The Malayan Emergency and Its Impact', Paper presented to the Seventh Conference of the International Association of Historians of Asia, Bangkok, 22-26 August 1977.

————, 'The Police and Political Development in Malaysia: Change, Continuity and Institution Building of a "Coercive" Apparatus in a Developing Ethnically Divided Society', Ph.D. dissertation, Massachusetts Institute of Technology, 1977.

Index